To Amy
her with
admiration
Linda Williams

Screening Sex

A JOHN HOPE FRANKLIN CENTER BOOK

LINDA WILLIAMS

Screening Sex

DUKE UNIVERSITY PRESS

Durham and London

2008

To Paul

contents

acknowledgments

This book began as an amateur movie. In the mid-1990s I bought a video camera and amused myself by asking friends and colleagues—mostly people who knew and cared about film—to tell me about the most erotic moments they had encountered at the movies. Most people's answers connected to an earlier moment in their life, a moment in which they made a discovery, through movies, of a "realm of the senses" that they may or may not have already known. Some answers were long and complex, some short and simple, but they all revealed the role movies have played in our sexual coming of age and development, and they all demonstrated that screening sex was both a revelation and a concealment. I never finished my amateur movie. It was just a lark—an escape from seemingly more pressing projects. But the fact that, camera in hand, I could think of no more important question to ask than when and how movies had first turned us on eventually made me realize that the rather intimate question I had asked so many others was perhaps one worth asking myself. This book is my more scholarly and systematic, though no less personal and idiosyncratic, answer.

I thank all my initial interlocutors, those on camera and

off, who generously shared their observations and got me started along this path. I owe special thanks to three people without whom this book would not have entered its next stage: Ernest Callenbach, beloved editor, who gently coaxed me into writing my first draft; Zeynep Gürsel, who miraculously knew where to take it from there; and finally, Ken Wissoker at Duke University Press, my actual editor, who obtained three supremely helpful anonymous readers and then actually dove in himself to offer some timely advice. I count myself very fortunate to have had two editors in my lifetime who actually edit! Courtney Berger of Duke has also been great. I was lucky to teach a course on the topic under scrutiny here to a Berkeley undergraduate class in the fall of 2006. The participants' papers and class discussion taught me even more about what the book could be. Thanks to Ben Hadden and Gabrielle Guthrie, special members of that class, who also worked as splendid down-to-the-wire editors and as important contributors to the intellectual content of this book. Thanks also to Johnathan Lee for heroic indexing, and to Heather Butler for reading and critiquing early drafts. Laura Horak grabbed many of the images and tracked down sources. A great many other generous readers and listeners have provided important help: Brooke Belisle, Lauren Berlant, Karl Britto, Rich Cante, Irene Chien, Kelly Dennis, Jeffrey Escoffier, Marilyn Fabe, Sanjay Hukku, Edith Kramer, Sydelle Kramer, Russell Merritt, Catherine Mezur, Anne Nesbet, Amy Rust, Deborah Shamoon, Alan Tansman, Virginia Wexman, and Kristen Whissel. I also thank the editorial board of *Critical Inquiry* for advice on the first chapter, which originally appeared in that journal. I also thank the editorial board of *Cineaste* for permission to reprint "Cinema and the Sex Act" and an adapted review of *Shortbus*.

To Yuri Tsivian I owe the kiss from *Tonight or Never*. To Don Crafton I owe the reference to *The Paleface*. To Tom Gunning I owe the valuable information about John Sloan. To Charles Musser I owe a much improved understanding of Thomas Edison's *The Kiss*. Thanks also to audiences at the University of Oregon, Portland State University, the Chicago Film Seminar, the University of Oslo, the University of Bergen, the Stanford Humanities Institute, the University of Iowa Conference on Obscenity, the Berkeley Film Seminar, New York University, and Harvard University for hearing me out and asking the hard questions. Thanks also to the University of California–Berkeley Humanities Research Fellowship, which gave me invaluable time to write. Finally, I dedicate this book to Paul Fitzgerald, whose support, love, and good humor have been better than any movie.

introduction

This book is about a basic paradox of movies: on one hand, we screen moving images to lose ourselves vicariously in the bigger, more glamorous, more vivid world we see and hear on the screen; on the other hand, we screen moving images to reencounter our own immediate sensuality in that more vivid world. Much has been written about the way we lose ourselves or identify with those glorious, magnified images of human bodies in movement on the "silver" screen; much less has been written about the ways we reencounter our own bodies, and our own sensuality, in that process. Though it has recently become possible to speak of the sensuous pleasures of embodied viewing and of the shock of cinematic "attractions," it has not been easy to understand the sensual experiences of cinema outside the often crude parameters of the vocabulary of shock and sensation. This has been especially the case when the shock and sensation are caused by moving images of sex.

Movies move us, often powerfully. Sex in movies is especially volatile: it can arouse, fascinate, disgust, bore, instruct, and incite. Yet it also distances us from the immediate, proximate experience of touching and feeling with our own bodies, while at the same time bringing us back to feelings in these same bodies. This is one reason, I suspect, that little has been said that is very intelligent about the sexual experience of movies beyond pronouncements about the suspect voyeuristic nature of the medium and the implied turn-on that voyeurs seek. Unlike the novel, which began to describe explicit sex acts in the 1920s with such vivid modernist writers as James Joyce and D. H. Lawrence (and which continued to do so, for example, in the fiction of Henry Miller, John Updike, Philip Roth, Ian McEwan, and Toni Morrison), the American movie experienced what I will call in chapter 1 a long adolescence. During this prolonged adolescence, carnal facts of life were carefully—often absurdly—elided, but also, as a result, much wondered about. Only since the 1960s has sex ceased to be the officially unmentionable, invisible energy of so much that attracts us to film.

While a smoldering glance and a kiss followed by a slow dissolve used to be all the sex to be seen, since the 1960s American audiences have begun to expect to learn from the movies something about the quality and kind of sex that characters experience—whether simulated or real, heterosexual or homosexual, hard or soft core, protracted or short. It is perhaps not surprising, then, that one of the questions asked by online dating services is to name one's favorite movie sex scene. Today, we expect that to know what sex a person likes to screen is a clue to the kind of lover he or she might want or might want to be.

In asking when, why, and how America went from being a culture that did not screen sex to one that does, I will insist on the double meaning of the verb *to screen* as both revelation and concealment. To screen is to reveal on a screen. But a second, equally important meaning, as the dictionary reads, is "to shelter or protect with or as a screen." Movies both reveal and conceal. If the history of moving-image entertainment is one of a general tendency toward revelation, of a greater graphic imagination of sex, we must keep the stress on imagination. This story is never a matter of a teleological progression toward a final, clear view of "it," as if it preexisted and only needed to be laid bare. Sex is an act and more or less of "it" may be revealed but, as we shall see, it is not a stable truth that cameras and microphones either "catch" or don't catch. It is a constructed, mediated, performed act and every revelation is also a concealment that leaves something to the imagination.

As a way of presenting the range of films discussed here, consider two diametrically opposed examples of popular film from 2005. The first might be considered chaste, the second prurient, but the status of each is only

1: The very last shot of *Pride and Prejudice* (dir. Joe Wright, 2005)

relative to the comparison between them. The very last shot of the latest screen version of Jane Austen's *Pride and Prejudice* (dir. Joe Wright) depicts a scene that Austen never wrote: the now-wed Elizabeth and Darcy presumably on their honeymoon gazing from a balcony out to a body of water. She is in a negligee, he in shirtsleeves and breeches without stockings. The camera slowly tracks in to frame just the couple facing the water. Darcy stands and Elizabeth sits on the ground. At the beginning of a long, slow camera movement in, Elizabeth strokes the back of Darcy's exposed calf. This gesture, like the whole scene, with its relaxed, postcoital, intimate air, is unthinkable in Austen. As the view slowly closes in, Darcy kneels on the ground facing Elizabeth and asks her what he should call her now that they are married. Elizabeth's playful answer is that he should call her Mrs. Darcy "when you are completely and perfectly and incandescently happy." Facing her in profile, Darcy asks, "How are you this evening, Mrs. Darcy?" He then repeats this name each time before he plants a tender, leisurely kiss on her forehead, cheek, nose, and other cheek. Finally, as we continue to move in and as the couple faces one another in perfect profile, they kiss with slightly open lips. For two seconds the kiss is held, and the music surges (figure 1). Cut to black and credits as the music continues.

In this uncompleted kiss lies the essence of the romance of the movies—a romance predicated on the screening out of much of the explicit detail of actual sex acts. A Jane Austen movie would not be a Jane Austen movie if the camera held on this kiss a second longer. Indeed, some purists could argue that this luxuriance of a couple reveling in their physical enjoyment of one another, establishing the terms and language of their new intimacy, is anathema to the world of Jane Austen and goes too far. In many ways this kiss resembles the kisses I will detail in the first chapter of this book, from the era in Hollywood when a kiss was all the sex to be seen in movies. But it is not quite the same, for this version of *Pride and Prejudice* reinvents the form of the romantic kiss for a new era of movies in which audiences are presumed to know the physical details of what follows such a kiss. Unlike the kisses in the era of the Production Code, this kiss basks in the glow of the anticipation of the sex to come and even the sex that—as is implied by that stroke of the calf—has already been. It is an adult sex scene even though it is rated PG, and even though it displays only the beginning of a kiss and screens out many of the physical details of the sex its couple is nevertheless understood to enjoy.

Now let us turn to an X-rated film of the same year. *Pirates* (dir. Joone) was advertised as the most expensive porno of all time and represents an irreverent, affectionate takeoff on the *Pirates of the Caribbean* franchise. If it did not entirely substitute sex play for swordplay, *Pirates* is nevertheless determined to reveal what *Pride and Prejudice* conceals. In one scene, the naive captain of a sailing vessel reads in his cabin, wondering what his (female) first mate is doing to keep up the spirits of his crew: possibly improving their "oral skills"? Cut to the first mate performing fellatio on a crewman. The first mate has the patented porn female body complete with enhanced breasts, slim waist, long, bleached blond hair. The crewman has the patented male body complete with big pecs and a long, frequently erect penis. While ellipses figure in this scene, they work more to conceal the mechanics of how the couple moves from one position to another than to conceal explicit sex. The sex itself is performed so as to be maximally visible at every moment: fellatio, cunnilingus on a shaved pubis, and penetration, concluded by the conventional "money shot" of ejaculation onto the face of the woman. In a later scene another two characters, in the repetitiveness typical of the genre, enact a very similar sexual encounter, this one distinguished by even better lit, more visible penetration in which the woman's shaved pubis faces the camera so as to reveal even more clearly the in-and-out action (figure 2).

Pride and Prejudice was a prestige picture shown on big screens and favorably received by critics. *Pirates* was a prestige picture too. It was aggressively publicized and proudly touted an array of special effects. However, it was produced straight to DVD and the largest screens it showed on were oversized home entertainment systems. Its elaborate special effects

2: Penetration staged for maximum visibility in *Pirates* (dir. Joone, 2005)

only called all the more attention to the ways it fell short of being a "real" movie: atrocious acting, mispronounced lines, anachronistic tattoos on women performers. Where the PG film conceals sex and is all about the kiss as an entrée to what would not be further revealed, the X film reveals the very functioning and the hydraulics of sex. Whereas the first film is all about anticipation and does not complete the sex act it begins before the fade-out, the second is all about the climax of discharge and its kisses are primarily genital. I do not cite these two examples to argue for the failure or bad taste of the film that reveals the most or the countervalue of concealment. Both ends of this continuum exist in moving-image entertainment today, and both occupy positions in the story of screening sex I want to tell.

The question is: How did movies arrive at this juncture, not only of these two, conveniently opposed, examples of concealing and revealing sex, but of art house, mainstream, adult, simulated, and graphic instances of sex screened today on big and little screens? What is the history of the auditory and visual imagination of sex through the transition from an era of official ignorance to a more forthrightly acknowledged but variably represented carnal knowledge?

Raymond Williams, writing a quarter of a century ago about television, noted that it is one of the unique characteristics of advanced industrial society that drama has become so much an intrinsic part of everyday life that sheer quantity may have brought about a qualitative change: "It is clear that watching dramatic simulation of a wide range of experiences is now an essential part of our modern cultural pattern."[1] If Williams's point about the vicarious nature of so much of our dramatic experience is worth pondering—he tells us, for example, that people spend more time watching drama than they do engaging in the more basic biological function of preparing and eating food—then what can we say about the fact that many of us spend more time screening sex than we do having it? Sex acts—both graphic, as in pornography, and simulated, as in most mainstream movies and television—have not only embedded themselves in the dramas that we quantitatively watch so much more of but they have also become, to adapt Williams, qualitatively significant in how we learn and live our own sexualities.

Moving images are surely the most powerful sex education most of us will ever receive. But this pedagogy, while significant as such, has also always been something more than the simple lesson of how to "do it." Even if we live our lives never "having" sex, we learn to appreciate and enjoy certain sexual ways of being, certain forms of (mild or powerful) arousal by watching the mediated sexual contacts of others, whether smoldering glances, kisses, more overt forms of friction or complex scenarios of power, abjection, and need. It is this second-order, vicarious experience of screening sex that provokes this book. What precisely does it mean that we now have a ringside seat at the subtlest or most overt displays of passion, lust, humiliation, or even love? What changes have taken place since Thomas Edison first filmed a kiss in 1896? How did we screen sex then, and how do we screen sex now? How have we become habituated to various spectacles of sex? If, as Guy Debord once put it, "The spectacle is not a collection of images, but a social relation among people, mediated by images," then what kind of social relation has prevailed among audiences who have learned to sit together in the dark to screen these most intimate of relations?[2] What, in other words, is the history of screening sex?

There have been many studies of the social effects of lifted censorship and the rise of more explicit representations (especially in the form of arguments about the definition of obscenity or the demise of the Production Code). But such arguments have often blinded us to the kinds of mediated carnal knowledge that exist on American screens. They have often kept us from understanding the carnal appeal to the senses as something within, not beyond, the pale. Historians of cinema have told a compelling story of the rise and fall of the Hollywood Production Code and the institution of new kinds of regulations, but no one has told the story of screening sex as a history of the relation between revelation and concealment.

Screening Sex is about the ways sex acts have come into our movies. It asks about the nature of this vicarious social-sexual experience as movies began to reveal more sex. When, why, and how did moving images on the big screen, and eventually those on smaller home and mobile screens, come to figure once-taboo sex acts and sexual scenes? How did it happen, for example, that movie narratives began to hinge on such matters as whether or not characters achieve orgasm, or on the specifics of genital, oral, or anal sex, or on sex between people of different races or between people of the same sex? This book is unapologetically interested in and curious about those "dirty parts" in a rented videotape or DVD that will often freeze or break because they have been the most replayed. To dismiss these "dirty parts" as gratuitous—as not part of the cultural story of the history of movies—is to fail to write the formal and cultural history of those moving pictures which have sometimes been the most moving. It is also to link the representations of sex that move us to the related legal concept of prurience. In both cases sexual representations are deemed in excess of what should be allowed.

I will argue throughout this book that Supreme Court rulings notwithstanding, prurience has always been an important reason for interest in movies. To consider the history of sexual representation in American culture since the invention of moving-image technology is to recognize the remarkable degree to which acts once considered ob-scene (literally, off scene) because they had the capacity to arouse have come "on/scene."[3] I have coined the term *on/scene* to describe the way in which discussions and representations once deemed obscene—as an excludable hard core easily excised from supposedly decent public space—have insistently cropped up, and not only in the realm of pornography. In the face of the pervasive and nearly ubiquitous presence of many different kinds of visible and audible sexual acts and sexual scenes we should cease futile arguments about the definition of the obscene. We should consider, rather, the dialectic between revelation and concealment that operates at any given moment in the history of moving-image sex. It is a waste of time to continue to blame the increased sexualization of all aspects of American life on the rise of pornography. The now pervasive influence of pornography needs to be viewed, rather, as part of a much larger proliferation of all manners of screening sex, from chaste kisses to the most graphic and frenetic of penetrations. And this proliferation of moving sexual images cannot be understood apart from a social and cultural history of sex.

Sexual Revolution

Of all the political and social revolutions that were either promised or striven for in the tumultuous era of the late sixties and seventies, it is the sexual one that in the end wrought the biggest change. The sexual revolution in the sixties was inextricable from the larger goals of a pervasive counterculture of antiwar, antiracist, anticapitalist, and, eventually, antipatriarchal activity. With hindsight, however, we can discern a distinct thread of demographic, cultural, and technological change that can be labeled the sexual revolution and that came to some kind of climax in the late 1960s though reverberating throughout the next decade. This revolution overlapped with and was inextricable from the rise of feminism, the reduction—not the end!—of the double standard, and the emergence of gay and lesbian sexual communities. Feeding into this revolution was an earlier generation of sexual researchers: Wilhelm Reich, who first coined the term *sexual revolution* in 1935 and whose theories about the release of sexual energy in orgasm were influential; Alfred Kinsey, whose quantitative tabulations of orgasm and "discovery" of fairly widespread homosexual experiences led him to assert a more fluid continuum of homosexual and heterosexual acts in the late forties and early fifties; and, beginning in 1966, William Masters and Virginia Johnson, who, in *Human Sexual Response*, used the laboratory observation of couples having sex to revolutionize the understanding of the female orgasm as multiple and, in direct challenge to Sigmund Freud, as clitoral rather than vaginal. Almost immediately, feminists began to interpret the significance of these findings in relation to the phallocentrism of previous ideas of sexuality.

As Jeffrey Escoffier notes, another factor in the heady mix of sexual revolution was the battles over obscenity and pornography in a series of trials extending protections of the First Amendment into literature and speech in the 1950s and eventually into film in the early 1970s.[4] Here, then, is one way of measuring the overall change wrought by the sexual revolution: In the America of the mid-sixties, abortion, birth control outside of marriage, homosexuality, and the screening of pornographic films were all officially taboo. If they took place they did so in illicit, closeted ways. Whatever sex people actually had, there was, as the sociologists Kristin Luker and Anthony Giddens and the historians John D'Emilio and Estelle Freedman have all argued, a loose agreement that sexual intimacy was a private matter, best relegated to the marriage bed.[5] However, this secluded arena soon began to undergo change partly due to the new ease of birth control by women. Though we cannot attribute the sexual revolution to anything as simple as the new technology of the "pill," there is also no denying that at least for heterosexuals, the relative freedom from the procreative consequences of sexual relations made possible new kinds of sexual behavior.

When I first began taking birth control pills in my second year of college in 1966, I hid them in an emptied-out lipstick tube from the prying eyes of my mother whenever I went home to live with my family over the summer. Each morning, I would engage in an elaborate ritual of locking myself in the bathroom and extracting my daily pill from the lipstick decoy, carefully crossing out the date on a tiny, handmade, folded-up calendar prepared for each month. When I subsequently began to live out of wedlock with my boyfriend in 1967, my mother declared me a fallen woman, damaged goods. Polls show that as late as 1969, seven out of ten Americans were still opposed to premarital sex. I was judged, then—and not only by my mother—to be a bohemian minority out of sync with mainstream sexual morality. But by 1973, only six years later, I had become a majority. By this time, only 48 percent of those surveyed were opposed to premarital sex.[6]

Something had radically changed between 1969 and 1973. As I argue in the fourth chapter of this book, making love was for many in my generation also a way of opposing war; a "fallen" woman such as myself could rise again; abortions were legally obtainable after *Roe v. Wade* in 1973 and no longer left an indelible stigma; contraception was legal, and pills and condoms were freely available, even for teenagers. When attitudes and behavior change so radically in such a short time, the term *revolution* seems apt, even if the extreme utopian promises of free love or the replacement of war with love were easier said than done. Some have argued that an earlier sexual revolution had already occurred at the turn of the century, when Edison was perfecting his kinetoscope and filming the movies' first kiss. This earlier alteration in sexual relations displaced reproduction from its formerly central role in human sexuality to allow sexual pleasure in its own right to become a value within marriage. However, it did not also call into question either marriage itself or the fundamental power relations within sex. It is this calling into question of the quality and kind of sexual relations—plus the very fact that they come on/scene for scrutiny—that made the changes that began in the late sixties so revolutionary.[7]

Even if one considers the debates about pornography that raged within feminism a decade later as a step back from the embrace of a never quite "free" love, and even if one recognizes that the sexual revolution never meant a steady progress toward sexual freedom, there is no denying the new public prominence of sex, whether one applauded or condemned its popular proliferation in the form of visible sex acts. Beginning in the late seventies, fierce debates about the nature and function of a recently emerged photographically based pornography (magazines and movies) took place within feminism. There was a flood of discussion "for" and "against," but neither side of the debate could take place without an unprecedented level of explicit description or quotation. Feminists on both sides argued about the significance of specific sexual positions—who was on top, who was on the bottom, who was active, who was passive?

Male and female, straight and gay, young and old, some speaking mostly of power, others mostly of pleasure—all were compelled to "speak sex," which is not quite the same thing as speaking "about" it. Speaking *about* sex presumes a stable object of investigation; *speaking sex* implies that the very speaking forms part of sex's discursive construction, and discourses of sexuality proliferated exponentially in the midst of intensifying sex wars and pornography debates.[8] My 1989 book on hard-core pornography directly resulted from these debates and from a sexual revolution that made a feminist interest in pornography possible. The present book has little interest in revisiting those debates and no interest at all in chronicling the supposed rise of pornography—at least not as an isolated phenomenon unrelated to other moving-image traditions. However, this book will assume that a sexual revolution (with the ebbing and flowing that occurs in all revolutions) has taken place and that an intensified screening sex is one of its more important, and least studied, effects. Revolution, in other words, has been most manifest, as Eric Schaefer has noted, as a revolution in media.[9] So while individual sexual practices were undoubtedly affected by the sexual revolution—witness my own surreptitious use of birth control pills—my interest in this study is not so much in how behaviors changed but in how movies did.

When movies began to show more sex than ever before, a fundamental reorganization of the relation of public to private took place. One of the slogans of feminism was that the "personal is political," by which my generation meant to say that many intimate practices once considered private deserved airing on a public stage. The feminist anthropologist Susan Gal has written, "Activities such as wife-beating, which were considered a private concern a few decades ago, are now the subject of public legislation around the globe; conversely, consensual sexual activity among adults that was once more widely subject to legal prohibitions [for example gay sex] has become a private matter in many locales."[10] It is not that what was once private simply becomes public, but, as the historian Joan Landes has put it, that the "line between public and private is constantly being renegotiated."[11] The cinematic representations of sex that became public in the late sixties and early seventies reflected revolutions in sexual attitudes and themselves shaped our very experience of sexual relations. But this new publicity of sex took place at a time in which the very idea of a right to privacy around things sexual and reproductive was also growing. For example, it was not until the 1965 *Griswold v. Connecticut* Supreme Court ruling, which overturned a Connecticut law prohibiting the use of contraception, that the "shadowy right to privacy" began to be articulated as a constitutional right.[12] It is thus not accidental that the "publication" of sex discussed in this book emerged at the same time as the idea of the right to privacy. As we shall see in chapter 6, notions of publicity and privacy came crashing together many years later in debates about the publicity campaign for Ang Lee's *Brokeback Mountain* (2005). Rather than a relentless march toward greater and greater exposure of all things sexual, we see, especially in the acute period of sexual revolution and in its later reverberations, a dynamic tension between the two categories that prove essential to the analysis of this book: revelation, on one hand, and a newly discovered right to concealment, on the other. It is for this reason that the first four of the book's eight chapters concentrate on the late sixties and the seventies, the period of greatest destabilization and renegotiation of public and private. In this period conventions for the representation of sex in moving images became established for the world in which we still live.

A greater range of sexual options, of ways of being sexual, thus emerged in the wake of the sexual revolution even as feminism engaged in an important critique of the limits of those options for women. The story told here will thus not be that of a triumphant march toward unfettered sexual freedom. For with sexual revolution came a new increase in sexual discipline—a greater control over and monitoring of the sexual body as we came to expect to see, hear, and know more about it. It would thus be a grave error to trace a history of screening sex as a simple rise of explicitness. Such an account would not be true to what is both historically and viscerally strange and intractable about sex—the many ways in which it does not submit itself to visual and aural explicitness, its incoherence, its troubling enigmas.

One important effect of the sexual revolution has been that it is no longer possible to point to the "norm" of penetrative heterosexual genital sex (coitus—how quaint the term is beginning to sound!) as a primary definition of sex. Coitus has become one act among many as heterosexual and homosexual variations of anal sex, fellatio, cunnilingus, and wide varieties of fetishisms and sadomasochisms confound the very notion of what my second chapter calls "going all the way." The growing visibility or inference of wide varieties of sex acts—whether merely suggested, simulated, or served up as the real thing in hard-core pornographies—have complicated the notion of sex as a singular, visible truth that one knows when one sees it.[13]

Sexual Theory

If sexualities are, as Michel Foucault argues, historically and culturally constructed, if procreation, in the wake of the sexual revolution, is less and less the ostensible aim of most sex acts, and if sex itself has been increasingly recognized as a matter of many and varied perversions, then simply to chronicle the screening of sex as a progression from lesser to greater explicitness as various censorships fall away will not suffice. Sex screened since the sixties has become more graphic in some ways, but it has also become more heterogeneous and theoretically elusive—witness the controversy over the former president Bill Clinton's denial of having had "sexual relations with that woman," which was not simply a lie, but in the eyes of many revolved around the question of whether fellatio amounted to sex.[14]

Foucault's great insights about the historical constructions of sexuality through discourse are embraced in this book. In the first volume of his *History of Sexuality*, written in 1978 at what might be viewed as the tail end of the historical period of the sexual revolution, Foucault understands sexuality not as a force of libido to be repressed or liberated, but as a discursive form of entwined power, knowledge, and pleasure. His proposed history of sexuality, never actually written as outlined in this first volume, was to have been a history of proliferating discourses of sexuality centered on historically emerging figures: the hysterical woman, the masturbating child, the Malthusian couple, and the homosexual. The force of Foucault's thesis is to minimize the existence of sex as a preexisting thing—say as the repressed drive of psychoanalytic theory—and to see instead how apparatuses of sexuality wrap around the body and its sexual organs to produce different kinds of pleasures and relations of alliance.[15]

Foucault challenged what he called Freud's "repressive hypothesis"—the idea that sex is an inherent force that civilization necessarily represses—and thus deflated the understanding of the sexual revolution as liberation.[16] Though Foucault was in fact a firm supporter of most forms of sexual revolution, he argued that we flatter ourselves if we think that by speaking sex we overcome its prohibitions and therefore liberate it. Repression exists, but it is part of a much larger apparatus producing discourse. In fact, he argues that we cling to the notion of sex as repressed because it allows us to believe in the utopian possibility that "enlightenment, liberation, and manifold pleasures" are all linked—for example, that making love, as I frame it in chapter 4, may actually have something to do with opposing war.[17]

To understand the history of sexuality, Foucault argues, we need to think of the more slippery relations between a power that does not come from on high to repress but comes from below to conjoin discourses of knowledge and pleasure. Sex is rarely just repressed or liberated; it is just as often incited and stimulated and nowhere more so than by media. Perversions are "implanted" by the very same discourses that may seek to control them. So instead of deciding whether we should say "yes" or "no" to sex, instead of joining the loud chorus of voices confessing the various "truths" of sex, Foucault would rather we account for the very fact that sex *is* spoken and instead see "who does the speaking, the positions and viewpoints from which they speak, the institutions which prompt people to speak about it."[18] It is in the spirit of this putting-into-discourse of an intertwined power-knowledge-pleasure that I hope to relate the history of screening sex.

The rise of sexual explicitness in the movies cannot be viewed as a transgressive exception to the rules of previous repression, but as the continuation, in Foucault's sense, of a larger discursive explosion of perverse sexualities. In language that is itself blatantly sexual, Foucault tells us how the power that "took charge of sexuality set about contacting bodies, caressing them with its eyes, intensifying areas, electrifying surfaces, dramatizing troubled moments. It wrapped the sexual body in its embrace."[19] In the end these *"perpetual spirals of power and pleasure"* prove that modern society is "perverse, not in spite of its Puritanism" but "in actual fact, and directly, perverse."[20] Whether or not any of these perversions actually constitute new forms of pleasure, they have been historically "implanted" in ways that become acutely visible in late-twentieth-century screening sex. Fellatio, prolonged and multiple female orgasm, sadomasochistic excitement, and homosexual relations—all have clear moments of emergence in the mainstream and the marginal history of screening sex and all will be traced in this study, not as liberating transgressions, but as the two-edged swords of liberation and further disciplinary control.

Foucauldian enthusiast that I am, I do not find it possible to tell the story of screening sex without also drawing on at least some of the theoretical insights of psychoanalysis. Even as I have myself grown increasingly unsympathetic to the story of repression that psychoanalysis always tells, and of the way psychoanalytic readings always seem to be allegories of its master theory, I have not been able to forego some of these basic concepts. My first chapter on the kiss, for example, is founded on the notion of the "long adolescence" of latent sexual knowledge in which movies seemed to simultaneously know and not know about the existence of sex. Nor has it been possible to think about the orality of the movie kiss apart from the oral pleasures of infantile sexuality so acutely described in Freud's *Three Essays on the Theory of Sexuality*. Similarly, chapter 6 on the primal scene of supposedly perverse sexualities as they came on/scene in American film since the eighties has not been able to do without Freud's key concept of the primal scene and deferred understanding. However, if I cannot fully reconcile my simultaneous recourse to both Freud and Foucault, I can at least qualify the way I will be using their very different senses of the term *perversion*.

Perverse in its adjectival form literally means turned about, deviated from, a more "proper" direction. To engage in sex with an organ not destined for procreation is to Freud to engage in perverse behavior; it is a deviation from the "proper" direction and aim of sex. Yet he fully realizes that a kiss, or any other sexual act, might be "lingered" on a little longer than necessary to achieve simple "discharge" in copulation. Freud would like to rely on a model of perversion (lingering) and norm (proceeding promptly to discharge), but he cannot quite maintain the distinction. Much of the time, as Leo Bersani has argued, perversion actually becomes his model for the understanding of sexual pleasure *tout court*. For example, Bersani shows that often Freud's model of sexual pleasure accepts the existence of forms of sexual stimulation that seek not to be released in discharge, but remain to be pleasurably-unpleasurably increased as tension.[21] Sexual pleasure, in other words, is not the same thing as satisfaction and may rely on a certain "unpleasure" that prolongs excitement. Bersani beautifully describes Freud's two forms of sexual pleasure as, on one hand, an itch that can be satisfied by a scratch, and, on the other, an itch that does not seek to be scratched, that "seeks nothing better than its own prolongation, even its own intensification."[22]

This Freudian hesitation between the two models of sexual pleasure and excitement is one way of circumventing some of Freud's more normative tendencies and of making his theory palatable, and I hope useful, for analyzing the activation of new cinematic erogenous zones. We shall see in chapter 5, for example, how one of the most genitally oriented of all sexually graphic art films, *In the Realm of the Senses* (dir. Oshima Nagisa, 1976), is predicated entirely on an itch model of sexual excitement, while some of the kisses examined in the first chapter function, for all the kiss's usual role as foreplay, as concluding scratches.

Another theorist who has proven essential to this study is Georges Bataille, who shares Foucault's propensity to eschew the approach to sexual identity and to think rather of sex acts. You might call him the philosopher of ecstasy, or what the French call *jouissance*, which is sometimes translated as "orgasm," sometimes as "bliss," and most times not translated at all. Bataille helps us understand what makes sex sexy in his exploration of the complex dynamic between prohibition and transgression out of which emerges his notion of the erotic. Bataille explains the erotic in terms of the tension between continuity and discontinuity, rather than between individual and society or between nature and culture, as Freud does. Eroticism gives us a glimpse of the continuity from which we emerge when born and to which we return in death: erotic activity to Bataille is a paradoxical exuberance of life which, at the extreme, is akin to death.[23] In a phrase that I have found extremely useful for thinking about the transgressions of taboo that constitute many of the sex acts described in this book, he argues that taboo is essential to erotic signification: "Unless the taboo is observed with fear it lacks the counterpoise of desire which gives it its deepest significance."[24] In other words, transgression does not defeat, but only suspends, taboo. The truly successful erotic transgression is one that maintains the emotional force of the prohibition. As yet another theorist inherently skeptical of the liberatory claims of sexual revolution, Bataille's introduction of the relation between fear and desire will prove invaluable to those films discussed in the later part of the book which are determined to probe the relations between sex and death.

Embodied Screening and Mimetic Play

In what precise sense do we sexually feel when we screen sex? How are our bodies engaged through vision and sound in a kind of vicarious touch, taste, smell? In asking these questions I mean to keep in mind the bodies of the viewers sitting in the dark before the screen, as well as the moving images of bodies on the screen. Walter Benjamin's famous statement—"Everyday the urge grows stronger to get hold of an object at close range in an image, or, better, in a facsimile, a reproduction"[25]—speaks to the striking fact that cinematic reproducibility has made possible the close-range reception of highly intimate and once private sexual acts. Reproduction—in this case, let us say the filmic reproduction of a couple "having sex"—makes a new kind of "contact" possible, what Michael Taussig, commenting on Benjamin, calls a "palpable, sensuous, connection between the very body of the perceiver and the perceived."[26]

This kind of screening is symptomatic, in Benjamin's view, of profound changes in apperception that have severed earlier practices of auratic and distanced contemplation such as painting. Yet when it comes to the reception of sexual contents, culture critics and legal scholars often fail to invoke the lessons of theorists like Benjamin and Taussig and confuse contact with literal touch. Consider the following statement by the respected First Amendment scholar Frederick Schauer:

> Imagine a motion picture of ten minutes duration whose entire content consists of a close-up colour depiction of the sexual organs of a male and female who are engaged in sexual intercourse. The film contains no variety, no dialogue, no music, no attempt at artistic depiction, and not even any view of the faces of the participants. The film is shown to paying customers who, observing the film, either reach orgasm instantly or are led to masturbate while the film is being shown.[27]

This is Schauer's description of the kind of hard-core pornography that he believes does not deserve protection as speech precisely because its effect on the body is directly mimetic. Though the film described corresponds fairly closely (except for the color) to the single-reel, silent stag films once shown exclusively to men at bachelor parties and fraternal organizations, it also represents a kind of legal scholar's Platonic ideal of obscenity as that which acts directly on the body and that which can then be dismissed as "mere" prurience. In Schauer's imagination there is no real difference between screening sex and having sex, between watching and doing. Indeed, he argues that there is virtually no difference between the sale of such a film and the sale of a "plastic or vibrating sex aid, the sale of a body through prostitution, or the sex act itself. At its most extreme, hard-core pornography is a sex aid, no more and no less, and the fact that there is no physical contact is only fortuitous."[28]

Though I do not defend the artistic value of such a film, if indeed such a pure example of obscenity actually existed, I do argue that even this stripped-down, bare example of what Schauer wants to relegate to the category of the obscene must take into consideration the medium that necessarily distances the viewer from the heterosexual sex act screened.

In other words, it is not merely "fortuitous" that no physical contact exists between the viewer and the moving image: it is constitutive of whatever our relation to these images may be. Even if a viewer should have the reaction that the genre of pornography strives to achieve (arousal or satisfaction or one of many stages in between), there will always be a difference between screening sex and having sex, even when the viewer moves out of public theaters and into the privacy of the home, where the kind of reactions Schauer describes become even more likely.

What Schauer ignores is the medium in which these sex acts exist and the mediation enacted by social viewers. It is the mechanical reproducibility of film that makes possible the screening of the act of heterosexual intercourse that seems so close in space, if not in time. Schauer thus ignores what Benjamin appreciates: we do not simply imitate what we see, we play with it too.[29] Getting hold of something by means of its reproduced likeness is not the same as getting hold of the thing itself. If cinema, often cited as the quintessential example of the shock of modernity, contributes, as Benjamin argues, to the breakdown of the auratic "tissue of space and time" of religious or aesthetic experience,[30] then we might use Schauer's blunt and decidedly anesthetic example of the supposedly worst-case scenario to examine the consequences of such "shocking" images.

A common way of reading Benjamin's influential "Work of Art in the Age of Its Technological Reproducibility" has been to see it as a defense of the shock of moving images as antidotes to the inherent shocks of modern life. In this reading, the aura-destroying shock of cinematic images— Benjamin's favorite examples, writing in the thirties, were Charlie Chaplin, Dada, and surrealist film—might jolt viewers out of the numbness of modern life. Of course the risk was always that the numbing effects of shock would simply be treated with more shock in an escalating cycle often invoked in critiques of sex and violence in the media. In recent articles on Benjamin, Miriam Hansen suggests a way out of this impasse through a concept unfortunately excised from the most familiar third version of Benjamin's famous artwork essay: innervation.

Hansen explains that innervation describes a neurophysiological process that "mediates between internal and external, psychic and motoric, human and mechanical registers."[31] While we typically call sensation the experience of *taking in* phenomena that make us feel—that is, experience that moves from our outer senses, ears and eyes, into our bodies where we feel—we are less prone to consider the reverse direction: the transmission of energy from the inside of our bodies back toward the outside world.

This latter transmission is what Benjamin calls innervation, though the term only appears in a footnote to the lesser-known second version of his essay. Though only incipient in Benjamin's own thought, Hansen argues that innervation allows us to see mimesis as a two-way process, one taking in, but also reconverting "psychic energy through motoric stimulation" to extend back out toward the world.[32] In other words, a process usually understood as a mere taking in of sensation and, in the case of Schauer's example, a taking in that mimics the gestures and sensations experienced by those viewed, can be understood as a two-way street: our bodies both take in sensation and then reverse the energy of that reception to move back out to the outside world. Thus, instead of just absorbing shock, in this case the shock of eros, the body is energized as what Hansen calls a "porous interface between the organism and the world."[33]

In this "porous interface" we might also locate a process of habituation that socially integrates sexual sensations previously viewed as private or antisocial. Thus where sexual arousal was once deemed antithetical to all civilized public culture, now, through screening sex, our bodies are not simply shocked into states of arousal but habituated and opened up to this changing environment in newly socialized ways. In Foucault's terms we are disciplined into new forms of socialized arousal in the company of others, but in (Hansen's understanding of) Benjamin's terms we are more than just disciplined; we may also learn to play at sex the way a child might play at being a windmill or a train by incorporating more subtle forms of psychic energy through motoric stimulation. In his short essay, "The Mimetic Faculty," in which this child's play is evoked, Benjamin significantly does not argue that the child believes that he or she *is* the windmill or the train. Playing at being a windmill constitutes an habituation to a culture in which windmills are important; playing at being a train is the same for a different sort of culture; playing at sex, too, is a way of habituating our bodies to a newly sexualized world in which vicarious forms of sexual pleasure are now on/scene. The mimetic faculty is a kind of tactile training that habituates viewers to adapt to changing environments. What is lost in the decay of aura is potentially gained, then, in the scope of play—a play that is, as Benjamin puts it, "widest in film."[34]

Let us now come back to Schauer's rude and crude example of screening sex, which he believes induces its audience to a reductive state of mimicry. Since Schauer depicts the screening situation as one with paying customers—in other words, as a normal movie audience, not a private stag party or a home screening—we might consider the similarity of what he describes to an actual ten minutes of a public screening of a specific pornographic film, say, *Deep Throat* (dir. Gerard Damiano, 1972), which will be discussed in chapter 3. There are stretches of this film that offer a "close-up colour depiction of the sexual organs of a male and female who are engaged in sexual intercourse." In 1972 public screenings of this film could have been said to have "shocked the nation" with the spectacle, and the sensation, of close views of sexual organs in action. In its initial shock of screening sex, this moment was not unlike another moment in 1896 when Thomas Edison screened a kiss as part of a program of short films. In both cases an aura-shattering abolition of distance jars by a display of organs—mouth and genitals—in close-up.

However, if we factor in the two-way possibilities of innervation, we can move beyond shock, and also beyond the limits of Schauer's presumption of a knee-jerk response to moving-image sex as no different than sex itself. We then begin to see that a variety of responses are possible: shock, embarrassment, arousal, but also, and most important, imaginative play. My point throughout this book is that the imagination can play with the most concealed and modest as well as the most revealed and explicit of images and sounds, with *Pride and Prejudice* as well as *Pirates*. We thus underestimate the imagination if we think that it can only operate in the absence of, or only at the slightest suggestion of sexual representation. As a "porous interface between the organism and the world," my body before the screen is not simply excited then numbed, or numbed and then excited; rather, over time and with more screenings, it becomes habituated to diverse qualities and kinds of sexual experiences, including those which I may never have but with which I can feel and play.

In other words, even if movies do seem to invite us to crudely mimic the acts they show, our bodies are not quite the mechanistic mimics that Schauer imagines. Another way of thinking about the two-way street that innervation permits is to consider the film theorist Vivian Sobchack's insights about the embodied foundations of cinematic intelligibility.[35] Sobchack writes that to understand movies we must literally *make sense* of them. She observes that carnal responses to cinema have been regarded as "too crude to invite extensive elaboration beyond aligning them—for their easy thrills, commercial impact, and cultural associations—with other more 'kinetic' forms of amusement."[36] Sobchack comes to grips with the "carnal foundations of cinematic intelligibility" by characterizing cinema as a series of "embodiment relations"—modes of mediated seeing and hearing, and of reflective movement that are the very foundation of its expressiveness.[37]

Sobchack's phenomenological approach to moving images echoes

Hansen's and Benjamin's, but with the difference that she conceives embodied viewing as an intentional arc that originates not with the world but with the spectator. She notes that when she attends to a film the fact that she can see but cannot also touch, smell, and taste means that her body's intentional trajectory "will *reverse its direction* to locate its partially frustrated sensual grasp on something more literally accessible," which is her own "*subjectively felt lived body*." Thus, she writes, "on the rebound from the screen—and without a reflective thought—I will reflexively turn toward my own carnal and sensual being to touch myself touching, smell myself smelling, taste myself tasting, and, in sum, feel my own sensuality."[38] Writing about Jane Campion's *The Piano* (1993), she observes that when the male character, Baines, touches Ada's flesh through a hole in her black woolen stocking, she—Sobchack—feels a tactile shock. Though Sobchack does not literally touch Ada, the shock of watching this touch between others opens her "to the general erotic mattering and diffusion of my flesh, and I feel not only my 'own' body but also Baines's body, Ada's body, what I have elsewhere called the 'film's body.'"[39]

Notice, as Taussig might appreciate, that Sobchack does not say that she "identifies" with Baines as he touches Ada. She is not describing an objectifying male gaze that excludes the female pleasure in looking.[40] Nor is she describing a Cartesian perspective that reduces what is seen to a mastered, distanced object.[41] Rather, she describes a situation in which the camera and the sound-recording technology sees and hears like a body, so that our own bodies subsequently see and hear what that original "film body" does. Viewing and hearing thus makes for a material experience of embodiment; it is a series of *mediated* exchanges of our social bodies, the film's body, and the bodies on the screen.

The attraction that pulls us toward a moving image is thus not just of the eyes but also of the flesh, yet not of the flesh in the way Schauer imagines. Our entire sensorium is activated synesthetically, all the more so, as will often be the case in this book, when the moving image shows two (or more) beings touching, tasting, smelling, and rubbing up against one another. If these bodies are engaged in sex acts, as Baines and Ada are at this moment in this long tease of a film, then in watching them I am solicited sexually too. However, this solicitation is not Schauer's nightmare of pure mimicry nor is it just of the eyes, for one bodily sense translates into another. With Benjamin and Hansen's innervation, then, we have a model for taking in energy through motoric stimulation that extends back toward the world, and with Sobchack's rebound we have a model for taking energy from the image back into the self.[42] Throughout this book

I will operate on the assumption that screened sex has always been and is now even more central to our culture; whether it leads to Sobchack's commuted, diffuse encounter with one's *own* flesh, or to Hansen's Benjaminian notion of one's body as a "porous interface" extending back toward the world.

We begin, as is proper in western culture, with the kiss. "Of Kisses and Ellipses: The Long Adolescence of American Movies (1896–1963)," begins with Thomas Edison's 1896 *The Kiss* and ends with Andy Warhol's 1963 *Kiss*—a compendium of thirteen kisses that I take as the epitaph for the era of the kiss. Looking at this most publicly acceptable and ubiquitous of cinematic sex acts, this chapter explores the history and the phenomenology of the screen kiss beginning with early reactions to the anatomization, magnification, and repetition made possible by the close-up and the large screen. With Edison and Warhol as the alpha and the omega of screen kisses, I contrast each to the era of the Hollywood Production Code and to the time before the Code's prohibition against "scenes of passion" and "excessive and lustful kissing." Through the kiss we explore the nature of cinematic oral pleasures and the eroticism of their limits.

"Going All the Way: Carnal Knowledge on American Screens (1961–1971)," my second chapter, asks when and how it became not only possible but obligatory to show, in either simulated or explicit fashion, what happens between the sheets in mainstream movies. How, in other words, did American movies grow up and shift from adolescent kisses to presumably more adult displays such as those viewed in *The Graduate* (dir. Mike Nichols, 1967)? What constituted carnal knowledge on the screen in this period of sexual revolutionary, late sixties change? This chapter compares the form and function of the supposedly tasteful Hollywood sexual interlude—the familiar montage of musically accompanied abstracted snippets of simulated sex—to other forms of adult sexuality available in sexploitation, blaxploitation, and the avant-garde.

A single year, 1972, and two films, *Last Tango in Paris* and *Deep Throat*, are the main focus of chapter 3. In this *annus mirabilis* of screening sex, two Italian male directors—one from Italy, the other from New York—altered the expectations of American movie audiences of what sort of sexual feelings they might experience at the theater. One film was considered erotic modern art, the other crass hard-core pornography. But both confronted public, gender-mixed audiences with narratives that were unapologetically about sex from beginning to end. As a member of both these audiences I have tried to depict the spirit in which a whole generation of American moviegoers dared in 1972 to watch these two films in the company of others. A third film, one that I did not see "in the day," was perhaps even more groundbreaking, though to a more specialized emerging community of gay viewers. Wakefield Poole's *Boys in the Sand* (1971) was made a year before these other landmarks of graphic sex and served to validate and celebrate, while never exactly normalizing, the difference of gay sex.

With all the ejaculating penises brought on/scene in both heterosexual and homosexual pornography of the early seventies, and with all the end-of-Code, beginning-of–ratings-system films and their climactically simulated sexual interludes, it is only fair to ask about the fate of the representation of female orgasm. Chapter 4, "Make Love, Not War: Jane Fonda Comes Home (1968–1978)," moves both backward to the roots of the American sexual revolution and forward to mainstream American cinema's belated concern with female orgasm through the French and American careers of Jane Fonda. In films as diverse as *Barbarella: Queen of the Galaxy* (dir. Roger Vadim, 1968), *Klute* (dir. Alan Pakula, 1971), and *Coming Home* (dir. Hall Ashby, 1978) Fonda was the first female American actor in mainstream film to play characters whose orgasms mattered. These orgasms related significantly to Fonda's successive iconic positions as a sexpot, a feminist, and an antiwar activist.

Where hard-core, moving-image pornography is easy to make and has flourished since the seventies in its own parallel universe devoid of much art, art films that venture to depict unsimulated sex acts have been difficult to make, both aesthetically and financially (witness the rarely used American rating of NC-17). One film of the 1970s, Oshima Nagisa's Japanese but French-produced *In the Realm of the Senses* (1976), fully succeeded in combining hard-core sex with erotic art. As perhaps the only work of seventies international cinema to actually do what Anglo-American and European critics and directors had only dreamed of doing, this single film occupies the whole of chapter 5. I argue that it deserves careful discussion, both because it was groundbreaking and because its lessons prove essential to the growing group of contemporary films since the nineties belatedly following in its footsteps.

Every once in a while films come along that hit a sexual nerve with the American public. Chapter 6 focuses on the perverse provocations of the American screen since the eighties in two groundbreaking films: David Lynch's *Blue Velvet* (1986) and Ang Lee's *Brokeback Mountain* (2005). Because the sex scenes depicted in these films are of simulated, not hardcore, sex they reached large R-rated audiences. David Lynch's small-town mystery that begins with a severed ear and Ang Lee's cowboy movie about two sheepherders who fall in love brought primal fantasies of sex home to general American audiences, and not just the art house crowd. Sado-masochistic sexual rituals which had their first emergence in mainstream American cinema in 1986 had much the same impact, I argue, as the more recent staging of sodomitical sex in *Brokeback*. In both cases the simulated sex acts brought perverse sex to the American heartland—to a picture-perfect small Northwestern town and to the iconic wilderness of the western landscape. Through these two films, this chapter examines some of the ways in which American cinema became perverse through the staging of primal scenes.

Simulated sex films such as *Blue Velvet* and *Brokeback* scrupulously avoid the display of sexual organs. Hard-core art films, on the other hand, often flaunt the display of sexual organs and are thus refused R ratings. Chapter 7, "Philosophy in the Bedroom: Hard-Core Art Film since the Nineties," examines a new tradition of art film that has followed in the hard-core art tradition of Oshima. Since the nineties, a new wave of French, German, Italian, Asian, and British films has defied the soft focus erotic prettiness of mainstream Hollywood's sexual interludes discussed in chapter 5 and even the simulated perversions of chapter 6. Many of the films discussed here innovate by choosing to focus on sex that is aggressive, loveless, or alienated in precise opposition to both the cloying romance of the dominant Hollywood model or the wall-to-wall ecstasy of hard-core pornography. My goal in surveying these films is not to parse the good sex from bad, or to determine which graphic sexual representations have gone "too far" or "leave nothing to the imagination." Rather, it is to understand how very many and different imaginative ways there are of "getting graphic" as non-pornographic movies open up the question of the imagination of sex beyond the familiar formulas of simulation and the equally familiar formulas of hard core.

Screening sex in a new media era means no longer luxuriating before the magnified projections of the big screen; it means getting busy: pointing, clicking, typing, choosing, playing, and "interacting" with highly "manipulatable" and "converged" media on often quite small screens. My conclusion asks what the essential differences are between the experience of screening sex on the large movie screen in a public place and the experience before the small television or computer screen at home—or wherever we now take our increasingly portable screens. With these little screens spectators who have always engaged in play with moving images now become more like literal game players. And one of the things we are more or less expected to play with is ourselves. Masturbation before a moving image or virtual orgies, in which couples have sex with one another as well as "with" the bodies on the home screen, now becomes a possible practice of sex. In a new media era the point of pornography has become, more than ever, the expectation that we will "have" sex with ourselves through the image on the screen. Through a look at several key examples of cyberporn this final chapter comes to grips with what is new and what remains the same about screening sex in a new media era.

Obviously these chapters do not constitute anything like a complete history of screening sex. I have sacrificed general coverage for close looks at a few films in each era—works that have seemed to me to be either groundbreaking or symptomatic of given periods of moving-image history. Whether or not they were great cinema, these were films that we often went to see out of simple curiosity for sexual knowledge. Though this book is in no way an account of my own sexual autobiography through movies, I have sometimes found it useful to tell the story of my own, necessarily limited, experiences as a longtime avid moviegoer alongside what I have gleaned from critical reception and scholarship. The films discussed in this book are thus those that have literally and figuratively "made sense" to me as forms of carnal knowledge. In evoking and analyzing them I have tried to capture some of what it meant to have been there, in the dark, since the sixties when sex ceased to be a fundamentally illicit, screened out experience and began instead to be heard and seen on/scene. If I have distinct memories of screening a film, I try to recall them and to discuss the context of my historically situated reactions as a white, heterosexual, American woman who would have liked to have been a cosmopolitan sophisticate but who, apart from her experience of movies, often remained naive and provincial at the core. As my most crucial form of sex education I hope this study of screening sex captures something of the excitement of that learning. Yet beyond the early chapters, which correspond to my own learning about sex and coming to sexual maturity, this is not a story of growing maturity. If anything, as the later chapter on primal scenes suggests, it is a story whose plot keeps thickening as carnal knowledge proves not to be a simple progress toward explicit knowledge but rather, an enigmatic and elusive "event."

Wrestling awkwardly with her across the bed . . . I realized I was
. . . reconnecting with subterranean fountains of juvenile lust
that I thought had long since run dry. But no, they were there,
as effervescent as ever, the obsessive and utterly unreal images
of desire the movies implant in the adolescent mind. The beauty
that never fades, the kiss that never ends, the night of passion
that swells to crescendo on a Max Steiner theme and ends the
film balanced forever on a pinnacle of undying intensity.

—THEODORE ROSZAK, *Flicker*

1

of kisses and ellipses

The Long Adolescence of American

Movies (1896–1963)

Movie kisses were the first sex acts I ever screened. Before
I had my romantic first kiss, I already knew, from movies,
that one needed to tilt the head a little to avoid bumping
noses, but that if both kissers tilted the same way they would
still bump noses, so a complex choreography of bodies had
to be worked out in this simple act. I learned this from the
big screen, where kisses were greatly magnified in the garish
Technicolor kisses of Rock Hudson and Doris Day. But I also
learned some things from the little black-and-white screen
before which my mother and I sat watching TV movies on
warm summer nights when I could stay up late. I remember myself at fourteen in 1960 sprawled on the rug directly
under the television screen, my mother across the room in
her big armchair, both of us riveted to a repertoire of Hollywood kisses performed by luminous stars.

To a barely kissed teenage girl, the extreme close-ups,
swelling music, and mysterious fade-outs offered compel-

ling promises of a grand communion to come. If I could not exactly touch, taste, and smell as the kissers themselves could do, I could sense, through sights and sounds that seemed to creep across my skin, penetrate my entire body, and generate my own sympathetic puckers, how it might feel to kiss and be kissed. I remember these kisses today through a haze of nostalgia, much like that displayed in the finale of *Cinema Paradiso* (dir. Giuseppe Tornatore, 1988) when the hero reviews the screen kisses and embraces of the films of his youth. This Oscar winner for best foreign film concluded with a grand montage of all the kisses and embraces that had once been snipped by censorious priests from movies shown in a provincial Italian village after the Second World War. Like the graying hero of that film, I too sit mesmerized in the present by the gift of the old-fashioned movie kiss. And like that hero I register the double sense of the verb, *to screen*, as both a projection that reveals and a censorship that elides.

Now that it is not only possible but almost obligatory for American movies to show the sex acts that follow them, kisses have lost some of their allure. They have become mere foreplay, one sex act among many. Though they still punctuate movies and remain dramatically significant as the inauguration of sexual contacts, they no longer carry the burden—or the enormous electrical charge—of being the whole of sex that can be seen. The movie kisses of the era before the 1960s sexual revolution were both more infantile and more adolescent than the kisses of today—infantile in their orality and adolescent in their way of being permanently poised on the brink of carnal knowledge.[1]

This chapter begins with the cinema's first kiss: Thomas Edison's *The Kiss*, a silent fifteen-second film made in 1896. It ends with Andy Warhol's *Kiss*, a silent fifty-eight-minute answer to Edison from 1963. In between these two exemplars of screen kisses, I will address examples from the era of the Hollywood Production Code,[2] as well as from the pre-Code era. My primary goal is to taxonomize the filmic mode of the screen's first sex act. What is its role as textual punctuation—as period, comma, question mark, and, most important, as the dot, dot, dot of ellipsis? What can we observe about the tension and excitement generated by these reciprocal acts of oral pleasure?

1896: The Forty-Two-Foot Kiss

In the late 1890s Thomas Edison had begun to film short sequences of action for exhibition in his newly developed Kinetoscope—a peephole device for screening short segments of moving images. A popular New York musical play, *The Widow Jones*, had included a kiss between the widow and her suitor. In April 1896 Edison brought the two stars of the play into his Black Maria studio and filmed just their kiss. The fifteen-second film has been variously called *The Kiss* and, after the stage actors who performed it, *The May Irwin–John Rice Kiss*, and simply *The May Irwin Kiss* (suggesting that women held greater importance than men as either kissers or kissees).[3] It was filmed only two days before Edison had his first public projection of films, though it was not included in that first show. Charles Musser shows that the film's making was actually a publicity stunt for a newspaper, the *New York World*, which reported in a Sunday edition on the making of the film: "For the first time in the history of the world it is possible to see what a kiss looks like. . . . Such pictures were never before made. In the forty-two feet of kiss recorded by the kinetoscope every phase is shown with startling distinctness. . . . The real kiss is a revelation. The idea of a kinetoscopic kiss has unlimited possibilities."[4]

As this review suggests, these "possibilities" are caught up in the new viewing machine's ability to deliver increments of knowledge about moving bodies that, not accidentally, happen to be in the form of the cinema's first sex act. The title of this long news feature is "The Anatomy of a Kiss," and the opportunity for an anatomization of the forty-two-foot sequence seems to have been paramount. As Musser notes, the kiss may or may not have been the actual highlight of the play (the final act in which it occurred has not been found), but when finally projected in early May of 1896, it immediately became the most popular of the many short films shown.[5] Though it is possible to assume that a famous kiss in a play simply became a famous kiss in the new medium of projected film, it seems more likely that the existence of the film retroactively made the kiss important in all subsequent performances of the play.[6] The forging of the possibilities of an emerging medium thus took place through the close-up anatomization of a sex act that existed in the play but that did not necessarily constitute its highlight. It is significant, therefore, that the new technology of projection onto a screen in a darkened theater distinguished itself especially through the particular act of the kiss. As in so many other examples of "new media"—print, lithography, photography, video, and now digital technologies—the excitement of new technologies of vision went hand in hand with the excitement around newly mediated revelations of sex.

The film consists of a single, chest-up shot of Rice on the left and Irwin on the right mouthing what seem to be a few lines of dialogue from the play. Touching cheeks, coming close to the position of a kiss, but continu-

ing to speak out of the sides of their mouths, they abruptly pull apart and prepare for a theatrical smooch. Rice's preparation includes the familiar but now archaic gesture of lifting the mustache away from his lip—associated today with villains in melodramas (figure 3). He then cups his hands on the side of Irwin's cheeks, leans in, and plants a few pecks on the side of her firmly closed mouth. Irwin, for her part, leans up to meet him, but her hands, in contrast, remain at her side (figure 4). Toward the end, Rice's pecks briefly turn into little nibbles, and the film ends in medias kiss. Throughout the scene, owing to Rice's big mustache, we see more of Irwin's mouth and lips than of his.

A stage kiss if ever there was one, this kiss shares the former's divided attention: the partners must face one another to kiss and must face front to make the contact visible to the audience. Something of this divided attention persists in all movie representations of sex acts, torn as they are between the necessary close contact between bodies and the requirement to make that contact visible.[7] Indeed, this early kiss introduces many of the features that will prove emblematic of subsequent screened sex acts, not just kisses: first and foremost is the close-up that makes the osculation visible; second comes the mouthed dialogue that precedes the sexual contact, in this case drawing our attention to the kissers' lips—we cannot know what this couple says, although it is likely that the conversation negotiates the terms of the kiss; third is the convention that the man initiates contact and the woman receives it, even though she may well have orchestrated it all along.

This kiss is also noteworthy because it is so radically severed from the rest of the play's action, becoming what critics of graphic sex and violence might call gratuitous—a sex act that is there just for sex's sake, with no other narrative or dramatic purpose. As we have already seen, these terms are often deployed, especially in legal arguments about obscenity, to identify the so-called prurient sex that supposedly does not belong on any screen. I will argue, however, that once a culture decides that sex matters—and the fame and popularity of *The Kiss* certainly formed part of such a decision—sex for sex's sake is never really gratuitous. Indeed, it becomes one of the important reasons for screening moving pictures.

Of course, there is nothing sexy to us today about the brief osculations of two plump, middle-aged actors mugging for the camera. We tend to laugh, and audiences in the day seemed to laugh. The *Boston Herald* wrote of the Vitascope program when it showed in Boston: "Of the 10 pictures included in yesterday's programmes . . . there is no shadow of a doubt as to which created the most laughter. That kissing scene in the 'Widow Jones,' taken part in by May Irwin and John C. Rice, was reproduced in the screen, and the very evident delight of the actor and the undisguised pleasure of the actress were absolutely 'too funny' for anything."[8]

What does it mean that *The Kiss* was "too funny"? Does it necessarily mean that it was also not shocking? Laughter can be an expression of genuine amusement, or it can be a nervous release covering over shock. In this case it may have been a little of both. The little nibbles that follow the primary smooch are comic in two ways. First, like a great many sex acts, they have a mechanical, repetitive quality in themselves. Second, shown over and over in the repeated loops that comprised the primary way of projecting early cinema, they are literal forms of mechanized repetition.[9] Audiences could be amused or, as in the response articulated in the Chicago literary magazine the *Chap Book*, they could be offended: "Within a natural scale, such things [as kisses] are sufficiently bestial. Monstrously enlarged and shown repeatedly, they become positively disgusting."[10] What, precisely, did this author, the young painter John Sloan, find so disgusting? Was it possibly the middle-aged plumpness of the widow herself, and the less-than-imposing figure of her suitor? None of the criticism of the stage play makes such a suggestion. Was it simply the unseemly intimacy of *any* kiss so "monstrously enlarged"? Clearly this kiss agitated in a way that the kiss appearing onstage, or as a small image in the Kinetoscope, had not.

Siegfried Kracauer has noted that "huge images of small material phenomena" become in cinema "disclosures of new aspects of physical reality." Though Kracauer's preferred example of cinematic magnification is the famous close-up of Mae Marsh's twisting hands in the courtroom episode of the modern story of *Intolerance* (dir. D. W. Griffith, 1916), his description of these hands, "isolated from the rest of the body and greatly enlarged . . . quivering with a life of their own," is even more applicable to screen kisses, which especially quiver with a sexual life of their own.[11] Kisses, when stylized and elaborated by the Hollywood narrative cinema, would eventually become synecdoches for the whole sex act. Here, however, a kiss constitutes an unnarrativized attraction amounting to a revelation of the physical act to one critic, and a disgusting monstrosity to another.

In either case, what seems to be at stake is a visceral attraction or repulsion on the part of viewers. Fragmentation, repetition, and magnification make possible an anatomization that turns the kiss of *The Widow Jones* stage play into a culturally new combination of prurience and pedagogy. The psychoanalyst Adam Phillips has written that although conventions governing the giving and getting of kisses clearly exist in literature and life, "It is really only from films that we can learn what the contemporary conventions might be for kissing itself."[12] This 1896 film constituted America's first such lesson. It is a quintessential example of what Tom Gunning has called the "cinema of attractions."[13] The Lumière brothers' *Arrival of a Train* (1895)—the main attraction of the first public screening of a film in France—may be emblematic of a certain dynamism of the machine age, and Robert Paul's *Rough Sea at Dover* (1895), the British attraction at the first American public screening of projected films, may be emblematic of cinema's ability to capture the tumult of nature, but Edison's *The Kiss* is emblematic of a new kind of sexual voyeurism unleashed by moving pictures. Screening sex, learning how to do it through repeated and magnified anatomization, would henceforth become a major function of movies.

But there was another important kiss in early cinema, one that I want to take up here as a counterpoint to all the dazzlingly white, luminous, romantic kisses that would eventually be fabricated by Hollywood. Though it attracted considerably less commentary in its own day than Edison's *The Kiss*, Edwin S. Porter's *What Happened in the Tunnel* (1903) has recently garnered considerable discussion as an exhibition of the "miscegenation" that would eventually be officially forbidden in the Hollywood Production Code.[14] What happened in the tunnel? A white woman and her African American maid sit side by side on a train. A white man sits behind the white woman who is reading. When she drops her handkerchief, he picks it up and uses the occasion to flirt, take her hand, and come close (figure 5). The screen suddenly goes black for a prolonged period (figure 6). When the darkness finally ends, and the train has presumably emerged from the tunnel, we see that the white man has leaned over into the space of the two women. But the maid and mistress have changed positions, and we find him kissing not the mistress, but the maid (figure 7). As soon as light illuminates this kiss, he pulls back in horror and tries to hide behind his newspaper as the maid and mistress laugh.

In contrast to the May Irwin-John Rice kiss, this one is not displayed in close-up and cannot therefore be "anatomized." If the Edison piece is kiss as revelation, screening as the projection of something to see, the Porter scenario is screening as mostly concealment of what *could* be given to see but is not. For this kiss is almost entirely screened out—as so many aspects of sex, and certainly most interracial aspects of it, would eventually be for many decades under the Hollywood Production Code.

What Happened in the Tunnel is also less likely to elicit contemporary amusement. Even if the supposed joke is *on* the man and *between* the two women, it is premised on a racial devaluation of the black woman and her lack of appeal to the kisser.[15] The film theorist and historian Jane Gaines notes that the predominantly white audiences who paid to see this less-than-one-minute film did not really want to know what happened in the tunnel.[16] They were not interested in the visible anatomy of *this* kiss, but in the social embarrassment of the man punished for taking liberties with a white woman by the presumed unpleasure of kissing a black one. What happened in the tunnel for the man was the presumably pleasurable touch and taste of a kiss that he thought was of white skin. This man does not discover his unpleasure until sight informs him that he should not have enjoyed the sexual contact in which he engaged. Only when his kiss becomes visible does he cease to enjoy it. What the kiss is to the black woman is harder to imagine.[17]

5, 6, and 7:
Edwin S. Porter,
*What Happened in
the Tunnel* (1903)

Kisses, as we shall learn, are both public visual displays and acts of mutual touch and taste grounded in a proximity that, at the limit, precludes visibility both to the kissers themselves and to the audience (which cannot see lips, for example, covered by other lips). These kinds of discrepancies between sight and touch go to the heart of a great many cinematic sex acts. In the case of *What Happened in the Tunnel*, the camera's distance from the kiss, compared to Edison's, along with the occlusion of all but the very end of its "action," elides the usual movements of a kisser *toward* the kissed and keeps only the movement of this particular kisser *away* from the kissed.

We do well to keep in mind, however, how much this "comic" occlusion of the interracial kiss between the white man and the black woman finds its horrific mirror reversal in the decidedly noncomic threat of visible sexual contact between a white woman and a black man. This not-quite-seen interracial kiss structures countless scenarios of early cinema. It especially structures the landmark film *The Birth of a Nation* (dir. D. W. Griffith, 1915), where a threatened kiss offers a synecdoche of the genital sex act—the proverbial "fate worse than death"—for the sexually and racially endangered white woman.[18] Hollywood would soon proscribe any representation of black/white interracial sex acts—comic or melodramatic—but we should note how interracial lusts sit uneasily around the edges of what would become the Hollywood mainstream.

"A Kiss Is Just a Kiss"

If audiences today do not see much romance or eroticism in the screen's first kiss, they immediately recognize both these qualities in the surprisingly brief, but erotically charged, kisses of the Code era. Even though these later kisses do not chronologically follow Edison's, it seems best to turn to a few of them next, because they represent the kiss in its most rule-driven, codified form.

In the era of the Hollywood Production Code—roughly from 1934, when the Code began actually to be enforced, through 1966, when Code approval had become increasingly irrelevant and a new ratings system was on the horizon—it was prohibited for any movie to "infer that low forms of sex relationship are the accepted or common thing."[19] By "low forms of sex" the framers of the Code intended any "scenes of passion" that might be likely to "stimulate the lower and baser element." This language emphatically links physically "lower down" portions of the anatomy with lower classes. "Excessive and lustful kissing" is linked to other, worse, taboos: "seduction or rape," "sex perversion," "scenes of childbirth," "venereal diseases," or the exposure of the "sexual organs of children." In addition, in the section called "Costume," "complete nudity" and "indecent or undue exposure" are also forbidden.

The Code's prohibitions explicitly spell out societal taboos against displays of sex that were already familiar but that had never before been made so clear. However, it was not just the lower classes, the unmarried, the criminal, the homosexual, or the colored whose sexual contacts were made taboo by the Code, but also those of married, reproductive heterosexuals whose pregnancies, births, and sexual relations also became unrepresentable. Of course, long before the crafting of the Code, kisses were already the only visible sexual contacts possible at the movies. However, it was only after the Code's stricter enforcement in 1934 that unofficial rules about the duration and context ("excessive and lustful") of kissing came powerfully into play. From the origin of film through the late sixties, then, a kiss of variable length had to do the job of suggesting all the excitement and pleasure of intimate sexual contacts.

I will not argue in this chapter for the good old days of the Code, when eroticism flourished precisely because of the extreme constraints imposed on the display of sex, but it is important to realize how some of these restraints, absurd as they may seem today, could enhance the eroticism of a kiss. Eroticism, as Georges Bataille teaches, can be surprisingly complicit with the law, or the morals, that prohibit it. The fascinating story of the travails of the Production Code Administration's conflicts with producers, directors, and writers of the studio era, detailed in several recent books on film censorship, reveals an ongoing tension between what Bataille calls "respect for the law and violation of the law."[20] The Code that forbids carnal representation, lustful kissing, and the "attractive presentation" of "adultery and illicit sex" goes hand in hand with the excitement generated when hints of lust, adultery, and illicit sex nevertheless emerge.

According to a 1992 Gallup Poll the third sexiest movie kiss of all time—right behind Clark Gable and Vivien Leigh's in *Gone with the Wind* (dir. David Selznick, 1939) and Burt Lancaster and Deborah Kerr's in *From Here to Eternity* (dir. Fred Zinneman, 1953)—is that between Humphrey Bogart and Ingrid Bergman in *Casablanca* (dir. Michael Curtiz, 1942). This well-loved classic is about an exiled American saloon owner, Rick Blaine, who, like his native country, belatedly becomes involved in World War II. The cost of his involvement will be to lose, for the second time, the woman he loves. As if in compensation for his noble sacrifice, the film offers several memorable kisses, each a little more forbidden than the last. I will discuss the three most dramatic of these.

In *Casablanca*'s first major kiss, Rick asks Ilsa who she is and if she has loved before. "Only one answer can take care of all our questions," says Ilsa, and that answer is . . . a kiss cued to the song, "As Time Goes By," which swells on the soundtrack. This kiss perfectly obeys the strictures of the Hollywood Production Code: it is short (less than three seconds); it displays no open mouths; it contains nothing "excessive or lustful." The Code reads that "adultery and illicit sex, sometimes necessary plot material, must not be explicitly treated or justified, or presented attractively." Even this prohibition is technically obeyed since neither kisser knows at this moment that he or she is committing adultery. And should we happen to suspect that a further sexual act follows from this kiss, the film is careful not to help us imagine it. Of course we will eventually come to believe that the affair in Paris that begins with this kiss was a great love, but that impression is not yet present in this first kiss. Also, like a great many Hollywood kisses of the Production Code era, this kiss occurs at the end of the scene and is not itself seen to end. Without even the pause of a fade-out and a fade-in, an abrupt cut to the German advance on Paris cuts short the kiss. This will be the pattern for the whole of the film as war and kisses duel.

"You must remember this / A kiss is just a kiss, a sigh is just a sigh / The fundamental things apply / As time goes by": Dooley Wilson as Sam sings the words to this famous song before Rick and Ilsa clinch in the film's second big dramatic kiss. The three of them drink champagne in the bar of Rick's hotel in Paris after Sam has sung a few verses of the song, originally written in 1931 for a different era. The full version of the song makes a case for the simplicity of certain facts of life—"kisses" and "sighs," "moonlight and love songs"—that are "fundamental" in a world of rapid change.[21] In the part Sam sings, kisses and sighs are meant to represent eternal verities, "as time goes by." On closer examination, however, these verities prove rather enigmatic.

Rick will kiss Ilsa three times in this scene. Each time the couple will suddenly exist in its own hermetic world, and Sam will momentarily disappear. In the first kiss, the couple stands at a window speaking of their past lives as the sounds of war draw near. Rick kisses Ilsa, but the back of Ilsa's head blocks our view of their mouths. The kiss is punctuated by the boom of cannons. Attention is drawn away from the unseen lips to the threatening sound of war. Afterward, Ilsa will ask: "Was that cannon fire

8: *Casablanca* (dir. Michael Curtiz, 1942), the gentle kiss

or only my heart pounding?" Next the couple moves to a table to drink champagne with the again present Sam. Rick proposes, but Ilsa is worried and evasive. She strokes Rick's chin with the back of her hand (a gesture we will soon see Bergman repeat in a later postwar kiss with Cary Grant) and then begins the kind of avowal-of-love speech that seems designed to be interrupted by a kiss: "If you shouldn't get away, I mean, if, if something should keep us apart, wherever they put you and wherever I'll be, I want you to know that I. . . ." As she breaks off, her mouth invitingly open in the pronunciation of "I," Rick puts his hand on her cheek and kisses her. In profile this time, we can finally see their lips come together (figure 8).

The couple about to kiss in a Hollywood film before the late sixties is usually bathed in a glow of "romantic" light. The conventional Hollywood three-point lighting scheme of key (usually slightly from above), fill (a light that evens out shadows), and back (the "halo" effect that comes from behind the head) is the basic formula that creates this glow, but especially on the (white) woman, who is almost universally more luminous than anyone else on the screen. The whiter she looks, the purer she seems, even though her presence in the film may also evoke carnal desire. As Richard Dyer writes, "Idealised white women are bathed in and permeated by light. It streams through them and falls on to them from above. In short, they glow."[22] It is not surprising that the Nordic Ingrid Bergman, the object and subject of illicit carnal desire in many of the kisses explored here and below, glows relative to the servile Sam,[23] whose blackness can only shine, not glow. She also glows relative to the darker skin tones of Bogart's Rick in this particular kiss. Though there is a little light on the top of his forehead, most of his face, and especially his hand, appear several shades

darker. Indeed, all white women in Hollywood films glow with a light that works to purify the darker lusts their kisses may evoke.[24]

Once again, cannon fire punctuates the kiss and "As Time Goes By" surges. But the kiss itself, described as "gentle" in the script, remains relatively undramatic. Under the impression that they will soon leave Paris together, Rick does not have the same urgency as Ilsa. All the more reason, then, Code notwithstanding, for Ilsa to demand a more dramatic, less "gentle," more "final" kiss. This time she even orders it: "Kiss me. Kiss me as if it were the last time." The relatively short Bogart rises high in his seat in order to take into his mouth the upper lip of the relatively tall Bergman—in profile. Hard bodily pressure, which Ilsa returns, signaled by her placement of her own hand over his, constitutes the essence of this "big kiss" (figure 9). As we have already seen, the logistics of filming two faces with mouths pressed tightly against one another often preclude seeing much of what transpires once lips are locked. This is especially true of the kisses of the Hollywood Code era. The best one can do is to observe where one set of lips is positioned before it encounters another, and, if one is lucky enough to experience the full duration of the kiss, to observe where they are located at the end.

But, of course, we are usually not so lucky to see a kiss all the way to its end. Here, for example, just as we begin to take it in, a quick camera tilt down averts our gaze from the lovers' faces to Ilsa's hand as it accidentally knocks over her glass (figure 10). Music, sounding like cannon fire, pounds ominously. We now notice that because Ilsa had never drunk to Rick's previous "here's looking at you, kid" toast, her champagne spills. Like the earlier scene's quick cut to the German invasion, this interruption also gives us no time to enjoy the kiss's full passion. Indeed, it casts an ominous shadow on its carnal pleasure.[25]

We might dub the frequent practice of the interruption of Code-era kisses *osculum interruptum*. Since any kiss that lingered was in danger of seeming "excessive and lustful," interruptions were frequent. On the whole, during the Code era, the mark of excess could be anything longer than three seconds. *Interruptum* could then be accomplished by fade-outs or by cutting away to a new scene or by interrupting our view internally within the same shot, as in this camera tilt down to the spilled champagne. Ironically, the tradition of interruption—of looking elsewhere while the kiss itself may continue—can give rise to the illusion that kisses might actually endure, but just out of sight.

The last big kiss in *Casablanca* offers yet another variation of *osculum interruptum* in the form of an ellipsis.[26] Ilsa sneaks into Rick's room above his café late at night. She is desperate to obtain the letters of transit for her husband, Victor Laszlo, to leave Casablanca. When Rick arrives, she first asks him to put his feelings aside and to aid the resistance hero. When he refuses, she pulls a gun. Rick welcomes it, "Go ahead shoot me, you'd be doing me a favor." She then weeps and turns away. Rick hesitates a moment, then quickly comes up behind her, and Ilsa collapses in his arms.

Getting ready for the kiss, we are learning, is often more dramatic and more teasingly erotic than the kiss itself. If we think of the kiss as the synecdoche of the whole sex act, then this part standing in for the whole has its very own form of foreplay. As in Edison's *The Kiss*, it often consists of two faces held close together, on the verge of touching. When two people are seen in profile looking at one another at close range, their eyes cannot take in the whole of the face at which they gaze without a certain survey-

11: *Casablanca*,
prekiss: "If you
knew how much I
loved you"

ing movement up and down or from side to side. This movement, which
cannot be captured in stills and which Bergman performs magnificently
here, seems to hover on the brink between looking and touching. Silhouetted in profile, face to face, the couple's mouths and noses almost touching, the music surges once again as Ilsa says "If you knew how much I
loved you, how much I still love you. . . ." Again, her words are interrupted
by a kiss initiated by Bogart (figure 11). As usual, the music of "As Time
Goes By" soars, but in a minor key, reaching no concluding chord. The
image dissolves, in medias kiss, replaced by a long shot of a searchlight.
Why, we ask, are we looking at a searchlight when we could be still looking
at what is, after all, the *big kiss* of the film? Have we again cut to the next
scene as with the kiss that was interrupted by the German invasion?

Not quite. After holding on the tower and searchlight a while, we see
Rick in the following shot, dressed exactly as before, still in his apartment, gazing at the searchlight tower. It is as if the film has blinked and
looked away momentarily, but it has not left the scene entirely. Time has
passed, we do not know exactly how much, but Rick's next line, "And then
. . . ," spoken to Ilsa discovered seated across the room, indicates that the
dramatic scene between them continues, but that the full action of the
kiss—and whatever may have been its aftermath—has been elided. We
cannot tell what has transpired in the ellipsis between the time of the kiss
and the time of Rick gazing at the searchlight. What we do know is that
the couple's conversation still centers on the same topic that initiated the
kiss—Ilsa's continuing love for Rick.

An ellipsis is a rhetorical figure of speech in which a word or words required by strict grammatical rules are omitted. In conventions of printing

or writing, an ellipsis is a literal gap indicated by three sequential dots that omit words that could, by the logic of what comes before or after, be present. In both instances, the missing words are implied by the context. The context, in the case of *Casablanca*, is the kiss—indeed all the kisses—begun and never seen to be completed by Ilsa and Rick throughout the film.[27] Ellipses happen all the time in movies, frequently within the same scene, usually accomplished by single cuts from shot to shot. But ellipses are especially frequent and felt *as* ellipses—noticed as dot, dot, dot—when they elide sex acts. An ellipsis that occurs in the middle of a kiss, and returns to the couple in the same space and at an unspecified later time, is as close as a Code film can get to the suggestion of otherwise unmentionable sexual contacts. What do we infer in this case? How, for example, do Ilsa and Rick now behave toward one another?

Certainly they are now relaxed. Rick is unmussed, but he is smoking and contemplative as he gets the story of Laszlo's unexpected return from Ilsa while standing at the window. In the process of this story we learn that Ilsa had been married to Laszlo only a short time before he was sent to the concentration camp, that they had kept the marriage secret to protect her from similar persecution, and that the nature of her relation to Laszlo was more hero worship than carnal desire. Respect and affection, not passion, mark the relations of the licit couple. (At one point we see him kiss Ilsa with fatherly affection.) Ilsa, too, is now relaxed, and she nestles (postcoitally?) in Rick's arms as she tells him, infamously, to do the "thinking for all of us." Later Rick will explain to Laszlo that Ilsa came to his apartment to get the letters of transit, pretending she still loved him: "I let her pretend."

Is this what the Production Code calls an "attractive presentation" of "adultery and illicit sex"? Obviously a lot depends on how one interprets the ellipsis and Rick's "I let her pretend." Film critic Richard Maltby argues that the film neither confirms nor denies Rick and Ilsa's affair, thus "refusing to take responsibility for the story some viewers may choose to construct."[28] Code enforcers let it go, probably because it does not lead, in the end, to the union of the adulterous couple. Maltby cites a letter from the Code administrator Joseph Breen to Jack Warner in which he observes that the scene in Rick's apartment "seems to contain a suggestion of a sexual affair. . . . We believe this could possibly be corrected by replacing the fade out . . . with a dissolve, and shooting the succeeding scene without any sign of a bed or couch, or anything whatever suggestive of a sex affair."[29] In other words, Breen believed that the dissolve to a later moment could allow the filmmakers to ever so discreetly deny what they were simultaneously indicating. The fact that Rick will ultimately decide that their little affair (whether construed as possible or actual) does not amount to a "hill of beans" when weighed against the larger world struggle, plus the fact that Laszlo ultimately "gets the girl," even if she does not love him, means that a physical relation can be suggested as long as it is also possible to deny it.

Sexual desire ultimately exists in this and many other Code-era films so that it may be sublimated to a more purified, ideological, and aesthetic "good"—whether the good of the family or, in this case, the good of the American and European struggle against fascism. Desire and sexual pleasure as positive values in themselves have no legitimate, acknowledged place in the era of the Code, though they certainly sneak in around the edges. This, of course, is the special, perverse pleasure of watching sex in movies of this period: sex can never be indulged in for itself, and for this reason it must remain exquisitely ambiguous what exactly transpires between Rick and Ilsa.

It is easy to ridicule a Code that works so hard to keep us from inferring what its very obfuscations and interruptions cause us to suspect. But this is how eroticism works in the Code era. It is no accident that the most erotic of the kisses in which Rick and Ilsa engage is the one most fully adulterous (by this time they *both* know that Laszlo lives). This may also be why the two other movie kisses—that in *From Here to Eternity* and that in *Gone with the Wind*—have also been deemed among the sexiest. They, too, are structured on internal conflicts between illicit sexual desires and the demands of war, whether the Civil War or World War II. Code kisses are memorable, it seems, not because they are necessarily performed by sexy men and sexy women (has Humphrey Bogart, with his perpetually wet lower lip, ever been, objectively speaking, sexy?), but because they are intrinsically structured around conflicts between sexual pleasure and taboo.

It is not necessary, however, for the desire-enhancing taboo to consist of strict patriarchal laws such as the one forbidding adultery, nor that the taboo be one actually written into the Production Code. The kiss that will often seem the most erotic need only be placed in tension with an internal resistance to its pleasures. Remarkably, the male actor of the Code era who has most often embodied these internal resistances, and who thus often participated in the most erotic (and neurotic) kisses, is the superficially wholesome, middle-American James Stewart. Stewart's most famous kiss is certainly the virtuoso 360-degree slowly encircled one performed with Kim Novak in Alfred Hitchcock's *Vertigo* (1958).[30] A less acknowledged erotic kiss, however—and one not yet overtly rebelling against Code limits—occurs in Frank Capra's well-loved family melodrama *It's a Wonderful Life* (1946).[31]

Here Stewart's George Bailey reluctantly pays a call to his former sweetheart Mary (Donna Reed). They are obviously drawn to one another, but George's goals in life are college and travel, and he knows that Mary is capable of miring him in the sort of small-town family life his adventurous goals vehemently resist—and that Capra's film ultimately celebrates. When George "happens by" Mary's parlor one summer night, he rudely begrudges her the visit, and Mary ironically taunts her nosy, interfering mother with the claim, very far from the truth, that George "is making violent love" to her. But when an old beau of Mary's phones her from New York, the call provides an occasion for George and Mary to put their heads together before the mouthpiece and receiver of an old-fashioned telephone. In the conversation, George's nose and mouth touch Mary's hair (figure 12). As he senses her presence, he becomes simultaneously aroused and enraged, fearing the entanglement she represents and desiring her all the more for that fear. He eventually drops the phone midconversation and faces Mary directly: "I don't want . . . to get married. I want to do what I want to do!" Violently shaking her, George gradually transforms the shake into an embrace, and the embrace into a tight kiss that proves Mary's comment to her mother correct: he *is* making violent love to her (figure 13). Moreover, the kiss is exceedingly long, or at least we infer that it is since a cut to Mary's mother, who had been spying on the pair, scurrying upstairs at this naked display of passion, keeps us from seeing much. This shot is followed, in a radical ellipsis, by Mary and George emerging from a church, married. A kiss between sweethearts that leads directly to marriage can hardly be called taboo. However, George's internal resistance to Mary's charms enacts the violent tension between fear and desire that renders this kiss, so little of which is actually seen, one of the most erotic of the entire Code era.

Orality

Physically, a kiss is the "juxtaposition of two orbicularis oris muscles in a stage of contraction." *Orbicularis oris* is the "sphincter muscle" around the mouth that shapes and controls the size of the mouth opening.[32] Used for talking and facial expressions, and capable of four distinct types of movement, this muscle is also central to kissing. As we have already seen

It's a Wonderful Life (dir. Frank Capra, 1946)

12: George's nose and mouth touch Mary's hair as they share the phone

13: George and Mary do make "violent" love

in the previous examples of kisses, every bit as exciting as the muscular locking of lips is the dramatic moment of transition from distant to more proximate forms of communication: from, say, talking face to face, where the muscles have one function, as George and Mary do through the device of the telephone mouthpiece, to, at the opposite extreme, "locking lips" or "sucking face."

The original function of these sphincterlike muscles, before they were employed to talk or to kiss, was to sustain life by sucking milk. In silent films, where pantomime often takes the place of spoken words, and mouths take on an allure far beyond their function in speech, we are often dramatically reminded of the mouth's originary, nonspeaking function. The fact that silent cinema existed in the era before the Hollywood Production Code outlawed "lustful," "excessive," and "adulterous" kisses means that silent films often allow us to watch the anatomy of whole kisses and to better observe the rather blatant oral pleasures of these uninterrupted osculations.

Consider, for example, the kisses of two of the most famous lovers both on and off the silent American screen: Greta Garbo and John Gilbert in *Flesh and the Devil* (dir. Clarence Brown, 1927). When Gilbert's dashing, young Austrian officer and Garbo's sophisticated (and unbeknownst to Gilbert, married) baroness first find themselves alone in a moonlit garden at a glamorous Old World ball, their romance is literally and figuratively kindled by a match intended to light a cigarette. In their secluded spot, already drawn close and framed in a tight shot, Gilbert's Count Leo speaks: "You are very beautiful." "You are very young," Garbo's ironically named Felicitas replies, protruding slightly parted lips. Should we wish to consider such things in a silent film in which words are seen but not heard, it is possible that the "realistic" motivation for this first protrusion of her parted lips is the pronunciation of the unheard word *you* (figure 14). But, of course, the beauty of silent films is that the realistic motivation for any gesture is often beside the point. We are in a realm of mute eloquence. Garbo's lips part and protrude because she is the seductive vamp, and vamps are oral beings who thrive on sucking the lifeblood of those they seduce. Unlike many a previous silent-screen vamp, however, she does not merely seek to destroy her prey. She, too, is caught up in the fleshy pleasures by which the devil tempts.

Any kiss requires that the kissers first face one another.[33] One of the reasons smoking has been somewhat slower to fade from the American screen than from public life may well have to do with its usefulness in creating the proximity for kissing. The cigarette, moreover, offers an eloquent prefiguration, as well as an occasional upstaging, of the kiss to come. Holding one up to her face, Garbo awaits the light for which the awestruck Gilbert fumbles. She places the cigarette dead center between puckered, proffered lips, as if teaching him with it what he might later do with his tongue (figure 15). Then, while still awaiting the light, she suddenly removes the cigarette from her mouth and places it in his. Gilbert's whole body responds to the oral intrusion, drawing erect and slightly back as he recognizes her bold invitation. Already probed by the moist cigarette that Garbo herself has "kissed," Gilbert nevertheless proceeds with the increasingly unnecessary business of lighting the match. Its purpose, when lit, is to dramatically illuminate their faces. But this illumination is more for us than for them. They themselves have moved beyond the stage in which sight matters to the more proximate senses of smell, taste, and

Flesh and the
Devil (dir. Clarence
Brown, 1927)

14: Garbo's lips
protrude on the
unheard word *you*.

15: Garbo places
the cigarette, as
if teaching Gilbert
what he might
later do with his
tongue

touch. To signal this, Garbo blows out the unnecessary match, and Gilbert finally gets the point: "You know," he says, "when you blow out the match that's an invitation to kiss?"

Once again, in this silent film, we do not bother to think about how Gilbert could have spoken these words with a cigarette planted dead center in his mouth. We have been transported to a realm of suspended sexual anticipation that has already forgotten about mouths as organs of speech. We have also forgotten about cigarettes as objects for smoking. Gilbert discards the still unlit cigarette and finally takes Garbo in his arms. The kiss that follows is cast in the shadow and shows only their silhouetted forms pressing together. It is not the kind of kiss that shows us exactly what the mouth and lips do, but this is not because any Code prohibits it. Indeed, everything that has gone before has conspired to make us believe that these two glamorous beings face each other, as Code era kissers cannot, with parted lips.

Itching and Scratching

"No one who has seen a baby sinking back satiated from the breast and falling asleep with flushed cheeks and a blissful smile can escape the reflection that this picture persists as a prototype of the expression of sexual satisfaction in later life"[34]: Sigmund Freud's once shocking thesis that infantile sexuality is observable first, in the child sucking at the breast and second, in the substitute gesture of "thumb-sucking (or sensual sucking)" can help us ponder some of the perverse pleasures of screen kisses.

According to Freud, the mouth is the first of the child's erotogenic zones to be activated. Thumb, lip, or toe sucking is a sensual, autoerotic pleasure that excites the mucous membrane of the mouth similar to the way the lips and mouth were once stimulated by the warm flow of milk.[35] Repetitive sensual sucking of a part of the child's own body thus becomes detached from the satisfaction of original nourishment to become a "labial zone" of pleasure in its own right.[36] The kiss is an act of sexual intimacy in which the mouths prefigure the later joining of other body parts. In this teleological way of thinking, a kiss anticipates, but does not yet arrive at, a more advanced, adult stage of genital sex. But it is also an act of intimacy that recalls the earlier act of maternal breast-feeding in which one erotogenic zone—the mother's nipple, her milk—excites another—the infant's mouth.[37] Sucking at the breast, and the more frequently ignored maternal side of this equation, giving-to-suck, are thus arguably at the origin of all sexual pleasures to come.[38]

But how exactly do we understand this sexual pleasure to come? Freud often asserts that the goal of sexuality—its defining instance—is a release in genital discharge. This is the "end pleasure." Freud defines perversion as any sexual activities that either "extend, in an anatomical sense, beyond the regions of the body that are designed for sexual union" or "linger over the intermediate relations to the sexual object which should normally be traversed rapidly on the path towards the final sexual aim."[39] Freud's terms are inadequate, both to his own discussion of sexuality—since he fully realizes that a kiss might be "lingered" on a little longer than absolutely necessary to achieve "discharge" in copulation—and for our examination of movie kisses, since all movies before the late sixties must censor any reference to "normal" sexual acts and (perversely) substitute kisses in their place.[40]

Motives of decorum and decency dictated that movies of the kiss era necessarily fixate on the infantile and perverse orality of kisses. Kissing too long, kissing posited as the sole visible sexual act, necessarily becomes, as Freud says of pathological symptoms, obsessive and repetitive.[41] In the love scene that follows Garbo and Gilbert's first kiss, for example, languorous kissing soon becomes dangerously vampiric. It lingers. The excess of the affair is measured in what may be one of the silent screen's longest kisses (nearly twenty seconds). Its carnal pleasure for the viewer is complicated, however, by several factors: First, the viewer's knowledge that a man we soon learn to be Garbo's husband, the Baron Von Rhadan, may be approaching; second, a sudden cut to black that seems to interrupt the kiss, but which actually proves to be a new point of view as the baron's hand slowly opens the bedroom door and then clenches into a fist when the space opened discloses the ongoing kiss; finally, as the long osculation continues, we resume something like our original view, but this time subtly reframed so as to make Garbo's already dominant pose more obviously vampiric as she "drinks" from Gilbert's lips while turning her eyes to encounter the baron.

In identifying the "perversity" of oral stimulations that have no further issue in a film, I do not meant to suggest that these films *should* "progress" to genital stimulation, that it is perverse that they do not. Rather, I want to stress the paradox of an era in which supposedly innocent kisses must constitute the be-all and end-all of sexual pleasure. In pre–Code era kisses this means that adults must sometimes behave as if they were orally fixated. Consider a moment, late in this same film, when Garbo, ever the seductress, having used a variation of the earlier light-my-cigarette trick to seduce Gilbert's best friend, now finds herself married to him but still lusting after Gilbert. The three friends are taking communion from a pastor who suspects Garbo and Gilbert's adulterous intentions. As the communion wine passes from person to person, the pastor turns the cup slightly so that the new drinker's lips will not touch the place where the previous lips have lingered. But when the pastor passes the cup from Gilbert to Garbo, to the shock and outrage of the pastor, she boldly turns it back so that her lips will touch where his have. In this orally fixated film, even the Old Testament pastor smokes a pipe adorned with the ceramic figurine of a seductive woman. Of course, Garbo's defiance of the forbidding pastor will seal her fate as a willful sinner who deserves her ultimate death by drowning. But before this end, we have run the gamut of the perverse pleasures of the mouth.

The point is not to accuse kiss-era films of their perverse orality, but to see this perversion as a model for understanding sexual pleasure *tout court*. For example, Leo Bersani, in a discussion of Freud, argues that often the "pleasurable unpleasurable tension of sexual stimulation seeks not to be released, but to be increased."[42] Thus a model of tension and release is complicated by the existence of sexual excitations that augment pleasure in ways quite distinct from simple "discharge." Pleasure, in other words, is not the same thing as satisfaction and may rely on a certain "unpleasure" that prolongs excitement. Bersani beautifully describes Freud's two forms of sexual pleasure as, on one hand, an itch that can be satisfied by a scratch, and, on the other, an itch that does not seek to be scratched, that "seeks nothing better than its own prolongation, even its own intensification."[43]

The itch (augmentation of excitement) and scratch (satisfaction in discharge) models of sexual pleasure operate in all forms of sexual contact. It would therefore be a mistake to view the kiss as the itch and genital sex as the scratch. We shall see in chapter 5, for example, how one of the most genitally oriented of all graphic art films, *In the Realm of the Senses*, is predicated entirely on an itch model of sexual excitement, while some of the kisses examined here function, for all the kiss's usual role as foreplay, as concluding scratches. Indeed, in the extremely limited repertoire of sexual acts permitted in the era of the kiss, kisses positioned at "the end" function as scratches, while kisses such as those we have examined in *Casablanca* and *Flesh and the Devil* function as itches. The itchier kisses, however, seem to teach us the most about a sexual excitement that, as the montage of kisses and embraces that concludes *Cinema Paradiso* shows, does not teleologically lead to "end pleasure" but may be, as Bersani suggests, a circle leading back to the polymorphously perverse sucking child.[44]

Reciprocity

The kiss is a relatively late form of oral eroticism—what Adam Phillips calls a "craving for other mouths"—that is central to adolescence but that also returns us to the "primary sensuous experience" of smelling and tasting another person first learned at the breast.[45] What is remarkable about the kiss, however, is that it can be simultaneously given and received. Unlike so many other sex acts that depend on penetration—one convex organ fitting into another concave one—the kiss is a contact in which one can touch the other with the *same* body parts—lips, tongue, mucous membrane—with which one is touched oneself. It is thus unique among sex acts in its great potential for reciprocity.[46] D. W. Winnicott stresses the mother's sensitive adaptation to the infant's needs and her ability to provide the "illusion that her breast is part of the infant,"[47] while Jean Laplanche stresses the interpenetration of the "vital (lifegiving) order" with the "sexual (pleasure-giving) order" to stress the mother's reaction, an activity that he describes, at the limit, as a kind of maternal seduction.[48] But even allowing for a nongenital maternal "seduction" in the nursing situation, the incommensurability of the "partners," the absolute dependency of the infant, and the dissimilarity of the organs—mouth and breast—mitigates against anything like egalitarian reciprocity in the nursing situation.

In the adolescent or adult kiss, however, each mouth is equipped with the same parts: receptive mucous membrane of the lips and a tongue that can retract or probe, not to mention saliva and, unlike in the baby, teeth. Unlike heterosexual intercourse, mouths and tongues can interpenetrate in a potentially mutual give-and-take.[49] This may be one reason why women are the great connoisseurs of romantic kisses—not, as has sometimes been suggested, because of an innate female predilection for soft-core, soft-focus romanticism, but because kisses are so potentially egalitarian.[50] There are few other (equipmentless) sexual acts in which a woman can be both penetrator and penetrated.

This is not to say that all kisses are fully reciprocal sexual acts. One could say, for example, that Gilbert "kisses" Garbo before the fade-out in *Flesh and the Devil*, for it is true that Gilbert, the man, in the end takes Garbo, the woman, in his arms, though all the rest of the kisses in this film offer the spectacle of the woman as the dominant kisser. In a certain heterosexual orthodoxy very much at work in American screen kisses all the way through the sixties, it may be the patriarchal job of men to initiate kisses, but it is frequently the job of the woman to teach, invite, or even order the man to kiss ("Kiss me, kiss me as if it was the last time").[51]

A kiss takes place in time; the probe of a mouth or tongue can lead to a later answering probe—or not. A kiss is both a sex act in itself and, as Phillips puts it, a "performed allusion" to one.[52] Such is the dilemma, and the glory, of the adolescent era of the kiss as the be-all and end-all of movie sex before the sixties. For even in Garbo and Gilbert's example of a pre-Code, "lustful," open-mouthed kiss—the sort that would be banned after 1934—even in a kiss that serves as a prelude to what is clearly meant to be seen as a torrid and destructive love affair, all that we will ever see of this affair will be . . . more kisses. To be sure, these kisses will be in horizontal positions, take place in what is obviously a boudoir, and manifest a mood of postcoital familiarity. Even so these kisses remain all we see.[53]

Consider the very next love scene in *Flesh and the Devil*, which follows immediately on the fade-out from the first kiss. After an intertitle proclaims, "No one had ever loved before . . . Leo was sure of it," the film fades into what seems to be Garbo's boudoir. She reclines languorously on a divan while Gilbert lounges on a rug with his head resting first on her lap, later on her breast. He smokes in undisguised postcoital relaxation (his cigarette finally lit!). It could be days or only a few hours since their first kiss; the ellipsis that separates the two scenes does not allow us to tell exactly. The couple is fully dressed, but Gilbert's high and tight military collar is undone, and the couple is intimately reveling in the kind of feet-off-the-floor reclining position that would, six years hence, become taboo in all American films. Long past the stage of needing an oral toy to bring them together, they now kiss freely and deeply. Garbo's luminous Felicitas has only to direct her lips down, and Gilbert's Leo only to direct his up, for them to meet (figure 16). Nor does obscure lighting this time prevent us from seeing the position of their parted lips. Later they will be discovered in flagrante delicto by Garbo's husband as she watches him enter the room (figure 17). Though it is obvious that in between the first kiss and these more intimate ones, something has transpired, both the fade-out that ends the first kiss and the fade-in that begins this next series of kisses elide these further acts.

The context of this ellipsis, unlike those of *Casablanca*, thus allows us to presume that genital sexual acts have transpired. Though the camera has, again, looked away, this particular postcoital aftermath does not preclude the possibility of all sorts of intimate, adulterous relations, for very soon Gilbert will learn, just as Bogart did in the Code-era film, that he is an unwitting adulterer. Indeed, the main difference between pre-Code and Code kisses, besides their obvious duration and the position of mouths and bodies, is how much further sex can be presumed to have taken place in the ellipses. Pre-Code ellipses are more likely, as in *Flesh and the Devil*, to build a long sexual affair into the fade-out/fade-in. Alternatively, they might punctuate the elided sex with a rhetorical flourish, as the train whistle that follows Marlene Dietrich and Clive Brooks's first kiss in *Shanghai Express* (dir. Josef von Sternberg, 1932). In this film, the whistle does the affective work of the missing coitus, literally letting off steam.

A particularly interesting example of the use of ellipsis as a rhetorical

Flesh and the Devil

16: Garbo need only direct her lips down

17: Garbo's long vampiric kiss while she discovers her husband at the door

flourish in the pre-Code era to point lasciviously to the beyond-the-kiss that we do not see occurs in Mervin Le Roy's romantic comedy *Tonight or Never* (1931) with Gloria Swanson and Melvin Douglas.[54] Like *Shanghai Express* this film occupies the fascinating transition period between the institution of the Code (first promulgated in 1930) and its gradual enforcement by 1934. Swanson plays a glamorous opera singer whose performances have been accused of lacking passion. To remedy this lack she determines to have an affair, choosing a handsome man who has been following her. This man (Douglas) is a famous American opera impresario whom she mistakes for a gigolo. Maneuvering her way into his apartment, she is prepared to be seduced by him for the sake of her art. When he discovers her belief that he is a gigolo, he acts the part, locking her in the room and passionately kissing her. This first kiss is rough and fast: Douglas

Tonight or Never
(dir. Mervin
Le Roy, 1931)

18: Swanson
points to bruises
and demands a
more tender kind
of kiss

19: The kiss for
which Swanson
has asked

leans over the diminutive Swanson and pushes down hard; the camera tracks in fast to a close-up, the camera movement, as much as the kiss itself, conveying the roughness. Afterward, he holds her at arm's length to scrutinize her reaction and throws her roughly down onto the divan. However, he is also somewhat relieved to see that she is scandalized by his roughness. Lying back on the divan, she invites a new kind of attention by pointing to potential bruises on her arms (figure 18), providing his cue to employ a more tender kind of kiss to make better her hurts.

Throughout the rest of the scene, Swanson alternately invites and repulses Douglas: "Let me get up . . . I really don't want to get up. I don't want to love a man . . . that is I do." He forces the issue with the eponymous ultimatum: "Tonight or never," giving her three minutes, until the clock on the mantel chimes ten, to make up her mind. If she remains in his apartment after three minutes pass, she will "have to take the consequences." After further verbal sparring that neatly devours three minutes in this rather talky adaptation of a Broadway play, she begs, in yet another example of the woman inviting and/or instructing the kiss: "Before I go, please kiss me just once, sweetly, tenderly, as if we really belonged to each other." They do kiss as if they really belonged (figure 19). But whereas the camera plunged forward into their first, rough, quick kiss, this time it coyly pans right to the clock on the mantel as it chimes ten. Almost immediately Swanson, offscreen, is heard to say, "Please call a taxi," and Douglas is heard to answer, teasingly, "It's too late!" Fade out.

Again, the look away from the kiss is a major cliché of so-called classic American movies that hints at what cannot be shown. Before the Code was fully enforced, such hints were stronger (compare this dialogue, which clearly suggests that Swanson *will* spend the night, to the cut to the searchlight in *Casablanca*, which leaves us wondering). However, both types are limited to the display of oral pleasures that become more perverse the more they are asked to substitute for a "normal" progression to heterosexual genital acts.

Eating the Other

We have seen that all screen kisses share a connection to infantile sexuality born of hunger and derived from the original oral gratification of sucking, in effect, of eating (or drinking) the other. Some of the most memorable kisses seem to understand that a primal hunger lies at the root of these oral pleasures. Phillips writes, "When we kiss we devour the object by caressing it; we eat it, in a sense, but sustain its presence."[55] The difference between the adolescent kiss and infantile sucking, then, is that the kiss is a kind of "aim-inhibited" eating. Like a gum-chewer, the kisser never swallows what he or she craves—although Garbo's vampiric kiss and sexualized communion come perilously close.[56] Some of the most arresting screen kisses are thus not surprisingly related to eating.[57] To return then to some of the quicker kisses from the era of the Production Code, when this devouring dimension was necessarily tempered by specific prohibitions against open-mouthed, "lustful," and "excessive" kisses, let us consider a kiss between Cary Grant and Ingrid Bergman in Alfred Hitchcock's *Notorious* (1946). Famous for the ingenious way in which

20: *Notorious* (dir. Alfred Hitchcock, 1946), Bergman and Grant begin the scene with a big, full-bodied kiss on the balcony

Hitchcock circumnavigates the length restrictions that had developed to counter the possibility of supposed excess, this film systematically mixes its kisses with hunger and thirst.

On assignment in Rio to spy on a ring of Nazis, Bergman's Alicia and Grant's Devlin begin to fall in love. She is eager, but he is cautious because of her disreputable past. Everything in the following scene seems to run in reverse. It begins with a big kiss on the balcony of Alicia's hotel. The kiss is full, lengthy (about four seconds), and uninterrupted (figure 20). It is very much the kind of big crescendo kiss that one might expect as the finale of a love scene or even, unfinished, as a film's final clinch. Indeed, it is as if Hitchcock has chosen to reverse the usual way Code-era films build up to the big moment of the scene-ending kiss, thus proceeding to a scene of separation that will leave the kissers still hungry for one another. After this kiss, still holding one another close in a long, continuous embrace, they begin to discuss dinner. Nibbling on Devlin's cheek, fondling his earlobe with the back of her fingers,[58] Alicia resists going out to eat. Devlin, more practical, says, "We have to eat." In answer, Alicia describes the chicken she will cook for him as their mouths and noses taste and smell each other. The decision to stay in and eat is coded as a decision to have an affair. (So of course it will have to be interrupted. But Hitchcock cleverly gets around some of the usual features of the *osculum interruptum*.)

With the big kiss already performed—hanging there as an invitation to eat more—the scene proceeds to perform dozens of small kisses and nibbles of the sort that would, more typically, lead up to the big one. No other Hollywood director of the Code era, to my knowledge, has managed to get away with so much kissing for so long. From the balcony the en-

Notorious

21: Still kissing,
Grant slowly extri-
cates himself

22: Devlin pulls
away from the last
kiss, leaving Alicia
at the door hungry
for more

twined couple moves into the living room of Alicia's hotel, where Devlin makes a phone call and picks up a message to report to the office for their espionage assignment. They neck all the way from the phone to the door where Devlin pauses for a last kiss, all the while subtly pulling away (figure 21). The consummation of either meal—the sexual one they are already tasting, and the chicken one they are discussing—is deferred. The genius of the scene is to make the kisses do double duty: they both advance the plot and prolong the itch, even while beginning with the kind of long, fulfilling kiss that might otherwise count as a scratch.[59] Devlin's exit is a master touch: he pulls away from the last possible kiss, leaving Alicia alone at the door, still hungry for more (figure 22).

When Devlin eventually returns with the news that their assignment will be for Alicia to seduce the Nazi villain, both lose appetite. Alicia substitutes the lesser oral satisfaction of a drink for Devlin. They will not get to kiss again until the film's climax, when Devlin rescues Alicia from the villain who has been slowly poisoning her. The couple thus remains hungry—Alicia quite literally must starve herself to resist poisoning by the Nazi husband who discovers her espionage—until the very end, when Devlin escorts Alicia from what is meant to be her deathbed, and they resume their mutual nibbles. Just as a child sucks greedily at its mother's breast, so these two grown movie stars inhale, suck, and taste one another, sustaining each other as objects of mutual oral desire.[60]

The Senses, Close and at a Distance

Film viewing offers a vicarious pleasure in which senses perceived "at a distance"—sight and hearing—are substituted for more proximate senses of contact—touch, taste, smell.[61] When I engage in a kiss, I ultimately give up this distance for proximity as the face of the person I kiss comes closer. Siegfried Kracauer cites Marcel Proust's famous description of a kiss from *The Guermantes Way* to show how perspective changes as we move into close-ups: skin surfaces become like aerial photography, eyes become like lakes or volcano craters, and the "prison of conventional reality" is broken apart to reveal new possibilities.[62] Proust's kiss points to some of the more disturbing qualities of the close-up's magnified view. In a many-paged description of his narrator's kiss of Albertine, the girl of his dreams, we encounter this description:

> In this brief passage of my lips towards her cheek it was ten Albertines that I saw; this single girl being like a goddess with several heads, that which I had last seen, if I tried to approach it, gave place to another. At least so long as I had not touched it, that head, I could still see it, a faint perfume reached me from it. But alas—for in this matter of kissing our nostrils and eyes are as ill placed as our lips are shaped—suddenly my eyes ceased to see; next, my nose, crushed by the collision, no longer perceived any fragrance, and without thereby gaining any clearer idea of the taste of the rose of my desire, I learned, from these unpleasant signs, that at last I was in the act of kissing Albertine's cheek.[63]

As he approaches the pink cheek he has so longed to smell and taste, the narrator discovers to his dismay that the entity that had been the visual Albertine breaks up into fragments. Where his sense of sight had been in need of a certain distance, the more proximate senses give only parts;

some are even foiled by proximity itself, and for Proust's narrator, who clearly wants to see as much as he feels, the anticipated possession of the girl never quite materializes.

The lesson for the movie kiss, however, is not quite the same as for Proust's narrator. Indeed, though the camera brings us close to the two kissing faces, so that the eyes may seem, as Kracauer notes, like lakes or craters, we never arrive at the point where nostrils and eyes seem "ill placed" because *our* eyes never cease to see, *our* nose is not "crushed." For the viewers of the movie kiss, the integrity of the kissed object never breaks up, even in close-ups as tight as the one held on Montgomery Clift and Elizabeth Taylor in *A Place in the Sun* (dir. George Stevens, 1951). From our vantage point looking on from outside the kiss, we see how the two faces fit together to become one—a view that eluded Proust's kisser. Indeed, this narrator is so focused on the imagined visual possession of Albertine that he seems not to realize that the pleasure of a kiss resides in this shift to another register of sensation in which "having at a distance" is no longer possible. In the magnified moving-image close-up of the kiss, what the person who watches lacks in the senses of touch, smell, and taste is gained, in a compensatory way, in the close vision that falls short of the breakup experienced by Proust. In other words, the film kiss partially satisfies, for its viewer, the desire of Proust's narrator to hold onto some semblance of the picture of the whole of the face that he kisses. This visual pleasure taken in an act that is inherently about other senses gradually becomes institutionalized in film history as kisses become the key punctuation marks of narrative films.

Kisses thus allow us to cop a look, so to speak, at those who cop a feel. But this does not mean that we vicariously kiss even if, as I have maintained, we learn a great deal about kissing from screening these sex acts. In the introduction I noted Vivian Sobchack's argument that to understand movies we must literally "make sense" of relations of embodiment, by which she means that cinema consists of modes of seeing and hearing, as well as of physical and reflective movement that constitute the very foundation of its expressiveness.[64] In other words, our own sense of touch is invoked when we watch touching on the screen. But our touch, as I also argue in the introduction, does not simply mimic what we see on the screen. My mouth may pucker, my tongue may move, but I do not myself kiss. Rather, one bodily sense translates into another, energies transmute, and I experience a diffuse sensuality. Proust's narrator may experience the loss of sight as he moves closer to Albertine, and he passes that frustrated sense on to his readers. But Sobchack suggests that spectators who watch the mediated sexual encounter of embodied beings are, unlike Proust's hapless narrator, able to feel with their other senses what only seems intrusive to Proust. Sight commutes to touch, not literal touch, but our own senses make sense of the vision of touch in our own flesh in haptic ways that cannot be reduced to sight alone.

Andy Warhol's Kiss

The films of Andy Warhol stand outside the mainstream of silent and sound, Code and pre-Code films we have so far examined. But because many of his early, silent, avant-garde films so single-mindedly anatomize specific sex acts, whether those actually seen—as in *Kiss*, or *Couch*, or *Blue Movie*—or those placed just off the scene—as in *Blow Job*—they offer a fascinating commentary on the more conventional Hollywood, as well as the more conventional pornographic, representations of these acts. Nowhere is this more the case than in his 1963 film *Kiss*, his first film to be publicly projected in a theater.

In this compendium of thirteen kisses, each one is longer than any of the kisses—Code and pre-Code—that had come before in mainstream movies. The film adds up to fifty-eight minutes when projected at the designated, silent speed of sixteen frames per second.[65] Though this film's length does not approach the truly epic proportions of some of Warhol's other early films, it is undeniably the one irrefutable epic of kisses.[66] *Kiss*'s quasi–slowed-down effect and concentration on the sole action of kissing makes possible an abundance of the sort of detailed anatomizing that appeared so striking to the first critics of Edison's *The Kiss*. Whether or not Warhol actually based his film on an archival viewing of Edison's film,[67] he intuitively returned to Edison's basics: the oral attraction of the kiss itself, bypassing the long history of Hollywood kisses that required so much laborious plotting. Indeed, as originally projected at the Gramercy Arts Theatre—an underground New York theater—the film resembled Edison's original even more: Each one of the original one hundred-foot camera rolls of a kiss was shown individually, thus over time constituting a kind of serial. Only later were thirteen of these more numerous kisses spliced together and projected as a single film, yet leaving all the rough beginnings and ends of each roll. By returning to the roots of the screen kiss and Edison's waist-up close-ups, Warhol's film offers a glorious epitaph to the era of the kiss.

Each kiss is already in progress as its respective black-and-white roll begins. Warhol adopts a tight two-shot close-up, holds on it for as long as the one hundred-foot roll of film lasts (approximately three minutes for his motor-powered 16mm Bolex). Only in one instance does the kiss end before the film runs out and white leader obscures our view. If the rule against excess in the Code-era meant that no kiss could last very long, and that most would conclude a scene followed by an ellipsis, then Warhol's strategy is to give us the long middles that strictures against excess had prohibited. In addition, his sixteen-frames-per-second speed institutes what Stephen Koch calls a *ritardando*—not exactly slow motion but a marked slowing down that lends both fascination and extra time to anatomize.[68] No ellipses, discreet lookings away, or fade-outs mar our fixed regard, but only a technological limit.

Without preliminary credits or title, the initial reel simply begins, first as blank white leader, then followed by a black-and-white, contrasty, and very close close-up of an ordinary man with a mustache, wire-rimmed glasses, well-groomed, longish hair, and tie.[69] He occupies the upper right-hand side of the frame, bearing down in three-quarter profile in an open-mouthed kiss on a slightly younger, attractive woman with long hair and a headband, leaning back into the lower left side of the frame. The man pushes down in rhythmic motions; the woman receives the kiss and pushes back up (figure 23). The kiss itself is almost constant; that is, the "juxtaposition of two orbicularis oris muscles in a state of contraction" is continuous throughout the hundred feet of film at least until the very end. Yet within this one long kiss there are lots of little ones—small gives and takes, tensions and relaxations, suggestions of drinking and being drunk from as we see neck muscles swallowing what must be mingled saliva (figure 24). In and out, up and down they move in a dreamy routine that is uncannily defamiliarized by the slight slowing of the action. In this kiss alone—a kiss in which the man's bristly mustache may offer homage to Edison's John C. Rice—the action is broken off before the camera roll ends: the woman pulls back, smiles, and shows teeth.

The second kiss appears a little less clearly focused at first. It repeats the man-on-right (super), woman-on-left (supra) positions, and the woman looks quite a bit like the woman from the first kiss (it is in fact Naomi Levine, Warhol's star kisser). But this new man is almost comically active. His left hand strokes the side of the woman's face and her ear, and he seems not too particular about where his kisses land—on both sides of her mouth, above her upper lip, below her chin. Even more shocking by Hollywood standards is that his tongue is visible (figure 25). At one point he takes the woman's entire chin into his mouth; at another point he rubs

Kiss (dir. Andy Warhol, 1963)

23: The man pushes down, the woman pushes back

24: Neck muscles are visible swallowing

25: Visible tongue

26: The man rubs his chin into the cleft between the woman's mouth and chin

his chin into the cleft between her mouth and chin (figure 26). His voracious enthusiasm exaggerates the orality that we have seen Freud isolate
as the original pleasure of kisses and in Garbo's vampiric "drinking" of
Gilbert. But Warhol's orality is crude: without the glamorous lighting, it is
both more real and, due to the effect of the *ritardando*, uncanny.

The first two kisses offer up a new messiness and longueur, reminding
us not only that kisses are fundamentally oral pleasures but also of Freud's
other point that mouths are the entrance to the digestive tract. Saliva must
be swallowed, tongues are visible and active, even teeth—those unmen-
tionables of the Hollywood kiss—are on display. The third kiss offers a
contrast in mood: Even though the kissers' relative positions are the same,
with the woman on the left leaning way back, the man on top leaning way
down, this kiss, despite the conventional attractiveness of its couple, is a
study in inertia and boredom. Although hands stroke and lips kiss, nothing else seems to happen between the kissers.

The fourth kiss breaks the pattern in a number of ways: by occurring
between two men, by offering a camera position that shows us more of
the couch on which all couples sit, by revealing a painting of Jackie Kennedy on the wall behind. The kissers are two slender, shirtless youths,
one quite adolescent and fair, the other a little older and dark. In strong
contrast to the boredom of the previous couple, they avidly rub against
each other. The darker, older youth occupies the top right, the younger,
fairer youth the lower left, and he might initially be mistaken for a woman
given the context thus far of heterosexual kisses and his long hair (figure
27). But even before the camera dramatically pulls back to reveal both
naked torsos stripped to their jeans, we suspect that they are males.[70]
They have Adam's apples, and the young man on the left has his eyes open,
as most of the women in Warhol's kisses, and indeed in most of the kisses
we have discussed, do not (figure 28).[71] There is an activity on the part
of both kissers that marks them, in contrast to Hollywood's depictions
of relatively active male kissers and relatively passive female receivers of
kisses, as men. (In a later kiss another two men, both with their shirts on
this time, will face off in remarkably erect, egalitarian positions, kissing
straight up, neither one leaning back, neither one giving more than he
receives in intense, muscular kisses of absolute reciprocity concentrated
on the lips alone.)

In *The Philosophy of Andy Warhol*, Warhol writes: "Sex is more exciting
on the screen and between the pages than between the sheets anyway."[72]
His *Kiss* pays homage to this idea by sustaining a fascinated look that is
also cool and analytical. His real interest, like that of the audience in the

Kiss

27: Two young
men kiss

28: Pull out on two
very active male
kissers, one with
eyes open

era of the kiss, is not in seeing, like actual voyeurs, what happens between kissers in real life, but in seeing what happens on the screen when these acts are projected. (Warhol himself was rarely in the room when his films were shot.) By slowing down, by skipping the beginning and the ends, by taking Edison's original fixed close-up and just holding it there, Warhol bypasses all the coy business—dialogue, twirling mustaches, telephones, cigarettes—used to motivate the oral relation. Instead he lingers on the perverse essence of the kiss's orality, the fixation on mucous membranes designed for digestion, showing neither beginning nor ending. Yet despite all the rule-breaking of Warhol's long, sometimes lustful, sometimes comic, always perverse kisses, it is also as if he decided to respect the formal rules of what I have been calling the long adolescence of American movies before the breakdown of the Production Code and before the inevitable effects of the sexual revolution made the kiss just one of many possible sex acts.

None of Warhol's kisses looks exactly like any of the Hollywood kisses that appear after the end of American cinema's long adolescence,[73] but they anticipate them. Yet, they are kisses that we know *could* lead to further sex acts. But if there is a privileging of the surplus perversion of a proto-gay kiss, there is also a respect for the rules of the era of the kiss in limiting action to just a kiss.

Like so much else in Warhol's art, *Kiss* portrays both limit and transgression. The kissers kiss as if they have bodies, not just mouths. Even though we do not generally see much of the rest of the bodies, we know by the rhythms of the movements, the abandonment of concern about whether the kiss even lands on the mouth, the voracious openness of the mouth as one orifice among many, that there is a whole body attached. And in this respect *Kiss* most defamiliarizes us from the conventions of the kiss era, making us wonder, over fifty-eight long and absorbing minutes, what on earth we are doing—and what we have ever been doing—sitting in the dark, screening kisses. By beginning after the beginning and ending before the end, Warhol's kisses offer a fitting epitaph to and celebration of a time when the kiss was all the sex that could be seen.

Conclusion: "Kiss Kiss, Bang Bang"

I have been arguing that ever since Edison filmed and screened a kiss, viewers have responded viscerally, though not necessarily imitatively, to what they see. I have also suggested that this response is not the same as experiencing a kiss itself. Rather, "on the rebound" my body is "moved" and "touched" by other bodies whom I watch tasting and touching one another. Of course, a fight, a blow, a stab, an explosion—any of the various forms of mayhem and violence to the body that the screen can convey—will also synesthetically solicit our bodies.

The late great film critic Pauline Kael wonderfully encapsulated these two major sensations of the movies in the title of her second anthology of film criticism, *Kiss Kiss, Bang Bang.*[74] Sex and violence, kiss and bang, are the primary attractions that draw us to, or repel us from, popular movies. But they have occupied very different positions in American cinema history. Consider, for example, another Edison film made one year before *The Kiss. The Execution of Mary, Queen of Scots* (1895) was also based on a well-known Broadway play, and it also depicts a small fragment of its play's sensational action. However, instead of bringing into closer view an act that had already been seen on the stage, it showed an act of violence that the stage play had not: Mary's beheading by an ax.[75] The play had ended with the curtain descending as the ax was raised above Mary's head. The film begins with Mary being blindfolded and ends with the executioner brandishing her severed head. Through the miracle of stop-action photography, which substituted a dummy for the male actor who played Mary, we see the Scottish queen lose her head.

In this first American example of the special effects of violence, there was significantly no equivalent to John Sloan's objection to the sensational display, the prototype of so many cinematic acts of violence to come. One reason may be that *The Execution* was photographed in long shot and only exhibited in Edison's Kinetoscope. Thus no effect of "monstrous" magnification permitted the same kind of "anatomizing" of the act of beheading that occurred with the stages of the kiss.[76] But even though they are parallel sensationalisms addressing the carnal being of spectators, both arising at the very origin of cinema, kisses and bangs have occupied very different positions in American moving-image history. The Hollywood Production Code would formulate strict prohibitions on the display of both that would more or less endure until replaced by the Motion Picture Association of America (MPAA) ratings system in 1968, and both sensationalisms became more graphic with the lifting of the Code. When the Code ended (officially in 1968, though it was slowly dying throughout the decade) and mainstream American films began to exploit both of these formerly suppressed sensations, violence almost immediately developed, with great flourish and style, into one of the country's most popular export items. Violence became, as H. Rap Brown once put it, "as American as cherry pie."[77]

Sex, on the other hand, while it came insistently on/scene at about the same time, has never seemed quite so American. As we shall see in the following chapters, it was more often an import item. Unlike violence, always faked in fiction film, sex bifurcated into two radically different forms: hard core (explicit, unsimulated) and soft core (simulated, faked). Not until the early seventies would hard-core sexual displays become familiar viewing to large numbers of Americans, male and female alike. Another way of looking at this difference between the status of sex and the status of violence is to say that a certain spectacle of violence revealing the aggression to or penetration of one body by another—in the form of various kinds of fights, along with displays of blood, wounds, and even inner organs—has become a normal part of the movies. However, the mainstream has not as easily absorbed a similar spectacle of sex—also often a penetration of bodies—even though in its own exclusive form, cordoned off as the separate genre of pornography, it is arguably the most enduring and popular of all moving-image forms.

With Edison's *The Kiss* and *The Execution of Mary, Queen of Scots*, we thus see the inauguration of a double standard between mediated sex and mediated violence. The great realist film theorist and critic André Bazin has pondered the paradox of this double standard in the following consideration of the limit cases of both sex and violence: "If you can show me on the screen a man and woman whose dress and position are such that at least the beginnings of sexual consummation undoubtedly accompanied the action, then I would have the right to demand, in a crime film, that you really kill the victim—or at least wound him pretty badly."[78]

Bazin's point is the similar pornographic impulse of each act. To go all the way in the depiction of sex—not just the kiss but the consummation to which the kiss tends—would also require going all the way in the depiction of violence: not using the dummy's head, but, for consistency's sake, a real decapitation. To Bazin, these are true obscenities that the cinema simply should not show. Interestingly, he goes on to link them as related orgasms: "Here death is the negative equivalent of sexual pleasure, which is sometimes called, not without reason, 'the little death.'"[79] This French *petite mort* links the involuntary shudder of pleasure to the involuntary shudder of death—both are spasms of the ecstatic body "beside itself."

In linking the spasm of sexual orgasm, which Bazin, rather like Freud, sees as the telos toward which sex acts tend, with death—the telos toward which violence tends—Bazin stresses the limit case of cinematic realism. A realist theorist who in every other way celebrates the ability of cinema to directly present life as it is, without the intervention of language codes or the hand of the artist, Bazin here acknowledges, as does the title of Kael's book, the sensational power of a medium that deals in the extremes of sex and violence. His ultimate fear is that "real sex," like "real death," will lead audiences back to the abuses of the Roman circus. His theoretical point is that cinema is founded on just such an illicit glimpse of real bodies and real objects of the world. In the cinema a nude woman can be "openly desired" and "actually caressed" in a way she cannot be in a theater because, he writes, "the cinema unreels in an imaginary space which demands participation and identification. The actor winning the woman gratifies me by proxy. His seductiveness, his good looks, his daring do not compete with my desires—they fulfill them."[80]

Yet if the sex scene *does* gratify by proxy (if not exactly in the male/subject, female/object teleological progress to orgasm that Bazin suggests, but in the more diffuse and rebounded way I have been indicating), we are seemingly plunged into pornography, a realm Bazin abhors. The liberal realist who admires the documentary quality of narrative cinema in many ways and who believes "there are no sex situations—moral or immoral, shocking or banal, normal or pathological—whose expression is *a priori* prohibited on the screen," nevertheless argues that as far as sex goes, the "cinema can say everything, but not show everything." If we wish to remain on the level of art, "we must stay in the realm of imagination."[81]

The problem, of course, is that every kiss in every film is already a kind of documentary of that particular, intimate, and yet still publicly acceptable sex act in a way that an act of violence, which is usually faked, is not. In or out of character, two people must really kiss in a film close-up. The kiss or caress has, as Bazin notes, the potential to "gratify by proxy." But everything is organized in scenes of violence so that actors, even though they may touch in a relatively intimate fight, do not really hit, knife, or shoot one another the way they are expected to kiss and caress. Bazin recognizes and is embarrassed by the inconsistency of his argument. Writing in 1956 in direct response to the provocations of Roger Vadim's Brigitte Bardot vehicle, *And God Created Woman*, which (following reluctantly in the tradition of John Sloan) he calls a "detestable film," he realizes that his remarks have also brushed off a good part of the contemporary Swedish cinema. His only recourse is to claim, weakly, that the "masterpieces of eroticism" do not cross a certain line. But as Bazin clearly foresaw, times were changing: the sixties were about to happen, and the argument that masterpieces never go too far sexually already rang hollow as movies would take on the challenge of "going all the way." Many so-called novelistic masterpieces had already described a great deal about sex, not leaving it to the imagination. And Bazin honestly admits at the end of his essay that the situation of the writer may not differ all that much from that of directors and actors. So he concludes simply: "To grant the novel the privilege of evoking everything, and yet to deny the cinema, which is so similar, the right of showing everything, is a critical contradiction I note without resolving."[82]

These are the honest and intelligent words of a great film critic grappling with the unprecedented realism of the new media form of the twentieth century and its special relation to both sex and violence. These words tell us that cinema is capable of delivering new forms of violence and forms of intimacy that were just beginning in the late fifties. In Bazin's time, no less than in our own, filmmakers, critics, and society have not agreed on the correct place of sex acts mediated by moving images. Since Bazin wrote this essay the kinds of images that worried him have increased exponentially, and his frank examination no longer satisfies. But it must constitute the necessary starting point of any observations about screening sex, even just a kiss.

> The Code has become the loose suspenders that hold up
> the baggy pants of the circus clown. It allows the pants to
> slip dangerously, but never to fall.
> —STANLEY KUBRICK, 1959

2

going all the way

Carnal Knowledge on American

Screens (1961–1971)

In the early sixties new forms of carnal knowledge, beyond kisses, were creeping onto American screens. As Stanley Kubrick puts it in this chapter's epigraph, the pants of the circus clown were slipping in the last decade of the Production Code, though they would not fall completely until hard-core pornography became a public obsession in 1972. This chapter asks how American movies in the period 1961–71 begin to "go all the way" in sexual portrayals. What does going all the way mean, anyway? To answer, we must first turn to the type of film that would always offer models of sexual sophistication to Hollywood: the "foreign film." A growing number of independent theaters operating outside the restrictions of the Production Code cropped up in the late fifties and early sixties. My mother—with whom I had watched kisses— would never have taken me to such a theater. It was beyond her cultural and financial reach. But through the auspices of a friend's mother I came, in 1961, to see my first foreign films at an art house in Berkeley, California.

The two films I saw were in blatant violation of the Hollywood Production Code. They not only displayed simulated genital sex in the form of the rhythmic grinding of hips but they showed it taking place on the ground, brutally. Both Ingmar Bergman's *The Virgin Spring* (1959), which had won an Academy Award for best foreign film, and Vittorio De Sica's *Two Women* (1960), for which Sophia Loren won an Oscar in 1961, portrayed gang rapes of young virgins. In *The Virgin Spring* two ragged and brutish goatherds in medieval Sweden rape and then kill the beloved blonde daughter of a well-to-do farmer as their uncomprehending younger brother looks on. In *Two Women* renegade Turkish soldiers rape an Italian woman and her daughter in the chaos of fascist defeat in war-torn Italy. Long before any ratings system had been devised to signal the need for "parental guidance" or "restrictions" on viewing, my fifteen-year-old self was intrigued, aroused, and disturbed by these two films.

I might have wished for a gentler awakening to the visual knowledge of genital heterosexual sex through more romantic, or at least more conventionally erotic, scenes.[1] But this is how it goes with carnal knowledge, which never arrives at the exact moment we are ready to learn about it, but always too early or too late. Nor do we know exactly from where this knowledge comes: does it arrive as an intrusion from the outside, like a seduction or a rape (in this case from foreign movies), or as a latent knowledge that seems to have always been present from the beginning? Is there ever a right moment to "get" sexual knowledge?

These two vivid rape scenes, viewed within a year or so of one another and constituting the whole of my visual knowledge of genital sex at that time, condensed over the years into a single scene. I recalled a dark-haired girl lying on her back on the ground (the woody scene of *The Virgin Spring* predominated over the bombed-out church of *Two Women*). The girl's legs were forcibly spread apart and a dark man pressed himself between them.

This was not the first time I had felt sexual arousal before a depiction of sex. I had already read the "dirty parts" of writers like James Joyce, D. H. Lawrence, and Henry Miller. However, as André Bazin knew (see chapter 1), to *screen* a dramatic simulation of (coerced) genital sex was a very different thing from reading about that, or any kind of sex, in a novel. The power of the impression derived not only from the vividness of seeing real bodies in acts and positions that were still unspeakable in polite American society but also from seeing them magnified several times over on a big screen. These larger-than-life bodies struggled against one another in a panting clinch in which the grinding of hips and repetitive, pulsing rhythms—rhythms related to but also quite different from those familiar to me in dances or fights—were strikingly in play. Suddenly, the rhythm stopped and the couple became terrifyingly still. The dirty man's face was desperate and ecstatic, the girl's was frightened and wild-eyed. But perhaps most burnt into my memory was a moment at which the image seemed to plunge out of focus, as if melting. This loss of focus seemed to suggest the girl's own loss of consciousness, even an ultimate loss of self, at the still unseen moment of genital penetration.

A Melting Loss of Focus

Looking at both films today, from the "mature" side of carnal knowledge and with the aid of video and DVD, I find that I totally invented this "melting loss of focus." Neither director actually blurs the image. Quite the contrary: Bergman holds close and unblinkingly on the face of the blonde girl after she has seemingly been penetrated, concentrating on a forced intimacy with her second rapist (figure 29). De Sica, on the other hand, begins his shot of the raped girl at a distance over the shoulder of the turbaned, Turkish rapist (figure 30). Then, as if in place of the violent genital penetration that we are never positioned to see, we rapidly track forward to a close-up of the wide-eyed girl's pained and startled face (figure 31). Instead of obscuring the face of the traumatized girl with the loss of focus that I remembered, De Sica's camera moves rapidly, violently, toward her to better register her shock and pain. By penetrating the initial distance between the camera and the girl, the film itself simulates a kind of rape.

How to understand this discrepancy between what I remembered of the rape scene and what I now know was revealed there? My memory of a "melting loss of focus" is what Freud would call a "screen memory"—a false memory that replaces the actual events (in this case those visible on the celluloid). Freud writes that seemingly indifferent memories of childhood often function as substitutes for much more meaningful, but often disturbing, later events. These indifferent early memories thus conceal, or screen out, the memory of later events. But they also are a way of revealing them at the same time.[2]

My personal screen memory can help us understand a dynamics of screening sex in which even the most explicit of images may not yield a

29: *The Virgin Spring* (dir. Ingmar Bergman, 1959), rape of the blonde girl

Two Women (dir. Vittorio De Sica, 1960)

30: Rape of the dark-haired girl

31: Close-up

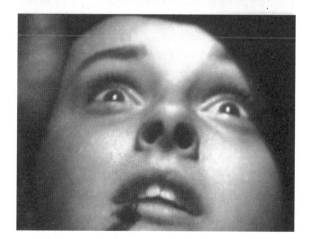

clear understanding of carnal knowledge, but only slow intimations. In this memory, the word *melt* used to describe the two rapes I had condensed from De Sica's and Bergman's films may have functioned to screen out the images I was not quite ready to see—the images that may have intimated more carnal knowledge than I was ready at that time to understand. At the same time, however, my very choice of the word belies the fact of my total sexual ignorance since it already signals an awareness of the sexual heat—the literal warming of my own body that I nevertheless did feel and about which I probably felt ashamed.

Even the most graphic moving images of sex acts rarely provide knowledge that we fully understand when we first see them in our youth. Nor can the memory of the supposed moment in which a not-yet-comprehending child watches parental sex ever be retrieved as it really happened. In this chapter I will argue that carnal knowledge came to American screens at the end of the Code in some of the same ways in which it comes to the child: in deferred, partial ways, never at the right time, and almost never as a clear revelation. It might seem that the history of screening sex would be one long progression toward a greater revelation of the naked facts of sex. In fact, however, this screening offers a complex dynamic of revelation and concealment (whether in my own memory play with the film or in the film's own strategies). It is also a dynamic of a deferred knowledge that either comes too late or a shocking knowledge that comes too soon and upon which one, like Bergman's uncomprehending younger goatherd, simply gapes.

Freud himself vacillated quite a bit about whether the primal scene was a real memory of observed parental coitus or a projected fantasy.[3] Either way, like my unreliable memory of these movies, it is not an *im*mediate event but, precisely, a mediation. In the case of the violent moving sexual images that I misremembered, it may be helpful to think of them as a kind of seduction or rape that assaults me from without, but which eventually gets lodged in my interior. Jean Laplanche and J. B. Pontalis offer the best Freudian explanation of these questions about the timing of the knowledge of sex. In "Fantasy and the Origins of Sexuality," they refine Freud's own vacillations about the fact or fantasy of the primal scene with the notion that the origin of sexual knowledge in the subject is not reducible to either a real event—say seduction by an adult—or to an imaginary scene totally made up. Rather, the trauma of seduction into the knowledge of sexuality takes place in the not quite locatable fantasmatic interval between two real events—one that occurs before the child has sexual knowledge, and another that may be perfectly innocent and nonsexual but which triggers a deferred reaction to the first.[4] The illuminating point for our discussion of how American movies began to show adult sexual knowledge is that this knowledge is rarely grasped in a single "aha!" moment. Sexual knowledge seems to be that which initially breaks in on us from the outside before we are ready for it but which also sets itself up in us as a kind of inner foreign body—"an internal alien entity" that provokes excitement.[5]

If some part of me wants to posit the traumatic scene of the rape of two very different teenage girls in foreign films as a primal scene in which an innocent child (me) witnesses a violence not understood as sex, then the most important point of this comparison is that like the primal scene this knowledge was deferred. I neither lost my virginity at the movies in 1961 watching rape in foreign films nor had it preserved by the elliptical conventions of the era of the kiss. The visual knowledge of sex did not become embedded in me in a single, dramatic, hymen-puncturing scene, but in numerous instances of pushing the limits of whatever codes held sway throughout the decade.

As foreign films, the two works I cite above came, by definition, from the outside to seduce or offend impressionable Americans who did not yet expect to see more than a kiss at the movies. It would take a sexual revolution and a great many changes in the business of making and selling movies for American audiences to begin to screen sex in homegrown product without feeling shocked or assaulted by simulated scenes of going all the way—whether coerced or consensual. Many of the intellectual and social·changes that made up what came to be called the sexual revolution took place as early as 1960 (the year of the marketing of the pill). Indeed, the term itself had been introduced as early as 1935 by Wilhelm Reich. Nevertheless, the real changes in the way large numbers of people actually lived their sexual lives did not occur until the late sixties and early seventies as the pill revolutionized the sexual practices of women in college, as courts overturned literary censorship, and as sexologists began to study sex scientifically.[6] I will discuss the sexologists and women's reactions to them at greater length in chapter 4. Here, I want to indicate the full range of cinematic carnal knowledges available to American audiences screening sex in this intense period of transition. In this chapter, then, I will address the various ways *American* movies, not the foreign seducers that had given rise to my initial screen memories, changed in the period 1961–71 as the Hollywood Production Code was challenged from many different directions. The types of film examined include the changing Hollywood displays, of course, but also independently produced sexploitation films, Blaxploitation films, and the avant-garde, all of which constructed very different codes of intimacy.[7]

Many film historians have told the story of the demise of the Production Code and of the rise of a more permissive era of the Motion Picture Association of America's (MPAA) ratings system in 1968.[8] These historians have pointed out how the sexual revolution, the beginnings of the women's movement, a divisive war in Vietnam, and a growing generation gap contributed to radical changes in Hollywood. I will not repeat here the complex story of historical, industrial, and social changes that brought forth a knowledge of the carnal in a wide variety of film forms. Suffice it to say for the moment that the new ratings system would classify films according to their supposed suitability for different audiences, instead of attempting to make all films acceptable for general audiences—although a self-imposed "adults only" category had existed in nonmainstream film since the teens, as Eric Schaefer has shown.[9]

The ratings system established in 1968 would initially offer a way for producers and distributors to signal to audiences which films were suitable for children and which for adults. Eventually many more distinctions would be forged (PG-13, NC-17). Along with these classifications, the MPAA contributed to, but never itself supervised, the X category, which initially held some hope of constituting an actual category of adult cinema with sex, but not only with the paramount goal of inciting prurient interest, which is what X became by the early seventies.[10]

Carnal Knowledge

Carnal comes from the Latin *carnalis*, or flesh. The knowledge of flesh that would come from the movies would eventually extend far beyond the narrow dictionary definition: "The act of sexual procreation between a man and a woman; the man's penis is inserted into the woman's vagina and excited until orgasm and ejaculation occur." Also known as sexual intercourse, copulation, coitus, coition, and sexual congress, carnal knowledge refers to the procreative, heterosexual sex that most Americans once considered the only true and proper sex, but which the ongoing sexual revolution would expand to include all manner of what Freud once called perversions. It might seem archaic to continue to use such a biblical term in an era that would soon celebrate so many "diff'rent strokes for diff'rent folks."[11] Nevertheless, it is worth retaining for several reasons: first, the films of this period are often quite literally about carnal knowledge as a knowledge that descends below the erotogenic zone of the mouth—the erotic focus of the era of the kiss—to the genitals; second, the term evokes the embodied knowledge that is not only of flesh pressing against flesh on the screen but also of our own carnal awareness as we watch; third, the term was employed as the title of a film discussed below.

The carnal knowledge to be discussed here does not necessarily come as a unique *identification with* any one body on the screen, but as a series of *mediated* exchanges between our bodies, what Vivian Sobchack calls the "film's body," and the bodies on the screen.[12] I have argued in the previous chapter that images of bodies taking sensual pleasure in one another invoke both our more distant senses of sight and hearing and our more proximate senses of touch, taste, and smell. However, it had been one thing to feel my own sensuality "on the rebound," as Sobchack formulates it, in relation to the publicly acceptable display of a kiss; it was quite another to feel it when sitting in the darkened public space of a movie theater while screening simulated (or even real) scenes of genital carnal knowledge. If this was not yet the shock of watching close-up genital sex acts aimed at arousal that would come with the arrival of hard-core pornography onto public screens, it was nevertheless a new kind of sexual address. American movies, taking their cue from the more sexually sophisticated Europeans, tentatively groped for ways to depict going all the way, while still staying on the safe side of the line between obscenity and titillation.

There are two primary registers of affective response to screened sexual acts (in both the revealed and screened-out senses I have been stressing). The one with the most impact and the one to which we film scholars always give precedence is the visual, by which I mean what we see and how we respond to these visual cues. The other register, which we too often ignore, is aural, which is harder to isolate given the ambient nature of sound, and which has no equivalent, for example, to a close-up; although certainly it makes a difference whether sounds are miked in ways that make them sound close or ways that make them sound far.[13] Music, as we shall see in the following, is often the most prevalent accompaniment to sex acts in Hollywood films, as well as a way to cover over what might appear to some as the tasteless grunts and moans of sex. But before movies got to that point, they used the aural register of talk, talk, and more talk.

Much the way adolescents talk incessantly of sex long before they ever have it, many of the early Code-challenging films of the fifties and early sixties seem to have been infected with a kind of sexual logorrhea. *The Moon Is Blue* (dir. Otto Preminger, 1953) set the trend. It had been a popular, if minor Broadway play revolving around the endangered purity of a young woman spending an evening in the apartments of two older bachelors. The comic "adult situation"—an innocent woman finding her virginity endangered—had already been the source of countless screwball comedies of the thirties. What was new here, and the reason for the denial of Code approval, were the words *virgin* and *sex* casually tossed about by the dispassionate virgin herself (Maggie McNamarra) in endless discussion with the two bachelors (David Niven and William Holden). Thirteen years later, in a much darker comedy and in a film that would prove to be instrumental in finally dismantling the power of the Code, Mike Nichols's *Who's Afraid of Virginia Woolf?* (1966) also talked sex. The words were now stronger and referred directly to genital sexual acts—"screw you" and reference to a party game called "Hump the Hostess"—but in the end, nobody was seen screwing, and it remained in some doubt as to whether the party guest, played by George Segal, really did hump his hostess, played by Elizabeth Taylor.[14] Jack Valenti, engaged in negotiations on behalf of the Production Code Administration with the producer Jack Warner, would later comment that "it seemed wrong that grown men should be sitting around discussing such matters."[15] But of course this is precisely what his MPAA would continue doing for years to come, with the difference, as Kirby Dick's delightful documentary on the MPAA, *This Film Is Not Yet Rated* (2006), shows, that now the discussions would take place in secret and would include quite a few women.[16] The temporary compromise that led the way out of the impasse between Code authorities and producers regarding *Virginia Woolf*—to label the film as "suggested for mature audiences"—would pave the way toward the new ratings system.[17]

But even after the institution of the ratings system in 1968, Hollywood still seemed more comfortable talking about sex (in risqué R-rated films) than it did screening simulated sex acts. Paul Mazursky's *Bob and Carol and Ted and Alice* (1969) is typical of the new ratings-era tendency to talk sex. It is a satire of two married couples flirting with the new lifestyle of "liberated" sex. The hipper of the two couples, Bob and Carol (Robert Culp and Natalie Wood), attends an Esalen-style encounter group and wants to share its newfound liberation with its more conservative friends, Ted and Alice (Elliot Gould and Dyan Cannon). One harmless affair leads to another (neither shown, both endlessly discussed), and by the end of the film we find the two couples in bed together in Las Vegas, seemingly on the verge of a wife-swapping orgy. But there they just sit, covers chastely pulled up over Wood's and Cannon's breasts as the anticipated climactic orgy peters out in self-conscious giggles. Finally, the friends put back on their clothes and leave the room to attend a not-very-hip Tony Bennett concert.

As late as 1969, even the new Hollywood of the post-Code era seemed more comfortable talking about carnal knowledge than showing it. The two brief love affairs chronicled by *Bob and Carol* are verbally analyzed but pointedly not shown. As in *Virginia Woolf*, the only carnal knowledge evident are two new words added to the lexicon of sex talk—*orgy* and *vagina*. Verbal satire, whether savage as in *Virginia Woolf*, or gentle as in *Bob and Carol*, was the preferred way of addressing adult situations during the transition from the Code to the new ratings system. Mike Nichols, an important director in this transition, proved particularly adept at this kind of witty satire.[18] His aptly named 1971 film *Carnal Knowledge* was made in the early stages of the new ratings system and received an R. Litigation around it would also lead to an important Supreme Court decision in 1973 that declared—contrary to a Georgia court's ban on the film—that it was not obscene.[19] Like *Bob and Carol*, *Carnal Knowledge* put sex at the front and center of its narrative, yet also like it, satire worked against the production of erotic heat.

Carnal Knowledge is about the sex lives of two Amherst College roommates of the late forties, played by Art Garfunkel and Jack Nicholson. Over the course of the next two decades they compete for sex with the same coed (Candace Bergen), marry, have affairs, divorce, and endure middle age. Although the screenwriter, the cartoonist Jules Feiffer, describes the film as "what happens between a man and a woman before, during and after they have been in bed, over a period of years,"[20] the emphasis is on the verbiage of the *before* and *after*, not the activity of the *during*. The film focuses especially on what the two male friends *say* to one another about their sex lives. No woman really speaks except to say what a man wants to hear. Though Garfunkel's Sandy is romantic and Nicholson's Jonathan is a Don Juan who only seeks sexual conquest, both fundamentally fear and dislike women in this often telling satire of American manhood.

Sandy, who embraces the outward trappings of the sexual revolution, eventually takes up with a younger "hippy chick" (Carol Kane), grows long hair, and imitates a hip sensitivity for which he seems too old. Jonathan,

32: *Carnal Knowledge* (dir. Mike Nichols, 1971), Jonathan is serviced by the prostitute who can (verbally) make him hard

on the other hand, grows more deeply misogynist with each failed affair. The film's final scene finds him visiting a prostitute (Rita Moreno) who services him through a carefully scripted monologue designed to make him hard (figure 32). The monologue is spoken directly to the camera and is intercut with Jonathan's satisfied facial reactions. It reassures him that he is "a man who inspires worship because he has no need for any woman . . . [a man] who is better, more beautiful, more powerful, more perfect (you're getting hard!), more strong, more masculine, more extraordinary (it's rising!), more virile, domineering, more irresistible (it's up in the air!)." Jonathan is thus depicted as a man who must resort to the hollow, overrehearsed praise of his virility from a woman he can never trust. Nichols's film is biting and bold, speaking of sex more than any previous mainstream American movie. But it also, like a great many films of this transition era, remains as visually reticent as his own earlier *Virginia Woolf*.

Sexual Interludes

It was yet another film by Nichols that would emerge as the major pioneer in screening sex for the transition out of the Code, beyond talk, though it, too, was not without its own share of Code-challenging words (*seduce* and *affair*). Made in 1967, the last year of the Code, *The Graduate* became the highest-grossing film of that year. Its great popularity contributed, along with other, more sexually frank youth-oriented films, to the Code's demise and the rise of what would come to be called the New Hollywood.[21]

The film tells the story of Benjamin (Dustin Hoffman), who returns home from college to a shallow and materialistic Los Angeles suburb. He falls into a sexual affair with the wife of his father's business partner and the mother of the girl he will eventually want to marry. Benjamin's predicament is gently satirized, while the older woman's lust for him is somewhat more harshly satirized in Anne Bancroft's deadpan, feline performance as Mrs. Robinson.[22] Nichols's portrayal of the affair between Benjamin and Mrs. Robinson became emblematic of the new Hollywood's grafting of French New Wave stylistics onto a music-infused, youth-oriented Hollywood cinema.

In a justly famous scene, Benjamin has been maneuvered into a hotel room by the predatory Mrs. Robinson. When he hesitates, caught between guilty despair and desire, literally banging his head against the hotel room wall, Mrs. Robinson's accusation that that he may still be a virgin spurs him into decisive sexual action. Rescued by masculine pride, the previously whimpering Benjamin authoritatively slams shut the hotel door and (we presume) takes charge sexually.[23] But we do not immediately see what he does. Darkness, the great ally of all directors venturing into the unknown of cinematic carnal knowledge, fills the screen and is further thematized by the famous Simon and Garfunkel song "Sounds of Silence" ("Hello darkness, my old friend . . .").

The sequence that follows unmistakably reveals a newly adult sexual content of the sort strictly forbidden by the Production Code: an adulterous affair that we understand to stretch out over the summer. But just as unmistakably, the sequence will cleverly screen out most views of this physical connection. Indeed, even before Benjamin closes the door, a war between illumination and darkness has been fought, with Mrs. Robinson winning the first round. But in the second round, Benjamin slams shut the door and takes charge. The lights go out; darkness rules as the familiar song about darkness, lack of communication, and alienation begins.

Clearly we are being teased about what we will and will not see of this adulterous affair. This is precisely the sort of scene that would have constituted the central ellipsis of a film like *Casablanca*. Mrs. Robinson asks, "Would this be easier for you in the dark?" But after the film plunges us into this deep darkness and holds on it, suddenly the bright illumination of light reflected off a swimming pool floods the screen. Illumination permits us to see again, but what we see is an evasion of what we expect. Instead of Benjamin and Mrs. Robinson in the hotel room, we seem to cut away—again as in a Code-era film—to a seemingly unrelated, and brightly illuminated, image: Benjamin sunbathes alone on an air mattress in the blue shimmering light of the family swimming pool. He soon climbs off the mattress, emerges from the pool, puts on a white dress shirt, and heads into his parent's house. Incongruously, however, in the very next shot, still in the white shirt and bathing trunks, he exits from a hotel bathroom back into the bedroom with Mrs. Robinson, who unbuttons his white shirt and strokes his chest. We thus cut away from the potential carnality of the sexual moment in the hotel room—the site of the affair—to the pool and from the pool back to the carnality of the hotel room, though now to a different moment, not to the sexual act we expected to witness when the lights first went out.

Instead of showing the quality and kind of sexual relations that Benjamin and Mrs. Robinson enjoy, the film thus chooses to extend and thematize the initial war between illumination and darkness but, much like the later *Carnal Knowledge*, to concentrate on the *before* preparations and the *after* dressing and departures, never the *during* of sex. In a tightly and cleverly edited sequence, the first half of which is accompanied by "The Sounds of Silence," we see busy dressings and undressings, comings and goings. In the latter part of the sequence, it is Mrs. Robinson who moves around the passive, fixed object of Benjamin in various beds.[24] After several transitions that continually throw us off guard about where we are, and after a transition to a new Simon and Garfunkel song, the sequence ends with a shot of Benjamin diving into the pool and leaping up onto the air mattress (figure 33). In a quick match cut, this plunge onto the mattress turns into a plunge onto Mrs. Robinson back in the hotel bed where the sequence began (figure 34). This graphic match between the forceful plunge onto the air mattress and the equally forceful plunge onto Mrs. Robinson is as close as the film ever gets to carnal knowledge. But even here, we do not linger in the bed. The sequence ends back in the pool where Benjamin, now alone on the air mattress, is asked what he is doing by his irate father. "Just drifting," Benjamin replies, as normal time, space, and sound finally resume.

In technical film parlance this sequence is what the film theorist Christian Metz would call a bracket syntagma: "Brief scenes given as typical examples of a certain order of reality but without temporal sequence, often organized around a concept."[25] The concept here would be something like "Benjamin and Mrs. Robinson begin a summer affair that takes on a cer-

The Graduate (dir. Mike Nichols, 1967)

33: Benjamin leaps up onto the air mattress

34: Benjamin's plunge onto the mattress turns into a plunge onto Mrs. Robinson

tain routine in Benjamin's ever-drifting life as he mechanically moves back and forth between home pool and hotel bed." We do see glimpses of flesh in the repeated scenes of separate dressing and undressing, but we do not, except for the brief moment Mrs. Robinson strokes his chest and the brief lunge that conflates the air mattress with Mrs. Robinson, see the couple's flesh together in the same shot. Nor is *our* flesh appealed to through the connection of theirs. Indeed, their carnality and ours are rather strenuously avoided in ways that prolong, in a different manner, some of the elliptical cutting away of the era of Code kisses.

going all the way   81

I have described the clever ellipses of this sequence of *The Graduate* in some detail because they are emblematic of the way in which Hollywood would go about signaling its new sophistication about sex, its new willingness to enter the bedroom and to display carnal knowledge, all the while remaining elliptical about sex. By conflating the single instance of Benjamin and Mrs. Robinson's first sex with the rote gestures of its later extension, the sequence avoids fleshy connection, reduces intimacy to habit, and smoothly skips over the details of Benjamin's loss of innocence. His loss of innocence is, of course, ours, but it is a loss that evades carnal knowledge. My point is not that Nichols should have shown more of the affair in this or any of his other films of the transition era—for example, more of the hostess actually being humped in *Virginia Woolf* or forms of nonverbal erotic pleasure in *Carnal Knowledge*. It is simply that in choosing this elliptical formulation, *The Graduate*, which seemed so boldly to challenge the still-in-effect Code by showing an adulterous affair, forges a trope that would prove very popular in mainstream American cinema as a "tasteful," discreetly concealing, way of suggesting carnal knowledge. Carnal knowledge is thus *revealed* (we are certain the couple does have sex; there is no coy fade-out or narrative obfuscation such as that in *Casablanca*) and *concealed* (we are not asked to confront the visual fact of genital action). Indeed, Hollywood's whole way of baby-stepping toward adult content resembles the new adulthood of Benjamin himself, the twenty-one-year-old boy-man shamed into having sex to prove a maturity that he does not really possess. I call this kind of montage "Hollywood musical sexual interlude."

An interlude is generally defined as anything that fills time between other performance events regarded as more significant. In theater history, it was a short humorous play performed between the acts of a more serious miracle or morality drama. But one of the term's primary meanings is also musical: the instrumental music played between the sung parts of a song. Either way, an interlude offers a break with the normal flow of drama or music. In movies before the 1960s it was conventional, in addition to the usual scoring of Romantic music throughout a film, to add interludes in the form of songs sung by performers within the narrative (e.g., Dooley Wilson singing "As Time Goes By" in *Casablanca*). But in the 1960s films began to appropriate a new model for importing a wide range of pop music into their very fabric, and these New Hollywood films moved away from "monothematic scores"—single themes that returned in dramatic situations—and toward "multi-theme" formats including what Jeff Smith calls "interpolated songs": new or old pop songs that underscore the film, often to highly edited montages.[26] The popularity of the song could thus contribute to the popularity of the film. It could also, it was soon discovered, sell a great many soundtrack records. This move to underscore movies and even to sell them with entire compilation scores proved especially attractive to younger audiences tuned into the music of, for example, Simon and Garfunkel. These lyrical montages (in some ways prefigurations of music videos) tended to stop the narrative flow of the film to "sell," or at least to let viewers enjoy, the song.[27]

Though none of the scholars who discuss interpolated pop songs in films address their use in what I am calling musical sexual interludes, it is significant that it is precisely in these lyrical montages—montages in which music amps up and narrative slows down—that a palatable form of carnal knowledge first found its way into mainstream American film. Indeed, the conjunction of music and sex, as opposed to the presentation of sex acts with little or no music, is enormously important in the history of cinematic sexual representation. Just as kisses in the silent or sound film almost never occurred without soaring music, so it would prove extremely rare for post-Code Hollywood films to depict carnal knowledge without the added affect of music.

When the sounds of sex became audible for the first time without the cover of music, and when the kind of affective control offered by musical interlude was not deployed, a new kind of nakedness became available to films, even when the characters having sex remained clothed. It was this aural nakedness that proved so disturbing in my audiovision of the rapes in Bergman's and De Sica's films. The smooch of a kiss, the smack of a slap, the slurp of fellatio or cunnilingus, the whoosh of penetration, not to mention the sighs, moans, or outright cries generated by sexual connection, make the sex seen seem all the more proximate to the viewer-listener. Though sound by its very nature cannot be framed and brought into close-up the way the image can, the sounds of sex become important confirmation of the reality and instantaneity of the sex depicted. The cinema sound theorist Michel Chion indicates that points of synchronization between sound and image serve to give the audiovisual flow of a film its phrasing, "just as chords or cadences, which are also vertical meetings of elements, can give phrasing to a sequence of music."[28] Chion's book does not discuss the sound of sex, but his remarks on screen violence seem remarkably appropriate to thinking about screen sex:

What is the most important object in audiovisual representation? The human body. What can the most immediate and brief meeting between two of these objects be? The physical blow. And what is the most immediate audiovisual relationship? The synchronization between a blow heard and a blow seen—or one that we believe we have seen. For, in fact, we do not really see the punch; you can confirm this by cutting the sound out of a scene. What we hear is what we haven't had time to see.[29]

The physical blow represents one kind of basic human bodily connection, but so, too, does the bodily penetration of kisses and other sex acts. Where Hollywood sound cinema was quick to provide sound effects for the physical blows of fight scenes, it was not equally quick to provide sound synch points for carnal encounters. Indeed, the trope of the musical sexual interlude seems expressly designed to screen out components of sex acts that were nevertheless becoming necessary to show. The rape scenes in *The Virgin Spring* and *Two Women* had not softened the nakedness of their penetrative blows with music, and this raw aural component of sex certainly formed part of their impact on me. Hollywood's new practice, however, would be to situate the spectacle of sex as an affectively controlled interlude distanced by the effect of editing and music. Though I prefer the term *sexual interlude* to Metz's semiotically inspired mouthful, *bracket syntagma*, we do well to recognize that *bracketing off* carnal knowledge from the rest of the film is precisely what the music and editing of the sexual interlude does. Within this bracket, intimate sexual relations reside in a different register of time and space.

Not all sexual interludes operate as chastely as the influential early one of *The Graduate*. For example, two years later, the 1969 X-rated *Midnight Cowboy* (dir. John Schlesinger) would solidify the trope of the musical sexual interlude while showing quite a bit more flesh. This Academy Award–winning film was another pioneer of the adult New Hollywood. In this early phase of the new ratings system, X did not yet necessarily connote, as it tends to today, the stigma of hard-core pornography, for the simple reason that hard core had not yet become as visible as it would in 1972. All it meant at this point was that a film was not rated and that no one under sixteen could see it. Many of the films so labeled were not, in fact, pornography, but did have a degree of simulated sex, or sexual situations, still unusual for the Hollywood of that era.[30] Over time, however, as mainstream films of all types sought to avoid a rating limiting viewership and as hard-core films eagerly seized on this category as a way of marketing their explicit sexual content, X came to signal a low-budget focus on sexual content that went beyond the pale of mainstream sexual acceptability.[31] In 1969, however, X only meant no viewers under sixteen, and it coexisted with quality indicators such as *Midnight Cowboy*'s Oscar for best picture.

Schlesinger's film does not avoid the sight of naked bodies together on a bed—though it studiously avoids what would come to be called "full frontal nudity" for both the man and the woman. In a scene with interesting parallels to *The Graduate*, a younger man—in this case Joe Buck (Jon Voigt), a hapless would-be male prostitute failing abysmally at earning his living—is taunted (much like Benjamin) into proving himself sexually with a more sophisticated older woman. Delighted to have finally been hired to earn what he hoped would be easy money, Joe is suddenly humiliated by his inability to perform. The scene begins with Joe and his wealthy client naked under the sheets. "It happens," she notes matter-of-factly and then invites him to pass the time playing Scrabble.

When the letters *g-a-y* turn up as a word in their game, Joe, like Benjamin, sees his manhood threatened and suddenly draws on hidden reserves of virility. It does not seem accidental that once again a memorable instance of Hollywood carnal knowledge is prompted by a young man's need to prove his masculine potency—just as Hollywood itself was doing. In an extended segment, the couple writhes to what appears to be a mutually enjoyable climax that culminates first, with a close-up of Joe's face, exhibiting purposeful effort and satisfaction in his final thrusts, and then with a close-up of the woman's face, fallen off the bed, upside-down in ecstatic abandon.[32] Unlike *The Graduate*, which repeatedly cuts away from the scenes of sex, this film offers more graphic views of the naked couple in the hotel room bed. This sex is portrayed as a heroic struggle, something like whole-body arm wrestling, in which Joe, by delivering pleasure, "wins"—not the girl, but the money and his own heterosexual self-respect against the homoerotic implications that mark his real relationship with his buddy Ratso (Dustin Hoffman). So while there is no shortage of flesh pressing against flesh—including what would later become the cliché of female fingernails clawing a male back at a moment of sexual intensity (figure 35)—each gesture of this sexual encounter is presented as an excerpted highlight rather than as a continuous action. Shots are arranged chronologically, but the action, while not as radically discontinuous as in *The Graduate*, nevertheless remains fragmented. Joe's buttocks clench at one moment (figure 36), his face at another (figure 37); Joe is on top at one moment, his client at another; one of her legs wraps around him at one moment, her ringed hand claws his back at another.

Also as in *The Graduate*, what really unites the discontinuous fragments is the nondiegetic music that controls the mood and distances us from

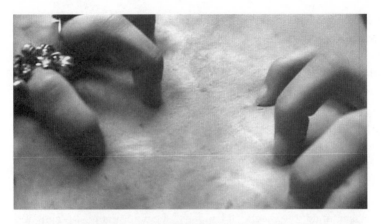

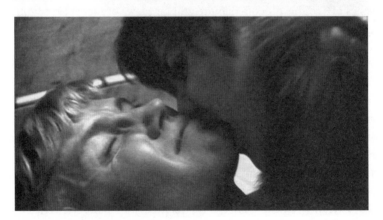

Midnight Cowboy (dir. John Schlesinger, 1969)

35: Female fingernails claw a male back

36: and 37: Joe's buttocks clench at one moment, his face at another

the diegetic sounds generated by the couple. Even without a popular song to hum later, we are once again in the realm of the musical sexual interlude.[33] In this case a crescendo of brass and percussive orchestral music offers a climax that augments and partially replaces that of the couple. Its triumphalism is tempered by the plaintive and folksy harmonica that underscores the entire film and adds a tone of melancholy. The music is reminiscent of Aaron Copeland–style celebrations of the cowboy virility Joe Buck has come to New York to perform—too late, it will turn out, to save his friend Ratso.[34] For, as in *The Graduate*, the sex that proves Joe's virility is not that of an intimate relation that really matters in the larger, more important romances of both movies (that between Benjamin and Mrs. Robinson's daughter in the first, and the repressed romance between Joe and Ratso in the second).

The sexual interlude in *Midnight Cowboy* offers fragments of action that signal a concept: "Joe finally proves himself the heterosexual stud he has wanted to be." The interlude simultaneously *spectacularizes* and *ghettoizes* its carnal knowledge by making a display of the body in the throes of sex, but by cordoning off this display into a carefully circumscribed space-time. Though it does not stint on the display of flesh, and is thus remembered as a breakthrough, the very form of the sexual interlude cuts the scene off in tone, mood, and style from the rest of the film. And this style, if not always the content, would remain, with some exceptions noted below, the dominant code of intimacy in mainstream American films to the present day. Later, as the formula solidified, it would become particularly useful when filming the sex scenes of established stars more leery of graphic sexual display than aspiring ones.[35]

A few of Hollywood's musical sexual interludes would occasionally exceed the effect of bracketing. A particularly subtle and effective example from the early seventies is an act of marital sex performed by Julie Christie and Donald Sutherland in Nicholas Roeg's *Don't Look Now* (1973). In this justly famous scene, a couple who has recently lost a child resumes relaxed and intimate sexual relations after what we are led to believe has been a hiatus. As is typical of sexual interludes, the music amps up and the sexual action is constructed in a tightly edited montage of sexual gestures. In this case, however, the sequence is structured on shots of the naked couple having sex on the bed of their Venice hotel room, intercut with postcoital shots of them later dressing for dinner, reflecting on the experience they have just had. The effect is to offer small tentacles from the sex scene into the rest of the narrative and thus to begin, however tentatively, to bring the sex into the fabric of the film. Nor is this film shy of showing male frontal (flaccid) nudity. By showing the couple during and after sex and by integrating these two moments, Roeg's film exceeds the usual limits of the sexual interlude while still obeying its conventions.

At the time that Hollywood began to develop sex talk and sexual interludes, hard-core pornography still remained mostly underground. By 1969, however, a combination of sexploitation and hard core would emerge in what are called "white coaters" that purported to offer clinical advice to couples—as well as in stag shorts shown in early storefront theaters. Stags, or blue movies, as these illicit, underground films were then still called, were low-budget, excruciatingly silent (no musical interludes here!) movies for men only. They showed clinically explicit genital sex acts performed and shot to achieve what I have called "maximum visibility."[36] These films aimed directly at arousal and were viewed, more or less furtively, at private clubs and parties.[37] All films depicting sexual acts in this transitional era defined themselves, in one way or another, in relation to the overt prurience of these still-illicit hard-core stags. Most mainstream Hollywood films, even those of the post-Code New Hollywood I have been examining, tiptoed cautiously around this territory—a territory itself very much in flux and about to mushroom, in the very late sixties and early seventies, into a new quasi-legitimate feature-length porn industry. But before we get to the flowering (or as some would have it, excrescence) of that industry in the next chapter, let us map the other forms of carnal knowledge available in the sixties outside the Hollywood mainstream.

(S)Exploitation

As early as the 1920s independently produced films exhibited in a separate market of itinerant road shows offered stories about drug addiction, miscegenation, abortion, nudists, strippers, whores, pregnant high school girls, and all the other issues and "problems" unrepresentable within the limits of the Production Code. Exploitation originally meant that, lacking other salable items—such as stars or high production values—these films were sold (exploited) on the basis of a special "carnivalesque ballyhoo" of normally forbidden topics and spectacles.[38] Later, in the 1950s, the term was expanded to indicate any low-budget movie with a topical bent aimed at social problems not treated in the mainstream—films distributed independently in limited numbers of prints. Most of these films were framed by often-questionable didactic messages meant to prevent the sensational acts depicted.

The independent *sex*ploitation film derives from exploitation. This sub-genre thrived throughout the sixties and into the early seventies in many of the same independent art houses screening the sort of European films that had made such a big impression on my adolescent self. Eric Schaefer has shown that sexploitation films were often American imitations of the racier aspects of European films. For example, Ingmar Bergman's *Summer with Monika* (1953) had been exploited in the United States in a short-ened, dubbed, and luridly advertised version called *Monika, the Story of a Bad Girl*.[39] No one took me to these films, and I remained ignorant of them until long after their popularity had peaked. The main point of these homegrown soft-core American sex films was to exploit so-called adult situations and, above all, to expose more female flesh than could be seen in a mainstream film. Russ Meyer's *The Immoral Mr. Teas* (1959) is considered the precursor of the sexploitation genre, though the film lacks the erotic tension, displacements to violence, and general luridness of the sexploitation films of the sixties, including Meyer's own.

More typical of mid-decade sexploitation is Joe Sarno's *Sin in the Sub-urbs* (1964), about two bored and sex-starved suburban housewives who become involved in a club orchestrating orgies. One housewife becomes a hopeless alcoholic and nymphomaniac as she finds herself too much alone on long winter nights; the other, a mother with a teenage daughter, finds herself, at the film's climax, in the midst of an orgy, performing sex on the floor before a masked and robed audience. The orgy's ringmaster announces her performance with another masked woman as "the greatest animal act on earth." The housewife soon recognizes, however, that the woman she is performing with is her own daughter. The film leaves this mother at the end alone on the floor crying hysterically, abandoned by her daughter, who has announced her intention to go "far away" from a mother too busy pursuing sexual excess to love her.

Both mother and daughter have sought illicit sex to make up for the missing love in their lives—the daughter neglected by her mother, the mother neglected by her husband. The sex itself, however, including the climactic orgy, amounts to no more than a few kisses—though the fact that it transpires on the floor in the context of sex talk, including the above double entendre about bestiality, makes it seem quite lurid. In point of fact, audiences do not actually see any more flesh in this film than they would see three years later in *The Graduate*, but unlike that Hollywood version of an adult theme, *Sin in the Suburbs* cannot cordon off one or two sex scenes into discrete interludes. Sexual display is the very raison d'être of this kind of sexploitation. Instead of contained musical sexual

38: *Vixen* (dir.
Russ Meyer, 1968),
Vixen's lurid dance
with a dead fish

interludes, loud, discordant jazz music deployed in the sex scenes spills over into the rest of the film, lending a sexual intensity to even the most ordinary acts of housewives and daughters suffering from the ennui of suburban neglect and isolation.

Sexploitation films thus offer a different tone and feeling compared to Hollywood. Hyperactive musical scores and poor sound recording or dubbing combine with portrayals of perverse, illicit sex to invent a rich repertoire of what Schaefer has called "strategies of evasion." These strategies distinguish themselves both from the Hollywood musical interlude and from the direct representation of penetrative sex in hard core.[40] Frenzied dancing, writhing, drinking, and close-ups of ecstatic female faces were typical sexploitative methods of indicating sexual activity without necessarily revealing more of the act of sex than in Hollywood.

Russ Meyer's *Vixen* (1968) is a particularly popular late-decade expansion of these practices whose date happens to coincide with the end of the Production Code. Vixen (Erica Gavin) is the buxom, pleasure-seeking wife of a Canadian bush pilot (all puns, of course, intended) who has uninhibited sex with just about everyone who comes her way. She mounts a Mountie, a millionaire fisherman, his ignored wife, her husband, even her own brother; she also does a lurid dance with a dead fish (figure 38).[41] Tellingly, however, she vehemently rejects the mere suggestion of sex with her brother's African American friend, whom she taunts mercilessly for having fled the draft of the Vietnam-era United States.

Sexploitation producers were so terrified of resembling hard-core pornography—and they did constantly skirt prosecution for obscenity in their

39: *Vixen*,
Vixen exhibits
convulsions
resembling those
of the classical
hysteric

vulnerable position outside the Code—that they would frequently displace the energy of genital coupling into a more generalized orgasmic abandon of the whole female body, especially, in Meyer's films, with jiggling breasts. Indeed, many expressions of female sexuality in these films verge on the clinically hysterical. Throughout *Sin in the Suburbs* the housewives abandoned to suburbia by their overworked, commuting husbands become depraved, sex-starved demons who collapse into hysterical laughter or tears at the drop of a hat. Similarly, watching Vixen's hands and face as she has sex with her many partners, we see involuntary convulsions that resemble that of the classical hysteric: a face frozen in a paroxysm of pleasure that looks like fear, hands bent backwards, fingers separated (figure 39).

These films tend to oscillate between a liberal ideology of sex as a natural, necessary outlet of human sexuality (housewives who simply suffer from the neglect of their husbands; Vixen as a wholesome, fun-loving woman who just happens to like sex), and the belief that this sexuality is unnaturally lustful and perverse, especially so in women. In this respect, sexploitation films prove perfectly symptomatic of the double standards of the sexual revolution. *Sin in the Suburbs* (1964) opts more for the scandal of perversion, leaving the depraved mother bereft of her daughter; *Vixen* opts more for an ideology of good, healthy fun, leaving Vixen ultimately in the good graces of the black draft resister and her own husband.[42] Either way, however, sexual intimacy in this genre is codified to make all sex acts seem dangerous, excessive, and, in their very convulsiveness, verging on violence.

Item number six under the category of "Sex" in the Hollywood Production Code of 1930 succinctly states: "Miscegenation (sex relationship between the white and black races) is forbidden." While miscegenation is usually understood as the mixing of *any* races, and while Hollywood cinema after *The Birth of a Nation* (dir. D. W. Griffith, 1915) certainly frowned on any such mixing, the odd parenthesis in the above statement clearly shows that it was really the mixing of black and white that raised Production Code Administration (PCA) alarms. As the film scholar Susan Courtney notes, these were the only "colors" regularly seen and named in the long history of the PCA.[43] Unlike the Code's prohibition against "excessive and lustful kissing" which left a little wiggle room for interpretation as to what constituted excess and lust, this prohibition sought to be categorical: visibly white and visibly black performers could not have "sex relations," period.[44] Of course, there was absolutely no clarity about what constituted black or white—many black characters were played in blackface; many passing black characters were played by white actors. Nor was there much clarity about the in-between category of "brown." Many white men would indeed have relations with "brown-," "red-," or "yellow-"skinned women without much ado, but the reverse had been taboo.[45] During the heyday of the so-called classical Hollywood cinema through the late sixties, a general prohibition, neatly summarized by Nick Browne, prevailed: "No nonwhite man can have sanctioned sexual relations with a white woman."[46] Taboos of interracial sex grew out of an American history that has covertly permitted white men sexual access to black women and violently forbidden black and brown men access to white women. However, the racist and sexist assumptions that undergirded such unequal access to sex generated taboo sexual fantasies with an important purchase on the American sexual imagination.

Even after the Production Code began faltering and Hollywood proved its liberalism with the approval of a miscegenous union of a white woman with a black man played by Sydney Poitier in Stanley Kramer's *Guess Who's Coming to Dinner?* (1967), the carnal display of sex relations was studiously avoided. (This film permitted one, very chaste, public kiss in a taxi.) To the African American inner city audiences who went to the movies in proportionately greater numbers than whites in the late sixties,[47] the mainstream stardom of an actor like Poitier seemed to have been purchased at the very price of his sexuality. Dubbed the "Sidney Poitier syndrome," this condition of being the lone black man in a white world with "no woman to love or kiss" was typified by the 1959 hit *The Fugitive Kind* (dir. Stanley Kramer).[48] Poitier and Tony Curtis costarred as escaped convicts handcuffed together, but only Curtis enjoyed a love interest once the cuffs were removed.[49] The brief interracial kiss Poitier was granted eight years later in *Guess* thus seemed like too little, too late.

What black audiences in the late sixties and early seventies were hungry for was the black man who was "bad," and to these audiences that meant two very good things: that he would get away with defiance of "the man" with none of Poitier's appeasement, and that he would be sexually irresistible to both black and white women. The mid-nineteenth-century figure of Uncle Tom had revolutionized white feeling toward the suffering of blacks through selfless, noble, and desexualized Christian suffering.[50] However, by the mid–twentieth century this same figure had become a negative emblem of emasculation to many emerging black nationals and impatient youth. Black audiences had already begun to celebrate new anti-Tom sensibilities in a range of performances by former black athletes in action-adventure films. At first these roles, often occupied by the former football player Jim Brown, simply emphasized virility through action. But soon some of these films began challenging sexual taboos.[51] Blaxploitation—the overt exploitation of racialized sex and violence—would prove the next logical step.

Blaxploitation describes a cycle of some sixty low-budget films that flourished at the box office between 1971 and 1974.[52] These were (more or less) independent films, aimed primarily at black urban youth still enthusiastically going to the movies at a time when white middle-class audiences were finding other distractions.[53] Often directed by, and always starring, blacks, Blaxploitation proved every bit as exploitative of sex as the sexploitation films it followed. Lacking big budgets and major stars, it offered violent action, a little more bodily exposure than the mainstream, and simulated sex acts that were more audacious than typical Hollywood sexual interludes. Most significantly, where sexploitation had spectacularized the female body, blaxploitation launched its initial cycle through the sexploitation of supervirile black male bodies. Only in a later cycle (beginning in 1973) did black female bodies offer a variant spectacle in films like *Cleopatra Jones* (dir. Jack Starrett, 1973) and *Foxy Brown* (dir. Jack Hill, 1974).[54]

Melvin Van Peebles's *Sweet Sweetback's Baadasssss Song* (1971) was the pioneer film most recognized for ushering in the popularity of the Blaxploitation cycle. It was also more genuinely independent than any of the films that would follow. Van Peebles heroically overcame all odds to write, direct, star in, score, and distribute the film.[55] One of the ways he managed to shoot this low-budget film was to claim to be making a hard-core "skin flick"—which by 1971 had emerged as an aboveground but X-rated genre. (This way he was also able to hire a mixed-race, nonunion crew and plug into independent distribution networks outside the mainstream.) The supposed camouflage of pornography proved especially apt. When the film was refused an R rating, Van Peebles exploited his X and sold the film with the slogan, "rated X by an all-white jury."[56] In more ways than one, then, *Sweetback was* a skin flick, though not one that corresponded to any known formula. Van Peebles delivered just enough of a rebellious X sensibility to satisfy his young, black male urban audience, though not so much as to encroach on the growing territory of then emerging hard core. While most critics have viewed *Sweetback* as noteworthy for ushering in an era in which a black man could be violent and even kill a white, I am interested here in its provocation to the once codified prohibition against "sex relations between the white and black races." How did Van Peebles deploy the vestigial taboos of the Code as a new kind of eroticization? To answer I propose to look closely at three of the film's five sex scenes.

Sweetback tells the story of a boy who grows up to become a sexual performer in a stud house. Its famous title sequence, which explains how this boy got his name, establishes a pattern in which the boy—and then man— sexually satisfies an obliging woman. A whore invites the prepubescent towel boy of the whorehouse into her room. As he lies down naked between her legs, we briefly glimpse his penis. She puts aside his cap and, as the script reads, "baptizes" him into manhood. But when the boy, played by Mario, Van Peebles's thirteen-year-old son, just passively lies there, she exhorts him: "You ain't at the photographers—move!" Gospel music ("Wade in the Water" followed by "This Little Light of Mine") accompanies her facial expressions of mounting pleasure until she fairly explodes with the line that baptizes him: "Ohhh! You gotta sweet, you gotta sweet, sweet back!" Throughout the scene, young Sweetback, father to the man, remains impassive.

A freeze-frame on this action permits the introductory titles to play, but we keep returning to the scene of the naked boy wedged between the naked whore's extended legs as she continues to voice her pleasure (figure 40). Eventually, a pullout from a close shot of her ecstatic face reveals that it is no longer a skinny boy between her legs, but a muscular, mature man played by Mario's father, Melvin (figure 41). In what will become a ritual gesture, he ceremoniously puts back on his cap—a freeze-frame concludes the scene on this gesture, one not unlike that of a cool gunslinger putting his gun back into his holster.

Sweet Sweetback's Baadasssss Song (dir. Melvin Van Peebles, 1971)

40: Young Sweetback is still between the whore's legs

41: Sweetback the man between the same whore's legs

Even before its credits roll, then, *Sweetback* puts naked black bodies engaged in (simulated) sex on parade. Though this first scene does not yet challenge the taboos against black-white miscegenation, it nevertheless aggressively eroticizes black bodies and does so with the added provocation of sex between an adult and a child. Item 9 under "Sex" in the Production Code read: "Children's sex organs are never to be exposed."[57] The whore's vociferous enjoyment hails the black boy into manhood in a near perfect illustration of Louis Althusser's description of how individuals are interpellated into ideology.[58] But what ideology is it that hails this boy-man with the name of "Sweetback" in a sex scene that constitutes neither the tasteful foreplay and bracketed interlude of the Hollywood mainstream nor the frenzied hysteria of sexploitation nor the maximum visibility of hard core? What, in fact, is meant by the very name Sweetback? The online

Urban Dictionary defines it as a "dude who is too smooth and fresh to go by any other, less respectful term." The second-listed definition, more apt for this context, is that it is "70's black slang for a large penis"—a meaning that Van Peebles himself has noted preexisted his film.[59] Even after the whore enjoins Sweetback to move, it is remarkable how very little pelvic (or any other sort of) movement Sweetback (young or old) actually puts into most of his supposedly studly performances.[60] We thus understand in some way that Sweetback's back(side) functions metonymically for his front, whose full view in an erect state would have made this film actual pornography.[61] Indeed, it is a frequent feature of seventies Blaxploitation that the eroticized black male ass consistently upstages even female flesh.[62]

The credit sequence ends with the sound of applause, which proves to be that of the audience in a sex club. We thus segue into a second sexual performance in this club, where the adult Sweetback works as a performer. This sexual performance also effects transformation, this time not from boy to man, but from woman to man. The act consists of a broad pantomime between a bearded black man and a sexy young black woman who parade themselves within a circle formed by the racially mixed audience of the sex club. But when the man undresses and lies down on the young woman, "he" proves to have breasts (still encased in a brassiere) and a black dildo attached to a harness. They pantomime sex in a way that is reminiscent of the credit sequence. Again, the "man" lies still, and the woman does all the moving, including the extension of her legs. Suddenly, the "man" pulls away from this coupling to pray. We understand from what follows that this prayer is to become a "real" man.

A smiling black man in a white dress and tiara magically appears in answer to this prayer. This "good dyke fairy godmother" waves a sparkler-wand. Through a combination of quick cuts and superimpositions, we witness a transformation of the praying person: the bra falls away and round breasts transform into a man's flat and hairy chest; the fake beard is pulled off and the real mustache of Sweetback becomes visible; the wand touches the dildo (shown very briefly in close-up), and it, too, disappears from the woman's body. Given this pattern of transformation from female to male, we could now legitimately expect to next see Sweetback's erect penis as the final touch—from dildo to the real thing. Instead, we *hear* what might be the appreciative response of a woman in the audience who screams in awe, possibly at this sight. But all we actually *see* is the face of one of the white cops overseeing the show. The transformation from emasculated woman with substitute penis to real man echoes the previous transformation from little boy penis to studly man's. In both cases, however, the sweet back stands in for, while strongly connoting, the unseen front.

Once again, a transformed and manlier Sweetback proceeds to perform sexually. And once again we do not actually see him do much: his naked back and buttocks move slowly over the woman. The audience, however, placed in a circle around the center of the room, cheers him on and, like the whore in the credit sequence, seems in awe of his performance. One black woman has her hands between her thighs, another smacks her lips and kisses both of the black men on either side of her; black and white men ogle the scene and urge Sweetback on as if he were in a wrestling match. Indeed, at the end, as he pulls back away from the woman on the floor, his arm is raised like that of a wrestling champion. But when the fairy godmother asks for a volunteer from the audience to be Sweetback's next partner and an eager white woman volunteers, a warning glance from the black club owner, responding to a shake of the head from the white detective, causes the offer to be modified to "sisters" only.

Thus *Sweetback* primes our anticipation of the vestigially taboo act of interracial intercourse while playing peekaboo with the male organ that would enact it. Sweetback's sexual prowess, visible almost exclusively through repeated mountings that show us his back and his celebrated "asssss," is exploited by the black club owner and shown in this same club scene to be at the beck and call of white cops. In the next sex scene, however, Van Peebles finally challenges the taboo against interracial sex, again in a public sex act performed on the ground before an audience. This occurs after Sweetback has beaten two white cops into a coma to save a black nationalist earlier beaten by these same cops.

Though Sweetback breaks free of domination by the man, he never seems to break free of the compulsion to perform sexually.[63] The big interracial sex scene, for which the performance in the sex club has prepared us, finally takes place when a menacing white motorcycle gang surrounds Sweetback, who is now on the run. Its leader at first appears to be a tall, leather-jacketed man. But once again we witness an abrupt transformation of gender, this time from male to female. When this man takes off his helmet, he turns out to be a tall white woman with long red hair. Challenged to a fight by this leader, Sweetback is asked to name his weapon. He does so with one word, "fucking."

The gang leader strides naked into the middle of the circle and lies down—rather noncombatively—on her back. Sweetback enters, also naked except for a derby hat and a white bow tie. But unlike his female antagonist, who is viewed frontally, we only see his "sweet back." As usual, he ceremoniously removes his hat and lies down between a woman's already spread legs. For once, however, he does not lie still. In the glaring lights of the motorcycles, surrounded by bearded, long-haired white men whose cheers for their "Pres" seem to cheer him on as much as their leader, he does finally "move," grinding on the woman in a prolonged scene marked by many edits that repeat gestures and superimpose multiple angles. Once he even changes positions, moving one of the woman's legs to gain a better angle. However, he moves slowly, methodically, and, as usual, with no apparent pleasure of his own, prominently displaying his now active back (figure 42).

The "Pres" alternately extends her legs and crosses her feet around Sweetback's back. Three times she cries out his name, echoing the voice heard from the black whore in the baptismal scene. Hailed as a stud by both black and white women and now recognized as such before an audience of only white men, Sweetback wins the contest by delivering yet another noisy orgasm to an easily pleased woman. And so the film finally delivers the interracial sex so anxiously diverted in the sex club (not to mention in *Vixen* and in countless other Hollywood flirtations with miscegenation). When it is over, Sweetback once again coolly puts back on his hat and withdraws from a woman's spread legs. But this time the scene ends with a very brief frontal glimpse of the naked (though flaccid) Sweetback (still in derby and bow tie) as the motorcycle gang roars off (figure 43).

Where gospel music had accompanied the first sex scene and blues the sexual performance in the club, and where jazz had been the typical music of sexploitation, here, strikingly, we hear only the sounds of sex and of the men in the gang cheering on their leader—as if they did not realize she had lost the contest as soon as she lay down on her back. Though the scene is a highly constructed montage marked by prolonged superimpositions, it is emphatically not a musical sexual interlude in any of the ways described above. Indeed, the presence of sound synch points for this carnal encounter lends this film some of the sense of the nakedness of the sex in those European art films that had so indelibly impressed me ten years earlier. With this scene, capped by the brief glimpse of full frontal nudity, Van Peebles dared to expose, literally and figuratively, an element of black empowerment frequently left out of civil rights agendas: the right for black men to have sex with white women; the black penis as a sign of power and potency. This briefly glimpsed front proves crucial to the film, yet is rarely noted by critics.[64]

The rest of the film focuses on Sweetback's protracted escape to the border. Mixed-race inner-city audiences (especially young males) roared

Sweet Sweetback's Baadasssss Song

42: Sweetback finally moves on top of the "Pres" and before an all-white, male audience

43: (53:01) Sweetback in derby and bowtie, glimpsed frontally

at the spectacle of a black man escaping the law and screwing his way to freedom.[65] Enthusiastic vocal responses aimed at the screen mirrored the many moments audiences within the film cheered Sweetback's sexual performances. The call-and-response format of much of the film's music, written by Van Peebles and performed by Earth, Wind, and Fire, itself elicited audience call-out ("You bled my Momma. You bled my Poppa. But you won't bleed me."). While white critics tended to begrudgingly admire the crowd-pleasing fabulation of the black man's revenge on "whitey," while simultaneously wincing at its crass overstatement, for once the more important critical commentary occurred within the black community.[66]

None other than the Black Panther minister of defense, Huey P. Newton, hailed *Sweetback* as the "first truly revolutionary Black film." Newton's long article, occupying an entire issue of the *Black Panther Party Intercom-*

munal News Service, whose target market was inner-city blacks, offered detailed, sometimes self-contradictory, close readings of all the film's sex scenes, each of which he argues should be interpreted not as "actual sex acts" but as "righteously signifying" sexual symbols. For example, despite the nudity and simulation of sex acts, Newton asserts that the first scene of "baptism" with the whore is "far from anything sexual." It is a "sacred rite" answered by a second baptism, this time in blood, when Sweetback beats the two cops who have themselves beaten the black revolutionary.[67]

In answer to Newton, Lerone Bennett Jr., writing for *Ebony*, argued that the film represented no liberation and no challenge to white stereotypes of blacks, but only its own stereotypical counter to the previous stereotype of the figure of the Tom. For Bennett, writing for a magazine whose target audience consisted of middle-class, upwardly mobile blacks, the opening baptismal scene was nothing less than the rape of a child, and the film's subsequent sexual performances were so many bogus "emancipation orgasms." "If f***ing freed," Bennett writes, "black people would have celebrated the millennium 400 years ago."[68] More important, perhaps, Bennett notes the woodenness of Sweetback's sexual performances, which to him missed an opportunity to portray "the black tradition of spontaneous sexuality." He insists that he is not opposed to the film's sexual explicitness per se, only to its manner: "The sex in this 'black' film is as cold and as white as snow—grim, manipulative, competitive, full of anxieties and hostilities." Indeed, it is "not explicit enough, it is not natural enough, *it is not black enough*." Worried that impressionable black viewers were taking Sweetback seriously as a sex symbol when the real opportunity had been missed to "make visible for the first time the lushness, the beauty, and the incredible variety of black flesh," Bennett is deeply disappointed that the film opted for a kind of vulgar intensity that could never "present sex as the human sacrament it is."[69]

Both Newton and Bennett address the stereotype of the hypersexual black male, but from different directions. Newton finds *Sweetback* liberating and revolutionary. Bennett finds the character a trap, a counterstereotype itself determined by the white man's stereotypes of the black man.[70] He notes Sweetback's own singular lack of pleasure and taunts that the only person who actually gives everything to sex, who holds nothing back, is neither "Sweetback the Sex Machine nor the black whores but the white female leader of the motorcycle gang. How does that black aesthetic grab you?"[71] Thus Bennett argues that Sweetback is entirely determined by the stereotype he is invented to counter.

Bennett certainly has a point. The white stereotype of the hypersexualized black man with a large penis is a figment of the white imagination. But the black imagination of the hypersexualized black man does not merely repeat that same stereotype. It is, as Mireille Rosello has pointed out about the working of stereotypes in general, a refunctioning that walks a tricky tightrope between two different stereotypes: the phobic stereotype of the black rapist who cannot control his slavering desire for white women and the counterphobic one of the kind, gentle, and asexual Uncle Tom.[72]

Thomas Cripps has written that sexual prowess is "the one racial stereo-type that few blacks ever bothered to deny."[73] I would like to respectfully revise this important statement. Historically, the figure of Uncle Tom, was deployed strategically by both blacks and whites in the nineteenth century to counter an earlier minstrel figure of the sexually promiscuous black buck.[74] The "anti-Tom" reinvention of this figure in the reconstruction era, most significantly revived by *Birth of a Nation*, put a new spin on the stereotype by presenting the comic minstrel as a melodramatic villain in perpetual lust after white women.[75]

Van Peebles thus had to counter two stereotypes. Uncle Tom was the most obvious. He writes in his manifesto-screenplay that when the idea for his film came to him, his primary goal was to "create a commercially feasible vehicle" and to "do something that wasn't Uncle Tommy."[76] It is entirely relevant, therefore, that he informs us that his inspiration for this film came to him while alone in the desert masturbating.[77] His version of the anti-Tom needed to assert sexual pleasure, but if it asserted too much and was not under control, it would fall into the stereotype of the white version of the anti-Tom. Peeble's anti-Tom thus had to emerge from a highly controlled form of sexual pleasure. As he writes, "I unbuttoned my fly, leaned back against the front fender . . . and pulled out my pecker and began to beat my meat. . . . some idea was lurking back there in my mind waiting for the coast to clear to be born."[78] Masturbating not merely for pleasure, or for cinematic inspiration, but perhaps to prove a certain potency through control, Van Peebles calls his crash method for creative inspiration "semen-shock." He compares this method favorably to the "racial-shock" of a film—recognizable as Stanley Kramer's *Home of the Brave* (1949)—in which a white doctor taunts a paralyzed black soldier into regaining the use of his legs by calling him a "nigger coward."

A stereotype of the black buck that functioned in the Reconstruction era to keep white women, black men, and black women in their place was thus in the early 1970s refunctioned by a black director to celebrate sexual performance in the form of a transgressive, quasi-pornographic tale. If we seek an answer for why Sweetback's glimpsed front rarely moves, why it is so often just coolly in control, just "there" between the women's legs, never taking and only giving pleasure, I think it might have something to do with the fact that it now has the burden of countering not only "Uncle Tommy," which any sexual performance could refute, but also the white-generated phobic stereotype of the black buck as first promulgated in popular culture by the likes of Thomas Dixon and D. W. Griffith. In *The Birth of a Nation* (1915), black men and so-called mulattoes thrust their pelvises at white women in wanton exhibitions of lust. The trick for the new generation of black men interested in black sexual power would be to perform neither "Uncle Tommy" nor the lascivious black buck, to show potency but not excessive desire or pleasure. It is thus not accidental that so many of the sexual acts depicted in the film are performed before the surprisingly approving gaze of white men. Van Peebles's accomplishment, though not as genuinely revolutionary as Bennett might have wished, is nevertheless to have redeployed the very taboos that once effectively policed the racial border in the service of eroticizing transgression.[79] Such was Melvin Van Peebles's complex masturbatory fantasy.

The persistence with which *Sweetback* positions audiences in the film for its many sexual performances alerts us to the fraught question of how audiences, themselves marked by signs of race and gender, might have responded to the sex. Three out of five times Sweetback performs sex before racially marked internal film audiences: the race- and gender-mixed audience in the sex club; the all-white, all-male motorcycle gang; and finally, the two white cops in the desert who are fooled into thinking Sweetback's knifepoint rape of a black woman is really lovemaking in the bushes. Each performance points to the affective dilemma of the theater audience's own response: Who should cheer, and who should be ashamed? Who might permit themselves to feel aroused, and who should be guarded against such feelings? Perhaps one reason for the exuberant cheering of young, black, urban audiences was the sense of release: where their parents' generation had felt the need to remain very guarded about showing arousal in any but the most strictly segregated situations, here, finally, was an opportunity to cheer on black sexual prowess even in one case vis-à-vis that most taboo object: the white woman. But in the agonistic arena of sexual battle, who wins and who loses?

Should I, for example, as a white woman, cheer when Sweetback brings the white woman motorcycle "Pres" to orgasm, or should I cringe at the passive way she lies down on her back to do battle? Should a black woman rejoice at the triumph of the black man, even if it is purchased at the cost of the humiliation (and later rape) of her counterpart on the screen? Or do these questions of opposed forms of pleasure and power look too narrowly at race and gender as identificatory viewing positions? Is the black stud who foils the cops and escapes across the border freed by his sexuality, or only further imprisoned by the need to perform his virility without ever losing his cool? These are questions without easy answers. The one thing they point to is the historic importance of a film that put the question of African American sex acts firmly in the public eye, right along with the issue of the black and white audience's response to those acts. Perhaps the most we can say is that Van Peebles's frequent hat doffing is a nod to both his audiences—those in and those at the film—as if to say "I know the cool new way to walk this tightrope."

The less fiercely independent Blaxploitation films to follow the trail blazed by *Sweetback* would make a point of delivering something a little more like "the black tradition of spontaneous sexuality" that Bennett called for. These films would also "make visible for the first time the lushness, the beauty, and the incredible variety of black flesh." Gordon Parks Jr.'s 1972 *Superfly* provides the quintessential example. Ron O'Neal's dope-pushing hustler hero casually leaves the bed of one of his white female customers at the film's beginning and later has luscious, spontaneous musical inter-lude–style sex in a bubble bath with a black woman he may actually love. The film even gives this couple a happy ending. Within the constraints of the gangster genre, a certain celebration of intraracial sexual pleasure had arrived in Blaxploitation, but perhaps only insofar as the films re-entered the supposedly tasteful realm of the Hollywood musical sexual interlude.[80]

The African American novelist Terry McMillan writes that before she saw Spike Lee's *She's Gotta Have It* in 1986, she had "never seen a real black couple in the twentieth century on screen making love before," nor had she seen "a black woman actually enjoying it."[81] Though McMillan seems ignorant of the early seventies history of Blaxploitation, her com-ment speaks to the anticipation with which African American audiences have greeted each rare sighting of intraracial sex. Henry Louis Gates Jr. has also noted that "honest and open explorations of the complexities of interracial sexual attraction have not been among Hollywood's strong points."[82] Like McMillan, Gates goes on to discuss Lee as the pioneer (this time writing about the 1991 *Jungle Fever*), skipping over what he calls the more "lurid and titillating" tradition of Blaxploitation. It is precisely in the "lurid and titillating" transgressions of early Blaxploitation, however, that one finds the most honest and open challenges to the taboos against miscegenation, as well as the deepest understanding of how these taboos, even when broken, structure the very nature of their violation.

Going All the Way in the Avant-Garde

The final location for the depiction of carnal knowledge outside the mainstream of American film in the sixties is the avant-garde. In the sixties proper I saw very few of these films, but I would make up for that lack in the early seventies when I moved to Boulder, Colorado, home to Stan Brakhage and a lively experimental cinema scene. In regular screenings at the Experimental Cinema Group (later renamed First Person Cinema) by filmmakers as diverse as Scott Bartlett, Brakhage, Bruce Conner, Jack Smith, Carolee Schneeman, Paul Sharits, and Andy Warhol I encountered another kind of carnal knowledge also caught up in the sexual revolution. Closest in some ways to the brazen revelations of hard-core pornography, avant-garde films did not hesitate to show explicit sexual acts, but they always pursued other aesthetic, political, and social goals in the process.[83]

Avant-garde films were also screened at the kind of private parties and clubs where stag films were shown until the late 1960s. But they had an ability, unlike the latter, to also travel to museums and art galleries. As rarified experiments in cinematic rendering of the texture of life,[84] they were often diametrically opposed to the clinical clarity of hard-core films, frequently interlacing carnal knowledge with flicker effects, fast cutting, superimposition, or the intentional lack of focus. Audiences for these films, like the audiences for pornography and sexploitation, often came to films with titles like *Loving* (dir. Stan Brakhage, 1957), *Blow Job* (dir. Andy Warhol, 1963), *Blue Movie* (dir. Andy Warhol, 1968), or *Lovemaking* (dir. Scott Bartlett, 1970) with built-in prurient interest and some expectation that if they were patient and looked hard enough they might glimpse aspects of sex that they could not see anywhere else. Sometimes, as in the promisingly titled *Blow Job*, they were pornographically disappointed.[85] At other times, as in Barbara Rubin's amazing *Christmas on Earth* (1963), originally titled *Cocks and Cunts*, or in Warhol's *Couch* (1964) and *Blue Movie*, they were gratified in prurient ways while also being offered all the familiar existential longueurs and formal challenges expected from avant-garde cinema. As Thomas Waugh and Ara Osterweil have both noted, these films simultaneously fulfilled and frustrated the sexual interests of their small but devoted audiences.[86]

Warhol's *Blue Movie* is of particular interest because, as *Variety* was quick to note in its review, it was not quite as underground as some of the previous films of the avant-garde (such as, for example, Warhol's 1963 *Kiss*). Indeed, it was the first theatrically released feature-length sound film to show explicit sexual intercourse.[87] The hard-core blue movies to which Warhol's title refers had been silent, short, and entirely illegal.[88] In contrast, *Blue Movie* was long and loquacious. What it shared with the stag film or blue movie was an unblinking look at unsimulated sex, but it was neither an old-fashioned, silent blue movie nor yet a feature-length, sound, hard-core work of pornography. Rather, *Blue Movie* had its very own way of going all the way, in particular a foregrounding of what we have already seen as a key issue of screening sex: the rendering of private and intimate sexual acts as public.

A remarkable number of the films discussed in this chapter depict sex performed for audiences within the film narrative. In *Sin in the Suburbs* an orgy arranged for an audience climaxes with mother and daughter unmasked to one another and to the spectators at the event. These spectators do not stay to enjoy the show. Public sex, as one might expect in a film that equates sex with sin, is tantamount to shameful, though still titillating, exposure. The words of the ringmaster who calls this coupling an "animal act" are apt: sin lies in the very absence of shame that permits a public performance. By 1971, with *Sweetback*, however, the performance of sex becomes an arena for a cool display of prowess. The black man shows his stuff to both the women he has sex with and the audience.

Warhol's *Blue Movie*, in contrast, does not have a literal audience inscribed in its narrative. But, as we shall see, the film is haunted by the specter of an audience. It is aware that its portrayal of unsimulated sex constitutes a publication of an act that had previously been taboo everywhere except in "blue movies." The film is about a man (Louis Waldon) and a woman (Viva) who spend a late afternoon and evening together. They undress, have sex, watch TV, eat, watch the sun go down, cook, wash each other in the shower, sing, and make inarticulate animal sounds. Throughout, they casually smoke, needle each other with an offhanded loquacious intimacy, talk and talk (about politics, the Vietnam War, acting, sexual pickups, not wearing bras, etc.). All of this takes place in the idiom of Warhol's late sound films, described by Wayne Koestenbaum as "lurid subject, cool presentation."[89] Viva (née Susan Hoffman), one of Warhol's many superstars, is a thin, beautiful, deadpan, "whine-voiced comedienne,"[90] the very opposite of Meyer's Vixen. Where Vixen is all busty, frenzied, working-class heat, Viva is sophisticated, world-weary coolness. Waldon is friendly, casual, and unlike many other Factory superstars, neither a man who wants to be a woman nor a man who likes men. The action takes place over the course of 133 minutes in the bedroom, kitchen, and bathroom of a New York apartment with a nice view of the skyline.

The sex act itself occupies about half an hour of the film's total running time. The couple slowly undresses as they lie in various positions on a bed. Usually their entire bodies are displayed within the frame. Never does the film cut, as a true blue movie would, to close-ups of body parts. A casual intimacy dominates; banal conversation accompanies even the sweatier, more strenuous parts of heterosexual intercourse. Like Warhol's earlier silent *Kiss*, *Blue Movie* is somehow more and less real in its representation of its chosen sex act. It is more real than mainstream cinema or sexploitation in its explicit display of full frontal nudity, erection, and penetration and in its depiction of awkward longueurs (e.g., the long time it takes Louis to get hard). It is also more real than blue movies in the synchronized sound that permits sexual grunts, interminable dialogue, and verbally explicit negotiations of sexual positions (as when Viva asserts that she will not suck Louis's "cock" because "it's boring"). At the same time, however, the film is less real than either the mainstream or the sex genres: acutely aware that it is not so much about sex as about the filming of sex, it poses the central question of what it means to perform sex for a camera and, through the mediation of that camera, to present sex to a film audience.

Unusual among Warhol films, *Blue Movie* has no drag queens, no male hustlers, no "perversions"—only a man and a woman alone in an apartment enjoying a leisurely fuck.[91] Yet of course the very fact that we can see them means that they were never really alone. For their sounds and images to be visible to us in the future audience, a camera and sound recorder (separate entities at this stage of 16mm film technology) had to be present, along with their operators.

Almost as soon as it begins—in medias res, like all Warhol films, with a clothed Viva and Louis already stretched out on a bed—*Blue Movie* explores the dilemma of the private act of sex performed for a camera and sound apparatus that make it public. Amid their small talk, Viva whispers something into Louis's ear in order, we assume, not to be overheard by the sound recorder. She then says out loud, in ironic complaint: "Maybe we should discuss it out loud at the next commercial break." Not much later,

44: *Blue Movie* (dir. Andy Warhol, 1968), Viva quips: "We don't want to see your ugly cock and balls!"

as they begin to caress and undress, Viva again expresses discomfort with the lack of privacy and asks Louis, "Why don't you ask someone in here to leave—all the ghosts?" Both complaints go uncommented on by Louis, but it is clear that their negotiation of the sex act is also a negotiation with the "ghosts." Indeed, Viva continually worries about how she might look, wishing at one point that she had worn a leotard "so I'd look sexy."

The long sex scene is marked by Viva's simultaneous self-consciousness about how she looks and her concern about how Louis looks with an erect penis when he finally takes off his shorts. "Oh! How disgusting," she exclaims, "right in front of the lens!" At this point their bodies are arranged perpendicularly, feet first, to the camera. In taking in the scene, we tend to look up their legs and bodies from the bottom to the top of the frame. Halfway up we discover Louis's now exposed, partly erect penis. Looking directly at the camera, Viva, whose own position in the scene is actually less favorably located for the sight of Louis's penis than is ours, explains, speaking both for herself and as if for us, "We don't want to see your ugly cock and balls!" (figure 44). And, in fact, she adjusts his top leg so as to hide the offending organs. Louis responds not by defending the beauty of his manhood, but by insisting on the fiction that they are alone: "Who's we? Me and you? There's nobody here but me and you!" (Later, however, a ghost sneezes, and Louis says "gesundheit.")

Viva and Louis navigate the pressures of having sex before a camera differently, Viva mostly with wisecracks and asides and Louis with what appears to be initial performance anxiety. For not only does Viva object to the fact that the lens sees "cock and balls," she objects to the fact that he is not hard ("How can you show that when it's not hard?" she questions, adding in her usual chatty way that hard-ons were considered comic in the Greek theater.) After a long kiss, and a rare silence, Louis puts his left leg between Viva's legs and rhythmically rolls into her, now apparently hard. But a doorbell rings and spoils the mood, giving Viva another opportunity to criticize him ("You're doing so poorly!"). Eventually, however, she climbs on top of his erect penis, they reverse positions, and he pumps on top of her. Though Viva never stops demonstrating her awareness of performing for a camera (saying at one point, "I think we should give a profile here"; and at another, "we should have organized orgasms"), she does respond to his pumping, pushing back up into him and working with him to achieve if not "organized," and certainly not visible, orgasms, then a certain concerted frenzy of motion whose passion can be measured by their sweat. Viva notes how they slip and slide and, when the passion subsides, cracks that they could use a dentist's suction machine to get rid of the excess liquid.

Viva's objection to, and Louis's complacency about, the ghosts is one of the couple's many running arguments. At stake in this argument are different assumptions about the privacy of sex acts, the appropriateness of having sex for a camera and tape recorder and, via these mechanisms, before an audience. Viva assumes that "we" do *not* want to see Louis's "cock and balls," but her eventual compliance suggests ambivalence. Clearly this "we" includes herself, the ghosts, and by extension, the "us" that marks for her an ambivalent obscenity. She invokes what William Ian Miller calls the "rules of disgust"—rules that in Judeo-Christian culture had deemed the display of lower portions of the anatomy obscene. The relaxation of these rules is the very substance, Miller argues, of intimacy.[92]

For Louis, however, the argument seems to rest on male pride: Can he get Viva excited enough to actually forget the camera? To the extent that she does seem to forget, he would seem to be successful in his own performance and the film a celebration of that success—just as the sexual interlude in *Midnight Cowboy* celebrates Joe Buck's success in giving pleasure to his female client. In Warhol films, however, we never fully forget the dimension of performance. Even after Viva has climbed on top of Louis and begins to be less critical of his sexual performance, she nevertheless suggests—again, to whom?—that a profile might be in order. The performance of genital sex for the camera, like the performance of kisses, *is* the sex; there is no more private, authentic moment. How it looks relates to how it feels, and Viva's constant references to how *she* looks are thus always more than a reference to how she might look just to Louis.

David James has noted of Warhol's "screen tests" that "the camera makes performance inevitable, it constitutes being as performance."[93] In his *Philosophy*, Warhol recalled that his purchase of an audiotape recorder

> finished whatever emotional life I might have had. . . . Nothing was ever a problem again, because a problem just meant a good tape, and when a problem transforms itself into a good tape it's not a problem any more. An interesting problem was an interesting tape. Everybody knew that and performed for the tape. You couldn't tell which problems were real and which problems were exaggerated for the tape. Better yet, the people telling you the problems couldn't decide any more if they were really having the problems or if they were just performing.[94]

Sex for Warhol was the "interesting problem." He was an admitted voyeur who felt like an outsider to all sex, but especially to his peculiarly exalted ideal of heterosexual sex.[95] *Blue Movie*, for all Viva's complaining, proves a most interesting solution to the problem of the performance of the private act of sex for a public audience. By forging intimacy around the very conflict of being filmed and sound-recorded in the act of sex, the film reflexively stages the dilemma of the performer and the audience in the spectacle of sex. Although the film sometimes halfheartedly attempts to present the tryst of Viva and Louis as that of an actual couple having an affair, the two cannot keep their stories straight. At one point Viva says, "I thought I was supposed to be your wife in this movie." Their sex, which is more extended and more real and hard core than in any previous American movie including preexisting hard-core pornography, only exists for, and because of, the camera and tape recorder that deliver this performance to the alternately bored and stunned avant-garde film audience.

Ironically, however, Viva and Louis's performance of sex achieves a simulacrum of the intimacy of the "authentic couple" through their very bonding opposition to the ghosts. This intimacy, which includes a long period of postcoital talk, cooking, and showering, and which is forged both with and against the recording apparatus, seems more genuine than any of the other forms of carnal knowledge I have so far examined.[96] Throughout the half hour in which the couple disrobes, verbally spars, wrestles around, and finally has sex, the only ellipses occur when the rolls of film run out; we see the image bleach out and go white, followed by brief darkness before again picking up the action at a slightly later point. Thus the temporal flow of this sex, although not without an occasional ellipsis at the seemingly arbitrary end of each roll of film, differs radically in duration and explicitness from any other discussed in this chapter.

If it were possible to have a degree zero of sex in movies, this is it. No edited montages, no superimpositions, no musical interludes attempt to stand in for the always elusive orgasmic moments of pleasure. Nor does the scene build to a dramatic climax of money shots. Yet Warhol does take his cue aesthetically from the blunt and often matter-of-fact older blue movies he so much admired. These films are often so haphazard in their orchestration of unfaked sex acts that they, too, neglect to offer dramatic climaxes and thus, screened today, often have an uncanny realism.[97] As we saw him do with kisses, Warhol simply shows the act with an unblinking, unprobing, unprurient eye although without maximally visible close-ups. It does not hurt therefore that Warhol chose to begin his film with the sex act rather than to build toward it as a payoff at the end. The real payoff of his film turns out to be the postcoital and emphatically domestic intimacy in which the brittle Viva becomes "soft." (Before they have sex Louis pleads, "Be soft so I can make love to you—soft, like an angel.")

Blue Movie was made in 1968 after Warhol returned from his recuperation from the wounds inflicted when he was shot by Valerie Solanas. Koestenbaum views it as his last piece of real art before becoming a kind of ghost in his own body.[98] After it was screened at the Garrick Theater in New York—soon to become the Andy Warhol Theater—it was seized by police, tried, and found obscene. Since then it has only been viewable on video at the Warhol Museum in Pittsburgh and on a bootleg video dubbed into German.[99] Though in today's pornographically saturated media environment *Blue Movie* would never be considered obscene, it has continued to be treated as such: it remains literally off scene so long as Viva has not consented to its screening. This way, it seems, she has had her revenge on those ghosts.

In *The Graduate*, just before he has sex with Mrs. Robinson, Benjamin makes a last-minute appeal to normalize their relation. "Would you like to go to the movies?" he asks. In 1967 Benjamin might have assumed the movies a place safe from the adult carnal knowledge in which he was afraid to engage. But as we have seen, the movies were becoming less "safe," more a place where scenes of passion, adultery, miscegenation, might now be glimpsed. By 1971 and 1972, however, going all the way would take on new meaning. No longer would it be a matter of the cordoned-off musical sexual interlude in the mainstream, such as that between Benjamin and Mrs. Robinson. No longer would the avant-garde or Blaxploitation be the only place to glimpse less contained moments of sex. Very soon "adult sexual situations" would become the primary reason for watching a film from beginning to end, whether in the new hard-core feature-length pornography exemplified by the ubiquitous *Deep Throat* (dir. Gerard Damiano, 1972) or in a new kind of sexy art cinema that was not entirely foreign.

3

going further

Last Tango in Paris, Deep Throat,

and *Boys in the Sand* (1971–1972)

Pauline Kael's famous review of *Last Tango in Paris* began with the following words: "Bernardo Bertolucci's *Last Tango in Paris* was presented for the first time on the closing night of the NY Film Festival, October 14, 1972: that date should become a landmark in film history comparable to May 29, 1913—the night *Le Sacre du Printemps* was first performed—in music history."[1] *The Rite of Spring*[2] had reportedly been the most notorious premiere in the history of music and ballet. What happened at that premiere in the Théâtre des Champs-Élysées in Paris was quite simply a riot. Almost from the very first notes of Igor Stravinsky's music and the very first steps of Serge Diaghilev's ballet the audience was shocked by the scenic and rhythmic evocation of pagan rituals with percussive intensities never before heard in classical music.[3]

Why did Kael, the most influential and astute film reviewer of her generation, compare a 1972 film by an Italian director working in France, and starring one of America's most famous actors, to a 1913 musical score and ballet performed by a famous dancer commonly considered to have been the defining moment of modern art?

Last Tango is about a twenty-year-old French woman (Maria Schneider) and a forty-five-year-old American man (Marlon Brando) who meet by chance in a Paris apartment, have sex, and continue to meet for more sex until their attraction dies. Though certainly not a ballet, it is a kind of arch, stylized dance of life and death, with a literal tango figuring prominently in one of its later scenes. Part of the audacity of Kael's review is the claim that a movie could have the same kind of cultural resonance as Stravinsky's and Diaghilev's famously dissonant, percussive works of music and dance. The comparison was certainly strategic. The film critic most famous for championing movies as a popular form was now claiming that film had finally come of age as high modern art.

It is hard not to ask: if the art of film was only then becoming modern, where had it been these last fifty-nine years? The implication could only be that film was behind the times, that it had not yet had its modernist break with classical traditions, even though it may have been the only art form actually born in the era of modernism. To make her audacious analogy, Kael had to ignore the cinematic avant-gardes of the 1920s, 1940s, and 1960s. This analogy only makes sense if one considers it a claim for the feature-length commercial narrative cinema, not for the avant-garde. But what specifically links the Stravinsky-Diaghilev-Nijinsky *Rite of Spring* with the Bertolucci-Brando *Last Tango* in Kael's mind is their embrace of a similar primitive eroticism.[4] In a telling phrase, Kael links the two through their shared "*jabbing, thrusting eroticism.*"[5] It is as modernist *sex* that the film is judged by Kael to be a "breakthrough." Modern art had often been connected with the unleashing of libido and thus with Sigmund Freud's theories on the importance of sexuality as a fundamental motive force in human life. Because of the Production Code, however, American films showing in regular movie houses had not participated in the explorations of human sexuality manifest in writers like James Joyce, D. H. Lawrence, Georges Bataille, or Henry Miller, or in visual artists such as Pablo Picasso, Egon Schiele, René Magritte, or Francis Bacon beyond the tame conventions of what I have called the sexual musical interlude. It is thus in this particular sense of taking on sexual themes in the non-romanticized, primitive ways of modern art that Kael claimed that movies had finally grown up.

Last Tango was certainly not the first film imported from Europe to screen adult sex beyond the kiss.[6] As early as 1959 Louis Malle's *Les amants* (*The Lovers*) had engendered controversy, not to mention significant litigation, with a long scene of adulterous lovemaking that was so intrinsic to the film that it could not—like Hedy Lamarr's brief nude scene in *Ecstasy* (dir. Gustave Machatý, 1933) or other European examples of risqué sex—be cut without doing extreme violence to the narrative.[7] And in 1967, the same year as *The Graduate*, Luis Buñuel's *Belle de jour* had structured its narrative around the multiple sexual encounters of an upper-middle-class housewife who takes up prostitution. None of these films were constructed in the bracketed-off, musically accompanied manner of the Hollywood sexual interlude.

Last Tango, however, differed. It had an unprecedented number of sex scenes (six) and a story revolving fundamentally around sex. But what was especially different about *Last Tango* was that it did not seem to be the usual foreign import. To be sure, it was directed by an Italian, shot in Paris, and featured the familiar French actor Jean Pierre Léaud and his compatriot newcomer Maria Schneider. But its star was Marlon Brando, the quintessential American male sex symbol of the late fifties and early sixties. His aging but still magnetic masculine presence did not allow American audiences to place the film's sexual scenes in the context of a foreign, supposedly Old World decadence. Though he speaks a little French in the film, all of Brando's important scenes, and certainly all of the sex scenes, take place in a very American idiom, some of which Schneider—who speaks in heavily accented English—cannot understand. It was thus at least partly the Americanization, through the body and voice of Brando, of a sexuality once associated with European sophistication that made the film seem such an astounding event for Kael.

Kael's *New Yorker* review was written on the occasion of the film's high-profile screening on the closing night of the New York Film Festival. It would help launch the film into wide distribution by United Artists, where it would rank sixth at the box office and eventually receive two Oscar nominations. The film's reception into the mainstream illustrates a distinctive American sensibility grappling with sexual scenes that went far beyond the interlude.

The first sex scene in *Last Tango* occurs in an empty apartment that Paul (Brando) and Jeanne (Schneider) are simultaneously looking over to rent. A few French words spoken by Jeanne serve to establish Paul's nationality. A phone rings and Jeanne picks it up in one room while Paul listens on the extension in another, moving closer, breathing on the line. No words are spoken directly before, during, or after they suddenly have sex right there in the empty apartment. Neither does music play, though a plaintive saxophone previously punctuated their mutual stalking around the apartment. Paul shuts the door, approaches Jeanne who has just picked up her hat to go, and carries her, in tough-guy style, to a blinded window. They have sex standing up, still wearing their bulky coats. We hear a rip when Paul presumably tears Jeanne's undergarment. Parodically one-upping Kael's musical comparison, Norman Mailer enthused, "in our new line of *New Yorker*–approved superlatives, it can be said that the cry of the fabric is the most thrilling sound to be heard in World Culture since the four opening notes of Beethoven's Fifth."[8] The couple is framed initially as full figures off to the left side of the frame with Paul's back to us (figure 45). Only after we have fully viewed this image of "the beast with two backs" from a distance, do we slowly move in a bit closer.

The sex is sudden, unromantic, and brute (the script describes them as "rushing like two dogs unable to stop").[9] Paul exhibits Kael's "thrusting, jabbing eroticism," Jeanne wraps her legs around him, and they almost topple over as they urgently press against one another seeking the leverage to thrust harder (figure 46). When they fall to the floor, Paul groans and convulses. The camera then pulls back, as if avoiding the intimacy of the moment, to appreciate the full view of two human animals who have been caught up in the violence of an ecstasy that has taken them, as the word itself means, to a state of crisis "beside themselves" (figure 47). They do not regain themselves until Jeanne melodramatically rolls several times over on the floor, showing her naked pubis in the process, landing some distance away from Paul (figure 48).

Last Tango's first "tango" exhibits a primitive passion, what Bataille in his writing on eroticism calls a "violence of the one" that "goes out to meet the violence of the other."[10] The unfurnished apartment, soon supplemented with a broken mirror and a bare mattress, will, for a few days, become Paul's crucible for constructing an *amour fou* in defiance of work, social identity, and family. Out of this he will attempt to build a purely physical relation with Jeanne, founded on the systematic transgression of the sexual taboos of bourgeois life.

Bertolucci has acknowledged the overt influence of Bataille's concept of orgasm as a "little death" (*petite mort*) at the time he began to write the script for *Last Tango*. Indeed, *La petite morte* was the film's original title.[11] It is not surprising, then, that Bataille's description of the "animal couple" reads like a description of Paul and Jeanne's first sex: "A meeting between two beings projected beyond their limits by the sexual orgasm, slowly for the female, but often for the male with fulminating force . . . there is no real union; two individuals in the grip of violence brought together by

Last Tango in Paris (dir. Bernardo Bertolucci, 1972)

45: The "beast with two backs" from a distance

46: Paul and Jeanne seek the leverage from which to thrust, nearly toppling

47: Two animals

48: Jeanne melodramatically rolls away

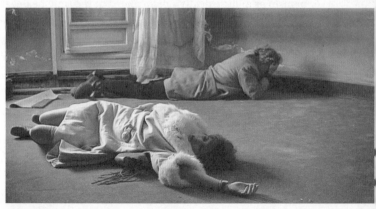

the preordained reflexes of sexual intercourse share in a stage of crisis in which both are beside themselves."[12] Afterward, they are just as alone as before.

Paul himself is already in a state of crisis precipitated by the unexpected suicide of his wife, which we learn about in the following scene. Death and decay haunt and propel his sexual acts, as his wife's still unburied corpse lies in a room of the hotel they own. Crude body functions also figure prominently in two of Paul's most memorable monologues, one about cow shit and another about pig vomit. The next time they meet they face one another, naked, and jokingly attempt to come without actually touching as Paul speaks only in animal grunts. In the following encounter, after Paul has told his childhood story of humiliation by cow shit, he moves away from the emotional intimacy of the scene just as Jeanne begins to tell of her own (happier) childhood. Hurt by his emotional and physical abandonment, Jeanne unzips her jeans and masturbates face down on the bed as Paul weeps in an adjacent room.

We do not know if Paul weeps for his wife, for himself, or for his failure to respond to Jeanne, which may itself echo the way he previously failed to respond to the emotional needs of his wife. What we do know is that the emotional content of the present relationship, haunted as it is by the past, cannot be the pure animal convulsion for which Paul wishes. For the first time in movies, as Kael's review would claim, complex emotional relations of ecstasy, alienation, and humiliation are enacted *in* the performance of the sex act itself.

Two of the most memorable of these sex acts are explorations of anal eroticism that illustrate Bataille's sense of the links between "excreta, decay, and sexuality," as well as the importance of desires tinged with fear. In the first of these scenes (the infamous "butter scene"), Paul asks Jeanne if she is afraid. She says she is not but, perhaps projecting his own fear onto her, he insists that she is. Next, he orders her to "get the butter." He pulls down her jeans, applies butter to her backside, and penetrates her anally on the floor, all the while remaining clothed himself (figure 49). In pointed defiance of the norms of heterosexual procreation, he accompanies this near violation with a verbal diatribe which he requires Jeanne to repeat: "Holy family, church of good citizens. . . . Where the will is broken by repression. . . . Where freedom is assassinated. . . . You fucking fucking family!" Hopelessly trying to inculcate in Jeanne his own sense of the necessary violence and violation of taboo, as well as his own closeness to fear and death, he acts out his existential despair by performing anal sex on her.

49: *Last Tango in Paris*, Paul penetrates Jeanne anally on the floor

The second anal scene is presided over by a dead rat that terrifies Jeanne and delights Paul. Paul gives Jeanne a bath and attempts to comfort her. But Jeanne is hurt and threatens to leave, accusing him of being too old and fat. Still naked in the bath, she taunts Paul with the news that she has found a man who will counteract the lonely confrontation with death that Paul insists is each of their fates. He argues that no man can offer her solace from solitude until "you look death right in the face . . . until you go right up into the ass of death—right up his ass—till you find a womb of fear. And then, maybe, maybe . . . you'll be able to find him." Like Bataille, Paul insists that the dissolution of personal identity in the face of death is necessary to any real eroticism and to any authentic being. Also like Bataille, he insists that "repugnance and horror are the main-springs of desire." When Jeanne counters that she has already found the man who will help her encounter the womb of fear, and that that man is Paul, he does not suddenly soften and embrace her as might be expected in a more conventional movie. "Get the scissors," he commands instead. Like his earlier "get the butter," we expect further violence to be enacted on Jeanne. But this time the anal penetration is digital and performed by Jeanne on Paul. (The scissors are just for him to trim her fingernails.) In this antiromantic, antigraphic climax, only Paul's face and voice register the violence of the act. This is his way of responding to her profession of love.

While Jeanne assaults Paul anally, he assaults her verbally: "I want to get a pig, and I'm gonna have the pig fuck you, and I want the pig to vomit in your face, and I want you to swallow the vomit. . . . I want the pig to die while you're fucking, and then you have to go behind him, and I want you to smell the dying farts of the pig. Are you going to do that for me?" Forcing Jeanne to enter into the "womb of fear," degrading her and himself with the signs of death and animal decay, Paul drives home his lesson that the urge toward love is also "an urge toward death."[13] In the next scene Paul finally confronts the body of his wife and speaks to her in a powerful monologue that mixes grief and disgust.

Only now, after the catharsis of confronting sex as death, does Paul attempt to connect with Jeanne beyond the womblike enclosure of the apartment. But now he is an ordinary middle-aged man with no special allure and Jeanne is hardly interested. In the tango hall into which they wander, they have their last tango—both a literal dance performed grotesquely by a very drunk Paul and a tango of sex in which Jeanne jerks Paul off under a table. Unwilling to believe that the relationship is finished, Paul becomes a stalker. Following Jeanne into the inner sanctum of her family home, he confesses love and asks to know her name. Jeanne speaks it as she also pulls the trigger of her military father's revolver. It is possible that Paul sought this fate of death at her hands all along.

Knowing that *Last Tango* would receive an X rating on release, Pauline Kael was determined to distinguish this particular X from more ordinary ones.[14] She writes:

> Many of us had expected eroticism to come to the movies, and some of us had even guessed that it might come from Bertolucci. . . . But I think those of us who had speculated about erotic movies had tended to think of them in terms of Terry Southern's deliriously comic novel on the subject, *Blue Movie;* we had expected *artistic* blue movies, talented directors taking over from the *Shlockmeisters* and making sophisticated voyeuristic fantasies that would be gorgeous fun—a real turn on. What nobody had talked about was a sex film that would churn up everybody's *emotions.*[15]

Like many others who have defended films with explicit sexual content, Kael downplays prurience, attaching that feature to other kinds of films: "Exploitation films have been supplying mechanized sex—sex as physical stimulant but without any passion or *emotional* violence . . . the physical menace of sexuality that is *emotionally* charged is such a departure from everything we've come to expect at the movies that there was something almost like fear in the atmosphere of the party in the lobby that followed the screening."[16] Exploitation films of the sort described in the previous chapter had prepared Kael to anticipate a simulation of sex. And it is obvious that the sex in *Last Tango* is simulated. But what she was not prepared for was the connection of sex with often powerful emotions, most notably with fear.

Before examining the nature of the emotions raised by the simulated sex acts of *Last Tango*, let us consider another critic reviewing another X-rated film in this very same year (1972) in yet another New York magazine. The writer is Al Goldstein, the journal *Screw*,[17] the film *Deep Throat* (dir. Gerard Damiano, 1972), and the review is just as full of hyperbole as Kael's.

> This week I am reviewing the very best porn film ever made, so superior to others that it defies comparison. The movie hits the all-time best score of 100% on the Peter-Meter,[18] not only for its raging raunch, but more startlingly for its wit, wild humor, fine acting and hilarious story. . . . Now I am blasé and bored with sexploitation flicks and can respond more to the passions provoked by a photo of a chocolate malted. Yet I was seized with yearning by the greatest on-screen fellatio since the birth of Christ performed before my very eyes.[19]

With *Deep Throat*, feature-length, hard-core, sound and color pornography emerged into the mainstream of American movies. Though it was hardly the first feature-length pornography to show on a big screen before gender-mixed audiences, it was the first to become a household name. It was every bit as recognizable in its own realm as *Last Tango* was in its, and the two films were often discussed in the same breath.

I take the unprecedented celebrity of these two films, emblematized by Kael and Goldstein's reviews, as the historical moment at which the American moviegoing public not only flocked to see sex on the screen but also massively recognized itself as interested in screening sex—not just an occasional sex scene in an occasional movie, but movies that were *all about sex* from beginning to end. We saw in the previous chapter that "carnal knowledge" became representable in the Hollywood mainstream through the bracketed sexual interlude in sexploitation through the often hysterical gyrations of female bodies, and in Blaxploitation through the virile presence of the black hero. Only Andy Warhol's avant-garde film *Blue Movie* (1968) actually portrayed a couple having unsimulated genital sex, though this quasi-underground film was seen by very few and soon disappeared from distribution. *Last Tango* and *Deep Throat*, the two X-rated movies released to general viewing four years later, were thus the first movies to spur a widely recognized public response to their unprecedentedly sustained sexual subject matter.

Al Goldstein's claim for *Deep Throat* is, of course, quite different from

Kael's for *Last Tango*. He does not compare his film to modern art. Nor does he argue that the sex portrayed in it expresses the characters' drives. But it is significant that both critics write hyperbolically about their chosen X-rated film, both favorably compare their film to more rote (s)exploitation examples, and both believe that with it the movies have arrived at a new peak of maturity. What Goldstein applauds in *Deep Throat* is a simplified and less emotionally threatening version of what Kael applauds in *Last Tango*: the spectacle of convulsive, phallic, heterosexual, but often nonnormative sex. But where Goldstein is not shy about describing the famous fellatio in *Deep Throat*, Kael is less specific about the anal sex in *Last Tango*.

Goldstein singles out the famous scene of Linda Lovelace performing deep-throat fellatio on the doctor who has discovered that her clitoris is located in her throat. "Hot white cum shot out and *Our Lady of the Lips* lapped it up. I was never so moved by any theatrical performance since stuttering through my own bar mitzvah, 'Stupendous!' was all I could shout as I stood up and spent my applause on the glory that mine eyes had just seen."[20] Kael, on the other hand, writes more generally of the shock produced by *Last Tango*: "This must be the most powerfully erotic movie ever made, and it may turn out to be the most liberating movie ever made, and so it's probably only natural that an audience anticipating a voluptuous feat . . . should go into shock. Bertolucci and Brando have altered the face of an art form."[21]

I link these two reviews because each in their own way takes note of a belated coming of age on American screens, whether in the new genre of hard-core feature or in the already existing but Americanized European "adult art film."[22] I also link these reviews because both foreground the question of audience response to real and simulated cinematic sex acts. Both Kael and Goldstein acknowledge their own visceral, physical response and thus, in a sense, model versions of response to their readers. Both even seem to be a bit stunned by the powerful ways they are moved. Kael writes of the "physical menace" of a sexuality that is so emotionally charged that it generated "something almost like fear."[23] At another point she notes that the first sex act performed by Brando "had the audience gasping and the gasp was caused—in part—by our awareness that this was Marlon Brando doing it, not an unknown actor."[24] Goldstein, for his part, forthrightly embraces the turn-on with his acknowledgment that the movie "hit the all-time best score of 100% on the Peter-Meter," though even he finds the need to sublimate his response into the "spending" of applause.

When critics write about films with sex, they are usually remarkably quick to assure their audience that it was not the sex that engaged them, but some other feature—the formal beauty, the acting, absolutely anything but the sex which is presumably too embarrassing to show interest in for itself. Kael and Goldstein's reviews are exceptional and mark an important moment of cultural criticism because they frankly acknowledge their own enthusiasm and/or shock without immediately turning away. I therefore take them as emblems of a wider cultural recognition of the seriousness of visceral responses that had previously been dismissed as "mere" prurience. When Kael admits that no one had ever imagined that a "sex film" could "churn up everybody's emotions," she was trying to differentiate Last Tango from other films with a presumably more exploitative use of sex by insisting that powerful emotions of fear and violence, not mere prurience, animated the audience. My guess, however, is that one element of the fear she describes was that audiences did not yet know how to react to a film that *also* aroused prurient interest. She thus grapples with the uncomfortable fact that representations of sex acts may mix with a wide range of emotions and cannot be cordoned off into "mere" prurience. Goldstein, on the other hand, seems to revel in the fact that what had previously been dismissed as mere prurience is now up there on a big screen for all to see. He is not interested in complex *mixes* of emotion, but in the spectacular visual display of what Freud would call "discharge."

Prurience is a key term in any discussion of moving-image sex since the sixties. Often it is the "interest" to which no one wants to own up. In *Miller v. California* (1973), one year after the shock of the release of both *Last Tango* and *Deep Throat*, the Supreme Court used the term *prurient interest* to solidify a legal standard for the definition of obscenity in the first prong of its definition: a work is obscene if "the average person, applying contemporary community standards, would find that the work, taken as a whole, appeals to prurient interest."[25] In such a case, First Amendment protections do not apply. However, this landmark decision did not then helpfully go on to actually define prurience in the ruling itself. Rather, in a footnote to the decision the Court had recourse to Webster's New International Dictionary describing it as: "persons, having itching, morbid, or lascivious longings of desire, curiosity, or propensity,. . . ." Further on, perhaps noting the vagueness of "lascivious longings," and the naturalness of "curiosity," it attempts to specify: "shameful or morbid interest in nudity sex, or excretion. . . ."[26] In other words, prurience is "defined" here as the morbid and shameful part of sexual urges that presumably also have a healthier and more natural side. Any sexual representations that were not the discreet, limited displays ending relatively soon, as the Hollywood sexual interlude tended to, or any sexual representation that prolonged the "itch" or that seemed to wallow in sex just for its own sake could therefore be deemed prurient.

In 1976 the noted First Amendment scholar Frederick Schauer would attempt to clarify prurient interest by excluding the above meanings of morbidity, deviance, or shame. He argued that what society wishes to prohibit with the concept of prurience is not the discussion of sex, nor the advocacy of sexual immorality, nor "deviant" practices. Rather, it is "that which shows erotic sexuality in a manner designed to create some form of immediate stimulation."[27] For Schauer, prurience is a purely physical reaction—what Kael calls the "turn on" and what Goldstein would measure with a "Peter-Meter."[28] Any work that, "taken as a whole," sexually stimulates can be said to incite prurient interest. Kael's vigorous defense of *Last Tango* seems to be, at least in part, an attempt to extricate the film from just such prurient interest in the name of more exalted "emotions."

The problem, however, is the line "taken as a whole." For Kael's major point about *Last Tango* is that the eros that turns us on *cannot* be extricated from other emotions displayed in the film and powerfully transmitted to the audience: fear, shock, despair, aggression. In contrast—even though Goldstein notes that his own emotions are not pure turn-on, but admixed with awe and admiration—his praise for *Deep Throat* is primarily centered on the celebration of prurient interest (in Schauer's new and reduced sense of the stimulation of male physiological response) uncomplicated by other emotions. Thus when moving-image sex acts are no longer elided, as in the tradition of "kisses and ellipses" discussed in the first chapter, when they are no longer cordoned off into neat sexual interludes, as in the Hollywood films discussed in the previous chapter, then, as in *Deep Throat*, they become the substance of the whole film. And when sex acts engage a range of other emotions, when the films that contain them are no longer confined to screenings in exclusively bohemian venues or art houses, then they begin, as did *Last Tango*, to become a part of the fabric of cultural life. This recognition is the gist of Kael's appreciation of Bertolucci's film and of Brando's performance in it. She cites, for example, Brando's willingness to display "the aggression in masculine sexuality," and our belief in the "insanity that grows out of it."[29]

Schauer worked hard to dissociate prurience from notions of immorality or deviance, but subsequent court cases attempting to clarify prurience have not always upheld that distinction. I have argued elsewhere that many elaborations of the definition of obscenity have tended simply to scapegoat "lasciviousness" or "morbidity" in the form of sexualities deemed deviant and to ignore the issues of "immediate stimulation" on which Schauer focuses.[30] The problem with prurience is thus twofold: its susceptibility to being identified as the shameful or morbid sexual practice of the deviant (someone *else*'s sexual practice, not my own) and the difficulty of isolating the "immediate stimulation"—or turn-on—from the rest. Sex is rarely ever "just" sex. Art films know this, pornography tries not to. Inevitably, sex mixes with diverse emotions (shame, joy, triumph, relief, morbidity, love, etc.). In what follows, I want to try to characterize what it meant to screen these two X-rated films "in the day."

Screening Graphic Sex

In the summer of 1973, I was a twenty-seven-year-old graduate student living in Boulder, Colorado. In that summer, almost a year after each film had already made its big splash in New York, I saw both *Last Tango* and *Deep Throat*. *Deep Throat* constituted the more memorable social occasion; I went to see it with a group whose camaraderie almost inoculated us against strong sexual feelings. This group formed when a bunch of us showed up for a screening of our campus art film society which was cancelled. On a whim we decided to go to the big city in quest of this much less artful film. *Last Tango*, on the other hand, constituted the more memorable private occasion: it forced my partner and me to recognize that the new intensity of passion we experienced after seeing it had something to do with the film. It was not easy for us to admit that our private sex had been influenced by a movie. All mainstream American movies that I had previously seen had either had a certain deniability built into them (e.g., Rick and Ilsa *might* have done it, but then again there was no clear evidence) or had deemphasized or bracketed the moment of prurience (e.g., Benjamin and Mrs. Robinson *did* do it, but my senses were appealed to in diversionary ways via pop songs and fancy editing, not the display of their flesh). In contrast, *Last Tango* and *Deep Throat*, not unlike Alex Comfort's explicitly illustrated how-to-do-it manual, *The Joy of Sex*—another cultural product of 1972—were focused on sex acts; there was no way to pretend that they were not about sex and that we did not feel what the Miller Test called prurient interest, however defined, however real or simulated were the acts themselves.

I insist on remembering these two films together because both did, in ways that I was not prepared for, turn me on. It would be all too easy to say that *Deep Throat* was trash and corresponded to Schauer's argument that there is no real difference between screening sex and having sex when the images of screened sex are fully graphic. Similarly, it would be easy to say that *Last Tango* made for high-class erotic art and thus was not, as Schauer polemically argued about hard-core pornography, "a sex aid, no more and no less."[31] However, it seems more important to recognize the degree to which any film that might be used as a sex aid is always both more *and* less than that. My point is that these popular, "household-word" movies of the early seventies rather more forthrightly than previous films could *become* sex aids, though of course never so much as when later released on video or DVD and brought into the home. But neither my partner nor I felt, as Schauer argued, that watching sex was having sex. Rather, I recall feeling prior to both films what Linda Lovelace says in *Deep Throat* about the nonearthshaking sex she had experienced before learning deep-throat fellatio: "Little tingles." To this extent you might say I mimicked my namesake as I saw mediated sexual action from what Walter Benjamin had called "close range." If I did indeed feel a more "palpable, sensuous connection"[32] between my body and those screened than I had felt before previous Hollywood movies, getting hold of this sex by means of its likeness did not mean slavish mimicry, but a new kind of play for which previous movies had not prepared me: actual fellatio in *Deep Throat* and simulated anal sex in *Last Tango*. There is no question that these acts rebounded in me and that I did reencounter my own body watching these acts, though not in Schauer's notion of direct correspondence.

Deep Throat, especially, constituted a kind of test. It was not a film that one went to casually like other movies, though it did try to present itself as if it were just another movie. I was an avid movie fan at that time, but the only time I ever drove forty miles to the metropolis of Denver and paid more than three dollars to see a movie was when my partner and I, another couple, and one other male friend went to Kitty's Theater on Colfax Avenue to see *Deep Throat*. In this era, before very many feminists had decided that pornography was a primary cause of the objectification of women, my friends and I dared ourselves to watch and thus, by implication, to watch ourselves watch.

Critics and commentators—everyone who was anyone—had already taken note of the experience of watching *Deep Throat*. Though only Al Goldstein had given it an unqualified rave, even those who disliked the film, such as Nora Ephron in *Esquire*, noted that it would be culturally derelict not to see it. For it was only with the explosion of hard-core features preceding and following *Deep Throat* that pornography became available to mixed audiences in public movie theaters. And not until the summer of 1973 did I see real unsimulated sex acts on a movie screen.[33] Now that moving-image pornography is familiar fare on the smaller screens of computers and televisions viewed primarily in the home, it is hard to understand the impact of mass American culture's first encounter with graphic sex in movies. To do so we have to again recognize, as with Thomas Edison's projection of the first screen kiss, the power of big-screen magnification before a public audience.

We have seen that the sheer size of the first public projection of a kiss, viewed in close-up, shocked some members of its initial audience. But this shock, quickly absorbed, cannot compare to that of the mass public screenings of *Deep Throat* and its memorable close-ups of deep-throat fellatio—producing ten- to twenty-foot erect penises on some screens. My friends and I watched these acts in a public theater with a large cross section of the American population: working-class men and women, middle-class businessmen, housewives, students, teachers, even older women. Afterward, we talked about the experience. Some of us were disgusted; some of us admitted to being turned on.[34]

When we are in the grips of the physical excitement of sex, we achieve a kind of intimacy with our own and others' bodies that, once past a certain threshold, allows us to relax what the historian and culture critic William Ian Miller calls the "rules of disgust."[35] Miller argues that whether or not sexual organs are intrinsically disgusting to sight, they have traditionally been associated with culturally debased "lower" portions of the anatomy that shame in Judeo-Christian culture had long compelled human beings to cover up. Genitals in particular produce liquid substances—menstrual blood in women, semen and urine in men—regarded by some cultures as polluting. These rules are not universal; some cultures flaunt sexual organs and sex acts quite avidly. But Western cultures have long tended to place sex acts off scene and to find their public display either disgusting or arousing, or both. What was changing in the culture to relax these rules of disgust?

Hard-core pornography was not unknown in the summer of 1973, even in public theaters. For several years already the theaters of Times Square and of a few other urban centers had begun to offer what the 1970 *Report of the Commission on Obscenity and Pornography* referred to as the "New Genre" of pornography—films that "graphically depicted actual sexual intercourse on the screen."[36] In these theaters, however, it was not only solitary men who were now screening sex. As Eric Schaefer has shown, a new kind of cheaply made 16mm hard-core feature was the real pioneer leading to the phenomenon that would become the 35mm triumph of *Deep Throat*. Sixteen-millimeter features could be made for a tenth of the budget of the old 35mm sexploitation films. Where the 16mm films had begun as plotless loops—so-called beaver films in which women displayed their wares—they soon expanded into features with men and women having both simulated and graphic sex, with the line between the two often marked only by whether a close-up of insertion was included. By 1970 these new films commanded the market with much greater profit return than the old stags. Small storefront theaters, not unlike the old nickelodeons of the early part of the century, began to cater to a "more varied clientele who viewed attendance at pornographic films as part of their participation in the sexual revolution."[37] Schaefer cites one example—the San Francisco Sutter Cinema—which had a special area for "lovebirds" who were "cordoned off from the single men."[38]

It was thus the 16mm format, used in such films as Bill Osco's *Mona* (1970), that had already pioneered the hard-core feature long before *Deep Throat*. It even had pioneered the spectacle of frequent fellatio, since much of its narrative concerned a "virgin nymph" determined to maintain her technical virginity through recourse to fellatio.[39] Soon 35mm sexploitation producers began to imitate the hard-core 16mm features while many of the 16mm producers shifted, Schaefer reports, to the professional 35mm gauge.[40] *Deep Throat* and the phenomenon of "porno chic" thus represented the convergence of a number of technological, cultural, and economic factors that were making the screening of graphic sex almost necessary to sexual citizenship in the early 1970s. As Gerard Damiano, speaking from his Florida retirement in the documentary *Inside Deep Throat* (dir. Fenton Bailey and Randy Barbato, 2005), says: "You had to be there. I'm thrilled that I was there. And I thank God I had a camera."

Deep Throat thus differed from the old tradition of the silent, men-only stags both in the repertoire of sexual acts (and especially the ascendancy of fellatio) and in the assertive publicness of its exhibition. *Mona*, *Deep Throat*, and the rush of hard-core films that followed were, as one influential *New York Times* article put it, examples of the new porno chic.[41] Whether or not the films exhibited in this era actually *were* themselves fashionably chic, viewing them was considered so. No longer—or at least not for a while—were public porn viewers furtive, no longer were raincoats placed carefully on laps. Celebrities of both sexes could be sighted at screenings.[42] Watching it, my friends and I felt, was almost a badge of honor.

The more radical fringes of Hollywood had long been acutely aware of the potential revolution of a new hard-core sensibility. As early as 1964 Stanley Kubrick had screened a pornographic film (undoubtedly a stag film) for friends at his home and audaciously suggested that one might improve on the genre by making such films under studio conditions.[43] In 1970 Terry Southern's satirical novel *Blue Movie* (not to be confused with Andy Warhol's 1968 film, but possibly inspired by it) described the making of just such a hard-core studio film.[44] By the time *Last Tango* appeared, then, the idea of adding "real sex" to a "real film"—not just in pornography—was on many minds. Norman Mailer, as we have seen, competed with Kael for encomiums with which to praise *Last Tango*, but he concluded his review in a fit of disappointment for its lack of courage, calling it a "fuck film without the fuck, like a western without horses."[45] To Mailer, the film copped out on the graphic sex that its subject demanded.

Men of a certain age and disposition—and that would certainly have included artists like Mailer and Kubrick—were likely to know the basic "dirty movie" conventions of the old "fuck films," and by 1972, when Mailer made his statement about *Last Tango*, he probably had a vague idea of what the presidential commission of 1970 was calling the "New Genre" of pornography.[46] But no one, not even *Deep Throat* director Damiano, could have known what the future of this genre would bring. To read the critics of the era is to be aware of a great sense of excitement, as well as of a certain apprehension and dread about the possible merger of hard-core sexual action with regular movies. What was imagined was no less than a new kind of mainstream film in which explicit sex acts would be integrated into narrative films: not just to deliver the required number of graphic sex acts that would soon prove de rigueur in the new porn genre but to expand the representative power of the medium into aesthetically ambitious realms of the performance of sex: *Last Tango* "with the fucks." In this imagined future, pornography as such would disappear, porn stars would cross over to the mainstream, and respected actors would consider the performance of sex acts part of the challenge of their craft.[47]

Of course quite the opposite occurred: mainstream movies did not accept the challenge, and pornography itself would devolve in the following decade into the parallel universe of mostly cheaply made, badly acted, and aesthetically impoverished sucking and fucking shot on video.[48] However, the fact of this failure should not keep us from examining some of the aspirations of the porno chic era.[49]

Damiano was a former hairdresser just learning how to make movies. He was restless to break out of the mold of the short underground stag loops, as well as out of the slightly more aboveground mold of pseudodocumentaries like *Sexual Freedom in Denmark* (dir. M. C. van Hellen, 1969) or his own *Sex U.S.A.* (1971). Like Mailer, Damiano saw the promise of a film like *Last Tango* and also regarded it as a failure of nerve: "Brando and Bertolucci copped out. . . . I would have added a few insertions and cum-shots." By adding precisely the parts of sex—"insertions and cum-shots"—not seen in the mainstream, Damiano proposed to "make it real."[50]

As long as the strict bifurcation between graphic "fuck film" and simulation (whether of mainstream Hollywood or European-influenced art film) was maintained, however, pornography would bear the burden of crowding all the sex that could not be seen elsewhere into its hour-plus time spans. In feature-length pornography, then, narrative is minimized, sexual numbers are maximized, and eventually a standardized genre emerged with a wide repertoire of sex acts.[51] In contrast to *Last Tango*, however, pornography offered a terribly limited repertoire of the moods in which these acts might be performed. Instead of thinking hard about the qualities and kinds of sex that might grow out of dramatic, or even comic, situations, pornography's primary concern was for the sheer quantity and maximum visibility of sex and, especially—and this is what was new and what Goldstein appreciated—for a visible climax in male ejaculation.

As we have seen, most of the sexual movements of human bodies had never been revealed in aboveground films. When cinema began to incorporate graphic depictions of sex, it had a great many aesthetic and dramatic choices to make about the representation of those acts. It could have begun to think about female pleasure more realistically; it could have found ways to show the many nuances of sex—friendly or hostile, playful or brute, fast or slow, sleepy or alert, nonorgasmic or multiorgasmic, and so on. It could have decided that erotic tension might be in play with dramatic plot. Instead, the emerging porn industry opted to obey the conceit that the hottest sex was the most visible sex. "Come shots" (or cum or money shots) would offer the extreme instance of this visibility. But the demand for visibility governed even the smallest gestures. For example, a female performer might pull her hair away from her face to better reveal the mechanics of the action of fellatio, or a male performer might put an arm behind his back while pumping to keep the arm from obscuring the in-and-out of his penis. Any gesture, in fact, that seems more designed for sexual display than for the performers' own pleasure can betray the erotics of the moment and make us aware, even if we might be grateful for the view, that the demand to reveal the graphics of sex overrules an often less visible erotics of the entire sensorium.

When Damiano asserted that he would have added a few "insertions and cum-shots" to *Last Tango*, he was applying the crude lessons of maximum visibility to an erotic art film whose complexities of emotion would have been ruined by such simple solutions. Yet, as Mailer noted, he also had a point: some of the sex acts simulated in that film, especially those that Kael noted conveyed "thrusting, jabbing eroticism," could have benefited from the sight of two, not just one, naked bodies and from the sight of some insertions, as long as they were not just the clinical sort invariably favored by porn. It is more difficult to believe, however, that the other hard-core convention of the visible external ejaculation could have contributed to the reality of Bertolucci's film. These shots would prove the most enduring of the conventions of the new pornography.

Cum shots, or money shots, as I prefer to call them,[52] are markedly unreal as depictions of the *practices* of mutual sexual pleasure. When they become the conventional conclusion to all sex acts depicted in pornography, the withdrawal (whether from mouth, anus, or vagina) that makes the ejaculation visible necessitates a dislocating shift from the proximate, mutual pleasure of touch to the more distant pleasure of sight, as if the couple compromises their own pleasures of touch for *our* screening pleasure. The film asks us to believe that the participants in the sex act, especially the woman who makes so much of the sight of the ejaculating penis, prefers, at that moment, to become more like a film viewer marveling at what she sees than like a sexual actor caught up in what she feels. As climax, then, the money shot is awfully one-sided.[53]

If Damiano's proposal for making the sex real in *Last Tango* disappoints, both as realism and as art—and, indeed, if *Deep Throat* disappoints from the same perspective—it is worth recognizing how very little thought had been given by anyone, with the possible exception of Andy Warhol, Jean Genet, and a few other avant-garde filmmakers of the 1960s, to making sex seem either real or aesthetically compelling in movies. It was almost universally agreed that *Deep Throat* was a badly acted film with a silly excuse for a plot. Ellen Willis, writing for the *New York Review of Books*, called it "witless, exploitive, and about as erotic as a tonsillectomy."[54] Only Al Goldstein—who may have been more honest than some of the other critics who reviewed it—seemed to think it was actually erotic. Nevertheless, it was precisely *this* film, and not some of the later, much better produced and acted porn features with higher artistic ambitions,[55] that not only delivered a mainstream theatrical audience to hard-core pornography but constructed these acts in ways still familiar to us today. And so, despite the fact that it has already been much discussed,[56] it is this film and its effect on audiences that still deserves our attention as we consider the rise of hard-core pornography on/scene in public theaters.

Deep Throat and Porno Chic Up Close

Deep Throat is about Linda (played by Linda Lovelace, originally Linda Boreman), an ordinary young woman with wholesome—not what would later become known as stereotypically pornographic—good looks.[57] She is a typical product of the 1960s sexual revolution. She considers sexual pleasure important to her self-fulfillment, but has missed out so far. She confesses to feeling "little tingles" when she has penetrative sex, but "no bells ringing, dams bursting, or bombs going off." After experimenting with a number of men to no avail, she goes to a doctor (Harry Reams) who informs her that her clitoris is deep in her throat (one early possible title for the film was *The Sword Swallower*).[58] Deep-throat fellatio is the "cure" immediately performed on the doctor.

Putting aside the many analyses that have been subsequently spun around this film, my own included, what I most remember about this screening was what most people remember about pornography when they first see it in a social group: how much we laughed. It would be a mistake to underestimate the function of this film's sophomoric brand of humor in making feature-length, publicly screened pornography palatable to its initial audience.[59] The film reassured us with the option of laughing rather than panting; or, if we did pant, the laughter helped disguise it.

Consider the film's first sex act. Linda arrives home to find her room-mate—played well by the porn veteran Carol Connors in the Joan Blondell mode of the older, more experienced woman—leaning back on her kitchen counter while a young man diligently "eats" her. What we see, however, is not so much a woman in the throes of pleasure as a woman blasé in the face of pleasure: "Do you mind if I smoke while you're eating?" she quips to her partner. The joke, such as it was, immediately defused our anxiety. Modeling a certain hip, casual acceptance, it put us in the same position as Linda herself, who, walking in on the scene, takes it in stride and simply sighs at the mild inconvenience. Music, too, defused the potentially fear-inducing erotic force of this and every other sexual act shown. Neither Connors nor her male partner exhibits much excitement in the medium-to-long shots (no close-ups) of cunnilingus. Nor has this particular sex act yet asked us to view an erect penis. Mild, rhythmic, mechanistic movements viewed at a distance rather than in close-up eased us into the display of graphic sex.

Linda's roommate next organizes an orgy to help her find the pleasure missing in her life. All of Linda's failed attempts to find pleasure in this orgy share in a similar atmosphere of competent but casual—even disengaged—sexual performance. We see perfunctory sexual acts—vaginal penetrations, a few external ejaculations, and even one act of fellatio (presumably not deep enough). Afterward Linda again confesses that she has felt no "bells ringing and dams bursting." By the time we get to the big moment of therapy with the doctor—the scene that finally does "ring her bell"—we have already been exposed to a good half dozen graphic sex acts casually performed with no great drama.

It might be possible to say that the absence of dramatic affect is simply bad pornography, especially if we accept the fundamental goal of pornography as the display of graphic sex acts for purposes of arousal. Compared to some of the much better made erotic examples of porno that followed, *Deep Throat* was, perhaps, bad pornography.[60] However, in a mainstream culture with very little experience of watching graphic sex in a mixed-gender public theater, this may be precisely the reason *Deep Throat* became the touchstone it did. Watching it eased audiences over the shock of what amounted to a kind of collective primal scene, played comically as an acrobatic freak show rather than as an emotionally challenging erotic drama.

I am not arguing that pornography by definition lacks eroticism, or that eroticism precludes pornography, but only that *Deep Throat*, the film that introduced the pleasures of hard-core pornography to mass audiences, insistently identified an apparently emotionally uncomplicated yet manifestly difficult-to-achieve end pleasure in its rhetoric of bells and bombs. In contrast, in *Last Tango*, when Brando tells Schneider that she would not be able to be free of that "feeling of being alone . . . until you go right up into the ass of death . . . till you find the womb of fear," and then had her put her fingers up his own ass, the scene was scarier to watch than anything in *Deep Throat*. Despite its lack of explicitness, it played on Bataille's notion of the erotic conjunction of fear and desire. *Deep Throat*, on the other hand, would show us many potentially disgusting and/or arousing penetrations—especially in the graphic oral penetration that constitutes its pièce de résistance. However, the whole force of its gimmicky narrative would be to teach the audience to relax its own automatic reflexes of disgust, much the way the good doctor would teach Linda to relax her gag reflexes in order to discover the pleasures of deep-throat fellatio.

Once again, Leo Bersani's distinction between the pleasure of the itch versus that of the scratch can enhance our understanding. Recall that

Freud presumed the goal of sexuality to be the discharge or end pleasure that releases tension, as if the goal of sex was the end of sex. Yet as we have seen, the tension of sexual excitement can be pleasurable in itself. Sexual pleasure is more than discharge. Bersani surmises that the "*mystery* of sexuality is that we seek not only to get rid of this shattering tension but also to repeat, even to increase it."[61] Following Bersani, I have been arguing that there are two poles of sexuality relevant to screening sex: the pole of the scratch, which emphasizes the telos of end pleasure, and that of the itch, which intensifies and increases sexual tension up to the limit case of what Bersani calls self-shattering and death.

In 1972 these two poles were neatly represented by *Deep Throat*'s athletic, pornographic emphasis on the scratch and *Last Tango*'s simulated erotic emphasis on the itch. Sexual pleasure in *Deep Throat* is a willed accomplishment with powerful parallels in the performative domain of sport. Just as a golf pro might instruct a golfer to relax into the swing, so the doctor instructs Linda to relax her throat to make possible the deep penetration that will scratch her itch. At one point he adopts the accent of a Yiddish grandfather in imitation of a familiar Alka-Seltzer commercial: "Try it, you'll like it!" At another point, he insists on the importance of "practice." As if this were not enough, the infamous *Deep Throat* theme song, discussed further below, kicks in with the following lyrics: "Now I'm going to tell the way it has to be . . . just relax your muscles and once you've hit that spot / keep right on pushing and give it all you've got." Practice— expressed as a contradictory mix of relaxation and effort—is required for pleasure to be achieved in the deep-throat climax.[62]

Vigorous deep-throat fellatio, in which the doctor presumably "hits" the invisible "spot" that precipitates Linda's pleasure, leads to the highly visible spectacle of the money shot that would become the sine qua non of all hard-core pornography for decades to come. *Deep Throat*'s money shot, however, is something more than visible ejaculation. Lovelace repeatedly takes what looks to be a nine-inch penis deep into her throat. Black-and-white small-scale reproduction cannot do justice to the impact of the sight of an engorged, giant, wet, vividly colored, erect penis repeatedly sliding into/engulfed by a mouth (figure 50).

But what especially marks this particularly famous money shot is an extraordinary montage in the manner of the Soviet filmmaker Sergei Eisenstein's famous Odessa Steps sequence in *The Battleship Potemkin* (1925), demonstrating that Damiano knew a thing or two about film after all. In a film with much poor acting and bad sound, the panache of this montage takes us by surprise. The sequence literalizes some, though significantly

not all, of the verbal metaphors Linda had used to describe her wished-for excitement. She had hoped for bells ringing, bombs exploding, and dams bursting. The rhythm of her performance of fellatio leading to the discharge of the money shot is augmented by increasingly split-second insertions of these metaphors: We see a bronze bell struck by bronze statues of men with hammers (figure 51); we see brilliant fireworks against a night sky (figure 52). Finally, at an increasingly fast pace that alternates the in-and-out of deep-throat fellatio (figure 53) and the take-off of a Cape Canaveral–sized rocket (figure 54), the two rapidly intercut shots seem to merge as the montage reaches a crescendo. Sounds (of bells, fireworks, and rockets) also merge with the music of the theme song. The veins of the penis grow taut, a milky substance covers its length, and we become aware, after the fact, that discharge has occurred (figure 55). Finally, at the end, Linda smiles (figure 56).

(facing page) *Deep Throat*

51: Bells ring

52: Bombs burst

53: Deep-throat fellatio

54: A Cape Canaveral–sized rocket takes off

55: Discharge has occurred

56: Linda smiles

Although Goldstein writes that "hot white cum shot out and *Our Lady of the Lips* lapped it up," the actual "shooting" of "cum"—an image that would soon be de rigueur in all hard-core pornography—is not seen. Rather, it is an illusion created by the convulsive montage. Though we do see Lovelace "lapping up" the ejaculate that gathers along the shaft, the montage itself interferes with the actual sight of the good doctor's penis in the act of coming. Of course, the other sleight of hand has been the illusion that somehow these pyrotechnics have rendered visible the pleasure and satisfaction that Linda seeks—as if we had actually seen her get scratched.[63]

Just as Edison's *The Kiss* had elicited excited enthusiasm at the prospect of the anatomy of a kiss, as well as shocked horror at the "monstrous" "bestiality" of the spectacle, so, too, did *Deep Throat* elicit a mixture of interest and disgust. The difference, however, was that very few of the critics who found *Deep Throat* offensive also called for its censorship.[64] For the most part critics worked hard to prove themselves able to assert critical sensibilities in the face of the unmistakable shock of "real sex" on the screen. Mort Sheinman's tongue-in-cheek comment that the film offered a "bold thrust forward in the history of contemporary cinema, plunging deeply into areas seldom, if ever explored on screen," was one approach that imitated the film's own humor. Vincent Canby's pan, on the other hand, was accompanied by an almost poignant rehearsal of the difficulty of writing honestly about pornographic films: "Like trying to tie one's shoes while walking: it's practically impossible without sacrificing stride and balance and a certain amount of ordinary dignity, the sort one uses with bank tellers who question a signature."[65] Dignity is what audiences who watch sex in public theaters run the risk of losing, especially if their bodies betray an interest that all the joking in the world cannot hide.

So what did my friends and I feel? I recall a mix of shock, disgust, amazement (how did the mouth and throat accommodate the shaft?), and "little tingles," all of which was tempered by the outright silliness of the whole spectacle at which we laughed heartily. I dutifully reported back to friends how boring and repetitive the whole show had been. And compared to *Last Tango* it was terribly clinical and unerotic. But undoubtedly the most fascinating part of this particular film, and indeed of all the new feature-length graphic porn of this era, was the novelty of fellatio as an ultimate sexual act rather than as an hors d'oeuvre before the main entrée.

Technically, according to laws that have only recently been struck down, fellatio is one of the possible meanings of sodomy, defined as any "abnormal" form of sexual intercourse. In John Updike's 1968 novel *Couples*, a wife asks her husband if he wants her to take him in her mouth. "Good heavens, no," he answers, "That's sodomy."[66] Historically, sodomy has especially been condemned when the supposedly abnormal sexual intercourse is between men, but it is a large category that includes all nonprocreative sexual acts between men and women as well. Fellatio, between men and men and between women and men, is one of those acts; so, too, is anal sex. But fellatio is most commonly described today (for instance in Webster's) as "a sexual activity involving oral contact with the male genitals." It is hard to imagine a sex act with more initial shock value than fellatio when graphically seen on the big screen. Even anal sex does not so dramatically bring organs of smell, taste, and ingestion up against organs of elimination. This shocking juxtaposition as deployed cinematically in *Deep Throat* literally put a pretty face next to the ejaculation and avoided the sight of the female genitals altogether. The hard-to-see inside of the female body into which the penis disappears during coitus was thus displaced by an easier-to-see female face and mouth that not only did not display disgust, but positively worshipped the man's bodily functions.

Fellatio was certainly not invented by the generation of the seventies but, hard as it might be to recall this in the post-Monica Lewinsky era, neither was it a sex act that before *Deep Throat* and the era of porno chic had much mainstream public recognition.[67] It is thus an excellent example of what Foucault calls the "implantation of perversions." It has gone from being a little-known form of sex whose initial disgust factor could not have been higher in the America of the pre-sexual revolution and which women of my mother's generation believed "nice" girls did not do (see, for example, Alfred Kinsey's discussion of dissensions in marriages over oral sex in *Sexual Behavior in the Human Male*),[68] to an unforeseen popularity, celebrated as the pinnacle of pleasure in *Deep Throat* and much of the hard-core pornography to follow. When it again surfaces as newsworthy in the late nineties, it is considered a much less intimate contact than genital sex, debated certainly for its propriety in the Oval Office but also, and most interestingly, for its status as a sex act at all. Though many were skeptical of Bill Clinton's claim that he "did not have sexual relations with that woman," it turned out the president and Lewinsky were not the only ones who did not define fellatio as sex.[69]

In *Deep Throat*, fellatio solves the anatomical problem of a clitoris that is not where it should be and that therefore cannot be properly "scratched." "Why you bugger, *there* you are!" says the doctor when he finds the clitoris at the end of his telescope in Linda's throat. Though he sees it, we do not.

This organ, unlike the normally visible penis, remains occulted throughout the film and thus offers narrative justification for not having sex in the prescribed, procreative missionary position. *Eating out, blow jobs*, and *giving head* were only then becoming familiar slang. Phillip Roth writes in a novel about the 1970s: "This is a generation of astonishing fellators. There's been nothing like them ever before among their class of young women."[70]

Foucault's notion of the historical "implantation of perversions" in which "scattered sexualities rigidified, became stuck to an age, a place, a type of practice,"[71] may not fully explain the mystery of the popularity of *Deep Throat* and its practice of deep-throat fellatio, but it does allow us to see how the public awareness of previously "disgusting" or obscene sexual practices can easily change once pornographies are on/scene. The British playwright and barrister John Mortimer, writing about Lovelace's death, recalled a 1970 obscenity trial for a novel entitled *The Mouth*, in which the judge asked a witness for the defense why anyone needed oral sex when "we've gone without it for a thousand years."[72] Had that judge been speaking after 1972, it is unlikely he would have been so misinformed.

Joel Tyler, who presided over the New York obscenity trial of *Deep Throat* in the winter of 1973, was another judge who learned a lot. Ignorant at the beginning of the trial about the meaning of the term *missionary position*, after the testimony of five expert witnesses he was eagerly instructing others as to its meaning.[73] Constantly at stake in this often hilarious trial was the question of the obscenity or nonobscenity of the display of fellatio and the perversion or nonperversion of the much discussed, though never shown, clitoral orgasm. An expert witness for the prosecution, one Dr. Levin, apparently a die-hard Freudian, testified that "a woman seeing this film may think that that is perfectly healthy, perfectly normal if you have a clitoral orgasm, that is all the woman needs. Now, she's wrong . . . and this film will strengthen her in her ignorance."[74] He went on to explicitly challenge the "extremists" in the women's liberation movement who called vaginal orgasm a myth. Levin also pronounced on the inherent perversity of acts of fellatio that do not serve as a "prelude to intercourse." As an end in itself, he expertly intoned, "this would be perversion on both sides."[75]

Judge Tyler, and probably everyone else at the trial, learned a great deal about the respective arguments of Freud, Kinsey, and William Masters and Virginia Johnson concerning the practice of fellatio and the relative merits of clitoral versus vaginal orgasm. Arguments for the defense centered on the instructional and liberatory value of explicit sex acts on the screen in improving the sex lives of individuals and couples; arguments for the prosecution centered on the inherent perversion and obscenity of such acts. In a famously long and vehement decision, Judge Tyler pronounced the film obscene and fined the theater three million dollars, concluding, "This is one throat that deserves to be cut."[76] To show that he was not an unsophisticated film viewer, however, he added that *Last Tango*, though he himself did not care for it, was not obscene.[77]

Obscene or not—judgments would go both ways in many trials throughout multiple states over the next several years—*Deep Throat* excited a great deal of sexual speech. Again and again it was oral sex that demanded the most speech, but almost never cunnilingus. Cunnilingus puts the mouth and face in conjunction with a sexual organ that is harder to see; it is embedded within labial folds that do not lend themselves to easy visibility. And so, cunnilingus, while certainly part of the repertoire of "diff'rent strokes" cultivated and legitimated by *Deep Throat*, is never offered as the climactic scratch, the discharge of end pleasure, despite the fact that the narrative conceit of the film is quite precisely Linda's quest for clitoral orgasm. The long history of the elisions, and occasional resightings, of the clitoris in medical and pornographic representation offers a fascinating tale.[78] Freud's own early-twentieth-century tale of the "immaturity" of the clitoral orgasm and the "maturity" of the vaginal one, which became such an issue in *Deep Throat*'s New York trial, certainly contributed to the elision of the clitoris from the turn of the century until the early seventies. But the era of the new pornography was also an era of one of the important resightings of the clitoris—in sexology no less than in the emerging feminism that Levin so discounted. It is thus worth asking how it is that an organ that got so much press in the sexology of the late sixties and early seventies only received a kind of lip service—literally a lot of talk and a few licks—in the pornography of this era. Shall we chalk it up to its small size relative to the penis and the physiological fact that it does not produce a dramatic liquid that can spurt as far? Or is there a deeper reason?

We saw in chapter 1 that Freud explained the pleasures of kissing in relation to the originary pleasure of the child sucking at the mother's breast. All intersubjective life, to Freud, has its beginning in this original relation between mother and child. Freud argues that sensual sucking, first connected to the stimulation of the warm flow of milk, becomes detached from the original satisfaction of hunger to become a "labial zone" of pleasure in its own right.[79] Sucking a penis and sucking a clitoris could thus potentially recall these mutual pleasures while producing in the body of the person "sucked" (kissed, licked, etc.) orgasmic pleasures.

I say potentially because, although the new heterosexual pornography of the seventies does show us these mutual pleasures in ways that definitively break away from coitus as the "proper aim" of sex, as Levin would have it, they rarely present the pleasures of sucking and the pleasures of being sucked as mutual. Nor do they present the female and male pleasure of being sucked as commensurate. Instead, we tend to think of the sucker as doing the work and of the "suckee" as receiving the pleasure. And since the only one of these organs with strong graphic presence is the penis, all pleasure seems to revolve around that organ in an entirely phallic regime that seems hopelessly stuck in what Luce Irigaray has defined as the phallic economy of the one, incapable of counting beyond that number.[80]

And yet, if we revisit the original scene from which Freud derives all subsequent sexual pleasure—the child sucking at the mother's breast—we might be able to rethink oral sexual pleasures as a more mutual give-and-take both from the point of view of the child and mother and from that of the adults who engage in oral sex.[81] When Freud theorizes the origin of all sexual pleasure as a refinding of oral satisfaction at the breast, he, too, sees it as a singular economy of the one—a pleasure for the child alone.[82] The pleasure of *being* sucked is elided in Freud, while in heterosexual pornography the pleasure of being sucked eclipses any possible pleasure to the sucker.

When Freud attempts to understand the pleasures of fellatio (nowhere does he tackle the pleasures of cunnilingus), he takes great pains to minimize the awareness of its perversion (in his terms) by referring it back to the innocence of the child sucking at the mother's breast.[83] The innocence of Freud's picture of originary sucking, which he uses to soften any perception of disgust or perversion in fellatio, seems to be linked to his own belief in the mother's (and the breast's) lack of sexual sensitivity in the act of nursing. Fellatio is an oral pleasure that refinds the pleasure of sucking the breast through the sucking of the penis, but he does not conceive of this pleasure as *also and simultaneously* the pleasure of being sucked. Too committed to insisting on the innocence of fellatio, he misconstrues its pleasures as one-way.

A breast produces milk that, when sucked, emerges in warm spurts that satisfy the child both as nourishment and as tactile, olfactory, and (perhaps) visual pleasure (Freud often stresses the importance of the breast as the child's first visual object—what Maria St. John calls the "ultimate home movie").[84] A penis when sucked or kissed, licked or "blown," also produces a milky liquid that emerges in warm spurts that can be touched, tasted, and seen. This liquid satisfies no need for nourishment, but those who suck and elicit it often enact a pleasure not unlike that of the child at the breast. They taste it, revel in it, and take delight in the way it appears and feels. The fellator thus reenacts the pleasure of the child at the breast, but the penis itself does not enact Freud's notion of the passive, nonpleasuring maternal breast. Rather, and especially in the new pornography inaugurated by *Deep Throat*, it often threatens to steal the show, to "go solo" in money shots that ignore the pleasure of the fellator by focusing excessively on the moment of external ejaculation.[85] The spectacular slow-motion money shot of the same year's *Behind the Green Door* (dir. Artie Mitchell and Jim Mitchell) makes for a famous example, even one-upping *Deep Throat*'s montage with optically printed, psychedelically colored doublings of the ejaculating penis.

In *Deep Throat* the conceit that Linda's clitoris is located in her throat allows the film to compensate the woman who fellates with a putatively deeper, nonoral, clitorally orgasmic satisfaction. The need to posit this fictitious satisfaction might be construed as the film's guilty conscience toward what is actually its physical elision of the woman's pleasure. The relegation of cunnilingus in this same era to an act of foreplay culminating in no dramatic climax and manifesting very little in either the oral pleasures of the sucker or the sucked might be understood as the historical moment in which the new graphic pornography failed to invest eros in that which it could not easily see. In this sense it is an escalation of the rule of maximum visibility in the face of an apparently invisible female pleasure.

A variety of factors thus converged to make *Deep Throat* the flashpoint of the new pornographic "implantation of perversions" and its new ways of speaking sex. An ordinary "fuck film" without the panache of these "diff'rent strokes" might not have created the ensuing scandal, might not have elicited so vehement a reaction from its New York judge, and thus might not have garnered as much hype. The very title *Deep Throat*, even before its Watergate resonance, added a sense of mystery and sophistication that lifted the film out of the Times Square circuit into a brief era of porno chic.

Deep Throat would prove to be the largest-grossing independent film of all time.[86] It offered an unprecedented spectacle of graphic sex on screen. In the end, however, the most significant show offered up by *Deep Throat*—to its Denver audience, as well as in its many screenings across the nation—was taking place in the audience: our social presence to one another at a public screening of graphic, unsimulated sex; our willingness not only to screen sex but to be seen screening it. And the sex that we saw there was offered, despite Dr. Levin's worries about the perversions of clitoral orgasm, as the telos of end pleasure corresponding to Freud's most orthodox conception of a satisfying scratch capable of discharging all tension. At film's end, Linda is happily satisfied with a lover whose penis is long enough to reach the clitoris hidden in her throat. Yet the act that produced this discharge is literally perverse, swerved away from conventional notions of carnal knowledge.

Last Tango, for its part, received cover stories in both *Time* and *Newsweek*, while stills of its one "nude" scene appeared in *Playboy*. Though it did not garner the unprecedented grosses of *Deep Throat*, it took in $16 million at the U.S. box office and, as David Thompson has noted, "there wasn't a more fashionable movie for the critics either to laud to the skies or snidely put down."[87] In New York, the film was exhibited at the unusually high ticket price of $5, exactly the same jacked-up price one had to pay to see *Deep Throat*. Both films eschewed conventional depictions of carnal knowledge and were thus perverse. But what was especially perverse in *Last Tango* was not the content (masturbation, anal sex), but the alignment of sex with the self-shattering end of life itself—the little death and the big one that greets Paul at the end.

Pornotopia is a place where, as Steven Marcus once wrote, it is "always bedtime."[88] In pornotopia people have well-lit, maximum-visibility sex for very long periods of time, ending in the discharge of money shots. Pornography is relatively easy and cheap to make: it simply needs to display precisely those details of sex so hard to see elsewhere. Erotic art, on the other hand, has proven much harder to make, which may be why there is a great deal of moving-image pornography and comparatively little sexually explicit erotic art. If we want to understand the differences between moving-image erotica and pornography, however, we need to see that they exist on a continuum of representations, any of which can be sexually stimulating. One end of the continuum aims directly at depicting sexual pleasures in the rhetoric of the scratch, conveyed as money shot discharge. The other end of the continuum is more interested in playing with these forms prolonging the tension in the rhetoric of the itch.

In the wake of these two movies, screening sex would henceforth form an inextricable part of the sexuality of adult viewers who could no longer claim sexual innocence at the movies. With the video revolution of the following decade, this screening sex would eventually retreat to the privacy of the home, but after 1972, "sex itself" could never go back to being as entirely private an affair as it had been before. All subsequent sexual relations would be complicated and informed by these indelible moving images.

Coda: Coming Out

The sexual revolution that *Deep Throat* and *Last Tango* represented was not just for heterosexuals. In 1969 a police raid on a Manhattan gay bar called the Stonewall Inn precipitated a riot that many claim was the flashpoint for the birth of gay liberation. At the center of this liberation was the "growing significance of the erotic in modern life."[89] The new graphic pornography in general and the subgenre of all-male pornography in particular constituted a crucially important part of this growing significance. At issue in that bar was the right of gays and lesbians to exhibit, even to flaunt, their sexual preferences. Gay pornography would prove a crucial aspect of this ability for homosexuals to be themselves. One simple way of looking at the emergence of gay pornography is to see it as an outgrowth of gay liberation: the throwing off of repression. However, as we have already seen with the straight pornography that privileged a wide range of sex acts once deemed perverse, the rise of graphic sex as a public spectator sport—gay or straight—cannot fully be understood as a simple lifting of repression that finally permitted more natural expressions. How natural, after all, is a money shot? Rather, the implantation of perversions came on/scene almost as aggressively as did supposedly perverse nonprocreative heterosexual ones in the early seventies. But in the case of sex acts between men and the rise of gay liberation, the dynamic of "reverse discourse" proved particularly important. Foucault argues that we do not live in a world of dominant and dominated discourses. Rather, discourse can be both an instrument of power (as in the term of abuse, *queer*) and a point of resistance to power (as when *queer* becomes celebratory).[90] Such was the case in the graphic celebrations of gay hard-core pornography.

In 1971, a year before *Deep Throat* seized the (hetero)sexual imagination of the nation to become the necessary viewing of all cognoscenti, a small film called *Boys in the Sand* (dir. Wakefield Poole) opened in Times

Square.[91] Not as prominent on the general culture radar screen (my friends and I had no idea), *Boys* nevertheless anticipated the impact of *Deep Throat* for the narrower but trendsetting and influential emerging gay community. Cinematically, it was also a much better movie. Like *Deep Throat*, *Boys in the Sand* was not the first (gay) hard-core feature film to show in a public theater, but, also like it, it was the first work of graphic moving-image pornography to reap giant returns on a very small investment. *Boys* had a much greater role in legitimizing the graphic sexual imagination of the gay community than *Deep Throat* did in the larger heterosexual mainstream. It was thus arguably, and for its numerically smaller audience, an even more important film.[92]

The rise of publicly exhibited feature-length pornography in the early seventies meant that sexually interested viewers had to be willing—as my friends and I had been—not only to *watch* mediated graphic sex acts but to be *seen* watching in public. To do so meant the suppression of the kind of overt carnal response that had been more openly solicited by the earlier stag films in the context of more private screenings. Arousal, whether leading to masturbation or impersonal coupling, could certainly occur in the public theaters of the 1970s, but it was not invited the way it sometimes had been in earlier stag films shown in often more ribald circumstances. However, if this suppression of audience sexual response was fairly common in the pornography that my friends and I went to see, it was much less common in the pornography watched by my only just then coming-out gay friends. As George Chauncey has noted in his history of gay New York, public movie theaters had often served as trysting areas as far back as the nickelodeons and extending into the unsupervised balconies of the movie palaces of the 1920s.[93] After Stonewall and the rise of an explicitly gay pornography projected in Times Square theaters, the use of theaters as cruising grounds pushed the notion of sexual interest far beyond what was exhibited at screenings of *Deep Throat* and its successors. John Waters, interviewed in the documentary *Inside Deep Throat*, offers the authoritative testament: "People weren't jerking off. Angela Lansbury might be sitting next to you!"

In theaters exhibiting gay porn, however, Angela Lansbury was most likely *not* sitting next to you. To be seen watching a film in these theaters could often be interpreted as a sign of interest in having sex on the spot. The atmosphere of the all-male stag party was converted in this situation from homosociality to overt homosexuality. The film historian Thomas Waugh tells of attending *Boys in the Sand* during the first week of its run at the Fifty-Fifth Street Theater in Manhattan. Newly arrived in New York and not knowing the protocol, he thought "people went to watch the film" and was shocked to find the person behind him more "interactive" than that. Waugh adds, however, that *Boys in the Sand* was such a standout film that more people watched it than usual.[94]

It is not surprising that gay pornography was in the vanguard of feature-length pornography. Wakefield Poole, the director of *Boys in the Sand*, had previously directed a ten-minute, avant-garde tribute to the art and photography—though not the films—of Andy Warhol. Richard Dyer has closely linked the "visionary, playful and self-reflexive qualities of underground cinema" to many aspects of gay and proto-gay culture.[95] Such qualities would mark pornographies with all-male action as different—in many ways far more chic and avant-garde than the much touted chic of mainstream pornography.[96]

The first episode (entitled "Bayside") of the tripartite, dialogueless *Boys in the Sand* opens with an out-of-focus image. We eventually discover a bearded young man with dark hair (Wakefield Poole's lover Peter Fisk) taking a long walk through the woods. The prolonged use of subjective camera emphasizes the play of light and shadow through the trees and immediately marks the aesthetic ambitions of the film as artier than most straight hard core. Music that resembles the more muted portions of Stravinsky's *The Rite of Spring* softly accompanies the journey and continues throughout the episode. When the young man emerges from the trees, he undresses and sits down at the edge of the sea. He gazes for quite a while at the water until what I shall hereafter call an apparition—a lanky, blond, naked man (Casey Donovan, aka Cal Culver, an icon of much early all-male pornography who will appear in each of this film's three episodes)— materializes on the horizon. In long shot, the apparition runs from the surf toward the bearded man, his penis flapping with each stride. Stopping before he reaches the bearded man, who has seemingly conjured him from the water, the apparition offers up his golden beauty first to the man's eye and then to his touch.

The first sex act is fellatio performed by the bearded man. It will eventually prove as graphically real and as climactic as that performed in *Deep Throat*, leading, as well, to a money shot. However, the way it is shot and performed can help us understand basic differences between gay and straight porn in these early years of porno chic. First, *Boys* takes its time. A fourth of the episode of "Bayside" passes before we arrive at the sex. This will be the case in the other episodes as well. Nor do we always see all of the action with maximum visibility. Initially, the bearded man's head blocks our view of the penis he fellates (figure 57).[97] Although a side view will soon confirm that the penis does indeed enter the fellator's mouth, it is neither the first nor the most prominent view (figure 58). A reverse angle follows, from behind the buttocks of the fellatee (figure 59). While the view of the buttocks presents the important other side of the body being fellated and introduces an anal eroticism central to much all-male porn,[98] it also prevents a more direct and clinical view of the graphic action of fellatio. An aura of mystery, rather than one of clinical clarity, hangs over the film.

Fellatio proves as fundamental to this episode of *Boys in the Sand* as it does to many episodes of *Deep Throat* and countless other examples of porno chic. However, the graphic pornotopia of a film like *Deep Throat*, which emphasizes unobstructed views of the act of fellatio in the more clinical manner of *scientia sexualis*, contrasts with what might be called the graphic erototopia of *Boys in the Sand*. Lighting is crucial. The sun-dappled, natural lighting of *Boys* means that shadows sometimes obscure graphic views. But *Boys in the Sand* also *plays* with its views of sex. For example, this first scene of fellatio does not, like those in *Deep Throat*, proceed directly to climax. Instead, it breaks off in a tease as the apparition pulls away from the bearded man and walks backwards into the darker woods. The camera moves into the dark woods much the way it earlier moved toward the dark anus, approaching a place of mystery.

This withdrawal from contact prolonging the initial flirtation is an early example of a fundamental convention of all-male porn that has no precise equivalent in the heterosexual genre: the long dance of flirtation in which two (or more) men cruise one another, simultaneously exposing their hard, or hardening, bodies, withdrawing to look and to let themselves be looked at before enjoying the movement from sight to touch. In this frequently prolonged dance of cruising, the taboo against male-male sexual contact is both inscribed and, gradually, overcome. Only after the bearded man catches up to the apparition deep in the woods, and only after some additional foreplay, does the fellatio resume. Although the encounter of these "boys in the sand" will encompass several other graphic acts that merge into one another, fellatio frames the entire encounter. In the even more dappled light of the woods, they kiss and stroke one another as the moving branches and leaves of the trees cast extremes of light and shadow on their skin (figure 60). The apparition removes a leather bracelet from the wrist of the bearded man and places it around this same man's penis and tes-

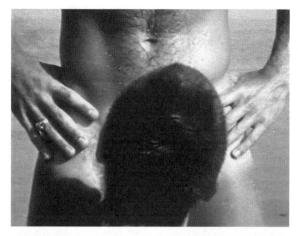

Boys in the Sand
(dir. Wakefield
Poole, 1971)

57: Fellatio without
maximum visibility

58: Fellatio with
visibility

59: Fellatio plus
anal eroticism

60: *Boys in the Sand*, the cruising couple kisses amid dappled light and shadow

ticles to match his own (already installed, metallic) cock ring. Their hands hold their penises against one another, emphasizing sexual sameness over sexual difference, and finally they resume fellatio. This time, however, it is the apparition who performs it on his knees before the bearded man, reversing the couple's original position.

More sunlight glimpsed through the trees signals an ellipsis. We now find the apparition lying on his back on a blanket in the woods as the bearded man fellates him. Again the graphic view is softened by the dappled light (figure 61). Eventually, they fellate one another in the sixty-nine position. After another ellipsis signaled again by sunlight through the trees (figure 62), the apparition politely brushes off the buttocks of the bearded man before first licking and then penetrating his anus. The pumping action that follows is vigorous, but the graphic view is again softened, in this case by the body of the penetrator, which casts shadows on the penetrated. As in heterosexual porn, a thrusting penetration eventually leads to a close-up money shot: here the apparition ejaculates onto the face of the bearded man and then considerately wipes it off—a gesture rarely seen in heterosexual porn and one that will soon disappear in all-male porn as well, as ejaculate becomes codified as the crucial proof of pleasure in both types. Next the apparition lies on his back and the bearded man stands over him, masturbating to ejaculation.

A final money shot climaxes the sexual action in a montage that anticipates the cinematic pyrotechnics of *Deep Throat*. As in that film, the buildup to the money shot rapidly intercuts with other images—in this case a staccato series of shots reprising the actions of the episode. These very quick cuts from previous fragments of the same scene mark the mo-

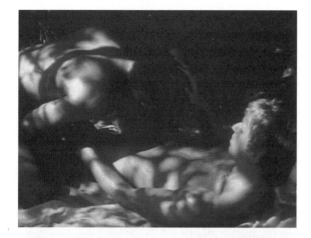

Boys in the Sand

61: A graphic view softened by dappled light

62: Ellipsis signaled through sunlight in the trees

ment leading up to the close-up display of ejaculation. Also as in *Deep Throat*, the rapid pace of the montage itself conveys the rhythmic convulsions of ejaculation. Although all-male pornography will punctuate its climaxes with money shots just as faithfully as heterosexual porn and may very well have influenced the creation of the convention in the first place,[99] orgasms tend to be mutual—one man's quasi-visible pleasure need not stand in for the other's the way the doctor's visible pleasure in *Deep Throat* stands in for Linda's invisible pleasure. In this case the ejaculation of the bearded man—the man whose fantasy this is, after all—is privileged over that of the apparition.

The episode ends with the bearded man's withdrawal from the scene. He removes the leather cock band from his penis and places it on the wrist of the apparition, kisses him on both mouth and penis, rises, and disappears into the surf. The circularity of the narrative seems perfect until we recall that the man who disappears into the surf is not the same one who first appeared out of it. Indeed, it is the original apparition who remains materialized, putting on the clothes and taking up the blanket of the bearded man who has vanished, as if to emphasize the interchangeability of the roles taken in this erotic fantasy.

As we have already seen, all pornography is utopian; all pornography takes place, as Steven Marcus has said, in pornotopia, the land where it is "always bedtime." But it seems fair to say that all-male gay pornography is more utopian, if only because the taboos that must be overcome to stage its pleasures are greater. Fire Island, where all the episodes of *Boys in the Sand* were filmed, is portrayed as a fantasmatic place where not only the taboos against the graphic display of sex are suspended but also those against the display of homosexuality. While *Deep Throat* exudes a happy-go-lucky ethos of "diff'rent strokes for diff'rent folks" and makes a point of embracing whatever kinky desires appear, the one desire that it rigorously eschews is that of one man for another. While the place of sex in *Deep Throat* might be a kitchen counter, a doctor's office, or a bedroom, the always-bedtime atmosphere of these places is easily achieved. In contrast, while the place of a more nonnormative sex in *Boys in the Sand* might be equally unconventional, it is negotiated more carefully; it is more aware of the greater taboos it breaks. As Rich Cante and Angelo Restivo have argued, the sex of all-male pornography is "always situated in relation to a public via mechanisms distinct from male-female acts, even when their setting is a private space."[100] In other words, the more fraught relation of male-male sex to a public means that this sex is more intensely utopian.

Each of the film's three episodes constitutes a silent erotic vignette with music in which an initially solitary man conjures the appearance of another through the sheer intensity of his desire. Poole has described the film as representing various stages in gay sexual relations. The first episode "centers on dreams, hero worship, and innocence," while the second episode is about "coming out[,] . . . the attainment of love[,] and finding a partner."[101] In this second episode, "Poolside," a man on a dock—Casey Donovan, the apparition from the first episode—reads about gay bar raids in a copy of a newspaper entitled *Gay*. Like the first, this episode also takes its time getting to the sex. The man walks on the dock and then moves to a more private, enclosed pool where he takes off his clothes and begins to masturbate. Later, inside the house he writes a letter, apparently in response to one of the ads in the newspaper. He swims naked and floats on an air mattress semi-erect. Days pass on a calendar; he runs on the beach;

suspense builds. Finally he receives a small package that contains a large white tablet, which he throws into the pool. Out of the raging bubbles created by the tablet a dark-haired lover (Danny Di Cioccio) emerges. According to Poole, audiences never failed to laugh and applaud the wish-fulfillment in the form of this apparition, who swims toward the conjuror and takes his penis into his mouth.[102] The couple proceeds to have athletic sex all over the pool deck: They engage in fellatio, ass rimming, and anal intercourse photographed from behind shrubs and furniture, in often quite dancerly poses, offering what Poole calls an intentional "voyeuristic feel."[103] No dramatic money shot climaxes the action, suggesting that in 1971 it was still an option, not yet the sine qua non of the genre. Afterward, the couple affectionately dries one another off, goes inside, and comes out dressed. Arm in arm they leave the private enclave of the pool surrounded by a high fence and emerge into the publicness of the community, still entwined, an overt couple. They pass the man with the beard from the first episode, who also has the *Gay* paper under his arm and who may be presumed to send off his own letter soon. Unspoken but clearly stated in this wordless episode is the advocacy of coming out as proud, happy, and sexually satisfied gay men.

A third episode, "Inside," explores a more hedonistic, fantasmatic, and forbidden terrain. A white man (Casey Donovan again) lazily wakes up with an erection inside an elegant house as sunshine streams in his window. Gazing out of the window, we see him establish eye contact, flirt with, and eventually have sex with an apparitional African American telephone repairman (Tommy Moore) to the accompaniment of a sitar and tabla. This apparition, unlike the others, does not seem to want to stick around, even for the length of time it takes to have sex. For each time the repair man abruptly appears, as he does suddenly on the living room couch, naked except for his repairman's tool belt (figure 63), he just as abruptly disappears (figure 64). Though the white man fellates him with gusto (figure 65), the apparition is always in danger of disappearing. Each time he does, the music changes tempo and a fast pan of the brightly colored windows of the elegant pine house signals a new fantasy.

Where the other apparitions remained—at least until the end of the sexual encounter as in the "Bayside" episode, and more permanently in the romantic "Poolside" one—this racialized apparition comes and goes; and he always goes before he comes. In the end, we become aware that he has been built primarily out of the white man's relation to a large, black dildo, which we later see him lubricate and sit on while popping amyl nitrate. In other words, this "inside" apparition gives the impression of being even

Boys in the Sand

63: The tele-
phone repairman
appears on the
couch

64: The repairman
disappears

65: Fellatio with
gusto

more conjured up—more fantasmatic—than the previous ones conjured out of the water in the open air. Always in danger of disappearing, the virile black man becomes all the more precious as the erotic fantasy of the white man. This means, of course, that the black man functions more as a sexual object than a sexual subject, more as what Franz Fanon has called an "epidermalized" racial essence than any of the other apparitions conjured in this film.[104] Undoubtedly, then, the black man is racially fetishized and reduced to his penis in the form of the black dildo.[105] Of course, all the male performers in pornography are at some point reduced to their penises, highly fetishized by the genre itself, and no more so than in all-male pornography. The fact that Moore, who plays the telephone repairman, is *more* fetishized is obviously a feature of racial attitudes of the era—attitudes we have also seen Melvin Van Peebles either challenging or reinforcing (depending on how one interprets the film) in the same year's *Sweet Sweetback's Baadasssss Song*.

Poole expressed pride in his "interracial cast,"[106] and perhaps justly so given the tendency in mainstream cinema to elide the sexuality of black people. He was breaking a color line just as emphatically as was Van Peebles and at approximately the same time. But to transgress a taboo is not to defeat it, as Bataille has so well argued.[107] The pornotopia of interracial desire is far from a happy-go-lucky place of immediate sexual gratification in which color lines fall away and everyone has sex with everyone else equally. Indeed, the extra erotic charge of the "Inside" episode of *Boys in the Sand* seems to be grounded in the vestigial taboos and prohibitions against not only male-male sex but interracial sex as well. A certain fear of interracial sex adds spice to the insistence on the acceptance of same-sex in this episode. These transgressions are not triumphant subversions since the flouting of a taboo fully recognizes the authority and power of the prohibiting law, but neither are they the same old racism that once functioned to keep the races apart or in relations of complete domination and submission.[108]

If *Deep Throat* is about the achievement of pleasure through practice and acrobatics, then *Boys in the Sand* is a lyrical, joyful celebration of a utopian place—Bayside, Poolside, Inside—where men take pleasure in one another in the face of normative taboos. In these fantasies without dialogue and synchronized sound, no one "teaches," "cures," or "initiates" another person into the joys of sex. And yet audience members who applauded and desired these apparitions, and who bonded with each other as a community in this very applause signaling mutually recognized desire, did certainly learn something about the joys of an out community intrinsically related to the practice of sex. An idealized, hypersexual male emerges in each episode from the conjuring imagination of a solitary desiring subject. The sex that follows serves to validate and celebrate, while never exactly normalizing, the difference of gay sex.

4

make love, not war

Jane Fonda Comes Home

(1968–1978)

With all the ejaculating penises brought on/scene in both heterosexual and homosexual pornography of the early seventies, and with all the end-of-Code, beginning-of-ratings-era films focused on young men proving their manhood in Hollywood's simulated sexual interludes, it is only fair to ask about the fate of female orgasm in mainstream Hollywood film. *Deep Throat* had purported to be about female orgasm by rather disarmingly acknowledging a problem that had not been previously disclosed in the mainstream history of screening sex: where to locate and how to depict female pleasures that did not necessarily coincide with those of the male? The clitoris, which as we shall see below was newly exalted as the primary organ of female pleasure by the sexologists, was not where it should be. "Why there you are! You little bugger you!" proclaimed the good doctor in *Deep Throat* when he found Linda Lovelace's clitoris in her throat. Deep-throat fellatio was the solution to the problem of this particular misplaced and misunderstood clitoris. Though more sober than this bogus doctor, the real sexologists were equally perplexed to find the female seat of pleasure so disconnected from the organs of reproduction. This was a conundrum, especially in Hollywood. Where to locate and how to portray a woman's pleasure? Ever since the fall of the Hollywood Production Code the main way to know if a woman felt pleasure was to listen to her.

Fast forward, for a moment, to this well-known scene from the 1989 romantic comedy by Rob Reiner, *When Harry Met Sally*. Best friends, and eventual lovers, Harry (Billy Crystal) and Sally (Meg Ryan) meet in a New York delicatessen and argue about male and female perspectives on sex. Sally views Harry as an affront to all women because he cannot wait to leave them after having sex. Harry counters that at least he leaves his partners satisfied. Sally doubts if they are satisfied since women often fake orgasm. When Harry disbelieves, Sally gives an aural performance of one right there in the deli. She pants, moans, shakes her head, musses her hair, and pounds the table, building to a rhythmic and ecstatic "Yes, Yes, Yes! Yes! YES!" as the whole deli watches in amazement and appreciation. After Sally has resumed her sandwich, an older woman voices the punch line to a waiter: "I'll have what she's having." Never mind that Sally is a repressed obsessive whose character would never do such a theatrical thing in a deli; the scene clinched the film's reputation as a classic romantic comedy in the post–sexual revolution era. Most of all, it clinched the by now well-known fact, here delivered in the mode of comedy, that women can often fake quite spectacular orgasms.

In the late 1960s and early 1970s, however, when the representation of carnal knowledge in mainstream films was still new and when Hollywood was tentatively devising new tropes for "going all the way," female orgasm was either overlooked or assimilated to that of the male. The possibly different rhythms and temporalities of a woman's pleasure were simply not acknowledged. How, then, did a different, female, form of carnal knowledge come to American screens? The answer may seem circuitous, but it proves to be inextricably tied to the context of the Vietnam War and emerging discourses of sexology.

"Make Love, Not War"

I was never a fan of the popular Broadway musical *Hair* (1967), or of the later film version by Milos Forman (1979). Its story about a young man drafted to fight in Vietnam whose countercultural friends fight against his conscription was altogether too happy-hippie for my taste. Hippie celebrants sang hopefully of the "dawning of the age of Aquarius," shed clothes, uttered forbidden words, and proposed to make love, not war. But if they were happy to make love, they were not really willing to *do* anything to stop war. The young man who is drafted goes to boot camp and is followed there by his hippie friends, one of whom takes his place just before he is shipped to Vietnam, where the friend is killed. My boyfriend had been drafted too; but with the support of his countercultural community, he had demonstrated against the war, joined the resistance, and refused induction. He would rather go to prison than fight an unjust war.[1] We made love *and* opposed war, in a way that made *Hair* seem frivolous. Just as its show tunes betrayed the very idiom of rock, so its politics avoided actual struggle. Facile as it was, however, *Hair* undeniably formed part of a late-sixties zeitgeist in which sex, drugs, and rock and roll seemed antiwar and political—not just consumerist—acts.

"Make love, not war" was a slogan that many of us chanted at the time of the Stop the Draft Week demonstrations against the Oakland Induction Center in 1967. Saying "yes" to sex in those heady days really did feel like saying "no," not just to war but to the kind of instrumental reason that had fatefully led to one of America's now-too-familiar quagmire wars. In those days sexual revolution was inextricably linked, as David Allyn's history of the era argues, to political revolution.[2] My draft-resisting friends and I were echoing the words of Frankfurt School theorists like Herbert Marcuse and Norman O. Brown who argued against the Freudian premise that sexual desire was in permanent need of sublimation if human culture and society were to persevere. Marcuse's *Eros and Civilization*, first published in 1955, had challenged Sigmund Freud's premise that sexual desire was permanently at odds with human society. Marcuse envisioned a liberation that would restore "the right of sensuousness," transform toil into unproductive play, and not simply release libido but utterly transform it.[3]

No longer used as a full-time instrument of labor, the body would be resexualized. The regression involved in this spread of the libido would first manifest itself in a reactivation of all erotogenic zones and, consequently, in a resurgence of pregenital polymorphous sexuality and in a decline of genital sexuality. The body in its entirety would become an object of cathexis and a thing to be enjoyed—an instrument of pleasure.[4] Sparked by Marcuse, turned on by music, marijuana, and psychedelics, a large part of my generation did see making love as part of a political act against war.

It did so especially in the face of an ever-escalating war whose injustice was driven home because of a draft that affected the entire population of young men.

But what was a woman's place in this loving alternative to war? Another slogan, not quite as popular in this period, was "Women Say Yes to Men Who Say No!" As one who *had* said "yes" to a man who had said "no," I was tempted to adopt it, too, before recognizing in it a whole patriarchal regime that wanted to make my sexual pleasure subservient to the only real political actor in the revolutionary scenario: the man. Gradually I realized that if I was to make love, not war, then, as the feminist cultural historian Lynne Segal notes, it "was going to have to mean something more than 'the freedom to get laid.'" It was going to have to mean, ultimately, "a radical rethinking of the whole area of sexuality and sexual politics."[5] What *was* a politically correct form of making love for a woman? Against Freud's dictum that civilization required a certain amount of discontent, Marcuse had encouraged the decline of genital sexuality and a "pregenital polymorphous sexuality," but what did that mean, exactly? For the answer to this question a whole generation turned to sexologists: the earlier work of Alfred Kinsey and the newer work of William Masters and Virginia Johnson, just emerging in the late sixties.

Sexology and Sexual Politics

Kinsey was a zoologist whose long crusade became the dissolution of the distinctions between normal and abnormal sex. While most people tend to believe that whatever they do sexually is what everyone else does, or should do, Kinsey discovered, at first just by interviewing married students in his famous "Marriage Course" at Indiana University in the late 1930s, that people actually did a great many different things.[6] The second lecture of this course, first taught in 1938, had already challenged Freud's orthodoxy about the vaginal orgasm. Throwing up a slide of a penis entering a vagina in his lecture hall, Kinsey very clearly pointed out that the reason for the woman's pleasure was not vaginal but clitoral stimulation.[7] Kinsey did not beat around the bush. From the very beginning he declared the Freudian orthodoxy of the vaginal orgasm wrong. The supposedly infantile clitoral orgasm was what really excited women. The married or engaged students admitted into his courses were decidedly interested in what Kinsey had to teach. And what he had to teach often derived from what he had learned from them.[8] Through ever-widening research, conducted in the form of extended face-to-face interview-style sexual histories, Kinsey came to believe that there was very little sexual activity that was abnormal, or perverse. In fact, he eschewed the word *perverse*, preferring the label *rare*.

Though Kinsey would democratically survey every possible aspect of sexual behavior, he would only count it as sex if it led to orgasm.[9] As a zoologist with an expertise in gall wasps, he valued measurability. Orgasms, which had the virtue of being countable, became his gold standard. From the very beginning, this meant that Kinsey's research, like that of most sexologists, was inherently androcentric. Though he could be remarkably nonjudgmental about the behaviors that might lead to orgasm—whether masturbation, hetero or homosexual relations—the countable orgasm was built to the measure of the male body. It would not be until he got to researching and writing his female volume, *Sexual Behavior in the Human Female*, published in 1953, that Kinsey would discover enormous dissimilarities between male and female sexual "outlets." For example, he calculated that the average male had experienced 1,523 orgasms before marriage, while the average woman had only experienced 223. After marriage, he calculated, most husbands achieved orgasm in almost all acts of intercourse, while wives did so only 39 percent of the time.[10]

Most pertinent to the history of screening sex, however, is the way Kinsey went about studying orgasms: he filmed them. Early in his research Kinsey had contrived to observe sexual activity live. He and Wardell Pomeroy had paid prostitutes to be able to watch them while they performed their tricks. But Kinsey found prostitutes unsatisfying subjects precisely because they faked orgasm. It was not always easy to observe their acts from the vantage point of a closet. Nor were the team's later efforts to observe furtive homosexual acts in toilets entirely satisfying as scientific observation. Inevitably, Kinsey turned to film in 1948, at first to test the theory of how men ejaculated, whether in dribbles or with projecting force. Clarence Tripp and Bill Dellenback, Kinsey's trusty photographers, paid three hundred men in New York City to masturbate to ejaculation. After collecting films of a thousand men masturbating, they concluded that in 73 percent of men ejaculate does not spurt but dribbles.[11]

Filming male ejaculation soon branched out into filming the sexual relations of male homosexual couples. By 1949 much of this filming moved into an attic room of Kinsey's home.[12] The subjects of these films were certain special "friends of the research"—those willing not only to give their sexual histories but now also to be observed and filmed. Just as Andy Warhol would give a screen test to just about anyone who wandered into the Factory, so Kinsey would film solitary or social sex acts with just about anyone who would let him. But he especially valued the "rare" ones and not only homosexual males. One of these was a gynecologist by the name of Alice Spears. Pomeroy reported that she was capable of "from fifteen to twenty orgasms in twenty minutes. Even the most casual contact could arouse a sexual response in her. Observing her both in masturbation and intercourse, we found that in intercourse her first orgasm occurred within 2 to five seconds after entry."[13] This was all the more surprising in that Spears had not had her first orgasm until she was forty and was in her sixties at the time of filming. Kinsey shot a total of seven hours of film with Spears performing with a great many different partners drawn from his entire team of male researchers, including himself.[14]

In filming sex, Kinsey was only doing what Masters and Johnson would later do with married couples in their laboratory. However, his way of doing it blurred the line between objective, distanced science and a much more involved, subjective participant observation. Nor did any of his funders, or the trustees of Indiana University, know what he was doing since the budget for filming was cleverly disguised under the category "mammalian studies" and did, indeed, begin as a collection of how other kinds of mammals "do it"—films of porcupines had been particularly valued.[15] No one knew about the human films until the 1972 publication of Pomeroy's biography of Kinsey. Had they known, Kinsey would have instantly lost his funding—as he would do soon enough anyway after the publication of the female volume. Kinsey's "attic films"—which meticulously recorded not only female orgasms but male-male and female-female homosexual relations, as well as scenes of sadomasochistic sex—are of obvious interest to any history of screening sex in America, and it is regrettable that the Kinsey Institute does not permit their study today.

For some, Kinsey's sexual proclivities, combined with his filming, utterly disqualified him as a scientist and made him complicit with criminals.[16] One recent biographer, James Jones, argues that from the very beginning Kinsey was a masochistic, homosexual voyeur possessed entirely by his demons. His real motivation for all his research, Jones insists, was to see if others were like him. Jones thus asserts that Kinsey's real interest was prurience, not science.[17] Jonathan Gathorne-Hardy, another recent biographer, disagrees with Jones and defends Kinsey's science. He does not deny that Kinsey had homosexual encounters, nor that he engaged in some masochistic acts, nor that he liked to watch. But he refutes the idea that Kinsey was a lifelong homosexual-masochist-voyeur, especially in the pathologizing, fixed ways that Kinsey's own research sought to loosen. He asserts, rather, that Kinsey was a bisexual who fluctuated on his own scale, but whose interest in diverse sexual practices is what enabled him to extract histories from homosexuals and other minority sexualities in the first place.

The gay media scholar Thomas Waugh argues, from a very different direction, that Kinsey's problem was that he did not admit to the prurience that inevitably informed his work and that Waugh himself believes should be a fundamental principle of "gay cultural and sexual research." Sexual science, Waugh insists, is inseparable from eroticism.[18] This may be a bit unfair to Kinsey, who could hardly have received funding as a proudly eroticized homosexual researcher. Waugh adds that Kinsey, in addition to being the voyeur and auditor, as well as sometime participant in a number of the films, was also their ultimate director, the grand metteur en scène.[19]

The question about ejaculation that led Kinsey to first film it was not unlike the epoch-making debate about the fast-trot of the horse: Was there ever a moment when all four feet left the ground? Only Eadweard Muybridge's photographs of 1877 could prove to Leland Stanford's satisfaction that there was a moment when all four feet did leave the ground, and so, as one poet put it, "we invent pornography."[20] We invent pornography, I have argued, never out of mere prurience but out of the quest for the truth of the body mixed up with prurience. Kinsey was a scientist *and* a sexually interested observer *and* a sometime participant in the sex he studied. We should no more dismiss his science than the eroticism that fed its interest. If Kinsey was a pornographer, he was interested in the kinds of things that were often faked in pornography by women who were paid to perform. His own "home movies" were thus, like Warhol's *Blue Movie*, a way to locate a truth of sex not otherwise rendered visible. However one judges Kinsey's objectivity or involvement, one only has to read the descriptions of orgasm in the female volume to recognize that behind all the graphs of respiration and blood pressure stands the kind of observation that could only have come from getting closer, from watching and screening. Kinsey writes:

Prostitutes who attempt to deceive (jive) their patrons, or unresponsive wives who similarly attempt to make their husbands believe that they are enjoying their coitus, fall into an error because they assume that an erotically aroused person would look happy and pleased and should smile and become increasingly alert as he or she approaches the culmination of the act. On the contrary, an individual who is really responding is as incapable of looking happy as the individual who is being tortured.[21]

He continues, "Fully 84 percent of the females in the sample who had masturbated had depended chiefly on labial and clitoral stimulation. . . . all the evidence indicates that the vaginal walls are quite insensitive in the great majority of females.[22] Kinsey thus concludes, contra Freud, that vaginal orgasm is a physical and physiologic impossibility that has no relation to maturity.[23]

Kinsey, however, was not in the business of fixing what was wrong with the sexual relations of married couples; his interest, as with gall wasps, was variety. With their first book, *Human Sexual Response*, published in 1966, the team of Masters and Johnson confirmed many aspects of Kinsey's groundbreaking work. Like Kinsey, they rhetorically stressed the similarities of male and female sexual response—viewing the clitoris, for example, as a version of the penis—while actually detailing some remarkable differences. For example, they noted that women could orgasm both more frequently and much longer than men.[24] Like Kinsey also, Masters and Johnson debunked the vaginal orgasm, asserting that "clitoral and vaginal orgasms are not separate biologic entities."[25] And finally, they also observed couples and filmed them, even placing internal electrodes to measure response. Perhaps most threatening to established hierarchies of male and female sexual response was their observation that "maximum physiologic intensity of orgasmic response" had been achieved through "self regulated mechanical or automanipulative techniques." The second greatest intensity was achieved through "partner manipulation," and a poor third was achieved "during coition."[26] Nevertheless, Masters and Johnson were therapists committed to the success of monogamous, heterosexual marriage, and all of their work was aimed at producing a more sexually satisfied couple. They thus closed down much of Kinsey's openness to varieties of sexual outlets, basing their study only on 694 white, middle-class heterosexual men and women.

There had been no major women's movement to absorb the lessons of Kinsey, but by the time Masters and Johnson reached print, feminists were immediately drawing inferences that may not have been consistent with the researchers' essentially masculinist and monogamous perspectives. Mary Jane Sherfey, a psychoanalyst who had studied with Kinsey as an undergraduate, was the first: "Theoretically," she asserted, "a woman could go on having orgasms indefinitely if physical exhaustion did not intervene."[27] This much Masters and Johnson would have agreed with, but Sherfey added, "neither men nor women, but especially not women, are biologically built for the single-spouse, monogamous marital structure."[28]

In a mood of even greater insurgency, the feminist activist Anne Koedt proclaimed, in a famous pamphlet widely circulated at radical meetings long before it was published, that if vaginal penetration was not the cause of orgasm, then women had been "defined sexually in terms of what pleases men; our own biology has not been properly analyzed."[29] According to this reasoning, what was needed was thus nothing short of a redefinition of women's sexuality and a rejection of former androcentric concepts of "normal": "We must begin to demand that if certain sexual positions now defined as 'standard' are not mutually conducive to orgasm, they [should] no longer be defined as standard. New techniques must be used or devised which transform this particular aspect of our current sexual exploitation."[30] Yet another feminist, Barbara Seaman, further drew out Sherfey's lesson of indefinite orgasm: *The more a woman does, the more she can, and the more she can, the more she wants to.* Masters and Johnson claim that they have observed females experiencing six or more orgasms during intercourse and up to fifty or more during masturbation with a vibrator."[31] No wonder Gerard Damiano had been able to weave an entire film around cultural anxieties about female orgasm. And no wonder Damiano had cried out, "Look at Jane Fonda in *Klute*; hard-core sex belonged in that picture."[32]

In pointing to the absence of hard-core sex in Jane Fonda's *Klute* (dir. Alan Pakula, 1971), Damiano was challenging the mainstream film industry to do what he had done: to show "insertions and cum-shots." The idea was unthinkable in 1973 when his words were spoken, but ironically it would be Fonda, much more than Lovelace, who would pioneer the representation of female orgasm in mainstream films. A further irony of this pioneer work is that it could not have been accomplished without an accompanying critique, even a deconstruction, of the kind of "insertion" plus "cum" shot that Damiano wanted to simply add to the mainstream film. In the rest of this chapter I propose to trace the advent of a new kind of female carnal knowledge in American movies through the career of a single iconic performer. I will argue that it was precisely Fonda's association with the antiwar injunctions to make love, not war that proved central to her role in the critique of the kind of phallocentric sex that flourished in the world of hard core.

The willowy Fonda, the daughter of Henry, himself an icon,[33] is perhaps

66: Jane Fonda in *L'Express* photo "speaking" to North Vietnamese in Hanoi. From *Letter to Jane* (dir. Jean Luc Godard and Jean-Pierre Gorin, 1972)

67: Fonda the workout guru. From *Jane Fonda Collection: The Complete Workout* (1989)

best known today for two roles played out not in film but in a highly mediated public life: first as "Hanoi Jane," the antiwar activist whose opposition to the Vietnam war was demonstrated in a highly publicized visit to Hanoi in July 1972 (figure 66);[34] second, as the guru of the home video workout, which, beginning in 1982, popularized aerobic workouts for women, utilizing the same video technology that would also bring hard-core pornography into the home. Fonda's highly disciplined, worked-out, but rarely sweaty body became emblematic of a certain do-it-yourself fitness that was every bit as big a household name as Linda Lovelace had been in the previous decade (figure 67). These two historically distinct features—a late sixties/early seventies antiwar activism whose slogan was "make love, not war," and a later early 1980s physical discipline that made her the queen of the workout—were bridged and linked by Fonda's fame as an American movie star of the late 1960s and early 1970s, the very first to play characters whose orgasms mattered. In Fonda's most famous film performances we thus encounter the dramatic convergence of a pro-sex, antiwar ethic that marked the late 1960s and early 1970s.

Jane Fonda's Orgasms

It is against the background of the indices of sexual revolution and feminist revolution discussed above—highly sexualized antiwar activism, new discourses of sexology questioning the cause of female orgasm, a further feminist revision of these discourses, not to mention the appearance of filmed sex acts as artifacts of sexual pleasure, knowledge, and power—that Fonda's orgasms take on significance. In concentrating on Fonda's orgasms in three films made between 1968 and 1978, I am not attributing to her any special status as a sex symbol. Rather, as we shall see, it was precisely when Fonda began to withdraw from the more kittenish sex-symbol roles of her early career that she emerged as an important actor whose performance of orgasms could be taken seriously. But let us first turn to the kittenish stage in *Barbarella: Queen of the Galaxy* (1968).

Fonda had been informed by the great stage director Joshua Logan that she would "never be a dramatic actress with that nose, too cute for drama."[35] It was this "cute" starlet who was invited to France in 1963 to make a film with the famous Roger Vadim, whose *And God Created Woman* (1956), starring Brigitte Bardot, had inaugurated a whole new era of sophisticated, if not exactly graphic, European screen sexuality. Vadim was a contemporary of the French New Wave artists, but unlike them, he was unabashedly commercial. He celebrated a particularly French kind of sensual pleasure in the first film version of *Les liaisons dangereuses* (1959), in a "racy" remake of Max Ophuls's *La ronde* (1964), and in the quite remarkable and little-known *The Game Is Over* (*La curé*; 1966).[36] Vadim's films glory in hedonism and the kind of titillation once synonomous with French movies. He rarely pictured graphic sex, but he was fascinated by female sensuality and did not always find it necessary, as Hollywood films of roughly the same era did, to punish female protagonists for their pursuit of sexual pleasure.[37] For a six-year period, overlapping with her career as a proto-Hollywood star in films as diverse as *Cat Ballou* (dir. Elliot Silverstein, 1965), *Any Wednesday* (dir. Robert Miller, 1966), and *Barefoot in the Park* (dir. Gene Saks, 1967), Fonda worked in France under the tutelage of Vadim, whom she eventually married.

To his great credit Vadim did not try to make Fonda into an American version of Bardot. What he did instead, with a screenplay authored by satirist Terry Southern, was capitalize on her American innocence, while asking her to disrobe in suggestive, but never frontally nude, ways. The credit sequence of *Barbarella* was emblematic: the space traveler Barbarella strips off her space suit while floating in her gravityless spaceship. In this futuristic striptease, the letters of the credits hide crucial body parts. The peeling off, or decorous shedding, of already skimpy outfits constitutes the primary visual pleasure of this film about an earthling ignorant of the old-fashioned sexual pleasures derived from bodily friction. Earthlings, we learn, had long ago given up such primitive distractions. But when a hirsute, virile representative of another galaxy insists on old-fashioned friction, Barbarella is pleasantly surprised. All we see, however, is Barbarella in a state of extreme, presumably postcoital, satisfaction. Another sexual episode, this time with the smooth, well-built flesh of the angel Pygar (John Phillip Law), further convinces her that old-fashioned sex has its charms. But like the first scene, this one, too, is elided: All we see, again, is a postcoital Barbarella, relaxed and humming, stroking herself with one of the feathers from Pygar's wings.

By the time Barbarella arrives at her third sexual encounter, this time with a bumbling revolutionary played by David Hemmings, she is eager to engage again in this supposedly retrograde activity. But this revolutionary, coyly named Dildano, is a modern man who insists that she engage in the pill-induced "exaltation transference." After ingesting the transference pellets, they face one another, fully clothed, and touch only their palms, which gradually begin to smoke as their faces reveal mild pleasure (figure 68). The climax for each appears to be a moment when their hair curls and stands up, though Dildano's hair curls more.[38] As in the early sex of *Deep Throat*, this scene is portrayed as only mildly pleasurable. Once again a female protagonist confesses, this time with disinterested body language, that sex is less than thrilling: no "bells ringing, dams bursting, or bombs going off." At one point a distracted Barbarella drops her hand, but then politely reengages.

Barbarella's plot is usually dismissed as a silly excuse to maneuver Fonda into various stages of undress. This it ably does, but the plot hinges on Barbarella's mission to locate and eliminate a "positronic ray," possessed by the villainous Duran Duran, which threatens the peace of the universe. It is thus to avert war that the future Hanoi Jane undertakes her mission. Barbarella thus makes love, the old-fashioned way (offscreen), and averts war (on-screen) by disarming the power-mad megalomaniac

68: *Barbarella: Queen of the Galaxy* (dir. Roger Vadim, 1968),
Barbarella and Dildano "have sex"

Duran Duran. But if *Barbarella* is strangely modest about the portrayal of sexual acts compared to the display of its heroine's body, it rather boldly portrays female orgasms not achieved through coitus.

Caught in the clutches of the villainous Duran Duran, whose peace-shattering weapon it is her mission to destroy, Barbarella is placed in a number of vaguely s/m torture devices. The most important is a futuristic version of an old-fashioned single-person steam bath from which only her head, neck—and later her upper chest—protrude. This rubber tent is attached to an organ (the musical kind) whose keys the villain plays. His plan is for Barbarella to die of pleasure from the sound vibrations caused by his playing. In "playing the organ" he thus proposes to "play" Barbarella herself—to death. What we then see is a nonexplicit extended "sex" scene in which the feminist inference drawn from Masters and Johnson is enacted: *"The more a woman does, the more she can, and the more she can, the more she wants to."*[39]

As Duran Duran begins to "play his organ" (figure 69), Barbarella sighs and her eyes widen as one by one items of her clothes are spit out at the bottom of the "Exsexive Machine." "It's sort of nice, isn't it?" she asks. "Yes," replies the sly villain, "it *is* nice . . . in the beginning." Though more of her upper body will gradually protrude from the steam bath–like contraption, it is her face that registers the surprise of successive degrees of pleasure as the music builds. "When we reach the crescendo you will die," promises the villain. Big death, real death, is supposed to follow the excess—exsex—of the little death (*petite mort*) of orgasm. But the more frenetically Duran

Barbarella: Queen of the Galaxy

69: Duran Duran begins to play his organ

70: Barbarella can match whatever pleasure the machine gives her

Duran plays the organ and the more the music reaches one crescendo after another, the more it becomes apparent that Barbarella can take whatever pleasures it offers (figure 70). In the end, it is only the machine that dies, not Barbarella. "Theoretically," as Sherfey put it, "a woman could go on having orgasms indefinitely."[40]

In this scene a finite, masculine concept of sexual pleasure as climax and crescendo—the quintessentially French and male concept of orgasm as a kind of finite *petite mort*—comes up against the lessons of Kinsey, Masters and Johnson, and feminist sexological revisions of female sexual pleasure as potentially infinite. The more the machine tries to kill her with pleasure, the more Barbarella relaxes and enjoys. Soon the tubes feeding the sound into the cubicle shrink, and the connections smoke and burn. Yet another mad male scientist's experiment has gone awry. "I don't believe it!" Duran Duran exclaims, "Wretched, wretched girl! What have you done to my Ex-

71: *Barbarella: Queen of the Galaxy*, Barbarella's face reveals Kinsey's insight that sexual response does not look like happiness

sexive Machine?! You've undone it! You've undone *me*! Look! The energy cables are shrinking! You've turned them into *faggots*! You've burned out the Exsexive Machine! You've blown all its fuses!" The snickering comic genius and campy double entendre of Southern's script is evident in every word of this monologue, but we barely hear the words—which appear superfluous compared to the ever-widening eyes, open mouth, and growing beads of sweat on Barbarella's face. This is one point in the film in which Barbarella/Fonda's face—not the game of peekaboo with her seminaked body—counts. And it is the expression on this face that prefigures all of Fonda's subsequent performances of orgasm. What it reveals is Kinsey's insight that "an individual who is really responding is as incapable of looking happy as the individual who is being tortured" (figure 71). Such is the first (American) face of female orgasm on the American screen.

While many have noted the campy sets and sexual innuendo of much of the film's dialogue, and while some have drawn a connection between the Exsexive Machine and Woody Allen's later "orgasmatron" in *Sleeper* (1973), no one has noted the sheer temporal duration of this scene or the fact that it only ends when the machine dies. Barbarella's pleasure endures as the machine steams up and sputters out. If the film carefully elides all views of heterosexual coitus as pelvic thrusting—more chastely, in fact, than American films of the same era—it does not elide the orgasm presumed the end point of sexual pleasure. Nor does it presume that this orgasm can be represented as a single climax. Rather, it is as an ongoing pleasure. In its own very sixties way, then, and in a way that will carry over in a much more serious mode into Fonda's post-sixties film career, the future Hanoi Jane uses her orgasmic capacity to expose the warlike villain and his death machine as impotent and to celebrate herself as orgasmically triumphant. Make love, not war, indeed!

In the introduction to his book about Victorian pornography, first published in 1964, Steven Marcus evoked an image derived from Masters and Johnson that he considered symptomatic of the new era of twentieth-century pornography on the rise at the time of his writing. Noting that Masters and Johnson had "discovered" the "orgasmic capacities of women," he points out the aptness of this discovery for an era of postindustrial advanced capitalism: "It can hardly be an accident . . . that the idea of large or virtually unlimited female orgasmic capacity should act as a centrally organizing image of our time. The notion of a multiply orgasmic female corresponds exquisitely to the needs of a society based on mass consumption. It is in effect a perfect image of mass consumption—particularly if we add to this image the further details that she is probably masturbating alone, with the aid of a mechanical-electrical instrument."[41] Fonda's Barbarella is not exactly masturbating alone, but she does have the aid of a "mechanical-electrical instrument" in the form of the Exsexive Machine. As such, she seems to be an important precursor of the image, already implicit in Masters and Johnson, of the future that so worries Marcus, perhaps as much as it worries Duran Duran: the multiply orgasmic woman in no need of heterosexual coitus to achieve multiple, uncountable orgasms.[42]

It would take another decade for mainstream Hollywood cinema to begin to depict the spectacle of an orgasmic woman in a serious vein. We saw in chapter 2 that the musical sexual interlude had been Hollywood's primary way of forging a supposedly tasteful suggestion of carnal knowledge while simultaneously screening out most of its physical details. However, the musical sexual interlude had little interest in the specificity of female pleasure. It was a way of taming and sanitizing the first representations of genital sex acts in American movies. Just as kisses in the silent or sound film almost never occurred without soaring music, so it would prove extremely rare for post-Code Hollywood films to depict carnal knowledge without affectively controlling, and reassuring, audience response with musical accompaniment. When we do get sex without the music, it usually seems more naked, more real, more like the zero degree of sex portrayed in Warhol's *Blue Movie* (1968).

Something closer to this zero degree is what we find in Fonda's post-*Barbarella* American film performances of orgasms. Indeed, it would first be through the discovery of ways of depicting nonorgasmic sex—often figured as "bad" sex displayed without music or bracketed editing and eschewing the celebratory, lyrical format of the sexual interlude—that Hollywood would eventually find a new way to portray sex beyond these conventions.

Bad sex in Hollywood had previously been portrayed as the sex the woman did not want to have. By the early seventies, however, it began to encompass another meaning: inauthentic or faked sex. Fonda here, too, would emerge as the pioneer. Her first Oscar-winning performance in *Klute* in 1971 was one of the first to complicate the sexually promiscuous figure of the femme fatale, usually a figure of villainy. In this film the woman is, in a more traditional sense and despite her promiscuous sexual activity, "good."[43] Having already proved that she could act in the 1969 *They Shoot Horses, Don't They?* (dir. Sydney Pollack), Fonda now proceeded to play Bree Daniels, a high-class call girl stalked by a mysterious killer and protected by a strong, silent cop named Klute (Donald Sutherland). Bree's orgasms, both faked and real, would matter to this narrative, though only the faked, "bad" ones would be directly shown. In an early scene, Bree has sex with a client. Pro that she is, she is fully in control of the orchestration of his pleasure through the semblance of her own. At the moment of her supposed orgasm she does a muted, but patently fake, version of Sally's exaggerated performance in the deli, while simultaneously glancing at her watch. Analytic sessions with a female psychiatrist make this point even clearer: Bree confesses that real sexual pleasure would threaten her control over the scene.

Both Molly Haskell's and Pauline Kael's reviews of *Klute* discuss this early sex scene. Kael complains that the timing is off: realistically, Bree would have looked at her watch before, not during, the faked orgasm. Haskell, for her part, notes what kind of toll such a performance exacts: "As any woman who has ever faked an orgasm knows, it's too easy to count as a great performance and too cynical not to leave behind some poison."[44] While both critics score important points in the evaluation of the film, my real interest here lies in the fact that these two influential women critics of the early seventies, themselves informed by discourses of sexology and its feminist critique, now find it possible to argue about the realism of a performance of (bad) sex. They recognize bad sex when they see it.

Good sex would be Hollywood's new, post-Code answer to bad. Good versus bad may constitute a terribly impoverished range compared to the sexual performances we have already seen emerging outside the Hollywood mainstream.[45] It is nevertheless fascinating to watch Fonda progress from the comic "exsexes" of *Barbarella* to the bad sex–good sex binary of her later work in *Klute* and *Coming Home* (dir. Hal Ashby, 1978). In *Klute*, Bree explains to her analyst that in her affair with Klute she is fighting having real orgasms for fear of losing her autonomy. Indeed, in a scene that might seem initially to be the good-sex antidote to the performed orgasms of sex with the client, Bree and Klute sleep on narrow adjacent mattresses in Klute's basement apartment after Bree has been frightened by a death threat. In the middle of the night Bree silently climbs onto Klute's mattress and seduces him.

The scene is striking in its stark simplicity. There is no fancy editing, no musical accompaniment, and only one ellipsis that takes us from a preliminary stage of seduction to thrusting man-on-top, woman-on-bottom missionary sex. Until we see the triumphant look of control on Bree's face as Klute expresses his (muted) pleasure, we may think that this *is* the good sex—at least she does not look at her watch. But the triumph is too smug, and she taunts him afterwards with the knowledge that she did not come: "I never do with johns." This is her way of asserting control over a man she feels tempted to love. Good sex is not shown, but it is hinted at in an extended bit of sex talk spoken by Bree in a long monologue to her analyst of which I excerpt a part:

> I enjoy, uh, making love with him, which is a very baffling and bewildering thing for me because I'd never felt that way before. I just wish I could let things happen and enjoy it for what it is and while it lasts and relax with it. But all the time I keep feeling the need to destroy it . . . to go back to the comfort of being numb. . . . I had more control with tricks . . . at least I knew what I was doing when I was setting things up. . . . It's so strange, the sensation that is flowing from me naturally to somebody else without it being prettied up. I mean, he's seen me horrible. He's seen me mean, whorey, and it doesn't seem to matter; he seems to accept me, and I guess having sex with somebody and feeling those sorts of feelings is very new to me.

Bree's words could almost be taken as Hollywood's best advice to itself on how to present sexual relations that capture a sense of a charge flowing between two bodies, without the buffer of musical interlude, without the abstraction of tight editing, and "without it being prettied up" in the usual Hollywood ways. *Klute* itself does not take that plunge beyond this verbalizing, but toward the end of the decade, Fonda would again perform brief, bad, nonorgasmic sex in yet another Academy Award–winning performance in *Coming Home*. This time, however, bad sex would be answered by good. And the portrayal of this sex would break the pattern of most previous Hollywood examples and address the question of whether what

Anne Koedt called "certain sexual positions now defined as 'standard'" deserved to be so defined.[46]

Hal Ashby's *Coming Home* is not an antiwar film of the late 1960s, but an elegiac antiwar film of the late 1970s that looks back at the late 1960s. It is about a Marine officer's wife living in California during the Vietnam War. Early on we see Sally (Fonda) have perfunctory farewell sex with her Marine captain husband (Bruce Dern) before he departs to Vietnam. In the dark of their bedroom, she lies still under his body. Her eyes are open and her hands are folded on his dog tags as he pushes tamely, passionlessly into her, emitting only a couple of muted grunts at the end. Sally does not fake orgasm; she simply holds still and passively takes what her husband gives. She is nevertheless clearly emotionally entangled with the only man she appears to have ever loved.

An adulterous affair will be the occasion to counter this bad marital sex, and shy Sally will become more independent.[47] She volunteers at the hospital and develops a friendship with Luke (Jon Voight), an angry paraplegic veteran who learns to channel his frustration and shame about his participation in the war into antiwar activism. After Luke heroically chains himself to the Marine base gate to protest conditions in the veterans' hospital, Sally asks to spend the night with him. In a scene almost perfectly designed to illustrate the argument of Koedt's "The Myth of the Vaginal Orgasm," she achieves her first orgasm with Luke, a man paralyzed and without sensation from the waist down.

The scene begins with Luke emerging from the bathroom of his apartment in his wheelchair with only a towel draped over his crotch. Sally, still in a trench coat, helps him onto his bed and turns off the light. "Turn on the light," says Luke, "I want to see you." What follows is almost a lesson in synesthesia designed for movies. Luke informs Sally that he cannot feel when she touches him (down there), but he can see. Sight, in a solution that neatly coincides with the needs of an audience screening sex, thus partly substitutes for touch in a sex scene that has a legitimate excuse to leave the light on.[48]

The first image after the light goes back on is a goldenly lit tight shot of the now naked couple in a clinch. "What can I do?" asks Sally. "Everything, I want you to do everything," answers Luke. This invitation to do "everything" implies a liberation from the usual temporality of a sex act that would progress through what Kael defined as a modernist "jabbing, thrusting eroticism" and predictably end (as did all sex acts in *Deep Throat* as well as in simulated films) with male orgasm presumed to signal the end of the female's pleasure as well. Without this usual telos, the trajectory of the encounter is up for grabs. We cannot assume what this sex will be. Thus when, in the next shot, we see a more distant view of Sally, her back to us astride Luke, we cannot assume that he is penetrating her. At this point, the polymorphous perversity of the body in its entirety—which Herbert Marcuse had called for in *Eros and Civilization*—seems to have a chance to emerge as the couple negotiates new ways of touching, feeling, and looking.

However we construe the sex that Luke and Sally have, it is emphatically not that of active, phallic thrusting into a passive receptacle. On the other hand, we do not ever see what exactly Sally does to pleasure Luke besides offer herself up to be seen by him. What we do see next is Luke kissing lower and lower parts of Sally's anatomy in what we can only assume eventually becoms cunnilingus. And what we hear is Sally's delighted, encouraging direction, "Oh softly!" It would seem that "jabbing, thrusting eroticism" is the last thing on her mind. Were this a scene from either a heterosexual or a homosexual porn film, the injunction from the penetratee to the pene-trator could only be the reverse: "Harder . . . harder!" "Softer" suggests a world of difference: a sex of delicacy in which less movement, force, size, and hardness might count for more. The following shot shows Sally's legs convulsing as they wrap around Luke's seriously scarred back (figure 72). We surmise from where her feet are that his face, not visible, must now be close to her genitals. A cut to her face reveals wide eyes and panting convulsive movements and a series of long "ohhhs" that are reminiscent of Barbarella's encounter with the Exsexive Machine (figure 73). When Luke says "You're so beautiful"—again asserting that his primary pleasure is visual—Sally for a short while just goes on convulsing, raising the ques-tion of when this sex act might end. It does end, however, after they have embraced and held one another for a while, when Sally says, perhaps un-necessarily, "It's never happened to me before." Here, finally, is the end-of-the-decade's good sex that answers both Bree Daniels's hurried sex with a client in *Klute* and Sally's passive, unresponsive sex with her husband at the beginning of *Coming Home*.

In her autobiography, *My Life So Far*, Fonda explains that she and Voight met with Vietnam veteran paraplegics and their girlfriends in preparation for their roles in the film to learn the various ways they had sex. In the pro-cess of the research they were surprised to learn that the men were occa-sionally capable of unpredictable erections. She writes that until learning this, "genital penetration was not something I had considered possible between my character and Jon's."[49] Nor was she interested in portraying this unpredictable and somewhat rare possibility. She was more interested

Coming Home (dir. Hal Ashby, 1978)

72: Sally's legs convulse as they wrap around Luke's scarred back

73: Sally's face during orgasm

in finding "a dramatic way to redefine manhood beyond the traditional, goal-oriented reliance on the phallus to a new shared intimacy and pleasure my character had never experienced with her husband."[50] Hal Ashby, however, was determined to portray the sex as precisely an achievement of rare penetrative virility. Voight, for his part, agreed with Fonda that the sex scene would be more adventurous if the assumption was that his character could not have an erection and the sex was thus nonpenetrative.

Thus began what Fonda calls the "Battle of Penetration." Ashby had already directed Fonda's body double in the nude scenes to move as if she was being pleasurably penetrated, while Fonda in her own flesh refused to match those actions. The climax of the battle occurred on the final day of shooting the scene when she was on top of Voight and Ashby yelled at her, "Ride him! Dammit! Ride him!" while Fonda, holding onto her concept of the scene, refused to play jockey. In Ashby's conception, Sally was astride Luke who had achieved an erection. In Fonda's conception, the climax of the scene was Sally's experience of oral sex. The double who acted in the long shots had been directed to "ride," while Fonda, in the closer shots, refused. According to Fonda, the two do not match. I would argue, rather, that they look like two phases of the couple's lovemaking, a first in which Sally is on top and could be riding Luke—but perhaps his thigh, not his penis—and a later phase that consists of cunnilingus and in which Fonda achieves orgasm. At this point Luke's body is outside of the frame, "below." From the evidence on the screen, I would say that Fonda won the battle of the depiction of this particular orgasm as resulting from nonpenetrative sex. However one sex scene in one Hollywood film could hardly win the larger war of gender equity in screening sex. Though Sally does give evidence of a prolonged and continuous pleasure that does not have the same rhythm and telos of phallic sex, her performance ultimately operates to restore a semblance of masculinity to an initially emasculated veteran. (Ron Kovic, the paraplegic antiwar vet who had served as the inspiration for the character of Luke, later told Fonda that the film had improved his sex life.[51])

Perhaps the only way to truly challenge what still remains the dominant phallic discourse of sex would have been to question the very notion of orgasm itself as the be-all and end-all of pleasure, or as the ultimate truth of sex for women. For in both these phrases is embedded the notion of a singular end pleasure—a climax, or as Duran Duran would put it, a "crescendo"—that contradicts the very notion of the polymorphous and the multiple.

As feminist researcher Annie Potts demonstrates, the language of orgasm, even the more female-aware language of sexologists such as Masters and Johnson, tends to be organized as a teleology of excitement, plateau, orgasm, and resolution in much the way it is performed by Fonda: as a transcendence that brings one back more fully and completely to the self though a beginning, middle, and end that often still privileges phallocentric models of thrusting and getting there, with men typically getting there too soon and women too late. Potts attempts to deconstruct the binaries by showing how the privileged term of presence (getting there) is dependent on the absence of a later "falling away" from presence, the return to absence, of the end of orgasm. Potts herself advocates a discourse of sex in which a climax would not be regarded as the only source of true intimacy. This general unfixing of pleasure from any specific organ is similar to Marcuse's call for a more general reactivation of all erotogenic zones, not just the genitals.[52]

It would be unfair to ask Fonda alone to point the way to a brave future of such deconstructed orgasm. Perhaps a simpler way to approach the problem of the figuration of orgasm(s) in film would be to recall Leo Bersani's argument that often the "pleasurable and unpleasurable tension of sexual stimulation seeks not to be released [as in a phallic, teleological discharge, in which excitement leads to satisfaction], but to be increased [as in a clitoral way of thinking of orgasm as an excitement that extends itself and, in Potts's terms, reintroduces the concept of desire]."[53] In other words, the hydraulic model of orgasm which views it as mounting tension concluded by an explosion of release can be complicated by another model of sexual excitations that seek nothing more than their own intensification and that might do so, as Sally requests, quite "softly." "Jabbing, thrusting eroticism" is thus one form of sexual pleasure modeled on what Bersani calls the "scratch;" it aims at satisfaction in discharge, at hitting the target, or the "spot" described in *Deep Throat*'s theme song. The scratch always presumes a thrusting and a targeted tactility of one erogenous zone on another. The itch, on the other hand, is much less specifically targeted; it is ultimately whatever manages to keep desire in play. The scratch model of orgasm has obviously been the dominant, phallocentric term of much sexology and much cinema. It took an antiwar movie about a paraplegic to begin to figure the pleasure of the itch: anticipation, prolongation, intensification—but not necessarily hard, not necessarily discharged—to tentatively begin to counter the dominant phallocentric model of going all the way in screening sex.

Coming Home received mixed reviews but substantial recognition at Oscar time (for both Voight and Fonda, as well as for the screenplay). Critics were divided by the lightning rod of Hanoi Jane playing a docile Marine wife whose political and sexual transformation moves tentatively in the direction of . . . well, Jane Fonda. They were also divided about the film's focus on Sally's orgasms, as well as its use of sixties rock music to underscore many scenes. Vincent Canby called the film "soggy with sound"—"a nonstop collection of yesterday's song hits."[54] Pauline Kael agreed, arguing that Ashby "has filled in the dead spaces by throwing a blanket of rock songs over everything."[55] David James, writing in the early nineties, has nevertheless made an important case for the film's use of rock and roll, pointing out that while there have been many American films about the devastation of American soldiers who fought in Vietnam—and no feature-length fictional films about the devastation of the Vietnamese—this film's "unequivocal assertion" that the invasion of Vietnam was "*wrong* distinguishes it from all other films made in Hollywood."[56]

What no one seemed to notice, however, despite both criticism and praise for the film's countercultural "underscore" of rock music,[57] was that music was for once *not* applied to the sex scenes. Indeed, the sex scenes were sometimes the only times in the movie when nondiegetic music did *not* accompany the action. Relative silence ruled, punctuated by the sounds of sex (the opposite of the musical sexual interlude's typical blocking out of such sounds), and that simple fact gave the sex scenes—admired or not—a more dramatically integrated status than the standard interlude. What some critics, Canby included, may really have been objecting to in his derogation of the film as a "women's picture" may thus not only be its politically tinged melodrama, but the post–sexual revolution mutation of a love story that details a woman's sexual pleasure without that pleasure being contained, as it had previously been, by kisses and ellipses or by musical sexual interludes.[58]

It is fascinating to watch American critics come to grips with an American—not European-inflected—screen sex that goes all the way, albeit in a simulated way. Kael, for example, undergoes an interesting change of mind in the course of her review. At first she seems to follow Canby's judgment and to trivialize the achievement-of-orgasm plot: "*Coming Home* started out to be about how the Vietnam war changed Americans, and turned into a movie about a woman married to a hawk who has her first orgasm when she goes to bed with a paraplegic." In the end, however, Kael does not deride the importance of this new "women's picture" subject matter. More organically, she argues that the film does not quite deliver on the logic and motivation of its sexual subject. Contrasting the look on Sally's face when she had open-eyed sex with her husband to the look when she also had open-eyed sex with Luke, Kael writes that the situation fairly demands that her husband discover her infidelity through the new way she would make love when they next have sex. In essence, this comment reduces to the question: Could the woman who now "really" makes love do so with a man who desperately wants to believe in the good of making war? Since the film does not depict such a scene, it, according to Kael, fails its subject.

Whether one agrees with Kael or not, the important point is that in the course of her review she begins to take the dramatic matter of the orgasm seriously, not just as something to be discussed (as in *Klute*) but as something to be screened and, more viscerally, corporeally understood. After initially making fun of the importance of Sally's orgasm weighed against the whole disillusionment of Vietnam, Kael implicitly recognizes that how Fonda has sex with her two different partners represents a new cinematic codification of carnal knowledge now demanding to be respected on its own cinematic and dramatic terms. Kael's insight is to see that that first climax required yet another sex scene with Sally's husband. Without directly noting that sexual performance had now become relevant to a mainstream Hollywood film with major stars, Kael tacitly acknowledges that a popular Hollywood film can use simulated sexual performance to express the complex psychology and drives of its characters and perhaps something more nuanced than simply bad or good sex. She also implicitly acknowledges, through her very demand for yet another sex scene, what Canby cannot admit: that screening sex, up to and including depictions of the quality and kind of orgasm, conjoins with interest in character and narrative and is now a valid expectation at the movies. Thus in 1978, five years after the American withdrawal from Vietnam, American audiences could finally understand the axiom forming the basis of my generation's activism: "Make love, not war."

In a recent documentary film by Rosanna Arquette, *Searching for Debra Winger* (2002), about the pressures of being a woman, a mother, and an actor in Hollywood, Jane Fonda provides the concluding interview. Throughout this film centered on well-known female stars who found plenty of work while young and much less work since they have hit their forties, Fonda and Vanessa Redgrave are the even more mature survivors whose life stories often serve as an inspiration to the questioning Arquette and her cohort. Fonda freely admits that she was a bad mother who never managed, as her own father had also failed to manage, to balance parenthood, family, and career—not to mention antiwar activism. But the point at which she becomes most animated, and the reason her interview concludes the documentary, is her vivid description of the eight or so times in her life at which she has entered the magic "circle of light" on the movie set when all eyes, all light, and all energy focuses on the main actor as a kind of "eye of the hurricane." When, in these moments of greatest fear and tension, an actor manages, perhaps just a few times in his or her life, to deliver a great performance, it is, Fonda claims, all worth it. What is important, however, is that she describes these performances in sexualized terms, first as bad sex and then as good: What if, she asks, you give too much in rehearsal and "blow your wad," leaving nothing for the shoot? What, she speculates, if in the actual shooting you "can't get it up"? On the other hand, she eagerly describes how thrilling it is to "hit your mark" with all channels open, like a "plane taking off," "like a dance, both with the other actors and the camera and loving your costar . . . it's this wonderful fusion . . . better than any lovemaking."

It may seem surprising that Fonda sexualizes the craft and the art of acting in such extremely phallocentric terms given her contribution to our understanding of orgasm as something more than "blowing your wad." Fonda is obviously still subject to the dominant discourses of sexuality and if "getting it up" and "hitting the mark" are the metaphors that work for her, perhaps we should not demand that she also tell us how she lets go and relaxes into it. Good feminist and antiwar activist that she has tried to be, Fonda can invent no better language. We can forgive an actor whose sexual performances were as crucial to the 1970s cinematic knowledge of sex and perhaps as important and influential in their own female sphere as Marlon Brando's animal sexuality was in that of the male. It does not seem accidental that the quintessential American sexuality of both actors was forged in relation to European, and specifically French-associated, movies. Both actors brought coming—each in their own, gender-based way—home to our movies.

> What does physical eroticism signify if not a violation of the
> very being of its practitioners?—a violation bordering on death,
> bordering on murder?
> —GEORGES BATAILLE, *Erotism: Death and Sensuality*

5

hard-core eroticism

In the Realm of the Senses

(1976)

Sex is too important to be left to the pornographers.[1] And yet, as we have seen, American movies only tackled the representation of hard-core explicit sex within the genre of pornography. Moving-image pornography as practiced since the seventies has had the primary goal of arousing viewers through the maximum visibility of normally hidden organs and acts that often verge on the clinical, with aesthetic considerations secondary. The rule of maximum visibility did not mean that pornography outlawed all aesthetic concerns; nor did it mean, on the other side, that erotic art necessitated a corresponding lack of graphic content.[2] Yet what we might call hard-core eroticism tempered graphic display with more subtle effects of line, color, light, and—in the performing art of film—subtleties of sexual performance that were much harder to achieve. In the end, moving-image pornography proved relatively easy to make and has flourished since the seventies in its own parallel universe in which art is not necessary (but can occasionally happen). In contrast, hard-core moving-image erotica proved difficult to make and did not flourish in this same time period.

The era of porno chic once seemed to open up a future in which art and porn film would merge and in which more films like *Last Tango in Paris* would be possible, this time, as Norman Mailer put it, *with* the "fucks." The utopian dream of the cinematic merger of the erotic and hard core— an eros that could include graphic sex as well as a pornography that might encompass the erotic—held that one day respected actors would take on the varied performance of sex acts as part of the challenge of their craft, while respected directors would take the depiction of the quality and kind of sex as a crucial element of their art. Cinema would then catch up with the grown-up concerns of other arts, like literature, to become truly explicit and adult.

We all know how that dream turned out: it was as if the bad karma of the long history of censorship—sixty-plus years of what André Bazin called "cinematographic lies about love"[3]—left the entire international film industry bifurcated into relatively artless films that would show sex in highly exhibitionistic, formulaic ways, and relatively artful films that would refrain from the explicit penetrations, convulsions, and secretions of actual sex acts. In the United States, the graphic category of adult X-rated films devolved into a repository for unsimulated but formulaic sex acts each culminating in a highly predictable money shot as the incontrovertible evidence of (at least) male orgasm. Less formulaic but simulated sex acts were explored in a few art films following in or anticipating the tradition of Bertolucci's *Last Tango in Paris*.[4] In the end, however, despite a few memorable glimpses of men's bodies in the late sixties and seventies—Donald Sutherland in Nicholas Roeg's *Don't Look Now* (1973) or Alan Bates and Oliver Reed wrestling homoerotically in the nude in Ken Russell's *Women in Love* (1969)—art and naked explicitness did not mix. What is more, in the simulated sex of the art film ridiculous double standards of undress prevailed: most male actors, like Brando, kept their clothes on, while most female actors, like Schneider or Fonda, took theirs off (sometimes, as we saw with Fonda, with the aid of a body double). Meanwhile, in Hollywood, the bracketed sexual interlude prevailed. *Last Tango*, which had seemed to represent the beginning of a new era of franker sex, proved to have been an anomaly by the end of the decade, at least as far as its influence in Hollywood was concerned.

But there was one film of seventies international cinema that actually did what Anglo-American and European critics and directors had only dreamed of doing. Oshima Nagisa's *In the Realm of the Senses* (1976) fused the graphic sex of hard-core pornography and the erotic narrative of mad love exemplified by the landmark *Last Tango in Paris* into a remarkable work of hard-core eroticism.[5] Explicit sex acts were deployed in this French-produced Japanese art film as part of a serious narrative in which the performance of heterosexual penetrative sex proved essential to the work's meaning. Because it consists almost entirely of an extended repertoire of graphic sex acts, even more than typically found in pornography (some twenty acts in almost as many different places), many critics were quick to identify the film with pornography. Since many of these critics also identified pornography with obscenity, the film was dismissed in many quarters. Some who defended the film, in turn, based their defense on its radical difference from pornography.[6]

Still others, including Oshima himself, defended the film as a radical extension of the possibilities of pornography and thus as a testing ground for challenging the very notion of obscenity.[7] He wrote:

> The concept of "obscenity" is tested when one dares to look at something that he has an unbearable desire to see, but has forbidden himself to look at. When one feels that everything that one had wanted to see has been revealed, "obscenity" disappears, the taboo disappears as well, and there is a certain liberation. . . . Thus, pornographic films are a testing ground for "obscenity." If that is the case, then the benefits of pornography are clear. Pornographic cinema should be authorized, immediately and completely.[8]

Pornography or not, Oshima's film has garnered important critical discussion among Western critics who know a great deal about Japanese culture.[9] My goal in this chapter will not be so much to understand this unique film as a stunning example of Japanese cinema (which it is), but as the first example of feature-length narrative cinema anywhere in the world to succeed as both art and pornography—as both genital maximum visibility and the erotic subtleties of line, color, light, and performance. This chapter is an argument about the importance of a film whose great influence has perhaps only begun to become evident since the late nineties, when a critical mass of new hard-core art cinema from Europe, Asia, and even, finally, from America, emerged to demand critical attention. Thus, although I will necessarily discuss this film within the context of its specific culture, my point about it is inevitably its transnational impact: a work of Japanese cinema powerfully influenced by, and in return influencing, Western film practices (the latter of which I will discuss in chapter 6). This chapter, however, is devoted to *In the Realm of the Senses* alone, the breakthrough film that would finally prove that explicit sex did not negate art.

I have no recollection of my first screening of *In the Realm of the Senses*. I know I saw it soon after it came out, but like the American film industry that had become so rigidly bifurcated between a graphic hard core and a less explicit mainstream and art film, I could not assimilate it to what I knew about either sex or movies. When I did go to see it, I did so in an almost furtive way, attending it, unlike *Deep Throat* or *Last Tango*, with neither friends nor my partner. Initially, in other words, I found Oshima's film at once too real, too hard-core, and too beautiful to fathom. Frankly, it scared me, and you might say I screened it out. Certainly the film's climax in literal and visible castration could easily scare. So even though this shocking ending fit rather neatly into then current Lacanian allegories of "lack" and castration, it seemed too literally so. Nor did the film's doubly foreign provenance fit into familiar categories. For not only was this an art film in a European erotic tradition very close to the mad love of the surrealists, Georges Bataille, and *Last Tango*, it also had an exotic Eastern eroticism that drew on the visual tradition of *shunga* art and geishan pleasure worlds. This tradition was highly stylized, formally beautiful, but also exaggerated and excessive. It was a form of hard-core art pioneered by such respected artists as Utamaro Kitagawa, Hokusai Katsushika, and Harunobi Suzuki that had begun in the eighteenth century (figure 74).[10] The film drawing on these traditions haunted me all through the late seventies and into the late eighties.[11]

Transnational Contexts

The film's reception in the West was influenced by the knowledge that it was based on a true story, already well known to the Japanese public, that had already served as the basis for another feature made the previous year.[12] In 1936 a former prostitute and geisha by the name of Abe Sada was accused of murdering her lover, a restaurant owner named Ishida Kichizo, and of severing his penis and testicles. In her highly publicized trial she testified that she had strangled him with his consent during sex and then performed a postmortem castration. In this era, the trial of a

74: Suzuki Harunobu, active ca. 1724–70. From Marco Fagioli,
Shunga: The Erotic Art of Japan (1998)

woman who claimed to live for love and pleasure alone struck a chord.
Sada was not the first woman in Japan to have her sexual story made public: adulterous women who killed men had been stock filler in newspapers
since the 1800s. However, the castration made her a figure of special fascination and perhaps surprising sympathy—she received a relatively short
sentence.[13] In the midst of a society gearing up for war and rapidly turning
fascist, the story of a couple who withdrew from all social contact to live
for love was taken to heart, especially among women.

Unlike the prewar masters of Japanese cinema—Mizoguchi Kenji, Kurosawa Akira, and Ozu Yasujiro—whose careers all flowered in the postwar
era, the younger Oshima was an iconoclast of the postwar generation who
radically broke with the aesthetic traditions of these great artists, saying,
"My hatred of Japanese cinema includes absolutely all of it."[14] This hatred
included the great traditions of melodramatic female suffering combined
with often exquisite formal beauty. It also included that cinema's heritage of sexual reticence, a heritage of the late-nineteenth-century Meiji
period,[15] which still imitated the cultural mores of the Victorian era long
after censorship in the West itself had begun to crumble.

For example, in an essay entitled "Sexual Poverty," written in 1971, five years before making *Realm*, Oshima critiqued the development in Japan of many new contemporary discourses of sexual science, whether books and articles about sex education, sexual frequency, sexual intensity, sexual sensitivity, even the size of sexual organs. Dubbing this numerical approach to sexuality "sexual GNPism" and linking it to the imitation of Western, American-influenced sexual culture,[16] he looks back to a "freer" sexual culture of the Edo period (1600–1868) grounded in the pleasure districts of the towns and in the communal-sex folk customs of the farm villages. While this might appear to place Oshima in a conservative camp harking back to the heyday of Japanese erotic arts, he is not so easily categorized. Asserting that both these traditional sexual cultures were crushed in the modernization of the Meji period, he places himself as part of a generation that sought a liberated, materialist view of sex, in short, a generation that not only believed in revolution but linked social and political revolution to sexual ones.[17] He concludes his essay with a call for a perpetual "renewing of our sexual communities."[18] Oshima's models for that renewal thus come from dual sources: an idealized nostalgia for premodern Japan and an equally idealized yearning for the post-1960s Western notions of revolutionary sex and politics behind the barricades.

Breaking with traditional Japanese cinema much the way the French New Wave directors had broken with an older tradition of so-called quality cinema, Oshima's embrace of Japan's sensual past included a parallel embrace of radical, Marxist-influenced, Western ideas, modernist aesthetics and, in the case of this particular film, even of Western financing. Though Oshima's politics and avant-gardism could sometimes make him seem like a Japanese Godard—a filmmaker whose metacinematic qualities he indeed did emulate in some of his earlier films—the narrative of this particular film, which is straightforward, is very un-Godardian.

If the story he chose to tell was uniquely Japanese, Oshima's chance to tell it in an explicit way came from decidedly Western influences. In 1972, which we have seen was a crucial year for both erotic and pornographic cinema in the landmark appearances of *Last Tango in Paris* and *Deep Throat*, the French producer of Argos Films, Anatole Dauman, offered Oshima funds to produce a pornographic film. Oshima had been a strong advocate of the Japanese soft-core pornography known as the *roman poruno* (or porno romance) begun in the early seventies at the Nikkatsu film company. His own past films had flirted with sexually daring, though simulated, sexual content and he had chafed under a cinematic censorship that still bore the influence of the puritanical Meiji Restoration and the American Occupation.

The necessary cuts to one of his earlier films, *Pleasure of the Flesh* (1965), enforced by the Japanese Motion Picture Code of Ethics Committee, had proven a source of shame to Oshima.[19] The unprecedented opportunity provided by Dauman to make a pornographic film with no strings attached and with an ample budget was certainly tempting. Yet, Oshima hesitated quite a while before deciding to actually make the film. What seems to have finally convinced him, three years after Dauman made the original offer, was his belief that other Young Turk Western directors were already doing it. In an article called "Theory of Experimental Pornographic Film," published soon after he made *Senses*, Oshima explains that he had learned from some colleagues just returning from the 1975 Cannes Film Festival that not only were serious pornographic art films being made but (in what was surely an exaggeration) "all the young directors are acting in their own scenes of sexual intercourse."[20] It was thus a combination of envy and masculine competitiveness that seems to have convinced him to finally make the film Dauman had offered to produce. That evening Oshima wrote in his notebook: "I will make a 'pornographic film'—not an average 'film,' a 'pornographic film' all the way." He clarified, "To me, a pornographic film was a film of sexual organs and sexual intercourse. A film that broke taboos was, to me, a pornographic film."[21]

Oshima thus resolved to do what no Japanese director had ever done and what no reputable director of art cinema in the West had ever done either: to make a narrative art film with frequent graphic displays of sexual organs.[22] He made this resolution under the mistaken impression that this kind of hard-core art film was already quite common in the West. This impression was based, at least in part, on the fact that France had legalized pornography. In fact, however, this kind of hard-core art was only a vague idea circulating around the potential of a newly emerged hard-core pornography.[23] Inspired by the revolutionary sexual freedom he imagined already existed in the West, Oshima did not then seek to imitate films like the 1972 *Deep Throat* and *Behind the Green Door*. Instead, he enlisted the cultural prestige of Japan's long-standing tradition of *shunga* art: paintings and woodcut prints from the once flourishing sex culture of the premodern Edo era, during which pornography became popular with an increasingly wealthy merchant class and a genuine flowering of the form occurred. After the Meiji Restoration in 1868, when Japan opened to the West, the new government banned all representation considered "injurious to public morals," which soon came to mean any kind of sexual content and nudity, all of which was often absurdly censored.[24]

When Dauman offered Oshima the means to outdo Western pornography, Oshima accepted the challenge—as American directors when offered a similar challenge a decade earlier by Stanley Kubrick had not. There seems no doubt that the existence of this once celebrated *shunga* tradition,[25] not to mention the special status and celebrity of Abe Sada herself, made his decision possible. Without the existence, however repressed, of this visual tradition, it is questionable whether Oshima would have had the political or aesthetic wherewithal to accept Dauman's offer. Nor does it seem accidental that the story Oshima chose to tell has similarities to the Western art film that had garnered so much recognition earlier in the decade: Bernardo Bertolucci's *Last Tango in Paris*. At first glance, in fact, *In the Realm of the Senses* seems a hard-core reworking of *Last Tango*: an older man and a younger woman withdraw from the world to explore an *amour fou* that ends with the woman killing the man.

To get around the Japanese censors, the film was shot in Japan with Japanese actors, sets, and crew, but on French stock. The negative was shipped to France for development and editing, which meant that Oshima had to shoot the entire film with only an occasional telegram to tell him how the rushes looked. Though he certainly wanted his film to be shown in Japan, he well knew that his real chances for exhibition lay in Western Europe and in the English-speaking world. He thus aimed his film at Western eyes or at those Japanese audiences who, like himself, were envious of what seemed to be greater Western sexual freedom.

So it happened that Oshima's "Japanese" film (shot in Japanese with Japanese actors) would enter his native country as a French import where it would be immediately seized by customs and not shown publicly until a third of its content had been expurgated.[26] Nevertheless, the device of French production had allowed him to make the film in the first place and to retain copies that were not expurgated for exhibition in Europe and the United States. Despite his clever ruse, however, Oshima was placed on trial for obscenity—not for the film but for the script, which had been published along with a number of photos, apparently shot at the time of filming. Twelve of these photos, described as "the poses of men and women engaged in sexual intercourse and sex play," along with selected written portions of the script, were accused of being obscene.[27] If they could not try the film as a Japanese product—though they could certainly expurgate it as a foreign import—the Japanese censors were determined to try the book in its stead. In his quite eloquent defense, Oshima did not, as many artists might have, claim that his film was art rather than pornography. Instead, as we saw above, he insisted that it *was* pornography and furthermore that pornography was useful for rendering the very category of obscenity meaningless: "When one feels that everything that one had wanted to see has been revealed, 'obscenity' disappears, the taboo disappears as well, and there is a certain liberation."[28]

Oshima's claim, in other words, was that an even greater obscenity is created by the kind of peekaboo offered by the obliteration of genitals (and particularly of pubic hair) so prevalent in Japan. He especially railed at the idea that his film was deemed obscene by censors who had never screened it. Though he won his case, the victory was pyrrhic and only applied to the book; the film itself remained expurgated and has still not been seen in Japan without little floating clouds obscuring views of genitals.[29] Oshima might have taken some consolation in the fact that even in its expurgated form, his film did well at the Japanese box office. At the Cannes Film Festival, though shown outside of competition, it immediately became the most talked-about film, necessitating thirteen extra screenings. Furthermore, throughout the film's subsequently long run in Paris, charter flights of Japanese tourists were organized with the express purpose of seeing his film.[30]

In the United States, the film ran up against some of the same problems it had encountered in Japan: a federal law against the importation of obscene materials. It had been scheduled at the New York Film Festival on 2 October 1977 and had, in fact, already been shown to the press a day before the regular public screening. After the press screening, customs officials informed festival organizers that the print would be seized if it were shown the next evening. The organizers then canceled the screening.[31] Thus, once again, *In the Realm of the Senses* was on trial, though this time not for long. Producer Dauman sued the commissioner of customs for New York as well as the U.S. government, and on 8 November the U.S. attorney's office withdrew its demand for the recall of all prints. *Senses* was thus shown after the festival in a special screening at the Museum of Modern Art, and then in most major cities across the United States. Just as Melvin Van Peebles had found his advertising campaign in the slogan "rated X by an all-white jury," so Dauman had found his in "seized by New York customs." The film was not rated by the MPAA but, like *Sweetback* and *Last Tango* before it, proudly exploited a self-assigned X. *In the Realm of the Senses* was thus a film that was destined to seem exotically erotic *wherever* it was exhibited, to Japanese no less than to European and American audiences.

True to Oshima's plan to make a film "of sexual organs and sexual intercourse,"[32] the first scene of the film begins in bed. The servant girl, Sada (Matsuda Eiko), refuses the cold hands and sexual advances of another woman servant in the communal sleeping room of the inn in which she works. The spurned servant takes her to spy on the master of the house having his daily morning sex with his wife. Sada's first glimpse of Kichizo (Fuji Tatsuya) thus occurs as an act of voyeurism on her master and his wife that is a typical feature of much *shunga* art (see figure 74). Sada avidly looks through a partly ajar door (figure 75). She sees the wife crouched before her husband as she dresses him. But the act of dressing soon turns into intercourse revealed in a close, side view of Kichizo on top, his wife on the bottom. Sada moves slightly in synchronization with the movements of the couple.

Kichizo first notices Sada when she wields a knife in rage against another servant. His very first interaction with her is thus to foil the knife that will threaten him repeatedly throughout the rest of the film. He briefly touches her hands and notes that they should be "holding something else" instead. That "something else" soon manifests as Kichizo's penis as he and Sada begin to have brief trysts stolen away from the watchful eyes of his wife. In the first, Sada only sits briefly on Kichizo's member before a geisha enters to officially entertain him; in another, Sada herself takes on the geisha role, playing the samisen and singing, as a geisha would do, but astride Kichizo as a proper geisha would not (figure 76). Her singing serves as a decoy: If the "geisha" sings, the wife presumes her husband is not engaged in sex. But Sada's singing is infused with sexual excitement, adding an audio dimension to the visual eroticism.[33]

Oshima now tells the rest of this story of sexual obsession almost entirely through graphic sex acts that often recall the poses of *shunga*. As we have seen, this tradition of graceful erotic woodblocks, crafted by some of Japan's greatest graphic artists, celebrated and exaggerated the sexual exploits practiced in Japan's pleasure quarters before the censorship of the Meijii era in the mid-nineteenth century. *Shunga*, which literally means "images of spring," flourished in Japan between the seventeenth and mid-nineteenth centuries and portrayed often explicit scenes of sex. They constitute a sexually graphic subgenre of *ukiyo-e*—or "images of the floating world."[34] Excluded from government, the wealthy, urban merchant class of this era assiduously cultivated hedonist pleasures: courtesans and wealthy male clients are depicted either in the throes of ecstasy—with gigantic

In the Realm
of the Senses
(dir. Oshima
Nagisa, 1976)

75: Sada spies
on the wife
and husband

76: Sada plays
the samisen
astride Kichizo

male genitals and abundant, detailed pubic hair—or as more casually bathing, eating, and drinking while also engaged in sex (figure 77). Oshima's depiction of Sada and Kichizo's sex often seems to resemble *shunga* in composition and pose. For example, in figure 78 we find the couple casually having sex outdoors while Kichi exchanges pleasantries with an old "grandmother" (figure 78). However, we see no exaggerated genitalia, not even the kind of extra length Western audiences would have already been familiar with in hard-core pornography.

The inn at which Sada works and over which Kichizo presides, as well as the inns to which they will later repair for their trysts, hark back to this floating world of pleasure where male clients were entertained by geishas. Oshima opposes this old Japan of geishas, courtesans, and pleasure seekers to a briefly glimpsed, but brutally ascendant, Japan of train

77: Utagawa Kunisada, ca. 1827. From Marco Fagioli, *Shunga: The Erotic Art of Japan* (1998)

78: In the Realm of the Senses, Sada and Kichi casually have sex outdoors while an old woman watches

travel and marching troops. He thus lends an air of doomed nostalgia to the events of his film not present in most *shunga*. In a telling scene much commented on by critics, Kichizo, who has chosen the route of sensual pleasure, is seen walking down a street in the opposite direction of marching troops hailed by patriotic, flag-waving women.[35] The troops grow louder and more numerous, pressing in on the solitary figure of Kichizo who in the end is almost flattened against a wall (figure 79). The new, efficient culture of Japanese modernism marches toward its fascist death,

In the Realm of the Senses

79: Kichi pushed aside by the new militaristic order

80: Sada fellates Kichi

while Kichizo, clinging to the ideals of a dying class, will choose another death, pursuing pleasure to the end.[36]

A good measure of how Oshima's *shunga*-influenced graphic depiction differs from the more urgent and clinical conventions of Western hard-core pornography can be found if we look at a particular sex scene. In contrast to the way Western moving-image pornography of the seventies is intent on revealing the exact moment at which pleasure becomes visible in the money shot, consider the way the first prolonged scene of sex between Sada and Kichi (as Sada soon calls him) builds to its conclusion. The couple pulls apart momentarily to look at one another in the dark room with its richly saturated colors. Kichi is naked, still erect, yet relaxed; Sada is in an open kimono and, as always, more intense. At this early stage of their relationship, she may also be a bit worried that Kichi has still not

81: *In the Realm of the Senses*, a minimal climax

come while it is implied that she has been in the throes of ecstasy all night. She leans forward to fellate him as he continues to lean back, lighting a cigarette. What follows corresponds in the act to the deep-throat fellatio of a film like *Deep Throat*, but with an important aesthetic difference. Sada, seen from the side at the left of the frame, enthusiastically takes the shaft deep into her mouth, while Kichi, propped on a pillow, looks on from the right. The sexual act is the very same as the famous moment in *Deep Throat*, but the quiet mood of relaxed intimacy and the inclusion of Kichi's whole body within the frame, as opposed to a close-up of just the woman's face and an ejaculating penis, could not be more different (figure 80).

The mise-en-scène of this fellatio is not arranged to exhibit the length of the shaft through repeated ins-and-outs of the penis and the oral ups-and-downs of the mouth that assure the exhibitionistic maximum visibility of hard core. Nevertheless, as in *Deep Throat*, we clearly see Kichi's vividly red, engorged, though normal-sized, penis. With no special gymnastics, Sada takes the penis into her hand and then into her mouth, moving assiduously over it as Kichi watches with slightly detached interest. "You are an extraordinary woman," he remarks. An extreme close-up of her face pressing down hard on his penis, accompanied by a small grunt from Sada marks an understated climax (figure 81) whose only visual evidence will be a small trickle of ejaculate that flows out of her mouth after she slowly pulls away to look at Kichi. This ejaculate does not fly or leap across the screen. It merely passes from Kichi into Sada and now trickles out as if a part of them both. There is no frenetic gymnastics, no enthusiastic licking, no ringing of bells, no rapid montage, no isolated shot of the ejaculating penis. Nor is there a loud theme song, or a formulaic repetition of the same signs of pleasure to signal the climax of subsequent sex acts (this, in fact, is the film's only detailed depiction of fellatio)—only a quiet conclusion to a night of lovemaking that needs some sort of end. The larger question of what constitutes the appropriate end to this couple's "realm of the senses" will prove crucial to the rest of the film.

Oshima's film thus avoids many of the qualities of a Western pornographic *scientia sexualis* familiar since the early 1970s in hard-core pornography. Does this then mean that it inserts itself into an older tradition of *ars erotica* to which *shunga* belongs? Precisely because these are images of real bodies in movement, not woodcarvings or paintings, it is not possible for them to imitate the physiological exaggerations that often occur in *shunga*, as in the physiologically improbable contortions of figure 77. Nor is it possible for Oshima, even if he were to hire the Japanese equivalent of John Holmes, to depict penises quite as immense as those in *shunga*. For this reason film scholar Peter Lehman has therefore argued that previous scholars of Oshima's film have overestimated the similarities between *Realm* and the *shunga* or *ukiyo-e* tradition Lehman hinges his argument on the fact that live actors cannot possibly equal the proportions of these penises.[37]

It is tempting, nevertheless, at least from a Western perspective, to place Oshima's film and its *shunga* influence within the older visual tradition of *ars erotica* in which pleasures are understood as accumulated practices and experiences.[38] Certainly much of the iconography of this film with its half-dressed lovers having uninhibited sex wherever they find themselves resembles the tradition of *ars erotica* that Michel Foucault argues is a product of ancient and non-Western cultures, one that passes on practices of pleasure as taught by a master to an acolyte. This iconography seems to contrast vividly with the more modern and Western tradition of a *scientia sexualis*, which aims at eliciting confessions of a more scientific truth of a sex that erupts and confesses itself without special—or at least conscious—cultivation. Do we want, therefore, to align Oshima's film with Foucault's *ars erotica* and distinguish it from the hot and hurried confessional pleasures of Western moving-image pornography which so often exists in relation to laws of the permitted and the forbidden? As we have already seen, the question is complicated by Oshima's belief that he was vying with Western and modern pornographic models. And it is further complicated by Foucault's own admission that strict dichotomies between the two traditions may break down when we come to consider the West's "pleasure of analysis" within the *scientia sexualis*, which may itself verge on "an extraordinarily subtle form of *ars erotica*."[39]

It is true that the story Oshima tells—of an older man who initiates a younger woman into the leisurely pleasures of sex—seems to operate within an *ars erotica* tradition of the cultivation and passing on of sexual techniques. In the beginning, as in this tradition, Kichi is the master guiding the less experienced Sada in the art of pleasure. One night he grabs Sada's heel from under the stairs as she descends to the bathroom. Deferring her need to pee—"It's supposed to be better," he says conspiratorially—he plays the role of the world-weary older lover who initiates Sada into the more rarified joys of unhurried sex. He tells her to slow down and not to try to serve what she presumes to be his urgent desire: "I want to feel your pleasure; we have all the time in the world." Making love until dawn in the scene cited above, Kichi remains perpetually hard. The film goes on to depict penetrative vaginal and oral sex that clearly shows explicit action. And like *shunga* prints it favors whole bodies in static long and medium shots, and even occasional overhead framings, over what the Western porn industry calls meat and money shots. Yet this distinction, which Joan Mellen makes much of, arguing for the art of whole bodies rather than the fetishization of body parts, does not hold exactly. Neither the *shunga* tradition, as in the example from a small book of erotic poses and anatomic details by Keisai Eisen from the early nineteenth century (figure 82), nor Oshima (figure 83) entirely eschew occasional close-ups of sexual organs.

Like *shunga*, Oshima's film glories in a variety of positions of the body and the genitals during sex. Like *shunga* also, the film often shows sex acts observed by third-party voyeurs or by servants who bring food and drink.[40] Also as in *shunga*, Oshima revels in the erotics of the deshabille. In contrast to modern Western moving-image pornography, bodies here are rarely completely nude; robes are open or half falling off, but they still do not function to hide sexual organs. Rather, they serve as curtains that pull back to reveal organs that persistently peep out. As in *shunga* also, sex often takes place on tatami mats on the floor, and any other place the couple finds itself. The Western tradition of the elevated bed, a special private place only for sex and sleep, does not operate.

As we have seen, however, Oshima's moving human bodies do not resemble the amazing contortions and the exaggerated organs and pubic hair of the *shunga* woodblock prints. While his bodies do entwine and wrap around one another, they do not defy physiology in either position

82: Eisen Kesei,
ca. 1822–1825.
From Marco
Fagioli, *Shunga:
The Erotic Art of
Japan* (1998)

83: *In the Realm
of the Senses*,
close-up of
penis

or organ size. Indeed, to the extent that Oshima can be said to operate within the visual tradition of *shunga*, we might qualify that he transposes its spatial exaggerations of size and position into temporal exaggerations of duration: Kichi almost never ceases to be erect, and Sada never ceases to find pleasure in this erection. The couple's pleasure is limited only by Kichi's endurance, which is remarkable.

Moreover, while Oshima knowingly operates within a tradition of explicit erotic art at one time well known in Japan, the systematic marginalization of that tradition throughout the nineteenth century as Japan sought to escape the colonized fate of other Asian countries meant that he could not count on Japanese viewers' ability to see his film. Indeed, *Senses* could not even count on Japanese viewers being able to see a film that would leave a much greater mark on Anglo-American and European audiences than on those of his own country.[41] It is not possible, then, to draw a direct line of influence between *shunga* and Oshima's film. To draw such a line would mean to ignore the fact that at a moment when much of the West was undergoing a radical proliferation of erotic and pornographic discourses of sexuality, Japan was still radically suppressing all evidence of its own artistically more prestigious hard-core traditions.[42] It is much more likely, therefore, that what looks in *Senses* like a continuation of a long-standing tradition of *ars erotica* is actually a more interesting routing of a nostalgia for this tradition though a very modern idea—perhaps even envy—of the presumed greater liberation of the Western pornographic imagination.

To provoke and challenge a Japanese cinema whose first fifty years had been marked by an extreme sexual reticence, and whose screens would not exhibit his film without blurring the views of all genitals, Oshima willfully forged a new synthesis out of elements of both *ars erotica* and *scientia sexualis*. This synthesis is most evident in Oshima's telling of the exceedingly modern story of Abe Sada. For if the director had simply wanted to reanimate the traditions of *shunga* he might have told one of the many stories of the double suicides of lovers depicted in these prints.[43] However, Sada's decision to live on after Kichi's death—perhaps, as Ruth McCormick puts it, to find other Kichis—is radically modern.[44] This couple does *not* choose the time-honored route of resolving the problems of lovers by dying together. Sada lives on instead to confess her story to both police and medical experts, most of whom commented on her unique sexual sensitivity. She is thus the very model of a woman whose sexuality was investigated under the clinical and scientific terms of a more modern *scientia sexualis*.[45]

Sada's story thus seems to be an amalgam of Western pornography's *scientia sexualis* and of Foucault's somewhat simplistic notion of a pan-Eastern and more ancient *ars erotica*. It has elements of the bottom-up confession of the secrets of a servant girl's knowledge of pleasure measured in relation to an absolute law of the permitted and the forbidden, and it has elements of the top-down initiation by a master of an acolyte to the intensities and qualities of pleasure through a connoisseurship of sex. If Foucault is correct in his observation that a Western *scientia sexualis* invents its own *ars erotica*, then perhaps this is what *In the Realm of the Senses* does. But we do well to note that both of these traditions for seeking the truth of sex, Eastern and Western, traditional and modern, are deeply androcentric in their very concept of what sex is. Whether understood as will to knowledge in which power and pleasure are intertwined or as techniques for the cultivation of pleasure, both correspond to essentially masculine economies. The master who passes on techniques of erotic arts is typically a man; and the medical expert who receives the confession of sexual secrets usually is as well. Oshima's synthesis of the two traditions is perhaps most noteworthy for reversing at least one of them.

Consider the way Kichi, who initially occupies the position of master, very soon cedes that position to Sada. Only in the first sex scene does he actually instruct her by telling her to take her time. Halfway through the film Sada takes the lead in initiating new forms of bodily ecstasy. The story of Sada is that of a woman who, once initiated by a master into the realm of the senses, learns to explore this realm according to her own, very different, economy of pleasure and who then brings the man along with her as far as he can go. She may resemble American pornographic heroines like Linda Lovelace in *Deep Throat* and Justine Jones in *The Devil in Miss Jones* (dir. Gerard Damiano, 1973) in her all-consuming need for the penis and in her initial status as an acolyte to a master of pleasure. However, she is unique in forging conditions for the achievement of phallic pleasure in collaboration with a man who gives himself up to her entirely. Her own near infinite capacity for pleasure will spur her lover on to the absolute limits of his own.[46] Oshima thus embraces neither the Western *scientia sexualis* of countable involuntary male convulsions, measurable in ejaculate and presumed to stand in for the whole pleasure of the couple in commercial pornography, nor the Eastern *ars erotica* of a master who passes on the secrets of pleasure to a disciple. Rather, he embraces what we might call a modern *ars sexualis* through the temporal medium of cinema. To understand what that is, we must think a little more about sexual timing and sexual violence.

The Bullfight of Love

In the previous chapter, mainstream American movies were seen to discover female orgasms as physically and emotionally satisfying climaxes that needed more time to perfectly coincide with the pleasures of men. A seemingly happy convergence of sexology and feminism, combined with a narrative of antiwar activism produced a new, simulated representation of sexual pleasure as a prolonged clitoral orgasm that was more gentle than the "jabbing, thrusting eroticism" that had so amazed Pauline Kael in *Last Tango in Paris* or the phallic exhibitionism that had so impressed Al Goldstein in *Deep Throat*. Jane Fonda broke new ground by portraying what could only be presumed as a clitoral orgasm in no need of penetration and in response to which she would significantly call out not the usual command, "harder," but the much rarer, "softly!" Fonda was portrayed as discovering her pleasure when she was freed to be out of sync with her phallically impaired lover.

In the Realm of the Senses also presents a different female orgasmic potential linked to an ethic of love rather than war. But Sada and Kichi's love will culminate in a warlike violence in which eros and thanatos converge. Theirs is an animal sexuality in which, as Georges Bataille famously puts it, "the violence of one goes out to meet the violence of the other."[47] Nor would Matsuda Eiko's Sada, in contrast to Fonda's Sally, ever call out for a soft touch. She demands that Kichi's penis be perpetually hard and perpetually inside her. Her fantasy is that the couple might be eternally and orgasmically in sync, and she will eventually fiercely call out to her lover: "I'm killing you!" In the end she will take control of Kichi's erection through the process of strangulation just as she will take control of his severed penis. Thus, where *Coming Home* depicts its female-centric orgasm through the effacement of the penis, *Realm* depicts its female-centric orgasm through the penis's visibility, exaggerated hardness, and perpetual readiness for action.

Given its violence it is quite remarkable how Oshima's graphically hardcore film refrains from organizing its sexual acts around the spectacle of male ejaculation so familiar in other hard-core verhicles. And even the one scene, which does end in ejaculation, constructs the act anticlimactically. Initially, Sada and Kichi aspire to the perfectly coincident meeting of male and female bodies "on time" at a moment of mutual readiness much like male-dominant heterosexual Western pornography. This pornography, as we have seen, works overtime to seem to match the woman's pleasures to the measure of the man's. Oshima's film seems to begin with this same goal, but then turns into the reverse: though it never abandons a fixed interest in the male organ as a source of pleasure for both the man and the woman (and is thus quite literally phallocentric), it shifts the temporal rhythms of pleasure away from the man, who first "teaches" Sada to slow down and take her time, onto the rhythm of the woman who, like Barbarella in the Exsexive Machine, has no limit to her pleasure. Toward the end it is Kichi who labors to keep pace and to coincide with Sada's prolonged and intense pleasures. Instead of the conceit of the male and female coincidence of pleasure at the moment of the visible male ejaculation, *In the Realm of the Senses* offers an even more impossible fantasy: to transcend the very finitude of climax itself. In place of a squirt of ejaculate as the sign for a supposedly mutual ecstasy of the couple, the film develops a long swoon that aims to abolish the separation between discrete individuals.

The primary difference between *Senses* and the pornography he both envied and productively misconstrued is not that Oshima's work belongs to a long-standing tradition of classy erotic art, while Western hard core constitutes a crass popular genre. Rather, it is that his film cultivates a new erotic-pornographic fantasy—one in which the woman's temporal rhythm of ecstasy is taken as the standard and the man aspires to meet it. It is in this quality that Oshima's film most differs both from the traditional top-down pedagogy of *ars erotica* and from the bottom-up confession of *scientia sexualis*.

This female-centered model of continuous sexual pleasure at first lends a relaxed casualness to the growing aberrations of Sada and Kichi's sexual encounters. If sex is ongoing then it need not always be the foreground of the narrative, but can also serve as a background accompaniment to other actions. The couple sings, eats, drinks, and converses—all the while having sex, sometimes highly aroused, sometimes only mildly.[48] Kichi savors mushrooms and other morsels dipped in the "sauce" of Sada's vaginal juices ("All we do, even eating, must be an act of love," says Sada).[49] He consumes a hard-boiled egg "laid" from her vagina; he matches Sada's oral acceptance of his ejaculate by licking his fingers dipped in her menstrual blood. They perform sex in a variety of moods as their intimacy grows. Sada even cuts off and eats a few strands of Kichi's pubic hair as a sign of her devotion, though also, I think, as a direct slap to the Japanese censors' special prohibition of any display of pubic hair. "It's as if he was yours," says Kichi of his penis. He jokes that the only time he gets a rest is when he goes to pee, while Sada jealously begrudges him even these few moments of necessary flaccidity.

Eventually, of course, the fantasy of unending mutual pleasure in the realm of the senses must encounter limits. Just as the womblike apartment of the couple in *Last Tango* is ultimately encroached on by reality, so Kichi must eventually pee and the couple must eat if life is to be sustained. Where most moving-image depictions of sex elide these more mundane bodily functions, this film's concentration on the temporal duration of sex acts lends a material grounding to these other bodily needs. Without funds, cut off from the food and shelter of Kichi's jealous wife, they rely on

Sada's infrequent sexual services to an elderly professor for income. But the pain caused to each of them by even these brief separations proves unbearable, and Kichi asks her not to leave again.

The film increasingly juxtaposes the glamour of the threat of violence with the pathos of old age and impotence. Sada wields a large knife (figure 84) and repeatedly threatens to cut off Kichi's penis so that he will not be tempted to have sex with his wife and so as to keep him inside her always. "If I cut him off will you die?" (figure 85). "Most likely," answers Kichi, matter-of-factly. But the allure of the knife remains, and Sada will eventually perform precisely this castration, though only after she has first killed Kichi by other means. The need to find the means to a violent love-death becomes increasingly urgent the more the film shows us the alternative of growing old. Early in the narrative, the specter of old age is embodied by an elderly beggar who recognizes Sada from better times when he was her client. "You were always so happy," he remembers. Sada eventually indulges him, but his penis, which cruel children have already pelted with snowballs and probed with sticks that wave Japanese flags, remains limp. Sada is kind; she strokes the organ in sympathy when it fails to rise and seems genuinely to regret its impotence. In another scene, during a mock wedding ceremony in which Sada and Kichi are entertained by geishas who join them in an orgy, a withered old man does a birdlike dance over the entwined youthful bodies (figure 86). Yet another old man in a restaurant informs Sada and Kichi that his penis is only good for peeing.

In contrast to the impotence of these old men, we see the greater potency of the aged female body. When an elderly geisha who entertains the couple at an inn notes that their continuous lovemaking in her presence is a "pleasure to the eyes," Sada invites her to have sex with the always obliging, though in this case not particularly eager, Kichi. The surprised geisha and Kichi couple awkwardly, in a scene that emphasizes the white pallor of her made-up, wrinkled face in contrast to the flesh color of the rest of her body (figure 87). Sada watches from close by, naked and crouched on all fours. Her face reveals a mixture of horror, fascination, and sympathy at Kichi's embrace with mortality. Afterwards he lies inert on the old woman until Sada slaps his buttocks to revive him. Kichi confesses that having sex with the geisha was like having sex with the corpse of his mother. In these powerful intimations of mortality both he and Sada seem to recognize the stakes of their own relation. "Everything must have an end," declares Sada. Faced with the combined spectacle of old men who can no longer get it up and an old woman who can, but whose desire has

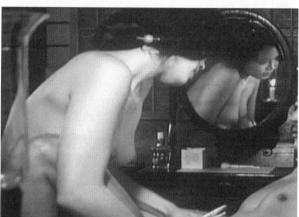

In the Realm of the Senses

84: Sada wields a large knife

85: "If I cut it off will you die?"

86: Old man dances over entwined youthful bodies

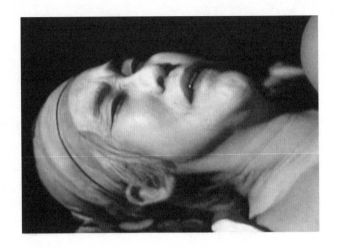

87: In the
*Realm of the
Senses*, the old
geisha's face

almost outlived her flesh, the couple seeks its own solution to the finitude of passion.

Kichi, however, remains understandably shy of the knife. After he has lapsed and returned to his wife, a jealous Sada, knife in one hand, penis in the other, threatens to cut. Kichi resigns himself: "I accept everything you ask, forgive me for having left you for three days," he says, and then invites her to punish him, though not with the knife: "Hurt me as much as you like." The couple now flirts more seriously with sadomasochistic acts in marathon sessions of lovemaking in which Sada is encouraged to "take the lead." After Sada introduces mild blows, Kichi suggests that they might try strangulation. Sada immediately invites him to strangle her. But when he finds no enjoyment in this act, Sada climbs on to his erect penis (always her preferred position), squeezes his throat with her hands, and articulates her pleasure to an increasingly red-faced Kichi: The subtitles read: "You can't imagine how good I feel; he's moving alone; it's so good!" It would seem to be the power to make Kichi's penis move inside her through her control of his strangulation that most excites Sada.[50]

Never does the violence of strangulation *replace* the act of sex. Violence enhances it, accompanies it and, in the end, makes the abandonment of the one to the other possible. For this reason it would not be exact to call Sada (despite the accidental resonance of her name to Western ears) a sadist,[51] nor would it be exact to call Kichi a masochist. The strict definition of both perversions entails the giving or taking of pain as substitutes for the sexual act. This does not mean, however, that their sex is without sadomasochistic elements.[52] The violence of strangulation will soon be taken to the extreme, not only to cause Kichi's swoon but his death. He will choose this death, in the short term, to avoid the aftermath of the pain of strangulation. In the long term, he chooses it to avoid the pain of a life that cannot be lived only for pleasure. At this point he is far from the masochist who seeks to prolong pain in pleasure; rather, he is a mortal man trying to prolong his ability to give pleasure. Sada will allow Kichi to die, even though it means that he will not survive to be hard again, thus giving up control over the pleasure he gives her for the sake of the final swoon, the "little death" that brings her to the brink of death and pushes Kichi all the way over.

"Eroticism," writes Bataille, "is assenting to life up to the point of death,"[53] and his book on this subject is full of insights applicable to the sexual violence of this film. Indeed, the Japanese title for the film, *Ai no corrida* (*Bullfight of Love*), would seem to allude to Bataille's infamous description of the pornographic evisceration of a matador's eye coincident with his heroine's insertion of the eye-shaped ball of a bull into her vagina in his pornographic novella, *Histoire de l'oeil* (*Story of the Eye*). Similarly, the French title of the film, *L'empire des sens* (literally, *Empire of the Senses*, from which comes the English title), echoes another French source: Roland Barthes's then popular semiological study of Japan, *L'empire des signes* (*The Empire of Signs*). Although *Ai no corrida* captures more of the Bataillian quality of the violence of an eros that extends "beyond the pleasure principle" into the domain of violence, violation, and death, both titles further suggest the strong Western influences on Oshima's film. Death, like orgasm, is for Bataille a violent wrenching of the discontinuous life of the individual into the continuity of the inanimate from which we emerge and to which we must return.

Eroticism, Bataille argues, constitutes a plethora of life that at the extreme tips over into death, into the domain of sacrifice, violence, and violation. It lies, like death, "beyond the pleasure principle." This title of one of Sigmund Freud's most confounding works exploring the limits of mere pleasure, reminds us, like Bataille, of the paradox that eros and thanatos are not necessarily opposites—that death is not simply the end of life but a return to the continuity of the inanimate matter of the universe. We saw in chapter 1's discussion of the orality of kisses that Freud's theory of sexuality is often caught between two different models of pleasure: one that is teleological and believes in the progression toward an end pleasure of release and discharge, and one that contains a certain admixture of unpleasure that does not aim at discharge but at a prolongation of sexual excitement and at the ecstatic itself. Leo Bersani, as I have had occasion to recall, refers to this distinction as the difference between an itch that is scratched to end it and an itch "that seeks nothing better than its own pro-longation, even its own intensification."[54] At the limit, this prolongation can become the "'desiring' destruction of objects in order to possess them internally."[55] Bersani argues, contra the discharge model that Freud some-times seems to espouse, that the destruction of the love object "appears to be inherent in sexual excitement itself" and that many phases of love, especially the pregenital oral and anal phases, produce sexual excitement through shattering fantasies of "incorporating or devouring."[56]

In the Realm of the Senses extends polymorphously perverse infantile fantasies of incorporating or devouring the other into the realm of the genital. Sada's desire, unlike that of conventional pornography since *Deep Throat*, is never to satisfy, or to discharge Kichi's penis into or onto her body. It is the more fantasmatic desire to incorporate this love object into herself and to prolong the violence of the one that reaches out to the vio-lence of the other. Kichi's death is not her actual goal. It is the gradually accepted by-product of their pursuit of a fantasy of pleasure that is not only coincidental ("on time!") but beyond time, merged into a new entity beyond their discrete individual selves.

I have been arguing, however, that the fantasy of perpetual ecstasy as it is played out in Oshima's film also acknowledges, as Freud, Bataille, and Bersani do not, the frequent temporal disarticulation of male and female pleasure. Kichi dies because he is unable to persist, as Sada and even the old geisha can, in an ecstasy that goes beyond the discrete, finite discharge of male orgasm. Sada lives because she is able to experience more and more excitation without discharge or end-pleasure release. After making love to the near corpse of the old geisha, Kichi had implored Sada: "Don't let our pleasure ever end."[57] His love-death is the result of the couple's at-tempt to accommodate Kichi's finite orgasm and temporal satiety to Sada's infinite satiety in insatiety—her ability to prolong ecstasy. You might say Kichi dies trying.

In the attenuated final scene, the couple meets back at their inn and strikes a bargain. Instead of the ever-present knife, which Kichi again makes Sada put away, he asks to be strangled, qualifying this by adding, "I want to give you pleasure." Sada makes him clarify not only that he desires her pleasure but that he desires his own strangulation because it keeps him erect. From this point on, the lovers play with the fine line between ecstasy and oblivion (the blackouts that cause Kichi to lose erec-tion). Bataille explains that on one hand, "the convulsions of the flesh are more acute when they are near to a blackout, and on the other a blackout, as long as there is enough time, makes physical pleasure more exquisite.

88: *In the Realm of the Senses*, Sada astride Kichi as she strangles him

Mortal anguish does not necessarily make for sensual pleasure, but that pleasure is more deeply felt during mortal anguish."[58]

In the first stage of this play with "mortal anguish," an ecstatic Sada thrills at her control of Kichi's penis; she feels it more intensely with each tug of the pink scarf that she now uses instead of her hands to strangle him. She faces the camera astride Kichi, her red kimono open. The top of Kichi's head is in the foreground (figure 88). While beautiful, the image is also explicit: we see Kichi's penis moving up and down as Sada moves over him. Though Sada cries out, "I'm killing you," in fact, she pulls back from the final squeeze to let her lover again breathe. In a hoarse whisper, he tells her to pull harder. When he involuntarily raises his hands to free his throat, Sada scolds him, saying she was near ecstasy. Now she ties his hands: "Do what you please," says Kichi. "My body is yours." Connected through penile penetration and the umbilical pink scarf about Kichi's neck, the couple fuses beyond the bliss of lovers to become like one body, not two.

The strangulation is both the means to Sada's ecstasy and to the violent death that will exempt Kichi from the fate of old men who can no longer get it up. Sada matches each thrust of her body over his penis with tugs on the scarf, gaining his assent each step of the way while making it clear to him that she will proceed even if it kills him. She asks if it hurts; he shakes his head no. She asks how it feels, and he says, "Like I'm part of you; our bodies have melted into one, bathing in a crimson pool."[59] Sada continues squeezing, and their bodies are reframed in a longer shot that shows them in the center of the room bathed in a crimson light (figure 89).

In the next scene, Sada waits, playing idly with an empty sake bottle,

*In the Realm of
the Senses*

89: "bathed
in a crimson
light"

90: Sada alone
in the stadium

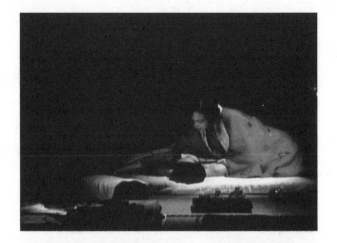

while Kichi, looking gray and fragile, sleeps. When he revives, we see the rawness of his neck and that he can barely stay awake to attend to Sada's desire. When he dozes, she slaps him awake. Though he tries mightily to attend to her sexual needs, he is soft. Sada masturbates herself with his flaccid penis; squeezes it hard to get a rise out of him, but nothing short of strangulation will make him get hard again. Kichi is ready for this, but in a raspy voice he admonishes her: "This time, don't stop in the middle; it's too painful afterwards." Sada crawls over to get the scarf, shakes him awake, and announces to a Kichi who already seems to be elsewhere that she is pulling. This time we do not see if Kichi's penis responds. Indeed, we do not see anything more of their coupling or of Kichi's death. All we see is a shot of the couple interlaced at an unspecified time, followed by a

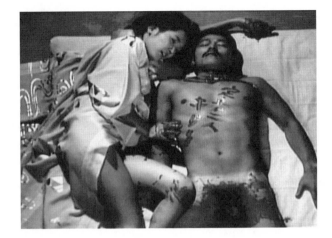

cut to Sada lying naked in the sun on a concrete platform in the middle of an empty stadium (figure 90).

In long shot, a man—it could be Kichi—is playfully chased by a young girl among the bleachers of the stadium. The girl repeatedly calls out in a singsong, "Are you ready?" and the man repeatedly replies, "No, not yet."[60] However one translates the question and answer of this children's game akin to hide-and-seek, it would seem to repeat elements of Sada's relation to Kichi, especially the quest for temporal coincidence, a coming together "on time!" that eludes the girl in the game as she tries to capture a man never quite as ready as she. Sada, still lying supine in the midst of this game but now seen in a close view, tries to speak, but no sound comes out of her mouth. In long shot again she sits up; the young girl and the man have disappeared. Alone in the vast stadium, she calls, "Kichi-san" in a mournful last cry to which there is no answer. The stadium, as Leger Grindon points out, could allude to the titular bullfight, and through that, to Bataille's deadly depiction of the game of love.[61]

Back in the room at the inn, Sada in her open red kimono stands over the lifeless body of Kichi, laid out under covers on a futon. Using the long knife with which she had repeatedly threatened Kichi's dismemberment in moments of anger and jealousy, she pulls back the covers and now performs the castration we have been anticipating and dreading all along. Though she does it with love, it is a brutal physical act. In close-up, we see her first slice off his engorged penis, then, this time without our seeing the cutting, his testicles. These bloodied objects drop on the mat beside Kichi's body. A final overhead shot reveals the final tableau: Kichi's supine, naked, castrated body with Sada in kimono alongside him. On his body, written in blood, are the words "Sada/Kichi. Two of us together" (figure 91). Suddenly an abrupt male voice-over announces: "For four days, carrying the part she had severed from his body, Sada wandered through Tokyo. Those arresting her were astounded that she glowed with happiness. The compassion of the people made her strangely popular. These events happened in 1936."

The film was widely reviewed. Some critics maintained they were bored, others were outraged, and some were enthralled. But almost all offered at least grudging admiration for the film's formal beauty and the performances of its primary characters, the *roman poruno* actress Matsuda Eiko as Sada and the "legitimate" film actor Fuki Tatsuya as Kichi. Many reviewers immediately saw resemblances or differences with the mad-love theme of *Last Tango* and/or iconic resemblances or differences with *Deep Throat* and its progeny.[62]

In laudable, but I think misguided, efforts to defend the film, more than one critic insisted, contra Oshima's own assertions, that it was not pornography because it did not solicit the arousal of its spectators. Joan Mellen and Ruth McCormick, both insightful close readers of the film, insisted that it did not seek to arouse. McCormick writes, for example, that it is "purified of any hint of the exhibitionism, objectification" of its Western counterparts.[63] Mellen similarly asserts that it "permits little vicarious arousal by a spectator. The participants have earned the right to sexual bliss; the audience is led to reflect on how and at what cost they have achieved this perfect sexual expression and is not meant to join in."[64]

I have been arguing, to the contrary, that *In the Realm of the Senses* offers a fascinating amalgam of Japanese and Western pornography and that neither of these traditions is free of what critics and legal scholars like to call prurience: *both* seek to arouse. The Eastern influence is not purer because it is more artful. *Shunga* woodprints were well known as sexual aids and stimulants. Some, such as the example reproduced here from Koryusai Isoda, even show couples consulting *shunga* books while engaged in sex (figure 92). I have not argued that Oshima's film descends in a direct line from *shunga*. My point, rather, has been that this film borrows elements of that tradition in conjunction with those of the West. We do Oshima an injustice if we think of his art as purified and of the filmmaker himself as one who wants only to make us think. To do so is to deny the obvious ability of this most lushly sensual of films to move us—whether to arousal or to horrified revulsion. Mellen's attempt to argue, for example, that frequent reframings to high angles distance and remove us from the

92: Isoda Koryusai, ca. 1770–1775. From Marco Fagioli, *Shunga: The Erotic Art of Japan* (1998)

action,[65] almost willfully ignores the many other in-your-face close-ups—close-ups of penis (attached and otherwise), vagina, and mouth, and the fact, as we have seen, that such close-ups also existed in *shunga*. The film thus both affords distance and brings us exceedingly close to objects of desire and terror.

Castration is typically viewed as a recognition of lack. The entire edifice of Lacanian psychoanalysis is grounded on this concept of the threatened loss of the penis as the foundation of human subjectivity—for both males and females. In this film, however, castration is imagined from the other side: not as the loss to the male but as the incorporation of the fetishized love object into the narcissistic self of the woman; as gain, in other words, not loss. Sada "glows with happiness." And her happiness depends on a breaking down of boundaries between ego and world; it is what Bersani calls a "psychic shattering" of pleasurable and nonpleasurable and what Bataille calls sexual plethora.[66]

Rarely does one experience so powerful a gender-bifurcated response as that which occurs in the public screenings of this film. All audiences gasp at the severing of Kichi's organs, but there can be no doubt that men gasp more, even clutching at their groins,[67] perhaps incorporating into their bodies the pain that the dead Kichi would feel were he sentient. They may also feel that the rug of the pornographic expectation of pleasure has been pulled out from under them in this final act. However, this rug has not been pulled out unfairly: the ending has been carefully prepared from the very beginning, and viewers familiar with classics of literary eroticism may not be surprised by Sada's final act.

What has not been prepared for in *Senses* is any *generic* cultural expectation by a public film audience of the kind of extreme shift between hard-core depictions of pleasure and special-effects depictions of violence. Neither the tradition of a Western moving-image pornography influenced by *scientia sexualis* nor that of a visual *ars erotica* prepares a social audience sitting in a theater for the violence of the film's end. Western audiences are so used to moving-image pornography in the mode of pleasurable discharge that *In the Realm of the Senses* disturbs by the simple fact of mixing (hard-core, unsimulated) sex with (simulated) violence. The shift to the special effects of violence is jarring and deeply disturbing precisely because moving-image pornography draws us into a belief in the hard-core reality of the bodies and organs it presents. The violence of this ending is thus much more wrenching than the usual acts of mayhem of films of action and violence.

Susan Sontag, in an essay about French literary pornography, has challenged the common notion espoused by many sexual liberals that sexuality is simply a "natural, pleasant function." This idea that sexuality is natural usually invokes the counteridea that obscenity is then a "fiction imposed upon nature"—a fiction imposed by a society convinced there is something vile about sexual functions.[68] Oshima himself, as we have seen, expressed much the same idea when he argued that obscenity might disappear along with the taboos against it if only pornographic cinema were authorized.[69] Sontag argues, in contrast, that the great pornographers, from Sade through Bataille and the authors of *Story of O* and *The Image*, reveal sexuality as an obscenity, as a primal notion of human consciousness, something "more profound" than a sick society's aversion to the natural body. Obscenity, she asserts, belongs "among the extreme rather than the ordinary experiences of humanity."[70] It is "one of the demonic forces in human consciousness—pushing us at intervals close to taboo and dangerous desires, which range from the impulse to commit sudden arbitrary violence upon another person to the voluptuous yearning for the extinction of one's consciousness, for death itself."[71] Of course Sontag was writing about high art literary pornography, not film.

It has long been something of an axiom in thinking about filmic obscenity that while it might be desirable to break the taboos against representing bodies, organs, and intercourse in literature or art, the inherently graphic nature of moving-image media lends the literal display of real bodies, organs, and intercourse a coarseness exemplified by Fredric Jameson's condemnation of the visual itself as a pornographic form of "rapt, mindless fascination."[72] Indeed, the received opinion about film has long been that its inherently graphic nature makes its pornography necessarily crass and mindless. Certainly a lot of it is. And certainly what Sade, Bataille, and Pauline Réage did with words can be more disturbing when real bodies act out the "extreme . . . experiences of humanity."

However, what might be called our cinematic imagination of obscenity has been terribly circumscribed by certain received opinions—opinions about sex, opinions about the realism, as opposed to the fantasy, of movies, opinions about the nature of the obscene itself. When Oshima decided to make a "'pornographic film'—not an average 'film,' [but] a 'pornographic film' all the way,"[73] he became the intrepid and solitary pioneer of a kind of hard-core art into which only a very few avant-garde filmmakers had previously ventured. No narrative film besides *In the Realm of the Senses* had ever come close to the literary tradition of hard-core eroticism. Just as it has been important to recognize pornography as a genre of pleasure among other film genres, so it is equally important to recognize the much more rarified achievement of this exceptional example of hard-core eroticism operating beyond the pleasure principle. We shall see in chapter 7 how this singular film would point the way, two decades later, to the contemporary explorations of new forms of hard-core art by filmmakers like Catherine Breillat, Patrice Chéreau, Michael Winterbottom, Lars von Trier, and others. To all of these younger directors Oshima's film would serve as the crucial benchmark.[74] Understanding hard-core film art is not a matter of parsing good sex from bad, or determining which graphic sexual representations have gone "too far." Nor is it a matter of invoking the old chestnut about the pitfalls of leaving "nothing to the imagination." Rather, as we have begun to see in this chapter and will further explore in a later one, there are many possible ways of getting graphic as movies open up the question of the imagination of sex beyond the familiar formulas of soft and hard.

Coda: Last Tango in Tokyo

A love story using the metaphor of the mortal bullfight the way *Last Tango* uses the metaphor of the tango, *In the Realm of the Senses* explores much of the same territory of Bataillian eroticism as the meeting place of sex and death as Bertolucci's film. Given the fact that Bertolucci's 1972 work launched the utopian dream of an X-rated art film that Oshima's 1976 creation was the first to realize in a truly hard-core fashion, a concluding comparison of these two landmark X-rated films seems important. Both films are about an older man and a younger woman who cut themselves off from the social conventions of an outside world to engage in an obsessive *amour fou*. Though Brando's Paul tells Schneider's Jeanne that she must go "right up into the ass of death" to discover the "womb of fear," Jeanne is never Paul's collaborator in the exploration of love-death. Instead, she simply becomes an uncomprehending instrument of his death. The lessons of love and death—what Kael called a "jabbing, thrusting eroticism"—all flow in one direction, from the man to the woman and in correspondence with male timing. At the moment in which the power shifts between the two—the moment at which Jeanne might have come into her own as an actual sexual subject—the relationship breaks off. When Paul tries to resume it, it is already too late. Where the derisive tango that Jeanne and Paul dance at the end of that film symbolizes the end of passion, the "bullfight" in which Sada and Kichi engage is a two-way street; it permits them to escape their times and to celebrate, through death and dismemberment, the psychic shattering of love.

Bertolucci's film both benefits and suffers from the presence of its great male star. While Brando's performance brought an undeniable complexity and vulnerable sexual energy to the role, his very stardom prevented the film from delivering on the premise of the dynamism of the sexual relation between Jeanne and Paul, leaving Schneider's naked Jeanne and Brando's clothed Paul unequally exposed. In the end, the overpowering presence of the male star unbalances the picture, leaving Jeanne, the woman who kills, a mere villain, with no real sympathy with his erotic quest. In contrast, as both characters and performers, Fuji Tatsuyo and Matsuda Eiko go the distance and defy convention.

Thus where Bertolucci's eroticism falters in the end and turns rancid, exposing Paul's conventionality, Oshima's succeeds in escaping, through a violent death that is also love, an even bleaker world of mounting war and fascism. The death Kichi embraces is shocking but beautiful in the way of what André Breton once called "convulsive beauty."[75] By the time Jeanne kills Paul in *Last Tango*, the "realm of the senses" they had inhabited in their furnitureless apartment has entirely dissipated. The cold violence of this murder is love turned to hate, while Sada's strangulation and emasculation of Kichi can be recognized as acts of love. The point is not to contrast the failure of mad love in the decadent West to its success in the East. Rather, it is to recognize the boldness of Oshima's hard-core erotic vision and the model it would provide for a new generation of eroticists to be explored in a later chapter.

Don't you fucking look at me!
—FRANK BOOTH in *Blue Velvet* (1986)

What the fuck are you looking at?
—ENNIS DEL MAR in *Brokeback Mountain* (2005)

6

primal scenes on

American screens

(1986–2005)

In the last third of Pedro Almodóvar's 2002 film, *Talk to Her* (*Hable con ella*), we are presented with a charming seven-minute, black-and-white silent film. Benigno (Javier Cámara), an effeminate male nurse working the night shift, describes this silent film to his comatose patient, Alicia (Leonor Watling), while giving her naked body one of its regular massages. Benigno adores his patient despite the fact that doctors say she is brain dead. As he relates the story of the film, called *The Shrinking Lover*, we see it on the screen: A slightly overweight man, Alfredo, watches his scientist girlfriend, Amparo, concoct a diet formula that he impulsively drinks. Soon after, while kissing Amparo, Alfredo shrinks slightly. He continues to shrink for the rest of the short film, until he is no larger, as the film scholar Marsha Kinder puts it, than a fetus or a tampon.[1] Failing to find the antidote for Alfredo's shrinking, Amparo can only care for him as if he were a tiny child. In bed one night, a Tom Thumb–sized

93: *Talk to Her* (dir. Pedro Almodóvar, 2002), Alfredo plunges into the giant vagina

Alfredo makes the Herculean effort of pulling the sheet off of Amparo's naked, sleeping body. He roams over its contours, climbs up and then rolls down the hill of a breast, descends the length of her body to the genitals, and jumps down to the V formed by her parted legs. There he faces a patently fake, giant vagina with curly, plastic-looking hair. He tentatively inserts an arm into the dark cavity, then briefly his entire torso, and comes back out for air, shaken (figure 93). Taking a final resolution, he turns to face the vaginal opening, removes his shorts and plunges naked into it. Soon only his feet protrude, then nothing. We see Amparo's face register fleeting pleasure and Benigno's voice-over concludes that the film's hero "stayed inside her forever."

With this silent film-within-a-film Almodóvar reveals the two major taboos of the contemporary art cinema that had already been challenged by Oshima Nagisa's *In the Realm of the Senses* (1976) and that would be more directly challenged toward the end of the century by the hard-core art film: an erect penis (impersonated by Alfredo himself) and an exposed vagina (the giant anatomically correct but patently fake labia, hair, and cavity that the famously gay Almodóvar must have had a lot of fun constructing). Of course, Almodóvar's clever circumnavigation of the rules for the display of sex only proves their power, especially when we learn that the comically obscene episode in a silent film recounted by Benigno serves as a screen for the much less benign act it conceals: Benigno's actual rape of the comatose Alicia. Later in the film we will learn that the half-mad and inappropriately named Benigno impregnated his patient this very night. The poignant insertion of Alfredo's body into his lover's vagina had thus concealed for us, and perhaps for Benigno himself, the actually coercive nature of the act. This silent film is thus a screen in the precise sense I have been using this word throughout this book:[2] it both reveals in explicit detail a phallic act of vaginal penetration while also screening out the violent and graphic coercion of rape that lies behind it.[3]

When I first saw *Talk to Her* I had already left the theater by the time I realized that the film had hoodwinked me into feeling sympathy for a rapist—into experiencing his act as he had deluded himself to experience it: as love, sacrifice, and a disappearing merger with the body of his beloved rather than sexual violation of an unconscious woman. As I laughed at the outlandishness of the fake vagina and the old-fashioned silent film acting, and at how the little man was a kind of surrogate penis "swallowed" up by his love's giant vagina, I was maneuvered into keeping sympathy with this most endearing of Almodóvarian protagonists. To this day, I am not quite sure how to react to the scene. Feminist consciousness has taught me to abhor what Carol Clover calls the "old style" rape films that invited the viewer to adopt the rapist's point of view and that often show the woman lying back and enjoying it.[4]

Almodóvar's portrayal of rape, to the contrary, *does* ask me, insidiously, without my even quite knowing it, to adopt a rapist's point of view. Only later, as Alicia becomes pregnant and the evidence points to Benigno, do I realize what has transpired. Yet by the end of the film, I weep at this rapist's graveside right along with his friend. Even more audaciously, the film goes so far as to portray the rape as having been a cure: the impregnation awakens Alicia from her coma, like a sleeping beauty.

Perverse Provocations of the Peek-a-boo

Almodóvar's challenge to political correctness in this screened-out scene of rape is typical of the kind of perverse provocation discovered in many European art films since the eighties. Rape is, in fact, a frequent act in Almodóvar's films. His first feature (*Pepi, Luci, Bom, and Other Girls on the Heap* [*Pepi, Luci, Bom, y otras chicas del montón*], 1980) depicted the rape of a virgin who sought revenge on her rapist not because she regretted the loss of "innocence," but for purely pecuniary reasons: he deprived her of the profits she would have otherwise reaped selling her virginity herself.[5]

Almodóvar's 1986 film *Matador* also features a rape—this time a failed one. It tells the story of a repressed, highly religious young man, Angel (Antonio Banderas), studying to be a bullfighter. To prove his manhood to his ex-matador teacher, Diego, he attempts to rape Diego's girlfriend.

Angel wants to be guilty of sexual crimes (rape and murder) to prove his masculinity against the suspicion of homosexuality, but he comically fails in his attempt. Pulling a Swiss army knife on the woman, he accidentally draws out the corkscrew. When he begins to go to the family priest to confess his would-be sin, he initially walks toward the confessional, but instead of confession to the priest, the next shot shows him in the police station confessing to the law. The detective, himself coded gay, assumes that it is Angel who has been raped but indulgently invites him, with not a little prurient interest, to "tell me how you did it." He thus incites Angel's further confession to all manner of invented sexual crimes.

Angel's confessions in quick succession to the priest, the police, and a therapist, each of whom takes a prurient interest in his (ultimately bogus) crimes, are almost a textbook illustration of Michel Foucault's assertion of the role of confession in constructing the "truth" of sex. The confession, Foucault argues, has long been a key technique of Western culture's quest for the truth of sex. But as confession moved from the confessional to the analyst's couch, it was "no longer a question of saying what was done—the sexual act—and how it was done; but of reconstructing, in and around the act, the thoughts that recapitulated it, the obsessions that accompanied it, the images, desires, modulations and quality of the pleasure that animated it. For the first time no doubt, a society has taken upon itself to solicit and hear the imparting of individual pleasures."[6] Confession thus becomes not simply the unburdening of guilt; it becomes an incitement to speak sex, to make it the motive force of our lives. Though Foucault refers especially to the great period of the formation of a "confessional science" that "took for its object what was unmentionable but admitted to nonetheless," he could equally be talking about Almodóvar's film.[7] *Matador* offers a knowing parable of Foucault's description of the role of confession in the "implantation of perversions." The aptly named Angel has committed no crime, but through confession, when faced with police pictures of sadomasochistic murders, he cannot distinguish between his own actions and desires and those of others. What he confesses to, in fact, are the sexual crimes of Diego, his teacher, who has taken up raping and killing women after retiring from the ring and losing the opportunity to kill bulls.

Teaching his bullfighting students, Diego explains what we later understand to be an account of the link between his sadistic pleasure as a matador and as a lover. "Chicks are like bulls," he explains, "you just have to hem them in." Gradually we learn that Diego is a sadist who finds his sexual thrill in killing female victims. But in the film's opening sequence the simplicity of this male voyeur-rapist-killer scenario is complicated by the presence of a female figure who is also a sadist; she lures men to their death and stabs them with a long hairpin. With the introduction of this second protagonist, Maria, the usual binary of the active, masculine voyeur-sadist who unleashes aggression on a passive, feminine exhibitionist-masochist is complicated. We are asked to look more deeply into the nature of the matador's art. A matador, we soon learn, does not simply hem in a bull and kill him. Rather, he must seduce the bull into charging at him; he must first open himself up to the bull as a target to then be able to kill it.

This more complicated seduction-aggression and masochism-sadism is what the film gives us in the opening scene. Maria seduces an anonymous man. She leads him up a flight of stairs, pulls on his belt, bites him playfully, and mounts him. We could say that he penetrates her, but her gestures are the more active in this simulated sex scene. And if she opens herself up to penetration by him, it is only to penetrate him eventually with a long and lethal hairpin. She exults over his expiring body, finally dead as a bull. In this scene the woman (*chick* is entirely the wrong word!) is the matador and the man the bull.[8]

Diego was therefore wrong: "chicks" are *not* like bulls, and in Maria he meets his match. In the sadomasochistic scenario it is not easy to assign fixed gender roles. Indeed, we might thus say that some "chicks" are like matadors, and that some matadors are like "chicks"—they find their destiny in being gored. Diego, for example, is acting out a perverse repetition compulsion: his desire is only partly to phallically penetrate; it is, more important, to be gored again, this time fatally, by a feminized bull.

This is exactly what happens when, during a tryst timed to coincide with a solar eclipse, Maria and Diego finally have their "Duel in the Sun" in a sadomasochistic love-death.[9] Diego dresses in his bullfighter regalia, and Maria, who has fetishized this regalia ever since she first saw him gored, spreads out his cape and sprinkles rose petals before a flickering fire. Soon she is on her back seminaked before the fire. In an over-the-top staging of a lethal sexual fantasy, Diego lightly strokes her pubis with a rose between his teeth and works his way up to her erect nipples, while the bolero "Espera me in cielo" is sung on the soundtrack. "Till now I have always made love alone," says Maria. "I love you more than my own death! Would you like to see me dead?" "Yes," replies Diego, "and I'd like you to see me dead." Easier said than done, however. Almodóvar plays this scene of love-death much the way Luis Buñuel and Salvador Dalí staged a similar scene in the avant-garde *L'age d'or* (*The Age of Gold*; 1930)—that is, both seriously and as the height of ludicrousness, taking seriously the very funny problem of how two matadors are to simultaneously kill and be killed by one another. In the end, it is not possible. Facing one another, they ecstatically fuck, each with a hairpin in hand. Maria uses hers first in the back of Diego's neck and, as with her previous victims, finds herself mounted on a dead man. "Look at me dying!" she enjoins, but Diego, whom she must now hold up, is past looking. She puts a gun in her mouth and shoots. But Diego cannot see. When Angel and the police arrive (guided there by Angel's telepathic ability to see these scenes of violence as if they were happening to him), they discover a beautiful tableau of the entwined, and dead, couple. The gay detective pronounces "I've never seen anyone so happy."

The perversions catalogued in this film are encyclopedic: voyeurism, fetishism, sadistic murder, and masochistic submission to death, not to mention necrophilia. By comparison, Angel's (failed) aspiration to rape seems strikingly "normal." The sex in *Matador* flirts with often politically incorrect manifestations of power and violence in sex. Indeed, the hallmark of sophisticated adult sexual representations in Western cinema since the eighties has just as often been a flirtation with the taboo of violence in sex rather than with the taboo of explicit sex itself. But here we encounter an important difference between the eighties and the seventies. Where a director like Almodóvar can make films that offer a compendium of perversions, and while the on/scenity of these perversions proves central to his work, his diverse sexual representations are not viewed, as they might have been viewed in the sixties or seventies, as liberations of formerly repressed sexual minorities. This is a major difference between the generation today working "in the realm of the senses" and that of Oshima or Bernardo Bertolucci. Almodóvar is not likely to believe that the mere expression of diverse sexual predilections will be automatically liberatory. Indeed, since the eighties art film directors face the much more difficult task of representing sex beyond the older dynamic of repression and release—beyond the language of revolution with which it had so long been associated.

Here, too, lies a major difference between the European and the American understanding of sex and sexual violence. Almodóvar's compendium of perversions is rendered with a light touch and a sophisticated sensibility even when dealing with a couple whose folie à deux consists of mutual destruction. He is, after all, the successor to Buñuel. However, when American cinema begins to engage with provocatively perverse material, it has no similarly light tone, except in the mode of outright comedy, which rarely takes sex acts seriously. Indeed, if the American films discussed in this chapter are perverse, and if they capture something important of what Anthony Giddens has called the "transformation of intimacy" of the contemporary post–sexual revolution era, they do so in decidedly American and melodramatic ways.[10] The American way, I will argue, does not so much play with sexual representations as treat them as crucial primal scenes—traumatic first witnessings of obscure forms of sexual pleasure that might not initially be understood as pleasure, indeed, that have previously been understood as pain. While there is no doubt that this sexuality has the qualities of plasticity and malleability of a modern sexuality cut loose from the requirements of reproduction and kinship—if it can be sadomasochistic, on the one hand, and queer, on the other—it is not also sophisticated and playful in the manner of the cosmopolitan Almodóvar. It thus seems important that in the two films which I offer as case studies of the American cinema's 1980s and beyond "implantation of perversions," this implantation takes place not in the metropolis but in the American heartland. It will take place in a picture-perfect Northwestern small town in David Lynch's *Blue Velvet* (1986) and in the iconic wilderness of the West in Ang Lee's *Brokeback Mountain* (2005).

In 1986, the same year that *Matador* hit the screens, American cinema had not yet assimilated sadomasochistic, violent sex into its repertoire of sex acts. Sadomasochist sex in 1986 was as new and traumatic to comparatively innocent American viewers in mainstream cinema as anal sex between men would be in 2005. Of course I do not mean to say that in an era that corresponds with the remarkable proliferation of video and DVD pornographies on/scene that S/M or anal sex between men was unknown or unrepresented. Anyone who paid attention to foreign film or to hard-core pornography—or even to a zeitgeist in which gays, transgendered people, sadomasochists, and others formerly deemed pathological assumed their place as proud sexual identities—would certainly have been aware of the existence of subcultures celebrating all of these sexual practices and in much more explicit forms than in these two R-rated films. But despite their careful avoidance of any direct view of organs and orifices, the sexual scenes depicted in *Blue Velvet* and *Brokeback Mountain* had a particularly dramatic impact on audiences who seemed to have no familiarity with screening perverse sex, especially sex acts enacted by mainstream stars and on big screens. I thus want to argue that these two films, more than any others belonging to the R-rated mainstream, have constituted crucial turning points in the American film audience's own witnessing traumatic sex acts.

Primal Scene 1: *Blue Velvet*

David Lynch is the only American art film director contemporaneous with, and as provocatively perverse as, Pedro Almodóvar. Like Almodóvar Lynch is a famously "weird" director with a cult status, but one who makes mainstream, studio films with major stars. Both have had long careers that have consistently managed to operate on the edge of sexual taboo. Also like Almodóvar, Lynch's sex scenes are audacious, less for their explicitness than for the unsettling feelings they generate. If, as I have argued, *Last Tango in Paris* brought violent, perverse sex at least partway home to American audiences through the mature body of the quintessentially American Marlon Brando, then Lynch's *Blue Velvet* brought it even further home to the mythical center of the American heartland, in this case the quintessential small American town of Lumberton. Though this north western town was meant to be contemporary, it iconographically constituted a throwback to the fifties—with white picket fences, stay-at-home moms, and a dangerous wrong-side-of-the-tracks neighborhood called Lincoln Street reminiscent of American film noir. The film provoked audiences with a surplus of what J. Hoberman called "psychosexual energy."[11] But instead of locating that energy in a mature man and his affair with a younger adult woman, *Blue Velvet* locates it in the more juvenile body of a postadolescent played by the soon-to-be-iconic Kyle MacLachlan and in his affair with an older woman played by the equally iconic vaguely foreign Isabella Rossellini.

What is perhaps most unsettling about *Blue Velvet* is how its innocent adolescent male hero feels sullied and shamed by his inquiry into the mysteries of adult sexuality. Teaching this film recently, I have discovered small but significant numbers of students, now in their mid-twenties, who vividly recall seeing this film not at the movies, but at home on video in the early nineties. Rather like the character of Jeffrey in the film, these then adolescents, and even some pre-adolescents, were sneaking a forbidden look at enigmatic adult sexual behaviors whose violence was both confusing and disturbing. These illicit home screenings point to a new way in which film was becoming an occasion for a new kind of primal scene.[12]

Contemporary reviews of the film also point to the fact that *Blue Velvet* was a key coming-of-age film for the generation of the late eighties and early nineties—a generation just as likely to see a film on the small home screen as at the movies.[13] "I'm seeing something that was always hidden," says Jeffrey Beaumont in *Blue Velvet*. So was the American audience, especially its young members. What they saw, I want to argue, amounted to an American primal scene in which a dark and nasty side of sex, a side long screened out of American movies, erupted into consciousness as the innocuous lyrics of a fifties love song about a girl's dress were transformed—in a way that only Lynch could do—into a sinister fetish.[14]

To the extent that the young viewers of this film were "too young" for the film's R-rated, adult content, their screening made them vulnerable to a perverse sex they were not prepared to witness. But as I have been arguing throughout this book, forms of carnal knowledge—whether in the life of the individual or in the American history of screening sex—never arrive at precisely the right time. They are forms of knowledge that cannot exist apart from fantasy. As the psychoanalysts Jean Laplanche and J. B. Pontalis put it, human sexuality is a "privileged battlefield between both too much and too little excitation, both too early and too late occurrence of the event."[15] Nor, as these interpreters of Sigmund Freud note, do we precisely know from where this sexuality comes—from what they call the child's own internal sexual "upsurgings,"[16] or from the external excitations and "seductions" of an adult (or, in this case, a grown-up movie with surprisingly infantile sexual content). The special fascination of *Blue Velvet* is to have dramatically staged this very question in a prolonged sex scene both participated in and witnessed by the film's young hero.

Young Jeffrey abruptly returns home from college after his father's sudden collapse at the film's beginning. While morosely walking through a field, he finds a severed ear, takes it to the police, and soon finds himself caught up in the mystery of what happened to its owner. That initial mystery leads him to further sexual mysteries connected to Dorothy Valens (Isabella Rossellini), the wife of the man whose ear has been severed. Jeffrey concocts a plan to sneak into Dorothy's apartment, ostensibly to learn about the mystery of the ear and the foul play done to her husband, who is being held hostage. When she unexpectedly arrives home, he must secrete himself in her closet, from which he observes what can only be described as a primal scene. Jeffrey's plan to "sneak in, hide, and observe" makes no logical sense in a mystery story short on explanatory plot. But considered psychosexually it makes perfect sense. As Michael Atkinson notes, "It's as if he's *looking* for a primal scene, to see his parents enact the forbidden ritual of sex."[17]

In analyzing his patients' dreams and fantasies, Freud at first believed he had uncovered memories of their actual seductions by adults. For a while this "seduction theory" served as Freud's best explanation for how sexual desire was introduced to the child: innocent children seduced into sexuality by perverse adults. Later, however, Freud doubted the veracity of these remembered scenes of seduction and developed the theory of primal fantasies that belonged instead to memory traces inherited from a mythical prehistory. In this theory, sexuality was a kind of unconscious psychic inheritance.

These primal fantasies included three different kinds of scenes: the primal scene proper—the fantasy of the child watching parental coitus; the scene of seduction—the fantasy of the child's seduction by a parent (usually the son by the mother); and the scene of the threat of castration (usually the classically oedipal threat to the son by the father). At first Freud thought that his patients had actually witnessed, or been subjected to, these scenes. But more often, as his thought developed, he was inclined to think of them somewhat outlandishly as a kind of prehistoric "phylogenetic" truth (the individual's ontologenic memory of the species) that underlay psychic reality.

The psychoanalysts Laplanche and Pontalis, unhappy with the unscientific nature of the idea of phylogenetic memory traces, adapted Freud's theory in a 1964 article to understand the primal fantasies as fantasies of origin that, like myths, appear to explain the basic enigmas of existence. For example, instead of viewing the primal scene as an archaic memory, they saw the imagined or real "scene of sexual intercourse between the parents which the child observes" as part of the child's own mythic explanation of the mystery of his or her existence.[18] Key to this observation is that the child interprets the act of pleasure as an act of violence, usually by the father on the mother. The primal scene can thus be said to mythically explain the enigma of the origin of the self—essentially how babies are made; the scene of seduction can then be said to explain the enigma of sexual desire; and the scene of castration can explain the enigma of sexual difference.[19]

To witness a primal scene, or for that matter to screen a film like *Blue Velvet* at "too young" an age, does not mean that one will be damaged for life and then, as in the case of Freud's most famous patient, have a dream of white wolves perched on a tree.[20] Behind this dream by the patient called "Wolf Man" Freud located a primal scene of parental sex "a tergo more ferarum" (from behind, like animals), which triggered the nightmare and the subsequent symptoms of extreme constipation and an inability to have sex with women except "from behind."[21] But it is far too simple to consider the primal scene itself as the cause of the patient's troubles. Rather, the primal scene proper is by definition a witnessing of sex from a time before the understanding of sex is possible. It is thus never clear whether it is an actual witnessing that is recollected, or a constructed fantasy. The Wolf Man himself, who in his later years had a great deal to say about his own analysis, believed that his real problem was not the trauma of having witnessed a primal scene, but rather an incestuous seduction by his sister.[22] As Sam Ishii-Gonzales points out in an interesting essay on Lynch's *Blue Velvet*, "It is not the actual observation of the primal scene at one and a half years which caused the disturbances in the Wolf Man, but something else that triggers a recurring nightmare."[23] The dream endows the primal scene with its newly discovered traumatic meaning (no longer just that daddy may be hurting mommy, but the whole, more recently acquired, awareness of seduction and castration). In this case, then, all the originary fantasies come into play. Freud sees the stillness and attentive gaze of the wolves as attributes of the dreamer himself—how the dreaming boy sees himself watching the primal scene. It is a scene of passive, immobile fascination (much like Jeffrey in the closet; also like audiences in the theater). By the age of four, then, the Wolf Man has already experienced both the fears of castration and a sufficient pleasure of seduction to understand, retroactively, that the spectacle he (may have) witnessed was an act of pleasure—not the act of violence he originally thought it to be.

According to these examples, it is not possible to know from where the knowledge of sex comes, nor precisely when it comes. It is too early at the time of the witnessing of the event, and it is too late at the time of the dream. Can it be said to come from the parents who enact the violent primal scene or who seduce the child or threaten castration, or is it the dream, fantasy, or daydream of the child? The answer is always undecidable, but the point is that the origin of desire is the enigma around which our *Blue Velvet* examples circle.

Blue Velvet's set piece is a twenty-minute scene that begins with young Jeffrey in the closet spying on Dorothy, the chanteuse. Dorothy pulls him out of the closet, threatens castration with a knife, and then begins to seduce him. When her husband's captor, Frank Booth (Dennis Hopper), arrives, Jeffrey is sent back into the closet to hide. From there he will observe the grown-up perversions—not coitus *a tergo*, but sadomasochistic violence and fetishism of the two characters who will increasingly function as his perverse parental surrogates.[24] In one tour de force scene Lynch's film thus stages all three of the primal fantasies in quick succession.

At first, however, it would seem that Jeffrey is just another voyeur hiding in a woman's closet—one with convenient louvers for spying (figure 94). His motives at this point are torn between the desire to learn more of the mysteries of adult sex and a contradictory chivalry that wants to "save Dorothy."[25] He first watches Dorothy speak on the phone to her imprisoned husband and child; he then watches her undress down to her black panties and bra. But this revelation is not presented as a typical striptease. The light is not flattering; Dorothy stands stiffly at attention against a wall while speaking on the phone; the conversation reveals her as a distraught mother and wife. She later throws herself on the floor to examine a frame hidden under a couch and crawls on the rug in an ungainly way. When she removes her wig, and strides to the bathroom down the hall to finish undressing, we, like Jeffrey, have the shameful feeling of having seen more than the conventional titillation we bargained for (figure 95).

Soon, in an abrupt fluctuation of mood typical of this entire scene, Jeffrey inadvertently makes a noise and Dorothy hauls him out of the closet at knifepoint. The vulnerable woman now becomes the potential castrator of another primary fantasy—the one that "explains" sexual difference (figure 96). She pricks Jeffrey lightly in the cheek and peppers him with questions: "Who are you?" "What do you want?" "Do you always sneak into girls' apartments to watch them get undressed?"—to which he can only answer, lamely but honestly, "I only wanted to see you." Still holding the knife, Dorothy now turns Jeffrey into the spectacle: "Get undressed. I want to see you." But just as soon as she establishes her knife-threatening dominance, she shifts roles again to become the seductress. As Ishii-Gonzales summarizes, Jeffrey is here confronted with each of the three primal fantasies; not in succession but in continual fluctuation.[26]

Jeffrey undresses down to a pair of cute red plaid boxers, and Dorothy orders him to come closer. Where she had formerly stood over him with the knife, she now abandons this position of dominance to kneel before him, her face at precisely the level of his crotch. Jeffrey responds with both terror and fascination at this mercurial woman dressed in a blue velvet robe, still holding a less and less threatening kitchen knife. Instead of more commands, Dorothy now asks another question, perhaps *the* question for a young man lurking in her closet and perhaps for a whole generation of "too young" viewers watching this film: "What do you want?" "I don't know," he whispers, again honestly. As if to show him what he might want,

Blue Velvet (dir. David Lynch, 1986)

94: Jeffrey hides in Dorothy's closet

95: Jeffrey's closet point of view on the anguished Dorothy

96: Dorothy with knife

Blue Velvet

97: "What do you want?"

98: Dorothy moves into position for fellatio

Dorothy puts her face close to his abdomen and begins to pull down his boxers to contemplate his penis (figure 97).

At this point—the point at which a fantasy of castration as the explanation of sexual difference turns into a fantasy of maternal seduction as the explanation of the origin of sexuality—we do well to note the discrepancy between what *we* are permitted to see of this spectacle and what Dorothy presumably sees. For this discrepancy marks the limits between the acceptable R-rated film that *Blue Velvet* occupies and the sort of NC-17 or unrated hard-core art film to be discussed in the next chapter. Dorothy's seduction of Jeffrey is precipitated by a concealed but strongly inferred act of fellatio. What we actually see has subsequently become the R-rated convention for the depiction of this act: a shot of Jeffrey's face looking ecstatic and another shot partially revealing an up-and-down movement of Dorothy's head that is in this case mostly screened out by Jeffrey's right arm (figure 98). Though everything in this scene is designed to make us believe in the presence of his erection and the action of Dorothy's mouth on it, its sight is nevertheless scrupulously avoided. Moreover, as long as the undressed Jeffrey keeps on his boxers, we are permitted to see his smooth young body from the front. But as soon as the boxers come off, everything is arranged so that we only see him from the waist up or from behind.[27] This is the modus operandi of the R-rated film: to hint at a view that is never seen.

It is against the backdrop of the still-hanging question—"What do you want?"—that we should consider the following, prolonged depiction of the primal scene. If we believe that Jeffrey tells the truth when he says he does not know what he wants, and if we believe he also tells the truth when he says he just wants to see Dorothy, then what happens next may be exactly what Jeffrey *does* want: to be neither the passive object of maternal castration nor that of maternal seduction but to return to the closet and the most passive role of all: that of the childlike observer of the primal scene of adult sex. From this position he can look at and hear the sex without himself having to enter into the scene. At a knock on the door from the expected Frank—the villain who holds Dorothy's husband and child hostage—Dorothy orders Jeffrey back into the closet. From this vantage point—and in the context of a film that will keep finding ways to return Jeffrey to this same closet—a primal scene of violent adult sex is observed.[28]

Frank enters the room in a fit of anger. He is already primed to play out a preordained script of sadomasochistic sex and ritual fetishism involving blue velvet and the inhalation of a mysterious gas intoxicant through a mask. Dorothy's role in this bewildering ritual is at one moment that of a mother who soothingly calls him baby, and at another that of a slut who calls him daddy. "Hello, baby," Dorothy begins. "Shut up! It's daddy, you shithead!" corrects Frank. As in the earlier shift from the fantasy of castration to that of seduction, roles can change rapidly. Frank sits on the couch with a glass of bourbon and Dorothy places herself in a chair opposite him. "Spread your legs. Wider!" he orders; "Now show it to me." Just as Jeffrey's penis was visible only to Dorothy in the previous scene, so now Dorothy's genitals are visible only to Frank, who constantly admonishes her not to return his gaze: "Don't you fucking look at me!" But Jeffrey *does* look. Unlike Frank, he cannot see between her legs; nor can we, since our point of view on the scene, with the exception of a few close-ups of Dorothy's face, remains closely aligned with Jeffrey's. What we do see is Frank. He places his gas mask over his face and moves to his knees

99: *Blue Velvet*, Frank on his knees before Dorothy's genitals

before Dorothy's spread legs while breathing noisily. The female genitals that loomed so comically large in *Talk to Her* are here, like the penis in the previous scene, concealed, yet they are the entire focus of Frank's attention (figure 99).

This sight, from which we and Jeffrey are so rigorously excluded, elicits Frank's abject regression to babyhood. "Mommy, mommy, mommy," he moans, and later, "Baby wants blue velvet," a piece of which Dorothy obediently places in his mouth like a pacifier. Yet this comforting fetish also elicits a shift to a monstrously aggressive violence. Frank screams, "Baby wants to fuck!" He hits Dorothy and admonishes her not to look at him. He throws her on the floor and threatens her with noisily snipping scissors close to her crotch (again invoking a threat of castration, though this time on a body with no penis to lose). He then places one end of her blue velvet robe tie in his mouth and the other end in hers, rubs his hand roughly between her legs, and finally climbs on top of her. He screams desperately while morphing back into the imperious daddy: "Daddy's coming home!" he repeatedly cries.

The scene is frenetic, violent, absurd, kinky, and nonspecific—we are never exactly sure if or how Frank discharges his monstrous sexual energy. Is it on or in Dorothy?[29] We do know that his reaction is triggered by the presumed sight, offered to Frank alone, of female genitals. But here it is not simply the Hollywood taboo on genitals that leaves us in doubt; it is the primal scene point of view—a point of view that is itself inherently in doubt about what exactly transpires between "daddy" and "mommy" from the immobile child's point of view. Just as Frank's words are often muffled by the blue velvet in his mouth, so are his actions occluded by camera angle or clothing. As Frank slowly calms down, a telling shaking gesture of the hand that had moved in the vicinity of Dorothy's genitals seems to try to shake off whatever uncanny thing he feels he has touched.

There is no mistaking the quality of the uncanny in this scene. The films of Lynch have often been described as uncanny, but this particular scene is almost a textbook illustration of Freud's description of the uncanny as "that class of the terrifying which leads back to something long known to us, once very familiar," but which has since become strange and alien.[30] Playing on the German meaning of the term, *unheimlich* (which literally means "not homelike"), Freud insists that it carries the dual sense of an unfamiliar thing that paradoxically belongs to the familiarity of home. Freud associates the uncanny both with the threat of castration and with his personal story of hastening to flee a neighborhood filled with prostitutes in a town in Italy, but inadvertently returning through the maze of streets to the exact same place. Like Jeffrey, who keeps fleeing and then returning to Dorothy's closet, he uncannily returns to the same place from which he would flee.[31]

And that place, the bedrock of Freud's definition of the uncanny, is finally this: "It often happens that male patients declare that they feel there is something uncanny about the female genital organs. This *unheimlich* place, however, is the entrance to the former *heim* [home] of all human beings, to the place where everyone dwelt once upon a time, and in the beginning."[32] "Love," it seems, is "home-sickness; and whenever a man dreams of a strange place that seems familiar, we may interpret the place as being his mother's genitals or her body."[33] Frank's frenetic line, "Daddy's coming home!" takes on both the sense of "coming" (his aspiration to virility) and also of a "coming home" to the female genitals from which "baby" once emerged. As the origin of the knowledge of sexual difference and thus as a recognition of castration, the trauma of the sight of female genitals can only be disavowed through the activity of the fetish, the film's eponymous blue velvet: and so "Baby wants blue velvet" oscillates with "Daddy's coming home!"

As "baby," Frank is needy and vulnerable, traumatized and fascinated by the same spectacle of female genitals that Almodóvar brazenly pictured giant-sized in *Talk to Her*. But provided with his fetish, this baby is soon emboldened and "wants to fuck" like "daddy," the phallic tyrant wielding his scissors over the female genitals and violently exerting total control. Overexalted and in control as daddy, pathetic and in need of reassurance as baby, Frank is trapped in the ritual oscillation between these two extremes.

It is striking how Lynch's film parallels Almodóvar's in its theatricalized confrontation with the "unheimlich horror" of the female genitals. As we have seen, Almodóvar built a giant vagina and had the silent film alter ego of his hero disappear into a vaginal "home" that dwarfed and engulfed him. At the same time, however, we have seen that this fantasy scenario screened out what we eventually understand as the violent transgression of the real adult "hero," Benigno, who through this screen disavows his actual rape of Alicia's comatose body. Only after the fact do we realize the heinous deed Benigno has committed. Lynch, on the other hand, avoids direct sight of this "unheimlich horror," but stages around its concealed presence a theatrical primary scene that reveals the violence of the sex act that Almodóvar occults. Both scenes are virtuoso screenings of sex in both their revealing and concealing senses.

If we understand Jeffrey's position to be that of the unknowing child witnessing the primal scene, and if we understand Frank's position to shift from helpless fetish-dependent baby to imperious daddy, then what are we to understand of Dorothy's position in the scene? We might suppose, as Jeffrey initially does and as the child watching the primal scene presumably does, that she is victimized by acts of pure, unwelcome violence: daddy hurts mommy. But there are moments of close-up, both before but especially after Frank hits her, in which we are privileged to see what Jeffrey cannot: that Dorothy exults sensuously in her role. When Frank finally calms down and leaves the apartment, Jeffrey, now back in his boxers, creeps out of the closet to comfort Dorothy who remains abjectly crumpled on the floor. He takes her to a couch and tries to cover her, but she will have none of his sympathy: "I don't like that," she explains. Instead, shockingly, she resumes the seduction she had earlier initiated (this time without the knife)—"Do you like me? Do you like the way I feel?"—soon escalating to repeated demands that Jeffrey hit her before the confused and ashamed young man leaves.

At one point, Dorothy is portrayed as out of her mind with fear for her kidnapped husband and son. At another, she acts out a perverse version of the mother role as Frank's mommy. At yet another point, she is a flirtatious and girlish "special friend" to Jeffrey. When she tells Jeffrey without any irony, at his next visit to her apartment, that "I looked for you in my closet last night," we know that she is a human being possibly beyond repair. At the end of the film her embrace of her restored son is a little too needy, just a little mad.[34]

Jeffrey will return to Dorothy's apartment, and even to her closet, and to his shame *and* excitement, he will eventually have the kind of (simulated) sadistic-aggressive sex that Dorothy asks of him. In this later scene, when they are naked on the bed, Dorothy asks him, for the second time, what he wants. Already on top of her, in missionary position, he happily answers that he is already doing what he wants. But Dorothy entices him into more primal games, whispering conspiratorially, "Are you a bad boy? Do you want to do bad things?" Now it is Jeffrey's turn to ask what Dorothy wants. "I want you to hurt me." When he refuses and suggests she might seek help from the police, she turns violently against him.

Or perhaps it is more accurate to say that the film itself turns violent: a candle flickers, the frame goes black, and Dorothy is heard to either say "Don [the name of both her husband and her child—she has also called Jeffrey this name before], hit me," or "don't hit me" as she chases Jeffrey out of her bed in a struggle that reveals their naked bodies in violent conflict. It is at this point that Jeffrey does, finally, hit her, at first spontaneously and then, cocking his arm for leverage, more deliberately. The film responds by showing a garish close-up of Dorothy's smiling, triumphant mouth— an exaggerated version of her head-back reaction to Frank's beating. The frame then turns white and, to the accompaniment of low animal noises, and with a superimposed hellish flame, we see their violent coupling in equally garish, grotesque slow motion. In the fade-to-black that follows, we hear Dorothy say, "You put your disease in me." At this point it is fair to say that Jeffrey has himself entered the fantasy of the primal scene in which daddy is seen to hurt mommy.[35] He has entered it now as daddy.

In a later scene, Frank will tell Jeffrey "you're like me," just before smearing lipstick on his own face, kissing Jeffrey, and beating him to a pulp. The same Frank who has repeatedly commanded Dorothy, and later Jeffrey, *not* to look at him, now commands Jeffrey to do just that. The evil father and the oedipal son in this way recognize one another across their perverse desire for Dorothy's "mommy."[36] The grotesque denouement of the film finds Dorothy's husband bound, earless, and dead alongside a corrupt cop who is also dead, but uncannily still standing. Jeffrey lures Frank into Dorothy's back bedroom, which gives him the occasion to grab a gun and hide, once again and now for the last time, in the closet, from which he will kill Frank, the perverse daddy whose position he has usurped. "I don't know whether you're a detective or a pervert," says Sandy, the "nice girl" who is domestically ensconced with Jeffrey in the film's final scene. Either-or, however, is not the mode of primal fantasy in which Lynch's film operates.

Fearing castration, succumbing to seduction, passively watching violent parental sex, killing the father, saving—but also fucking and beating—the mother, Jeffrey will have occupied all of the possible positions of the original primal fantasies. As Laplanche and Pontalis argue, fantasy is not the pursuit of an object by a subject, but rather a desubjectified participation in the very "syntax" of the sequence.[37] Jeffrey both passively and actively participates in fluctuating permutations of desire. Dorothy's question, "What do you want?" is never satisfyingly answered. If he does "save Dorothy" by killing Frank, by the time he does, he can no longer be the unsullied hero of the fairy tale. The film's end, which restores little Donny to Dorothy, Jeffrey to the nice girl Sandy, and even revives Jeffrey's ailing father, ambiguously pictures a robin that had been described earlier by Sandy as a symbol of goodness. But as no critic of the film has failed to mention, that robin is patently false and holds a large bug in its mouth.

Lynch's multiple variations on the primal fantasies of the origin of sexuality are a tour de force of a new perverse sexual ritualism introduced into mainstream American cinema. In a decade whose popular entertainment forms tended to be devoted to family fare, heroic rehashes of the Vietnam War, and other forms of action films, and in the very same year that Ronald Reagan welcomed the two-volume *Final Report* of the Meese Commission on pornography, which painted a dark and mostly inaccurate picture of a pornography industry devoted to horrific violence,[38] American film had finally, and unlike most pornography, tackled the dark side of sex. In this same year—1986—Adrian Lyne's *Nine and a Half Weeks* and Jonathan Demme's *Something Wild* would also explore sadomasochistic pleasures. The quality of these films is uneven (with Lyne and Demme's films more superficial pop entries). Nevertheless, they, too, bring focus to abruptly shifting sexual roles understood *as* roles and to sex understood as a scene of erotic possibilities tinged with threats of violence more than as a straightforward event. In these films sex could no longer be reduced to the simple positions of penetrator and penetrated or to clear outcomes of climactic fulfillment. Indeed, sex as presented in these films could hardly be understood as a kind of progress toward sexual maturity at all. If anything, they represented regressions to fundamentally infantile roles in which fantasy and desire are paramount. And as Laplanche and Pontalis teach, fantasy is not about a subject who pursues and then gets, or does not get, the object. Rather, it is all about desire's setting, about being caught up "in the sequence of images" with no fixed position in them. Their conclusion, that the subject, although present in the fantasy, "may be so in a desubjectivized form, that is to say, in the very syntax of the sequence in question," seems to be the very lesson of Lynch's film.[39]

It would be all too easy to argue, and in some ways Fredric Jameson already has done so, that the violent, fantasmatic scenarios on display in these films represent a debased narrowing of the transgressions of sex once envisioned by a sexual revolutionary counterculture.[40] Jameson identifies *Blue Velvet*'s violence and sadomasochism as the postmodern debasement of an earlier 1960s-style transgression. He thus faults the film, along with Demme's *Something Wild*, for its postmodern play with an evil (personified in *Blue Velvet* by Frank) that is merely a simulacrum and no longer really scary. He argues that the film's sadomasochistic materials "abolish the very logic on which their attraction/repulsion was based in the first place." Jameson sees the film as a parable of the end of the sixties, "a parable of the end of theories of transgression as well, which so fascinated that whole period and its intellectuals."[41]

In a sense, Jameson is right. *Blue Velvet* and the other films that usher in violent originary fantasies in the late eighties are not politically transgressive in a 1960s, modernist way. But does that mean, as Jameson seems to say, that their sex is therefore pseudotransgressive in a postmodernist way that is historically inauthentic, unimportant, basically not sexy? To do so would be to discount the experience of a generation that grew up not with *Last Tango*, *Deep Throat*, and *In the Realm of the Senses*, but with *Blue Velvet*, *Matador*, and *Nine and a Half Weeks* and in the shadow of the Meese Commission's own horrified discovery of a violent, sadomasochistic side to sex. In place of Jameson's dismissal of such films as mere symptoms of the loss of the sixties, we do better to take the primal scene seriously as the popular staging of a new kind of sex scene for a generation no longer aligned with the high-culture Marquis de Sade or with an idea of sexual liberation suited to the antirepressive ideologies of the 1960s.

When Foucault writes that "modern society is perverse, not in spite of its Puritanism or as if from a backlash provoked by its hypocrisy; it is in actual fact, and directly, perverse,"[42] he describes a general tendency to isolate, intensify, incite, consolidate, and implant "peripheral sexualities." These sexualities have then become "stuck to an age, a place, a type of practice." Sadomasochistic perversions and sexual fantasies that partake of originary fantasies of seduction, castration, and the primal scene begin to become "stuck" in the eighties American popular culture through these films. What was particularly unique to this age was a new understanding of sex as a desubjectified scene, more akin to an infantile fantasy than to an adult act with a telos of discharge. The one thing the sex of these sadomasochistic primal fantasies is not is something that can be clearly seen and heard and that in that seeing and hearing becomes automatically transgressive of previous repression. "Don't you fucking look at me!" says Frank repeatedly to Dorothy. Later, Dorothy says much the same to

Jeffrey. In a way, it is also the injunction to the audience in a film which, unlike *In the Realm of the Senses*, forbade a more direct look at sex.

Primal Scene 2: Brokeback Mountain

If sadomasochistic pleasures in American movies are now recognized *as* pleasures, however complicated they may be with pain, anal sex between men has previously been recognized, if at all, as only pain and humiliation, especially to the one anally penetrated.[43] Since *Deliverance* (dir. John Boorman, 1972) anal sex between men has been portrayed much as heterosexual rape was in the nineteenth century—as the fate worse than death that spoils the innocence and reputation of its victim.[44] This shame has been compounded, since the eighties, by the knowledge that anal sex is one of the ways in which AIDS is spread. On this count alone, Ang Lee's staging of pleasurable anal sex between two cowboys who spend a summer herding sheep high in the Wyoming mountains in 1963 and then conduct an illicit affair over the following twenty years has deep cultural significance. Over the fall of 2005 and continuing through the following year in the much publicized run-up to the Oscars, Lee's *Brokeback Mountain* (2005) became a major cultural event—something more than just a movie. Premiering at a number of major international film festivals (Venice, Telluride, Toronto) in the late summer and early fall of 2005, it benefited from producer James Shamus's platformed, gradual release, picking up steam, as well as controversy, along the way. As more people saw it, read reviews, and argued about whether it was too gay, not gay enough, too explicit, not explicit enough, Oscar-worthy or not, it became a touchstone, and not only for the gay community.

At stake in the film's reception were not only the quality of Annie Proulx's source story, or of Lee's direction, or of Heath Ledger's and Jake Gyllenhaal's performances, but something very much like a primal scene's first witnessing of a sex act initially understood by the inexperienced child as pain and only later as pleasure. Although *Brokeback Mountain* does not stage the primal scene as radically and fantasmatically as did *Blue Velvet*, Lee's more subdued, understated, realistic, and "tasteful" cowboy melodrama deals equally with primal fantasies of seduction, castration, and the primal scene of sexual witnessing itself. Consider two instances in which the primal-scene witnessing of Jack and Ennis's sexual relation takes place. In one, the boss Joe Aguirre (Randy Quaid), through binoculars, sees the boys romping around their camp partly undressed, while in another, Ennis's wife Alma (Michelle Williams) catches them passionately kissing through the window of her apartment door.

D. A. Miller, in a long complaint about the film, calls these images "vitri-fied" because they are views of "the Homosexual" viewed by another char-acter through glass. Miller argues that they tell us, for his taste too theatri-cally, that these are another's (homophobic) perspective. Miller's point is that "whenever the Homosexual is seen as such, it is not we who are seeing him, in *that* way. We are thus invited to distance ourselves from what the character looking through the glass thinks." To Miller this is an especially insidious disavowal of homosexuality itself: we think that the homosexual does not *mean* to be homosexual; the spectator does not *mean* for him to be so either. What is preserved, then, according to Miller, is just a *"vague homoeroticism, innocent and ineffable, that Jack and Ennis shared with us and the scenery on Brokeback Mountain."*[45] I will argue in what follows that this interpretation, while it may operate in these two instances as dis-tancing and may be true of a great many representations of homosexuals in movies, omits the film's primary sex scene in the tent, which is not "vitrified" and which challenges *us* to understand it in a fresh way, not as a preknown entity. Rather, we are invited to participate in a seduction into new sexual knowledge that operates in relation to primal fantasies.

I mention my differences with Miller now because some of the ideas that follow bounce off his emphatic dismissal of the film. It is not clear from his criticism if Miller wants the film to contain more explicit sex or if he would just prefer this "gay love story" to come more overtly out of a self-recognized gay culture rather than at least partly out of Proulx's heterosexual female imagination of sexual desires that do not, at their point of emergence, acknowledge themselves as gay. It is clear, however, from a footnote that Miller sees Lee's film falling short of French, German, Italian, and Spanish precursors of what he calls "homocinema"—a cinema capable of disrupting social and symbolic orders, as seen for example in the films of Jean Genet, Pier Paolo Pasolini, Rainer Maria Fassbinder, and Almodóvar. "Hollywood cinema knows only two options: to make homo-sexual desire invisible, in a closet intended for general use, or to make the Homosexual super-visible, as a minoritized 'problem.'"[46] I argue, to the contrary, that by staging a mythical primal scene in which homosexual desire emerges from something that does not preexist, and in also staging the threat of castration against which it emerges, that this Hollywood film precisely does not reduce homosexuality to a minoritized problem but makes it a fear, and a desire, sympathetically, and even melodramatically, felt by all. Thus much of the argument about how gay or not gay, how universal or minoritized the film is, seems misplaced on both sides. Much more important is how carefully Americans of all sorts not only watched this film, as I have argued about *Deep Throat* and *Last Tango in Paris* (chapter 3), but paid attention to themselves watching it.[47]

B. Ruby Rich's claim for the film was large: "Every once in a while a film comes along that changes our perceptions so much that cinema history thereafter has to arrange itself around it."[48] In extolling the beauties of the idyll the two men have on their mountain, Rich describes the "rural bliss of their primal scene."[49] In what follows I want to pursue the primary fantasy sense of this term, not only as pre-Edenic innocence but in Laplanche and Pontalis's tripartite sense of fantasies of sexuality's origin, now understood in queer terms.

"You know I ain't queer," says Ennis Del Mar (Heath Ledger) to Jack Twist (Jake Gyllenhaal) shortly after the two cowboys have had wordless, grunting (simulated) anal sex in their tent. "Me neither," says Jack, "It's nobody's business but ours." As the one who initiated the action, Jack will, over time, prove more inclined to accept this label, to publicize who he is with it in certain contexts. He will also die in the end because he does not keep his queerness as closeted as Ennis. At this point, however, what the two men clearly agree on is their sexual right to privacy—a right that did not exist for homosexuals in 1963, the time of the film's initial events. Indeed, the right to sexual privacy is a recently forged one that resonated in this 2005 film with the still-reverberating 2003 *Lawrence v. Texas* Supreme Court ruling that struck down sodomy laws.

Lawrence v. Texas

Over and over in the *Lawrence* ruling, the sanctity of home and bedroom, associated with the rights of the normal (propagating) family to privacy, is extended to homosexuals: "Individual decisions concerning the intimacies of physical relationships, even when not intended to produce offspring, are a form of 'liberty' protected by due process."[50] "It suffices for us to acknowledge that adults may choose to enter upon this relationship in the confines of their homes and their own private lives and still retain their dignity as free persons. When sexuality finds overt expression in intimate conduct with another person, the conduct can be but one element in a personal bond that is more enduring. The liberty protected by the Constitution allows homosexual persons the right to make this choice."[51] The majority in *Lawrence* is clear: the state can no longer criminalize private sexual conduct; if it does not assert the right to sodomy, it does assert the right to privacy.

The *Lawrence v. Texas* ruling overturned the conviction of two men who had purportedly committed an act of sodomy. This act was apparently viewed by two uniformed Harris County, Texas, male police officers, answering a call about a man brandishing a gun in an apartment. These officers discovered John Lawrence and Tyrone Garner in Lawrence's bedroom engaged in anal sex.[52] The specific Texas statutes that Lawrence and Garner offended defined sodomy as deviate sexual intercourse, namely, "(A) any contact between any part of the genitals of one person and the mouth or anus of another person," or "(B) penetration of either of these orifices with an object."[53] Texas law thus did not define the deviate part of the act as specifically homosexual, and this vagueness would prove an important part of the Supreme Court ruling overturning the previous ruling of *Bowers v. Hardwick*. In that nineteen-year-old earlier ruling, the majority had declared sodomy to be "heinous," "a disgrace to human nature," and "a crime not fit to be named." *Lawrence v. Texas* did not so much overturn this attitude of revulsion as it tempered it with a right to privacy.

"Sodomy is a word," says Gore Vidal, at the sound of which "everybody starts to vibrate like a gong."[54] Justice Antonin Scalia's near apoplectic dissenting opinion to the decision is just such a vibration and, unlike the majority, he says the word as often as possible. Scalia (correctly) points out that the majority had not been bold enough to assert that "homosexual sodomy" is a fundamental right, the way, for example, the 1973 Supreme Court had established abortion as a fundamental right. Rather, Scalia notes that the majority simply asserts that there is no justification for Texas's intrusion into the "personal and private life of the individual." He takes every opportunity to vibrate the gong in contrast to the euphemisms of the majority (who prefer terms like "private consensual act,"[55] "intimate conduct,"[56] "sexual practices common to a homosexual lifestyle,"[57] etc.). When Scalia catches the court saying that the "laws prohibiting sodomy do not seem to have been enforced against consenting adults *acting in private*,"[58] he asks what *other* kind of sex can there possibly be? The opposite of private sex, to Scalia, would be public sex, which is automatically obscene: "surely," he sneers, "consensual sodomy, like heterosexual intercourse, is rarely performed on stage."[59]

Yet the moment the two police officers intruded into the bedroom to become the witnesses of this "sodomy," they became a kind of audience whose very horror put in motion the machinery that would end in the highly publicized *Lawrence* ruling of 2003. Two years after that ruling, *Brokeback Mountain* staged consensual sodomy between two men in a very dark tent as a simulated R-rated movie sex scene available for viewing by all persons seventeen or older, or any age if accompanied by a parent or adult guardian. If I find a certain hypocrisy in the *Lawrence* ruling's exalted respect for the newfound privacy of homosexuals and a certain ugly honesty in Scalia's overt homophobia at the idea of staged, public sodomy, it is because the majority ruling seems unaware that its very assurance of privacy also constitutes a kind of publicity. If we have learned anything from the teachings of Foucault it is that discourses of sexuality, including so-called reverse discourses that do not embrace the acts named, are forms of publicity in which technologies of print, photo, film, video, and digital forms of pornography have been particularly important. Indeed, the rights of sexual minorities have not been gained without the loud publication of intimate sexual practices tied to particular forms of media. The history of minority sexualities in the twentieth and twenty-first centuries is indissolubly linked, as Michael Warner, Lauren Berlant, Gayle Rubin, Rich Cante, and Angelo Restivo have all argued, to its mediated publicity.[60] Indeed, between the 1986 *Bowers v. Hardwick* and the 2003 *Lawrence v. Texas* ruling, it is possible that the proliferation of gay pornography could have functioned as the single most important factor in the recognition and acceptance of homosexual practices on/scene.

The great irony of *Brokeback Mountain* is thus that in the wake of the triumph of the ideology of the privacy of consenting adults, and in the context of a film about two cowpokes who think their sexual pleasure is "nobody's business but ours," gay anal sex received its widest publicity beyond the contained world of gay pornography.[61] It is thus against the background of this liberal consensus about privacy in the striking down of sodomy law that we need to situate the concealed and revealed sex acts between Ennis and Jack. In what sense is this film also about primal fantasies, and how have these fantasies been queered?

Seduction

Perhaps the first answer to the above question is that the primal scene itself, the fantasy of parental copulation that Freud described, is already in its original form proto-queer. That is, before the dream of wolves that later introduces the fear of castration, the image of the boy's mother and father engaged in coitus *a tergo* is assumed by a pregenital male child who does not yet understand sexual difference to be taking place between sexually undifferentiated actors at the anus. Freud emphasizes that this position *a tergo* proves "especially favourable for observation," that is, favorable for the child to observe both the facial expressions of the mother and the penetration of the anus.[62] Thus the primal scene *a tergo*, as Lee

Edelman interprets it, gives "imaginative priority" to a kind of "proto-homosexuality."[63] Before the child needs to repress its identification with the so-called passive position of the mother, it freely identifies with the pleasure (or pain) that comes from the penetration of what he understands to be the anus. According to Edelman this pleasure could be both the doing of the act of penetration and the experience of being penetrated.[64] It is only in the later dream of wolves, a dream that takes place after the child understands sexual difference and the threat of castration that lies behind it, that the Wolf Man feels terrorized by what Freud called the boy's earlier homosexual enthusiasm.

With this primal fantasy in mind, how shall we understand the simulated public spectacle of sodomy as staged in *Brokeback Mountain*? How does this spectacle contrast with the liberal concept of sex as that which deserves privacy as articulated in *Lawrence v. Texas*? How does Lee's film show its two adult protagonists seduced into the pleasures of male-male anal sex despite their fears of castration and emasculation? How is the film audience also seduced into a curiosity about, perhaps even an erotic desire to see, this extremely occulted spectacle of seduction?

We have seen that Laplanche and Pontalis argue in "Fantasy and the Origins of Sexuality" that certain primary, original fantasies function as myths of origin that address basic enigmas related to subjectivity. After the primal scene of the witnessing of parental sex proper, they discuss the related fantasy of the origin of sexual desire. From where does it come? This origin is "explained," so to speak, by the fantasy of seduction. In this scenario, the child, having passed through puberty, recollects seduction as having come from outside, from the adult.[65] For example, as we saw in *Blue Velvet*, when Dorothy drags Jeffrey from her closet she asks him what he wants. "I don't know," comes his honest and perfectly innocent answer. Yet he does have some inkling of what he wants, or else he would not be there. Though Dorothy then seduces Jeffrey into wanting what *she* wants—ultimately for him to beat her in the act of sex—we recognize that she herself gets this desire from Frank. The real origin of desire remains inaccessible and deeply mysterious; in autoeroticism it is ultimately nothing more than an elusive matrix of memories that only become significant after the fact.

In *Brokeback Mountain* Jack and Ennis are also engaged in a primal fantasy of seduction that operates to explain the origin of an even more mysterious, and unwanted, homosexual desire. Ennis, like Jeffrey, thinks he knows what he wants: to marry a nice girl. But Jeffrey responds to the mystery of the ear and Ennis responds to the lure of the wilderness, and both young men find themselves seduced into something quite different.

Seduction begins in *Brokeback*'s very first scene. Robin Wood argues that a gay spectator would knowingly understand Jack and Ennis's first meeting as such.[66] In long shot, Jack arrives noisily in his decrepit truck and kicks the bumper. Ennis watches. Jack then leans against the truck, hands on hips and displaying himself. He takes a few steps toward Ennis, then watches, uncertain. In close-up, Ennis lowers his head, his face shadowed by his hat. Jack in close-up looks at Ennis with a hint of a smile. Ennis looks back and then lowers his head. "Heterosexual, or just not interested? Or just cautious?" asks Wood. Next Jack leans against the truck, one hand on his belt, the other stretched out ("invitingly?" comments Wood) over the bumper. He lowers his head to look in the truck window. The next shot shows Ennis reflected in this mirror. A final shot shows Jack shaving, using this same mirror "for the Boss, due to arrive? Or for Ennis?" asks Wood.[67]

These questions are real. Gay desire does not necessarily preexist in Jack any more than it does in Ennis. The scene of seduction is the place of the emergence of desire, but if we take seriously Laplanche and Pontalis's lesson about the always too early or too late nature of the upsurging of desire, then it must be seen to come both from within the subject and from without. Jack is not portrayed as already gay; neither he nor we can say where this taboo desire comes from, though it will, at some point, be recognized.

Seduction proper takes place in several scenes around the campfire long before the two men get together in the tent. Two lonely ranch hands find camaraderie high on a mountain, away from the world, caring for sheep. The closed-down, tight-lipped, and wary Ennis opens up to the more gregarious Jack. They talk, eat, and drink, but one of them must always spend the night higher up from base camp to guard the sheep. Sexual awareness emerges as if unconsciously from growing friendliness. Ennis, for example, speaks of the apple-sized balls of a coyote he saw on the mountain and soon after strips naked to bathe. Though Jack, viewed in the foreground, scrupulously avoids looking at him, we appreciate the effort it takes him not to look (figure 100). In a series of round-the-campfire scenes, emotional intimacy engenders subtle signs of attraction. Jack, for example, takes a piss and comes back to the fire pointing proudly to his rodeo-prize buckle, which is also to say in the direction of his penis (figure 101). Though this pointing to his prize buckle only precipitates a rousing

Brokeback Mountain (dir. Ang Lee, 2005)

100: Ennis bathes, Jack exerts effort not to look

101: Jack points to his belt after peeing

argument about the merits of rodeo riding, the emotion of argument itself moves them closer. When the shy Ennis speaks of his childhood, Jack observes that these are the most words he has spoken all week. Ennis self-mockingly adds that it was the most words he has spoken in a year. Under the influence of the bottle, Jack next breaks out in an exuberant dance imitating a rodeo rider "waving to the girls in the stands"—though the only person he waves at is Ennis.

Seduction continues at the next campsite as Jack plays his harmonica, Ennis speaks fluidly, and the two men now drink out of the same bottle.

102: *Brokeback Mountain*, Jack and Ennis face off

Jack loudly sings a hymn taught him by his Pentecostal mother, which leads to a discussion of sin in which Ennis confesses that though Jack may be a sinner who will go to hell, "I ain't yet had the opportunity." It is this confession of virginity that leads into the seduction proper. Too drunk to tend the sheep higher up on this cold night, Ennis falls asleep beside the campfire while Jack sleeps in his usual place in the tent. Halfway through the night, Jack orders a shivering Ennis into the tent with him.

It is dark in this tent and director Lee never lets us see exactly what transpires. Nor do we see facial expressions very clearly. We do see, and especially hear, a general sort of wrestling whose understanding depends a lot on our own state of knowledge. For example, we can surmise that when Jack reaches over and grabs Ennis's hand to pull it toward himself that what actually happens is that Jack brings this hand to touch his own presumably erect cock. All we really see, however, is Ennis's recoil and some rather intense wrestling. What interests me especially in the first part of the scene are two pauses in the action when Ennis and Jack face each other in momentary standoffs. In the first, Ennis, though locked in ostensible struggle to elude Jack's embrace, leans toward him ever so slightly and thus gives permission to proceed. At this point Jack removes the denim jacket in which he has been sleeping. In the second standoff, when it becomes clear that Jack is now undressing himself in preparation, Ennis struggles again as if to move away. At this point, Jack places his hands on either side of Ennis's face. Once again Ennis ceases his struggle, putting his own hands on Jack's face and mirroring him—with the difference that *his* hands form fists (figure 102). Again Jack interprets Ennis's stillness as acquiescence and proceeds to unfasten his prize rodeo belt buckle. Thus Jack is again the ostensible seducer, but at each new stage Ennis has given small signs of encouragement.

At this point, however, it is Ennis who takes charge. He turns Jack around, unbuckles his own belt hastily, spits into his hand, and thrusts into Jack from an upright position on his knees, *a tergo more ferarum*, as Freud would say. We hear both men grunt and pant, and much of our understanding comes from sound. The visual focus such as it is initially rests on Ennis's face and upper body in this nonexplicit (simulated) scene, but the camera soon tilts down to reveal Jack, face down on the bedroll, ass up in the air. The camera twice tilts up and down between each of their faces, neither ignoring nor focusing on the bodies that are between. A loud grunt suggests release, and a cut to the tent seen from the outside illuminated by moonlight ends the scene.

If Jack appears to be the initial seducer, the one who first knows gay desire and shows it to Ennis in the form of his erection, then we would expect Ennis to be the one seduced into this desire by the one who knows. But as we have seen, Ennis is not truly without knowledge; he gives permission at each stage of the seduction and, when the time comes, he expertly turns Jack over, lubricates himself with spittle, and commits the act of "deviate sexual intercourse" that got Tyrone Garner and John Lawrence in such trouble in Texas. But now, instead of two shocked and offended police officers, a very large portion of the America filmgoing public above the age of seventeen was led to understand, if not to explicitly see, what transpires. Proulx's depiction of the seduction is very brief, but it makes one further point clear: "Ennis ran full-throttle on all roads whether fence mending or money spending, and he wanted none of it when Jack seized his left hand and brought it to his erect cock. Ennis jerked his hand away as though he'd touched fire, got to his knees, unbuckled his belt, shoved his pants down, hauled Jack onto all fours and, with the help of the clear slick and a little spit, entered him, nothing he'd done before but no instruction manual needed."[68] What Ennis seems to "want none of" is not anal sex, but to be in the more passive "female" position in it—the position of the anally penetrated mother as understood by the Wolf Man in the primal scene. Later in the film we will see that Ennis, like the Wolf Man, prefers heterosexual sex *a tergo* with his wife as well. Compared to Proulx's abrupt lines, the film protracts seduction over its entire first third as we watch Ennis warm to Jack, slowly overcoming resistance. We cannot say where this desire originates, but the fantasy of seduction operates as America's first mainstream movie example of the seduction into homosexual desire.

Castration

In yet another impassioned argument against the universality of *Broke-back Mountain*'s love story—this time for seeing the film as a specifically gay "tragedy"—Daniel Mendelsohn asserts that while other star-crossed lovers may face familial or ethnic impediments to their union, they do not despise themselves for belonging to these familial or ethnic groups.[69] Capulets, for example, do not despise themselves *as* Capulets and Montagues *as* Montagues. In contrast, Jack and Ennis have been taught to fear and despise queers, and when they find themselves "seduced" into queer desire, they hate themselves for it, though Ennis, as we shall see, has reason to hate himself more. This self-hatred is generated in Ennis's case especially by what Mendelsohn calls a "grim flashback" from Ennis's childhood. It shows Ennis's father marching his two sons in slow motion to view the mutilated remains of an old queer cowboy who had been dragged by his "dick" until it fell off. Ennis's narration notes, "He made sure that I seen it," and the film makes sure that we see it by abruptly jumping closer. In voice-over, Ennis's narration adds of his father, "Hell, for all I know he done the job." This flashback, also part of Proulx's short story, published in 1997, a year before the University of Wyoming student Matthew Shepard was beaten and killed outside Laramie, goes a long way toward explaining Ennis's internalized homophobia as a fear of literal emasculation.

With this scene of castration serving as his own traumatic primal scene, Ennis is, as Mendelsohn puts it, and as Ledger plays the role, a man "tormented simply by being in his own body—by being himself."[70] For Ennis to be himself, that is, to own up to the queer desire into which he has been seduced, is in more ways than one to court the disaster of castration. However, castration here is not simply the fantasmatic paternal threat that psychoanalytic theory likes to posit as the originary explanation of the difference between the sexes. Instead, it constitutes a literal punishment specifically meted out to men who other men fear might lead them down that same path of seduction. The men who vehemently insist on repudiating the pleasures of the anus will punish men like Ennis (whose very name echoes this word) for being too much like presumably already castrated women. Castration here is something more than what Laplanche and Pontalis call the fantasy that explains the mystery of sexual difference to the heterosexual imagination; it also carries the added "horror" of being seduced into same-sex desire.

For a cowboy whose seasonal job is castrating cows,[71] literal castration makes for a familiar fact of life. After his first night with Jack, Ennis rides out to his neglected herd and finds a dead sheep whose eviscerated innards are a silent reproach to his "succumbing" to seduction. Each time over their long intermittent relations when Jack urges Ennis to join him in making a home together, Ennis is clear that such a venture risks the kind of emasculation-death that as a child he saw enacted on the gay cowboy. As he later says to Jack, "If this thing grabs hold of us in the wrong way, then we're dead." Immediately after learning of Jack's accidental death by an exploded tire, Ennis suspects, and the film pictures, another possible cause for his death: the blows of a tire iron, a classic tool used in gay-bashing. For Jack, "this thing" *had* "grabbed hold" of him the wrong way and the film shows us Ennis's imagination of Jack's death even as Jack's wife gives him the official story of an accident.

In the short story Ennis belatedly confirms his suspicion that "it had been the tire iron," not an exploded tire, that killed Jack, at the moment he hears Jack's father speak of Jack's plan to bring "another one" back to his ranch. We are left to infer that his involvement with "another one"—a character the film fleshes out briefly—is what brought on this murder.[72] But Proulx's story adds something at this point that the film excludes: a fear-of-castration backstory now involving Jack and his father.

Ennis recalls that Jack once told him that as a four-year-old he had been severely punished by his father for the minor crime of missing the toilet while peeing. His father was furious and whipped him with his belt. To further impress on him the magnitude of his crime, the father also pissed on Jack and then made him wash everything up. But what especially impressed Jack from this memory is that "while he was hosing me down I seen he had some extra material that I was missin'. I seen they'd cut me different like you'd crop a ear or scorch a brand. No way to get it right with him after that."[73] Proulx has Ennis remember Jack's recounting of the scene just after he has met this hard, grudge-bearing father. Her narrator summarizes, "Jack was dick-clipped and the old man was not; it bothered the son who had discovered the anatomical disconformity during a hard scene."[74]

That both Jack and Ennis endure the threat of castration from aloof, unloving fathers is obvious.[75] But where Ennis lives his life in paranoid terror of losing what the father threatens to take from him, Jack appears to live more comfortably, though also dangerously, having more readily accepted and lived with the evidence of his "loss." If castration is the fantasy that explains sexual difference, then it may, in this queer context, also function to explain queer difference. In this case perhaps it explains not just the son's "lack" vis-à-vis the father—notice that Jack does not only say that he is "missin'" what the father has but that the father also has an excess of "material," suggesting that the father's possession might not be the true standard of measurement. Jack's greater comfortableness in his own skin may thus derive from his ability to differentiate himself from a father he does not want to emulate. Here, too, Ennis has not "had the opportunity" that Jack has had.

Jack's relation to the paternal phallus thus appears to be less terror-struck than Ennis's. This may be what enables him, at a later point in the film—in a scene not included in Proulx's story—to reclaim the knife that carves the Thanksgiving turkey from his bullying father-in-law and to, at least briefly, take over from him the role of head of household.[76] In a parallel scene also set at the Thanksgiving dinner table, we see Ennis with his ex-wife Alma, their two girls, and Alma's new husband. Unlike Jack, Ennis does not take over the carving from this upwardly mobile supermarket manager whose noisy electric knife stands for everything Ennis abhors. Later, at this same celebration, Ennis turns violent at Alma's mention of the many fishing trips he took with his friend Jack, trips in which he never caught a single fish. Terrified that someone might be looking at him and catch out his queer desire, Ennis can only flee. He soon learns of Jack's death and retreats to the safety of his lonely trailer in whose closet he keeps their two shirts—relics of the idyll on the mountain.

The film's penultimate shot shows this small, cramped trailer closet containing Ennis's few possessions and the two shirts. They have been transferred from their deeply hidden place where Ennis found them in Jack's closet to a more prominent position on the swung-open door of Ennis's. In Jack's closet the blue denim of his own shirt had been protectively overlaid over Ennis's faded white, yellow, and blue plaid—both blood encrusted from the fight they had had at the end of their idyll. Even the sleeves of Ennis's shirt had been carefully inserted inside the sleeves of Jack's, "like two skins, one inside the other, two in one," writes Proulx.[77] When Ennis first discovers the two shirts, he indulges in the classic gesture of the fetishist—breathing in the smell, feeling the texture of the garments—while still standing in Jack's closet. Proulx writes, "He pressed his face into the fabric and breathed in slowly through his mouth and nose, hoping for the faintest smoke and mountain sage and salty sweet stink of Jack but there was no real scent, only the memory of it, the imagined power of Brokeback Mountain of which nothing was left but what he held in his hands"[78] (figure 103).

In a scene not included in the story, Ennis takes the shirts downstairs having folded them so as to render invisible his own shirt underneath. Nevertheless, Jack's silently sympathetic mother seems to understand the

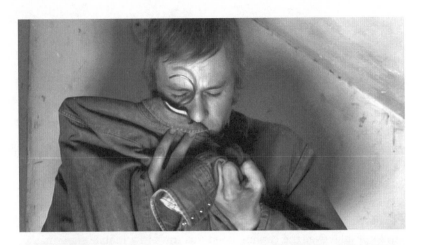

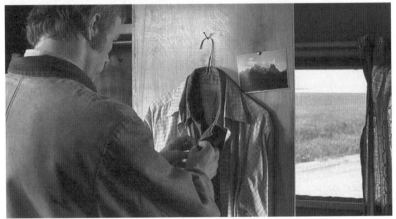

Brokeback Mountain

103: Jack's closet: Ennis discovers the two shirts and breathes them in

104: The two shirts, reversed, in Ennis's closet

relation he is hiding from the father who sits nearby. She carefully helps him place the two shirts in a brown paper bag, emblem, like the closets themselves, of a life of careful concealment. Jack's shirt is more out, as is Jack himself, while Ennis's shirt is carefully concealed underneath. But at the end, when we see Ennis's closet, we may also note something that the story also does not tell: that the relation of the two shirts has been reversed; now it is Ennis's lighter shirt that protectively, lovingly, envelopes Jack's denim one, which Ennis now carefully buttons. Just above the shoulder of the shirt hangs a postcard of Brokeback Mountain (figure 104). In this shrine to loss, Ennis has also memorialized a more open love that might have been.[79]

Compared to the tawdry glamour of Frank's blue velvet, the old work shirts of two cowboys could not be more humble, nor do they appear to have the same direct sexual function. Yet like Frank's blue velvet, these shirts, too, perform a fetish function (and the fact that these shirts have fetched over a hundred thousand dollars on auction through eBay would seem to attest to their enduring fetish value).[80] In the most classic Freudian sense of the term, all of these garments are substitutes for the relations their owners can no longer have. They are also disavowals of castration that are testimonials to the very lacks they may wish to deny. At the sight of Dorothy's vagina Frank demands his blue velvet fetish as a magical talisman to protect him from the threat of castration. He cannot have sex without his blue velvet. His fetish is not merely a necessary condition to the sexual object but, as Freud puts it, "actually *takes the place* of the normal aim" and thus, to Freud, would be judged not simply perverse but pathologically so.[81]

The two shirts, in contrast, do not operate as pathological substitutes. In the passage quoted above, Ennis seems to search for the talismanic function of the shirts as a means of evoking the lost object of the flesh and blood Jack, but he finds it wanting. This fetish will not, like Frank's, get him off. Jack's scent is not in the shirts, only the "memory of it, the imagined power of Brokeback Mountain of which nothing was left but what he held in his hands." Ennis's fear of castration, like Frank's, has reduced him to the possession of a fetish instead of "the real thing." But this fetish, unlike Frank's, does not take the place of "the normal aim"; rather, it serves to haunt him with the recognition of a lost opportunity of a real relation in which the sodomitical sex act would no longer be viewed, as Scalia views it, as a heinous "crime not fit to be named," but precisely as one of many possible "normal aims." Compared to Frank's, then, Ennis's fetish is more on the side of knowledge than of belief. He may wish to *believe* that Jack's shirt might substitute for the flesh-and-blood person, but he *knows* that it cannot. We might call it a fetish that works in the service of melodrama to evoke the acute sense of loss. This fetish evokes the melodramatic pathos of an avowal of love that is both too little and too late. Too little in that the shirts, though more prominently displayed and not literally hidden as they were in Jack's familial childhood closet, are nevertheless still in a closet; too late because they can only nostalgically evoke a frozen moment of the past and cannot facilitate the actual contact of skins.

However, the new position of the shirts, with Ennis's light one now enveloping Jack's darker one, does suggest that Ennis's own frozen and private memorial to lack has gained a new symbolic significance as now displayed in his own sad closet. For in placing his shirt over Jack's, he takes a baby step toward outing himself. No longer hiding underneath the embrace of Jack's shirt, Ennis's shirt now enacts, in place of Ennis himself, an engulfing embrace of Jack. What is most striking, however, is also the way this figurative, fetishistic embrace recalls an earlier actual embrace that took place when they were still young on Brokeback, saved in the film for the powerful statement of loss at its end. It is a flashback embedded in a late scene in which Ennis and Jack part for the last time after a bitter argument in which Jack famously wishes he knew how to "quit" Ennis, and Ennis urges him to do so. When Ennis breaks down in impotent self-loathing, Jack embraces him, precipitating a violent rage that only ends after Jack persists in the embrace and Ennis finally collapses to the ground with Jack's arms around him: "I can't stand this anymore, Jack," he says. Jack's embrace of Ennis at this point constitutes the typical embrace pictured in their relations, not unlike what we glimpse in the tent: A violent, reluctant, and conflicted Ennis gives in to Jack's amorous, persistent, and in this case nurturing embrace (figure 105). This embrace mirrors the shirts as initially found in Jack's closet: Jack's shirt, like his arms here, surrounds and "embraces" Ennis's. But this is not the embrace that has been saved for the end.

In a bold move, the film cuts from the above embrace to the smoking embers of a fire. A young Jack stands half asleep before an early-morning campfire on Brokeback, Ennis comes up behind him and puts his arms around him in a nurturing way usually more typical of Jack (figure 106). "Well, now you're sleeping on your feet like a horse," he says. "My momma used to say that to me when I was little." He hums a bit of a lullaby and sways back and forth still embracing the sleepy Jack with his right arm around his shoulder and chest. A long shot of the same pose memorializes this rare moment of intimacy and tenderness in which Ennis, for once, embraces and comforts Jack before bidding him good-bye until evening (figure 107). The moment has been conjured from Jack's memory as a happier alternative to the present scene of bitter farewell. In the remembered scene, Ennis embraces and comforts Jack and good-bye is only until nightfall; as Ennis rides off for his day's sheepherding on Brokeback, Jack looks after him. This view of Jack in the past fondly watching Ennis depart is smoothly linked to the departure in the present as an angry, bitter Jack again looks after him. It is the last time they will see one another.

Two departures by Ennis, both of them watched by Jack, thus follow

Brokeback Mountain

105: Jack's last embrace of a devastated Ennis

106: The "saved" memory of Ennis's last embrace

107: Long shot of Ennis's last embrace as used in the trailer

two embraces, one from the past and one from the present. And these embraces, in turn, echo the different positions of the shirt memorials. The first embrace, what I have called the more typical one, mirrors the position of the two shirts as they were *first* hung in Jack's closet: with Jack's shirt embracing and also hiding Ennis's. This embrace, in which Ennis is passive and Jack enfolds him, is still haunted by the threat of the father's discovery and punishment. It is the reason, as we have seen, for the near total concealment of Ennis's shirt under Jack's. The second embrace mimics the mythic and more precious "saved" memory from the past and the shirts as they are later hung on the door of Ennis's closet. This embrace is comparatively free of the father's threat, as evidenced by the mother's lullaby and Ennis's ability, for once, to enfold Jack in his own nurturing embrace. It is mirrored in the new position of Ennis's shirt placed protectively over Jack's. With the too-late revelation of this earlier embrace, we discover that this position may not be so new after all; it simply mirrors a past we have not yet seen that now comes to stand for what might have been.

In a heated exchange over the advertising campaign for the movie, the critic Mendelsohn, the same person who championed the film as a specifically "gay tragedy" about the closet, took producer James Shamus to task for seeming to market it as a universal, rather than a gay-specific, love story. Mendelsohn's primary evidence for his charge that Shamus chooses the universality route of obfuscation is that the words *gay* and *homosexual* are never used in the press kit and that the posters for the ad campaign did not show the two men embracing, thus falsifying the film's content. Shamus, for his part, defends the marketing by saying, "No mainstream film in history has been promoted with as open, proud, and insistent a celebration of the love between two men." Thus Shamus insists that the film is both a love story *and* a gay story and that it solicits every audience member's identification with the film's central gay characters. In their debate, Mendelsohn and Shamus occupy the two binary positions laid out by Eve Sedgwick's influential study, *The Epistemology of the Closet*: the always inadequate either-or of a minoritizing gay desire particular to a specific group of actual homosexuals (Mendelsohn's claim) and a universalizing view that sees homosexual desire in relation to that of other sexualities (Shamus's claim). Indeed, Shamus's claim is precisely that the film's reception, which he masterfully organized, participates in a cultural moment of "shattering the 'epistemology of the closet,'" a shattering that runs "the risk of destroying the nonuniversal, specifically gay knowledge previously hidden inside it."[82]

Of course any film advertisement, necessarily condensed, will attempt to appeal to the most universal possible demographic and will inevitably "falsify" a film's content in trying for the broadest possible appeal.[83] Mendelsohn's minoritizing requirement for the film's ad campaign would seem to translate to a poster that would show Jack and Ennis frontally embraced. Yet as Shamus points out, in a later reply not included in the *New York Review of Books* exchange, frontal embraces are not exactly de rigueur in even the most classically romantic of heterosexual ad campaigns (e.g., posters for both *Titanic* [dir. James Cameron, 1997] and *Pride and Prejudice* [dir. Joe Wright, 2005]). He notes, moreover, that the long shot of Ennis's embrace of Jack from behind (figure 107) is featured as the central image of the film's trailer, underscored with the lines, spoken by Jack at another point in the film: "It could be like this, just like this—always."[84] While I believe that Shamus's defense of his ad campaign is convincing— it does not falsify the film's gay content though it does try to universalize its appeal—the larger question of gay epistemology cannot be answered because, as Sedgwick's book eloquently argues, and as I have been arguing about *Brokeback*, the closet constitutes a place of deep contradiction not easily shattered. There is no definitive answer to an argument between minoritizing and universalizing views of homosexuality, just as there is no definitive answer between constructivist and essentialist understandings of sexuality.

If *Brokeback Mountain* is about the epistemology of the closet, then it cannot be about a proud proclaiming of gay love, a definitive emergence from the closet into the bright light of day. If the film is the product of a postcloset world, it is looking back on an era of the closet. As I have tried to show in the previous discussion of what hangs in the closet of each man, it is not about shattering the confinement of the closet; it is about glimpsing inside and discovering reasons for there being a closet in the first place. Ultimately, this movie's depiction of the closet concerns some rather small rearrangements of what hangs inside. But what is perhaps most important about this representation of the closet and the poster art that advertises it is that it does not aim to show us a bold image of illicit desire, but instead the tension between desire and the fear that inhibits but also eroticizes it. Nowhere does Georges Bataille's observation that the taboo "observed with fear" evokes the "counterpoise of desire which gives it its deepest significance" seem more apt.[85] Considered from the point of view of gay pornography, *Brokeback's* famous publicity still (figure 108) may seem a cowardly avoidance of gay sex; but from the point of view of an eros primed by the tension between fear and desire, it makes

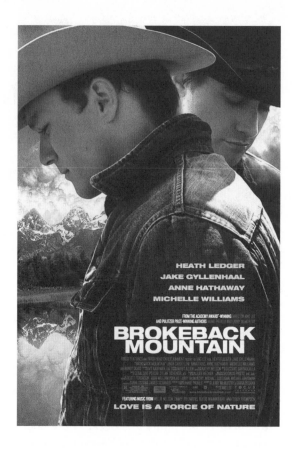

108: The movie poster for *Brokeback Mountain*

for a perfect one: the two men refrain from touch but seem tempted to come closer. The tension of the refraining is palpable, and the eroticism all the more powerful. Some fear—the fear that institutes the closet—is necessary to the historical understanding of this desire. Thus this particular image that refrains from touch takes on tension in the context of the trailer image and the primal sex scene of the film itself. And this is where I would finally disagree with Shamus. The trailer image of Ennis embracing Jack is not a "standard visual representation of erotic love," nor is it "open, celebratory, proud." Rather, it is a melodramatic what might have been, and it makes all the difference in the world that it is a position pictured, as Freud would put it, *a tergo*.

As for the larger argument for the minoritizing or universalizing view of *Brokeback Mountain*, it is—like the false binary of being inside or outside the closet, like the question of where desire comes from altogether, like the primal scene itself—undecidable. We do not know how gay desire suddenly becomes speakable or representable in a culture. One day homosexual desire is hidden, another day it is plain as can be. One day Jack and Ennis are just two cowboys vying for a job, another day they are already beginning a long dance of seduction. Human sexuality, as Laplanche and Pontalis note, seems always to be caught between the too early and the too late occurrence of the event. We cannot know where the upsurgings of desire come from. We are not, and we can never be, on the same wavelength about the origins of desire, the meaning of castration, the real or fantasmatic witnessing of a primal scene. But in 2005 American audiences encountered a film that powerfully enacted these fantasies in ways that hit home to American audiences, and not just the art house crowd. This is what also happened in 1986 with *Blue Velvet*. Both Lynch's small-town mystery of the severed ear and Lee's vast wilderness of the West brought primal fantasies of sex home to the American heartland.

When I was at university, the film club always showed *In the Realm of the Senses* at the start of a new year to get people to join. It was full of explicit sex. . . . That's the benchmark.
—MICHAEL WINTERBOTTOM, 2004

7

philosophy in the bedroom

Hard-Core Art Film Since

the 1990s

Although hard-core pornography had flourished in American movies during the so-called golden age of the seventies, and although Oshima Nagisa's *In the Realm of the Senses* (1976) had seemed to augur an era of hard-core art, in point of fact, by the late 1980s no more graphic sex appeared on large, theatrical screens. Hard-core pornography flourished in the eighties with the move into the home. Hard-core art films did not similarly flourish on either big screens or small. It would not be until the nineties that graphic sex would again screen in theaters. By this time critics got into the habit of distinguishing between two kinds of sex on movie screens: simulated, such as that of *Blue Velvet* and *Brokeback Mountain*, in which great care is taken to avoid the display of (especially male) sexual organs; and the unsimulated, in which male and female sexual organs are on display in action.

It is one of the goals of this chapter to replace the awkward term *unsimulated* with a more appropriate designation that American culture might finally be adult enough to abide: *hard-core art*. Critics resort to the term *unsimulated* to differentiate the sexual representations of art films with explicit sex from the cruder maximum visibility and overt intention-to-arouse of hard-core pornography, on one hand, and from the R-rated *simulated* sex of the mainstream, on the other. Under the Motion Picture Association of America (MPAA) ratings system that has replaced the Hollywood Production Code since 1968, films are given age-appropriate maturity levels that range from G (general, appropriate to children), PG (parental guidance), and PG-13 (parents strongly cautioned, no one twelve and under allowed) to R (restricted). R signals that a film "contains some adult material." Children may see these films only if accompanied by a parent. Adult material, though never designated as just sexual, is considered to encompass "strong language, violence, nudity, drug abuse." Thus simulated sex acts themselves are not necessarily defined as constituting this restricted category, though in practice they often are. The most recently invented category, NC-17, admits no one seventeen or under. Although this category does not necessarily imply just sexual content, it is in fact sex, and especially kinky, nonheterosexual sex and explicit (nonsimulated) glimpses of it that most often lead the MPAA to deploy the NC-17 rating. This rating is usually considered a commercial kiss of death. Sometimes, however, a film may begin with an R-rating, have a life on the large screen, and then be recut to correspond to NC-17 for later home viewing on DVD.[1] While short-duration female nudity is tolerated in some R-rated American movies, male nudity is not, and an acute double standard, brilliantly illustrated in Kirby Dick's documentary *This Film Is Not Yet Rated* (2006), also prevails in the simulated representations of gay and straight sex.[2]

It is tempting to rail against the hypocrisies of the MPAA and its continuing contribution to what I described in chapter 1 as the artificially "long adolescence of American movies." Initiated by the Hollywood Production Code, this adolescence is prolonged now in the MPAA's pathetic last gasp. Its system of assigning presumably age-appropriate labels avoids the outright prohibitions of the Code, but it has undoubtedly contributed to the continued arrested development of American movies and audiences. Given the stunted opportunities to explore explicit sex on-screen outside the realm of hard-core pornography, it is not accidental that most of the films discussed in this chapter, with the important exception of John Cameron Mitchell's *Shortbus* (2006), are foreign. Rather than fume at the MPAA's continued preference in American movies of graphic (simulated) violence over any kind of sex, I would like to champion the many ways in which diverse directors from many different countries have gone all the way. In this way I hope to suggest how American audiences might emerge from the infantilizing dichotomy of simulated/unsimulated, concealed/revealed into a wider range of possibilities.

Hard-core art films are the bold inheritors of Oshima's *In the Realm of the Senses* even if they no longer share the politics of revolutionary transgression marking that singular benchmark film. The films of hard-core art may be aggressive, violent, humiliating, desperate, alienating, tender, loving, playful, joyous, and even boring, but they are art films that emphatically do not shy away from explicit sexual content. It is something of a critical truism that artworks about sex that "leave nothing to the imagination" are inferior as art because of the pornographic expectations that seem to come with the territory. This idea has received its most extreme formulation in George Steiner's diatribe against literary pornography (one can only imagine what Steiner might have had to say about contemporary film and video pornography!). Steiner accuses pornographers of subverting the "last, vital privacy" of sex by doing "our imagining for us."[3] Pornographers, he claims, take away "the words that were of the night and shout them over the roof-tops, making them hollow."[4] He thus views the rise of what I call on/scenity—a public display of sex that loses the force of obscenity by virtue of familiarity—as an explicitness that leaves the imagination impoverished and that infringes on human privacy. I have been arguing throughout this book that sexual representations, whether simulated or explicit, do not necessarily rob the imagination of sexual fantasy. Steiner's presumption that explicit sex acts belong only to the privacy of the "night" fails to understand the ways words and images feed the imagination. Nor does it understand the historical changes taking place in the relations of the human sensorium to both the immediate and the mediated world.

Rather than complain that movies no longer leave anything to the imagination, we might do better to approach the imagination as a faculty that perpetually plays with the limits of the given. Christian Metz has described the cinema as a kind of "permanent strip-tease" whose "wandering framings (wandering like the look, like the caress)" can even take back what it has already given to see.[5] We do not necessarily need the old-fashioned ellipses of the era of the kiss for the imagination to do its work. There will always be ellipses, just not in the places we once expected them. Catherine Breillat, we will see below, offers ellipses in plot just as previous directors used to offer ellipses of sex. If explicit movies can be rich, complex, multitextured, and ambivalent, rather than banal, simple, and formulaic, then so, too, can the imagination that responds to them. In what follows I offer an initial typology of hard-core art film chosen from a range of possibilities.

Lyrical Sex

When the acclaimed British art film director Michael Winterbottom decided to tell the story of a love affair by concentrating almost exclusively on the sexual content of the relationship, his *Nine Songs* (2004) immediately became the most sexually explicit film in the entire history of British cinema.[6] In this film Winterbottom stages a very slight story about a man and a woman (Matt and Lisa, played by Kieran O'Brien and Margo Stilley) who meet at a London concert, have sex, and begin a relationship. The rest of the film portrays their attendance at subsequent concerts (nine songs from nine different concerts), intercut with further sex and small fragments of meals, holidays, pillow talk, and mornings after. All of this is framed by Matt's sparse voice-over recollection of the affair as he does climate research in the icy regions of Antarctica.

All of the songs in the film contribute to a lyrical portrayal of sex. Literally so, for each sex act behaves like a song with something akin to a song's duration, effusion of emotion, and economy of presentation. But despite this superficial resemblance both to the musical sexual interlude of Hollywood tradition and to the sexual number of hard-core pornography, none of the lyrical sex moments are matched up with or accompanied by the music of the songs. Instead of *adding* music to sex, which would have amounted to a sort of hard-core MTV, Winterbottom seeks to discover the lyricism within the sex, most of which is presented unaccompanied by the concert music, or with just a small bit of piano.

To appreciate *Nine Songs* one must abandon the expectation that the sex scenes will illustrate and thus become part of a larger plot and character development. Winterbottom's gamble—which only partly pays off—is that the sensual substance of a love affair can just as well be captured through sexual and musical lyricism as through dramatic event or extended dialogue. The sex scenes, like the music scenes, offer moments set apart from everyday life. Yet Winterbottom also keeps them remarkably separate, one from the other, respecting the different spaces of noisy pub-

109: *Nine Songs* (dir. Michael Winterbottom, 2005), Lisa casually caresses Matt's erection with her feet

lic concert performance and quiet private sexual encounter. The first line is spoken as voice-over as Matt flies over a frozen Antarctic landscape: "When I remember Lisa I don't think about her clothing or her work, where's she's from or what she said. I think about her smell, her taste, her skin touching mine." The film then invokes these sensuous qualities of the affair, with almost a third of the action taking place in bed.

The couple's sex varies from intense thrusting (man on top or woman on top), cunnilingus, fellatio, mild bondage (again, perfectly balanced with respect to tops and bottoms), and female masturbation with a vibrator. Though *In the Realm of the Senses* may have been Winterbottom's benchmark, he does not reproduce the mad love and sexual excess of that earlier film. Rather, he chronicles the male lover's recollections of the arc of a love affair that reaches its peak at about the fifth concert and that afterward fades, apparently more quickly for the woman than for the man. After the third song, while on a brief holiday, Matt declares his love for Lisa after plunging into the frigid sea, yelling "I love you." Lisa does not respond. Later, we see the couple in the bathtub. Lisa, facing Matt at the opposite end of the tub, casually caresses his erection with first one and then both of her feet (figure 109). The gesture speaks volumes about the casual intimacy and playfulness of this middle phase of their affair, but also, through the feet, about Lisa's slightly more cavalier attitude toward it. Following on Matt's profession of love, this scene suggests that while Lisa is seriously engaged in their lovemaking, she is not also equally in love with Matt. However, the physical part of their affair is still on its upward arc. In the next scene, Matt blindfolds Lisa and asks her to recount a sexual fantasy, giving her a prompt: "You're on a beach in Thailand. . . ." As he performs cunnilingus she recounts a fantasy of a woman and a man who have sex on the beach while looking at her. She then orders Matt to "come up here and fuck me." He puts on a condom and does.

Pausing to put on a condom would have been unthinkable in the taboo-breaking films of the seventies, just as it still is in most mainstream heterosexual pornography. Today, however, it is axiomatic. Putting on the condom automatically signifies two things that are historically new in the world of screening sex: first, the awareness of the danger of sex ever since the threat of AIDS became known;[7] second, the unmistakably recreational nature of the sex about to transpire—there is no question of procreation as a goal or outcome. (Compare the kiss between George and Mary in Frank Capra's 1946 *It's a Wonderful Life* immediately followed by their exit from a church, and followed just a few shots later by the children of this union.)[8]

On one hand, we can see that Lisa is the perfect sexual partner: adventurous, aroused, playful, and willing to ask for what she wants. On the other hand, we know that Matt is recalling the affair, apparently trying to comprehend a relation that we already suspect did not end happily. Indeed, the moment Matt's profession of love is not answered in kind by Lisa, we expect that the relation will not endure. In keeping with his determination to show a relationship *through* its sex acts, Winterbottom next shows Lisa confessing that sometimes when they kiss she wants to bite him hard enough to make him bleed. We see the couple next at a sex club, not at their usual concert. The rock concerts are Matt's passion, and Lisa will tellingly opt out of the next one. The sex club, however, seems to be her passion. She certainly seems more interested in the lap dances offered by these women than is Matt, who soon leaves. During this brief unelaborated scene, we hear a different kind of music: a woman in a recording sings the blues. Though it is only a snippet of sound, it forces the realization that all the other music in the live concerts has been by male rockers. Whatever Lisa's own song may be, it may not be any of the eight other songs we will hear in this film.

Just as we do not see Lisa's experience of the lap dance, we do not see the argument the couple most likely had later over Matt's departure. What we do see soon after is Lisa alone in bed with a vibrator as Matt forlornly looks on. We can only surmise that whatever the cause, the heady experience of the beginning of the affair has now lost steam. Lisa no longer seems to find Matt fulfilling as a lover. After Lisa orgasms she weeps, perhaps mourning what she now anticipates as the end of the affair. We may recall at this point that in most of their sexual encounters it has been Lisa who has been the first to pull away. Now Lisa will cling to Matt, but it is the clinging of the partner who best knows that the end is near and is mourning the relationship's loss. Soon after, the couple has the only argument we are privileged to see. It is over trifles: he put sugar in her tea; she has taken a pill too early in the day. Though they make up and have passionate sex (light bondage this time, with Matt blindfolded), all that follows is tinged with the melancholy of anticipated loss.

Matt's activities in Antarctica frame the film and serve as occasional metaphors for its form: "Antarctica," he says, "is an exercise in reductionism;" its cold landscape is visually juxtaposed to Lisa's warm flesh; like the affair, it is "claustrophobia and agoraphobia in the same place, like two people in a bed"—a phrase many critics seized on to analogize the film itself. Matt is the subject who speaks, and Lisa is the object about whom he speaks: "She was twenty-one, beautiful, egotistical, careless, and crazy." If Lisa often remains a cipher in terms of motivation, so, too, does Matt. The mere fact that he narrates the story does not give us any more access to what he is about as a character.

If we accept the film's premise that what we learn about the couple must come from the substance of the sexual relationship, we should not look for a narrative explanation for why Lisa leaves but to the sex itself. What we learn from its performance is that Lisa is more "out there"—both more sexually frank and more sexually demanding: she reads pornography out loud and speaks her sexual fantasies. Matt does neither. We also suspect, from the lap dance episode and from other hints about female friends, that she may be inclined to have sex with women. She is also clearly more drug dependent (we see her snort cocaine more than once, and Matt criticizes her for taking an unidentified pill). When Lisa demonstrates that she can satisfy herself through masturbation with a vibrator, the point is not the evil of technologically aided masturbation or a judgment on Lisa for engaging in it, but a way of showing the disconnect occurring between the once passionate couple. While it might be possible to invoke judgment on Lisa's withdrawal from heterosexual coupledom, especially given the sadness of the soon bereft Matt, we have nevertheless been witness to a highly nuanced chronicle of an affair presented and understood primarily through its many and varied acts of sex. To pay attention to this sex is to understand that sometimes the "hottest" sex in a relationship can occur after the potential for mutual love has been foreclosed. While this also means that a certain desperation enters into the proceedings, affairs can have this desperation, though rarely those depicted in movies.

Though the film does leave one hungry for more story, particularly for more of Lisa's, the development, mood, and execution of each sexual scene creates a coherent arc of relationship. Similarly, the way Lisa masturbates alone with a vibrator while Matt sits apart has the same emotional resonance of a scene that might show Lisa eating alone. Sex, like eating, is a bodily function with its own automatic pleasure and satisfaction. Indeed, Winterbottom is on record saying, "If you film actors eating a meal, the food is real; the audience know that. But when it comes to sex they know it's pretend. You'd never do that with food and so I started thinking we should make sex real."[9]

Like André Bazin, but without that critic's apologetic remorse about sexual realism, Winterbottom cites the age-old realist imperative: if one part of a film is real, then the rest shall be too. Like Bazin, he wants to introduce a level of documentary realism to a basic fact of human life— as basic as eating—that has been occluded in conventional movies. But where Bazin drew the line at real sex, arguing that if you showed real sex you must then show real violence and, at the limit, admit the morally unthinkable possibility of unsimulated violence, even murder, Winterbottom's example of food prompts us to ask if all the drugs and alcohol consumed in *Nine Songs* are real as well. My guess is that some are and some are not and that much the same thing can be said about the sex the couple engages in. Not every thrust that we see Matt make into Lisa is that of a certifiably erect penis, but we see enough of that penis to believe more in the authenticity of the rest. Nor does every moan that Lisa emits as Matt performs cunnilingus correspond directly to the moments that his lips touch her genitals, but we believe in them nevertheless. There is often a very fine line between the real and the performed in screened sex acts, just as there is with kisses and with food that could easily be spit out before swallowed, bourbon that is really iced tea, or cocaine that is powdered sugar. Nevertheless, Winterbottom's (documentary) portrayal of the sex of his (fictional) couple represents a significant assault on the heretofore fairly rigid division between pornographic hard-core sex and simulated art sex in feature cinema—a division that had only been truly broken previously in narrative film by Andy Warhol's 1968 *Blue Movie* and by Winterbottom's own benchmark, Oshima's *In the Realm of the Senses*.

Most critics have been quite careful to distinguish *Nine Songs* from pornography.[10] Even the notoriously censorious British Board of Film Classification gave the film an R rating. Nevertheless, this is the one film of all those discussed in this chapter that structurally comes the closest to conventional pornography. If pornography can be defined simply as a string of sexual numbers hung onto a plot existing primarily as an excuse for the sex, then, as I have argued elsewhere, pornography's closest genre affiliation is the musical in which the lyrical choreography of song and dance numbers resemble the rhythms of bodies in the sex act. *Nine Songs* thus merges the lyrical structure of the musical—in this case nine songs by popular bands—with the sex acts performed by Matt and Lisa. If the film *were* pornography it would be possible to say that it is the very first work in the genre to possess even half-decent music. However, *Nine Songs* is not pornography if we mean by that a genre intent on the maximum visibility of sexual function with the accompanying intent to arouse. Despite its undoubted display of graphic sex, and despite the fact that its display might arouse, it never focuses on the plumbing details of hard-core involuntary display. It is graphic, we might say, without being pornographic. *Nine Songs* represents one possible, lyrical direction for a new kind of hard-core art cinema. Winterbottom is an art film director who realizes, like Oshima before him, that not to speak sex in the realistic way of which cinema alone is capable is to leave out an enormous chunk of human life. Very few of the directors I will examine below believe they are striking blows for sexual freedom when they portray graphic sex. Yet all feel compelled, like Winterbottom, to be more "real" about the often paroxysmic life of the flesh than their predecessors.

Idiot Sex

Lars von Trier is another well-known contemporary art film director whose main subject has not previously been sex.[11] Nor is his Dogma-certified *The Idiots* (*Idioterne*, 1998; released in the United States in 2000) a sex film in the way of many of the other films discussed here. There is far too little sex in it for it to count as a major contributor to the new wave of sexual explicitness. Nevertheless, von Trier's decision to include a short scene of unsimulated penetrative sex in a "spastic orgy" (explained below) means that he regarded real sex as one of the measures of authenticity in the new wave of cinema he helped launch.

The so-called Dogma manifesto, originally signed by von Trier and Thomas Vinterberg in 1995 (hence the title Dogma 95), was first and foremost opposed to the stifling creative constrictions of big-budget, big-star, big-effects filmmaking. The manifesto's ten "Vows of Chastity" were aimed half-seriously at the restoration of "purity" to a medium that the original cosigners deemed to have been corrupted by complex cinematic effects.[12] Most of all, von Trier, Vinterberg, and the later joiners wanted to return cinema to a more spontaneous, emotionally authentic medium with neither fake blood nor fake tears by adhering to the discipline of the Dogma rules. The final words of the vow read: "My supreme goal is to force the truth out of my characters and settings. I swear to do so by all the means available and at the cost of any good taste and any aesthetic considerations. Thus I make my VOW OF CHASTITY."[13]

Von Trier's vow would seem to require, according to his own interpretation of the rules, that sex scenes, like crying scenes, derive from authentic feelings. Just as the director would expect the tears of a crying scene to be real, he would, in theory, expect erections and penetrations to be real as well—"good taste" be damned.[14] Liberated from commercial constraint by the "Vows of Chastity," von Trier was determined with *The Idiots* to emotionally and physically go all the way. What else could he do in a film that thematized the struggle to arrive at a core of authenticity through the technique of releasing one's "inner idiot"—literally acting like a mentally challenged spastic in both public and private places?

The film is about a commune of dissidents opposed to the inauthenticities of polite Danish society. They inhabit an old villa in an upscale neighborhood. Their leader, Stoffer (Jens Albinus), is a tyrannical, unbalanced, and charismatic dictator, not unlike von Trier himself, who seems to need to flirt with emotional disaster to create. Part performance art project, part political intervention into the well-oiled machinery of Danish society, Stoffer eggs the group on to more and more risky spectacles of "spassing" in public—restaurants, swimming pools, the door-to-door peddling of pathetic Christmas ornaments, even a scene in which they encounter a group of persons with real Down's syndrome. They regurgitate food, drool, get help going to the bathroom, and generally expose what look like involuntary bodily functions to the dismay of fellow citizens and to the appreciation of one another. It is never quite clear what this ultimate "spassing" performance might be, only that it is in process. Stoffer, for example, urges the group to take their idiocy back with them to their families and professions where, because they care more deeply about how they are regarded, it will be more meaningful. Many balk at this command. Stoffer himself sets the tone in a scene of total freak-out in which he runs naked through the streets of the staid neighborhood. Rebels with an ambiguous cause—and in this sense not unlike the Dogma movement itself—von

Trier's idiots seem less interesting when engaged in simple exercises to *épater les bourgeois* and more interesting when delving into more dangerous personal and interpersonal terrain.

Given the logic of a story about bodily "spassing" as a device for seeking authenticity, it is not surprising that one of the commune's celebrations should turn into a spastic orgy. At a birthday party for Stoffer, most of the "idiots" arrive in character. When asked to propose a game for the group to play, Stoffer proposes a "gang bang." "Sure, I'd love a spasser fuck," replies one of the women, who promptly disrobes and lies down. The others get naked too, and the men display erections amid a confusing tumble of bodies. When one naked woman flees the house, three naked men pursue her in a chase across the grass. But they clumsily miss in each of their attempts to tackle her. When they do have her on the ground, all dissolve in giggles. More spastic group grope than gang bang, the orgy glimpsed inside the house is brief, good-humored, and playful: out of a mass of intertwined bodies, we see only a brief moment of penetration. The willed spastic behavior of the group thus finds a correlative in the involuntary spasms of the sex act.

Since many of the actors were unwilling to perform real sex in the orgy, von Trier brought in professional porn performers who actually did the requisite penetration. If not in violation of the letter, these body doubles appeared in flagrant violation of the keep-it-real spirit of the "Vows of Chastity." Nevertheless, these very brief hard-core glimpses color the next scene of simulated sex. After all the faux idiots have performed their spastic orgy, two of the more genuinely troubled individuals get together: Josephine (Louise Mierite), who is later retrieved from the group by a father worried that she has not been taking her medication, and Jeppe (Nicolaj Lie Kaas), whose whole being never relaxes from a state of awkward dis-ease. Josephine had gotten naked at the beginning of the orgy, but had then fled the room. Jeppe, who had hovered about its perimeter, comes up the stairs half-undressed himself and sees the naked Josephine spassing.

In contrast to the free and easy, good-humored, and explicit sex of the orgy, in which a "spasser fuck" is portrayed as a frenetic, giggly grope, we now see two fragile people, already uncomfortable in their own skins, already uncomfortably close to their "inner idiots," touching one another awkwardly. Josephine stands facing a wall; she whimpers and issues inarticulate cries. Jeppe approaches her and then sits on the bed. Josephine goes to him and awkwardly touches his naked thigh. Though this gesture is an inquisitive probe into his sexual receptivity, it is, like many of the sexual gestures discussed in this chapter, not one that has been much seen at the movies. And this seems to be partly the point. This is a couple that seems to have missed out on the kind of carnal knowledge to be gained from screening sex. Jeppe, especially, seems not to understand that to move into the domain of touch is to give up some of the domain of sight: he keeps trying to see Josephine's face while smelling and feeling it at the same time. This holding close of faces, yet without the conventional fore-play of the kiss (the moment in which sight is typically given up), intro-duces a peculiar tension that makes strange all the other familiar gestures of heterosexual sex. Where in the orgy one might say that the idiots were fake (acting out idiot personas) and the sex was real, in this scene, the idiots seem more real and the sex is faked.

After a pause in which they look at one another and Josephine holds Jeppe's face in her hands, he awkwardly lunges. The lack of continuity between one shot and the next—one moment Jeppe has his shirt off; the next moment it is on—only enhances the sense of the spontaneity of the moment. Though all we see is the very conventional missionary position of a clothed man lying atop a naked woman, the physical connection, coming from such a space of awkwardness, is electric. Josephine professes love at one point, weeps uncontrollably at another, and seems to lose her idiot persona for something even more real: an intimacy both frightening and tender. It would be a mistake to conclude, however, that visual discre-tion here makes possible a nuance that the brute explicitness in the earlier scene does not allow. For it is the spastic, freewheeling, hard-core orgy (though censored in all American prints, with distracting black boxes placed over genitals) that provides the emotional context for, and contrast to, Jeppe and Josephine's intimate connection.[15] This connection will pay off further in the subsequent scene during which Josephine's father re-trieves his emotionally disturbed daughter from the commune and Jeppe throws himself helplessly on the departing car taking her away.

In the recriminations that follow the loss of Josephine to the group, Stoffer again challenges the members to take their contrived idiocy home to their real lives. One by one the more normal members of the band of idiots prove they lack the courage. Only Karen (Bodil Jørgensen), an older woman who has more sincerely entered into the activities of the group (and who, like Josephine, has an emotional fragility that puts her in close touch with idiocy), dares to do so, and with devastating personal conse-quences. In an excruciating scene we see her reunited with the family she had abandoned to join the idiots. In this scene we learn that following the death of her young child, she had walked out on her husband, mother, father, and sisters. As we watch her chew and then extrude the unswallowed cake and coffee served at this painful funereal family gathering, we realize that for Karen idiocy has high stakes. It deeply offends her family and seems to permanently burn her bridges to them. At the urging of her communal companion, Karen then leaves her family. The film ends at this moment of devastating idiocy.

The sex in this film is only a part of von Trier's larger plan of seeking greater authenticities of performance. It is just one of many bodily activities on which he seeks to refocus the attention of cinema. Though he cheats the most on his Dogma vows when it comes to sex, the attenuation of the sexual scene, the ability to see a moment of sex between two idiots beyond the familiar clichés of dominant commercial traditions, is nevertheless the most memorable aspect of this film. A long way from Winterbottom's lyricism, idiot sex seeks to unsettle our very expectations of sexual performance.

Urgent Sex: Last Tango in Lewisham

The acclaimed stage and opera director Patrice Chéreau has said in several interviews that he wants his film sex scenes to begin "where others normally end."[16] This means that they will have greater duration certainly, but also that they are constructed as dramatic wholes with gestures that function almost like dialogue, as a call-and-response in which body parts normally hidden come into play.

Chéreau's *Intimacy* (2000) is a French-produced film set in London, adapted from a novel by Hanif Kureishi. It is Chéreau's first film in English. In some ways it offers an anglicized and downscaled hard-core version of *Last Tango in Paris*—David Denby's review calls it *Last Tango in Lewisham*.[17] It features regular Wednesday afternoon meetings between a man and a woman who abandon themselves to passionate sex without so much as exchanging names. The man, Jay (Mark Rylance), will prove to be a head barman and divorcé who lives in willful, antibourgeois squalor while undergoing a midlife crisis. The woman, Claire (Kerry Fox), will prove to be a mother and sometimes actress married to a cab driver. Jay soon finds himself impatiently waiting for the appointed hour, but instead of developing a relationship and getting to know the woman, he surreptitiously follows her, witnesses her amateur theatrics, and strikes up an acquaintance with her husband and son. More emotionally needy than Claire, yet unable to show it, Jay cannot abide the fact that she seems content with their anonymous Wednesday assignations in which they barely speak. After his stalking nearly ruins her marriage, he makes a plea for her to stay with him. Instead, she has sex with him one last time and leaves.

The film opens with urgent, hurried, and explicitly penetrative sex between these near strangers. Much of the first scene shows them struggling desperately to get a better leveraged position from which to thrust at one another. The difficulty of obtaining the ideal leverage creates a kind of poignancy as the two bodies, so separate in the rest of their lives, work desperately hard to maintain an always imperfect physical connection throughout the prolonged scene. One way of registering the difference between 1970s art sex films and those of the new millennium is to compare this film's first sex scene to a similar scene of simulated first sex between Paul and Jeanne in *Last Tango in Paris*.

Recall that Bernardo Bertolucci's 1972 film also begins with an urgent, animal act of lust between strangers in an empty apartment, also ending on the floor, also emphasizing what Pauline Kael called "*thrusting, jabbing eroticism.*"[18] It is perhaps not surprising that what seemed shockingly real in 1972 now seems remarkably stylized and abrupt. Art film audiences, I would venture, have grown more familiar with a certain duration in the sex acts figured on-screen, whether from the often absurdly long, extremely graphic scenes of hard-core pornography or the tighter interludes of the Hollywood mainstream. Screened today, the *Tango* scene seems remarkably short (a little over two minutes) and arch, especially the moment at the end when Jeanne dramatically rolls away from Paul like an overly enthusiastic actor biting the dust.

Both of these initial acts of sex portray urgent lust between individuals who will fail to connect as enduring couples. In comparison to the stylized tango of Bertolucci, however, Chéreau's film emphasizes the vulnerability of the couple whose naked bodies exude a desperate desire. Nor does he invoke a nudity double standard. Claire has a slight belly and a melancholy need. Jay is slender with a receding hairline, a hungry look, and sad eyes. He undresses first. Where Bertolucci's camera holds his couple at a (respectful, goldenly lit) distance, the graphic sex of Chéreau's couple is seen in a cold, bluish light and from much closer views. These views are caught up in the urgency of the act, though not so much so as to imply the shakiness of a handheld camera that is itself in the action. We become aware through this closeness of the actual physical exertion involved: how the bodies pant and lose breath; how awkward it is to take off clothes in a hurry; how one or the other must occasionally rest before pushing on; how Claire's breathing is through her nose while Jay's outright pant is

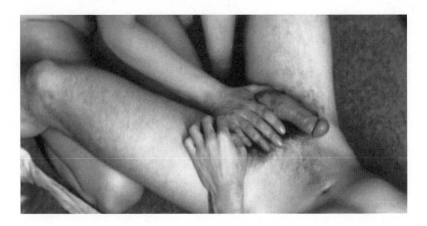

110: *Intimacy* (dir. Patrice Chéreau, 2001), Claire strokes Jay's penis against his body

through the mouth and partially voiced. Most of all, we become aware of the duration of the act (which, at three minutes in this first scene, is a full third longer than that in *Last Tango*).

The couple's second meeting is almost as wordless. They lunge at one another greedily while still dressed. They then stop abruptly, making a conscious effort to savor the experience, and to slowly undress. They kiss naked on their knees before one another. Claire strokes Jay's erect penis with the palm of her hand as he lies on his back. She begins at the base and strokes up its length, pressing it against his abdomen (figure 110). While I do not suppose that this gesture is at all uncommon in the gestural repertoires of heterosexual sex, I found myself shocked to see such an intimate gesture on film. So often in mainstream movies women's gestures seem organized to deny prior familiarity with the movements of sex. It comes as a surprise, for example, in Alfred Hitchcock's *Notorious* (1946) to see Ingrid Bergman using the back of her fingers to stroke Cary Grant's ear in a gesture of intimacy that speaks volumes about her character's sexual experience and the awareness of her own desire.[19] Similarly, the hunger, urgency, and desire of Claire's gestures are unprecedented in any known repertoire of hard-core cinematic representation. Though she strokes the erect penis, she does not offer the kind of reverential penis worship that so commonly occurs in hard-core pornography and which is usually designed to showcase the penis's outward extension from the male body in phallic display. Rather, we feel that she feels both the fleshy vulnerability of the organ as well as its pulsing hardness. Most important, the gesture makes us believe in the reciprocity of one touched body part to another.

In the next position, the couple is locked together in intercourse and ends up on their side, holding on to one another desperately. Unlike pornography, no effort is made to "get in" to see the sexual organs, yet to privilege the view of insertion and extraction, the previous shot of stroking (like the previous glimpse of penetration in European releases of von Trier's idiot orgy) lends credence to other acts that are less graphically penetrative. We believe, in other words, that this couple is connected, whether they really are or not. Chéreau's camera even backs off, adopting several more remote vantage points, including a final one that moves all the way down to their feet and then looks up their legs. From this perspective, each thrust by Jay yields small jiggles in the back of Claire's leg and thigh, which are wrapped around his body (figure 111). Their faces and chests grow flushed in the heat of their sustained grappling.

Compared to the hypervisible penetration and spraying ejaculate of the money shots of hard-core pornography that tend to isolate organs for individual display, this momentary connection emphasizes the desperate tenuousness of Georges Bataille's continuity that disappears back into discontinuity. We understand the poignancy of each half of the couple rediscovering themselves as separate beings. While *Last Tango in Paris* had also attempted to dramatize the urgency of the couple's need, its couplings seem comparatively stylized. Though one really needs the moving image to appreciate this, there is something quite touching about the way Fox's Claire finds herself with her left leg poised on Jay's ass (figure 112). The same leg that had jiggled in response to his desperate thrusting now returns to being just an ordinary leg, indicated through a tiny, mundane movement of her foot that reveals it to no longer be attached to the center of her pleasure. Jay's final and only line, "Next Wednesday, is that a Wednesday too?"—a minimalist question about the future of their connections—is left unanswered, adding a note of poignancy.

Neither tastefully erotic nor insistently hard-core, Chéreau's film surprises. It makes us realize how impoverished are the gestures and emotions of most cinematic sex acts. But here, perhaps, we need to examine our terms. How shall we describe what actors do when they have explicit sex in art films? Acting implies artifice, becoming precisely what one is not, though drawing on what one has been to create an appearance that is credible, that gets into the role. To act a scene of sex is, in these explicit

Intimacy

111: Each thrust by Jay yields small jiggles in Claire's leg

112: A leg and foot go back to being just that

moments, not only to engage in acts that act as though they were sex, it is also, sometimes, to have sex as well.

If an actor is asked to express grief—let us say to weep over the body of a dead lover—it is entirely possible that the actor will feel grief, not actually for the character posing as dead, but that a real quality of grief, possibly connected with some real loss in real life, will be conjured for the benefit of the scene, to make it true. The more genuine the tears, the more they come from within the body of the performer (rather than, say, as effects elicited by glycerin), then, presumably, according to this ethos, the better the performance.[20] In a sex scene, however, actual sexual intimacy with another person must take place, whether or not one really feels desire for that person or whether one really comes. This may be one of those occasions where the contemporary sense of the word *performance*—connoting an avant-garde edge challenging the more safely contained boundaries of acting and role—is more appropriate. If performance is the art of opening the body of the performer up to the physical and emotional challenges of the situation being performed, then Chéreau's film, along with those made by Winterbottom and von Trier, can be said to require the performance of sex: the physical motions and the accompanying emotions that might be more real than just acting.

Sexual Humiliation: Catherine Breillat's Philosophy in the Bedroom

Unlike Winterbottom, von Trier, and Chéreau, the French director Catherine Breillat has single-mindedly explored women's sexuality throughout a long career as both a writer and a filmmaker. Breillat began as a teenager with the publication of a novel, *L'homme facile*, which was immediately banned in France for its sexual frankness. She also had a small role in *Last Tango*. Since the mid-seventies she has continued writing novels, which often read like sketches for future films, and then making films from some of them. Her first film, *Une vraie jeune fille* (1976), an adaptation of her third novel, is the story of the erotic fantasies and sexual awakening of a brooding adolescent girl during her summer vacation from school back home on the family farm. This girl philosophizes before her mirror in voice-over: "I cannot accept the proximity of my vagina and my face." And indeed, the film follows through on this premise as she goes back and forth between attraction toward nascent sexual urges and powerful revulsion. Denied distribution in France, the film has only resurfaced in the 1990s along with a new wave of sexually oriented films and especially with the controversies surrounding Breillat's more recent, sexually explicit *Romance* (1999), *Fat Girl (À ma soeur!* 2001), and *Anatomy of Hell (L'anatomie de l'enfer* 2004).

In all Breillat's films, sexual desire emerges as a highly ambivalent phenomenon. It is often a powerful attraction, but it is also a source of shame and compromise. Most fundamentally, it is something that her female characters are destined to negotiate, both within themselves and with the men with whom they have sex. Self-conscious, self-reflexive beings contemplate themselves and wonder about the conjunction of conscious thought and intention with animal lust. Sex may be a pleasure, but it also causes pain and humiliation. The flesh is both sublime and ridiculous. To be a virgin is to carry around an enormous burden. To lose virginity can be a negotiation of enormous bad faith.

In Breillat's critical breakthrough film *Romance*, Marie (Caroline Ducey), a young elementary school teacher, is sexually spurned by the boyfriend with whom she lives—a coldly narcissistic male model. Proof of this boyfriend's lack of interest is dramatized in the limpness of his penis, which Marie tries unsuccessfully to arouse via fellatio. Humiliated, Marie leaves their bed late at night and prowls a bar. She seeks merely to prove her desirability to a man. Entering the bar, she ever so slightly brushes by a bronzed, golden hunk of a man seated at a stool (Paolo, played by Rocco Siffredi). As soon as she passes, we see him take her in with all his senses. He perks up, half rising from his barstool. They exchange looks and she glories in his interest. Their dialogue is an eloquent mating ritual in which each of them concocts a lie that may also be a partial truth: Marie claims to be married but restless; the man claims that his wife is dead and that he has not made love for four months.

Outside the bar, in Marie's car, the couple makes out eagerly. Marie's voice-over informs us how hungry she is for the "miracle of a stranger making love to her," for the access it gives her to a "pure, childish desire." However, the point of the film is never simply to depict this desire but rather to show how difficult, complex, and short-lived "pure" desire can be—indeed, how much it may be mixed with disgust, how much work must be invested in its achievement, and how complex the power-pleasure relations between male and female can be. Soon after Marie exults in the purity of her abandon, the lover, Paolo, who speaks with a thick Italian accent, requests that Marie give him a blow job (*faire la pipe*). In many films such a request would be used to mark the tawdriness of the affair or the male lover's lack of respect for the woman. Here, however, given our knowledge of Marie's earlier thwarted desire, she is not insulted. She only informs Paolo that she would be happy to do so, but not as their first sex and not in a car.

As in all her films, Breillat is as interested in the details of sexual negotiation as in the sex itself. Several scenes later the two lovers are finally in bed, negotiating again about sexual position. Throughout the scene, a naked, but ever cerebral Marie strains to remain emotionally faithful to her cold and absent lover while still seeking physical satisfaction with the warm and present Italian one. Siffredi, who plays the lover, is Italy's best-known male porn star, making here the kind of real crossover that American porn stars have only dreamed of making. In this scene, we see how thoroughly Breillat departs from the *Last Tango* double standard model of sexual display. The man's body—warm, bronzed flesh and prominently erect penis—is more on display than that of this pale, ethereal, and small-breasted woman. For once the man is body, the woman is mind, as evident in Marie's ongoing voice-over philosophical reflections on the sexual relation—a veritable "philosophy in the bedroom" in the grand tradition of the Marquis de Sade.[21]

The scene begins in the interlude between one bout of sex and another, at precisely the point at which postcoital conversation, and philosophizing, become possible. Paolo, somewhat reluctantly, puts on a new condom. Marie has evidently insisted on it though he protests that he has not had sex for four months and so is "clean." Marie observes that when they first had sex he hid the application of the condom, but that now he seems to flaunt both penis and condom. Like Viva in *Blue Movie*, she explains that she does not like "to watch cock." Nevertheless, she strokes his briefly, while still making small talk about the used condom, which she briefly holds up and verbally compares to the tampons she sometimes hides under the bed when having sex during her periods. Her voice-over explains that she is intrigued by disgusting things. She also opines out loud that condoms make guys go soft. She complains that many men (though obviously not Paolo) cannot get hard enough: "Look at any porno: Girls have to stuff limp cocks in them." This theme continues in a diatribe against badly shaped cocks—those that are too thin, too crooked, too pointy. When she turns her back to Paolo he asks if she wants it in the ass. She says not yet, but that she prefers not to face him during sex.

Only at the point that he penetrates her from behind does Marie stop talking. Given Marie's reference to porno, not to mention the presence of Siffredi himself in the film, a comparison of this sex scene to pornography seems in order. One obvious difference in Breillat's sex scene is the presence of the condom, discussed, argued over, and displayed in both its used and unused state. In contrast, condoms are almost never displayed—let alone argued over—in heterosexual pornography. In *Romance* this prosaic detail becomes an integral part of the drama of the couple's sex. A second obvious difference is the relative unimportance of genital sex once the erect penis has been registered as present. Instead of pornography's confirming close-ups of meat and money shots, *Romance* presents the couple's encounter in one long take that shows them on the bed—Marie on her stomach with her back to Paolo and Paolo on top. The camera pans a little to the right at one moment to take in their lower bodies; it pans a little to the left to concentrate on the couple's faces and upper bodies, and then continues to subtly shift attention between lower and upper halves, in tension, in the words of Breillat's earlier heroine, between "vagina and face."

Marie proffers only her back to Paolo and later refuses *la tendresse* of kisses or cuddling. Her withholding seems to be part of her larger project of remaining emotionally faithful to Paul, even as she seeks sexual release with Paolo. Her voice-over at the conclusion of the scene explains that she does not want to see the men who screw her: "I want to be nothing more than a hole . . . the more gaping the hole, the more obscene, the truer it is, the more I surrender. It's metaphysical. I disappear in proportion to the cock taking me. I become hollow. That's my purity." Marie has finally taken the sensual pleasure that had been missing in her life with Paul, but her pleasure in her new lover is guarded, ambivalent. Though she articulates a desire to disappear, in fact she seems to try hard not to give herself up completely to the experience. She cannot fully achieve what her philosophy in the bedroom desires.

In the rest of the film Marie will continue to seek the sexual release she cannot find with the man she loves, finding her greatest release, in Breillat's usual celebration of paradox, with her decidedly unalluring boss— the school principal—who applies the intricate knots of bondage. Though some form of conscious humiliation does seem to be a key element of all of her sexual experiences (most important in the sexual experience she is denied by the man she loves), this does not mean that Marie has found, like O in *The Story of O*, her inner masochist. Rather, as Liz Constable has argued, the experience of bondage with the older school principal—in many ways the exact opposite of her bossy control of Paolo in the scene described above—does not mean that Marie discovers herself through the perversion of a bondage to which she submits, but rather that she discovers a form of transformative rebirth to which she willingly surrenders, not as permanent condition but as part of an ongoing process of becoming a sexual subject.[22]

Breillat's 2001 film *Fat Girl* also deals with sexual humiliation and negotiation. But this time the sex concerns the initiation of two inexperienced sisters, one twelve and one fifteen. Anaïs (Anaïs Reboux) is the younger, and bigger, of the two. It is through her often reluctant eyes that we watch the seduction and defloration of her svelte and beautiful older sister, Elena (Roxane Mesquida). However, this is no ordinary, wistful, bittersweet end-of-innocence tale so typical of French films. Nor is it the sex-is-pure-humiliation that we have seen from directors like Todd Solondz or Gaspar

Noé.[23] Though the sex acts portrayed *are* humiliating, and even worse, they are never without ambivalent desire.

The two sisters are initially discovered in a very long shot walking and talking about sex and boys as if they had worlds of experience. Anaïs, the fat, younger one, tells Elena, the svelte, older one, that despite Elena's beauty she scares boys away. Elena vows to pick up a boy in the next café yet also insists that by retaining her virginity she remains exempt from the charge of "loose morals" leveled by her sister. Anaïs disputes the tactics of the technical virgin, saying she would like to be divested of her virginity long before she meets the man she wants. (We see her repeatedly singing a forlorn song about boredom in which she longs for someone, anyone—a man, a woman, a werewolf—to relieve her ennui.) During this opening conversation the two girls walk from an extreme distance into closer view, and we are surprised, given the apparent sophistication of their talk, to discover how very young they both are. At the café Elena, to prove the point that she does not scare boys away, picks up a young Italian law student (Fernando, played by Libero De Rienzo) and flirts with him while Anaïs eats a banana split. Each sister indulges in the ambivalent pleasure that seems to complete her.

Locked in battles of love-hate extending back to their infancy, these sisters alternate affectionate confidence with the typical cruelties of adolescence. Each indulges the other in her weakness: Elena comforts the unhappy Anaïs with more food; Anaïs makes possible her sister's sex. She pretends to be asleep when Elena invites her new boyfriend to sneak into the beach vacation bedroom they share at night. Anaïs both criticizes and envies her sister's sexual initiation. Playacting alone in a swimming pool earlier in the film, we see her enact a dialectic between innocence and experience: at one end of the pool she kisses the pylon of the diving platform as if it is her lover, acting the part of the shy virgin, she says that she is saving herself for him; dog-paddling in her awkward, buoyant flesh to the other side, she now acts the role of the worldly woman to the pool ladder, saying cavalierly that each lover brings something new. At night, however, she watches a similar dialectic of innocence and experience play out in Fernando's assault on her sister's virginity (figure 113). As in *Romance*, Breillat's principle of masculine carnality is another Italian with a big erection, though this time not one played by a porn star. Elena is torn between the same pretense to worldliness and an innocent desire to save herself for her future husband that Anaïs performed in the pool.

The two bedroom scenes between Elena and Fernando, with Anaïs as

113: *Fat Girl* (dir. Catherine Breillat, 2001), an Italian with a big erection

reluctant witness, constitute the dramatic core of the film. Elena both wants and fears the loss of her virginity. Her desire is tentative, hesitant; his is alternately cajoling and bullying. We have heard all the clichés before: She, on one hand, would like to love him, does not want to be a "cock tease," but worries that she will lose his respect. He, on the other hand, claims to respect and love her but needs proof of her love or he will be forced (out of physiological necessity) to turn to an older woman whom he does not love. What is new in this scene is the remarkable combination of duration with explicitness in the form of Fernando's initially looming erect penis. Out of this combination a banal scene of seduction takes on epic proportions in a prolonged battle of wills lasting most of the night. In this battle, the erect penis functions like a dramatis personae. All Fernando's actions, and all Elena's reactions, are governed by its visible presence in two scenes. He argues, for example, that she must trust him to "stay on the edge" and not to come. She is physically uncomfortable with its demands, especially when he presses it up against her. At the same time, however, she pitifully accepts his practiced lies that profess eternal love and the promise of marriage, promises which are made strange, and even more inauthentic, by his Italian accent. We know this is a line, but we understand that she wants to believe that the man to whom she will eventually give her virginity is the love of her life. How else can a young girl have access to sex but through the rhetoric of true love? Thus each time she rebuffs him and he turns away, she finds a way to give him new hope. Eventually, an unhappy compromise is reached "the back way."

What proves especially powerful about the scene, beyond the insistence

114: *Fat Girl*, Anaïs as witness of her sister's ordeal

of the penis, are the two moments in which the film cuts to Anaïs watching from her bed across the room. In both cases the shift to her distanced point of view occurs at the precise moment that most hurts her sister. In the first instance when Fernando tells how he has enjoyed humiliating other women who invited him into their bedrooms, though of course not Elena whom he respects, the cut to Anaïs punctuates his bad faith, for she perceives the violation despite its apparent lack of violence. In the second instance, when Fernando anally penetrates Elena, we again watch Anaïs's face as she hears her sister's muted screams and Fernando's noisy climax (figure 114). Thus the eventual sexual climax of the first bedroom ordeal is not viewed "in the flesh," but on the face of the empathic younger sister who registers its violation.

In the second bedroom scene, Elena more freely gives herself to Fernando, and Anaïs is on this occasion the silent judge and uncomfortable witness to her sister's actual defloration. We see Fernando put on a condom and climb onto Elena. She asks him to be gentle but he insists that "one hard push" is best. As he does push, we again cut to Anaïs: this time she is weeping and turned away from the sight of the couple. Behind her, in the distant background, we see the moving legs of the entwined couple and hear, once again, Fernando's loud climax. Thus the first daughter rids herself of the burden of her virginity while the second daughter weeps for her.

There have been countless scenes representing the loss of innocence in cinema. The mere fact that Breillat's film offers what appears to be more explicit sexual action is certainly not the sole cause of the originality and

philosophy in the bedroom 281

power of these scenes. But fragments of explicit sexual action, along with uncommon duration, allow the battle over the loss of virginity to become a more psychologically and emotionally accurate ordeal, both immediate and powerful in its effects on Elena, and distanced and refracted through the eyes of a sister who is simultaneously empathic, jealous, and sorrowing. The scene is true, sad, funny, and devastating all at once.

What happens next is shocking, yet in keeping with the film's lucid presentation of the brutality of sexual initiation and the conflicted desires of young girls. Once Fernando's seduction of Elena is discovered, the couple is separated and the family's vacation comes to an abrupt end. But the mechanics of how this happens are unimportant to Breillat, whose films, as noted above, have ellipses of plot where others have ellipses of sex. The sisters' furious and hopelessly noncommunicative mother declares the vacation over and sets out to drive them home. On the road, things turn ominous. Looming trucks pass the increasingly rattled mother and her disconsolate daughters. We begin to think that the film will end in a fatal accident.

Instead Anaïs now gets the seducer of *her* dreams. Unlike her sister, this will not be the man she must convince herself she loves and to whom she gives her heart, but a version of the man she conjured in her song of boredom at the beginning: an anonymous anyone, a "werewolf," who will relieve her of the burden of herself and of her ennui. Specifically, he is a big man with a crowbar at a rest stop. In short order he smashes the windshield of the car, kills Elena with a blow to the head, and strangles the girls' mother. Anaïs, who had been chewing taffy in the back seat when the violence began, continues chewing after the intruder has dispensed with her mother and sister. Urine runs down her leg. She slowly gets out of the car and walks backward, holding his gaze, saying, almost as an order as he begins the rape, "you are not going to hurt me." And indeed, she will emerge from the ensuing quick rape—counterposed to the prolonged psychological violation of her sister—seemingly less hurt, more intact.

Even on the ground with his body moving above her—no question of explicit sex in this scene with a thirteen-year-old actress—she continues to hold his gaze, unresisting but in her very stillness exercising a peculiar control. When he is done she simply removes the scarf he had used to gag her and holds still. The final scene shows police gathering evidence at the car as two policemen lead a stunned but still-living Anaïs out of the woods. A cop says she claims not to have been raped. Anaïs herself says, "Don't believe me if you don't want to," as the frame freezes on her face. It is as if in meeting her fate, the unhappy twelve-year-old virgin, whose untouched flesh had been like a "ball and chain," recognizes a perverse liberation—from family, from innocence, from the web of lies a young woman must enter into to rid herself of virginity, from her very imprisonment in her self.

Ending with this fearful symmetry of the defloration of the second sister, *Fat Girl* turns out to be a comparative study of the forms of humiliating sexual initiation and the damage they can do to young girls with no real power over their sexual fate. While the film is deeply feminist in its protest against this lack of power, its polemical point, like the point that bondage liberated Marie in *Romance*, is that the more truly violated of the sisters is the one who was not literally raped, the one who convinced herself to love her seducer. This puts Breillat in the provocative position of arguing that a quick rape is actually preferable to a long seduction, and that the raped sister exercises more control over her fate than the seduced one. As in *Romance*, Breillat is willing to show, sometimes quite explicitly, the sexual degradations women often endure in a quest for pleasure and intimacy.

It is not likely that any of the sex we see in *Fat Girl* is fully hard-core owing to the young age of the girls. Significantly, we do not see any of the penetrations. Indeed, in a subsequent film entitled *Sex Is Comedy* (2002), Breillat has made a point of staging a woman director shooting a scene very much like that with the Italian lover. Amusingly, she has the male character of that film walk around the set with an erect, prosthetic penis. Yet the view of this erect penis is as necessary to the tragedy of the one film as it is to the comedy of the other. No other director, male or female, has so effectively presented the complex circumstances including the "pressure" of an erection in which sexual pleasures are negotiated.[24]

American Hard-Core Art: The Orgasmic Imperative of *Shortbus*

American-produced films have not entirely been missing in action on the front of hard-core art, but neither have they exactly been pioneers. Stanley Kubrick's *Eyes Wide Shut* (1999) was raked over the coals by many critics for the digital insertion of clothed figures to obscure explicit sexual activity during a brief orgy. Kubrick's producers were terrified of receiving the kiss of death of an NC-17 rating and so inserted the robed figures in a scene that can now be seen in all its not very earthshaking glory on DVDs of the European release. On the other hand, the occasional film that does not bow to the requirements of the R rating can be excoriated as too brazen. Witness Vincent Gallo's unrated *The Brown Bunny* (2003), which received a hostile reception from critics at the 2003 Cannes Film Festival. A subsequent ill-fated billboard placed above Sunset Boulevard showing the star Chloë Sevigny engaged in fellatio with the director and costar Gallo did not help the reception of this film, which was not as bad as critics made it out to be when it was first booed at Cannes. American films that incorporate real sex into their narratives often run the risk of seeming like bad imitations of European angst (Gallo) or, as in Wayne Wang's *The Center of the World* (2001), about a young dot-comer who hires a prostitute to perform sex for him in Las Vegas, as too timid to deeply explore the sex that is their topic.

What no American film had hazarded was a story predominantly about sex—not just one sex scene or two—in an idiom that did not constitute a poor imitation of European angst but proved distinctly American. This is the great accomplishment of John Cameron Mitchell's *Shortbus* (2006). Unlike Gallo's dour film, *Shortbus* received a standing ovation when shown at an out-of-competition midnight screening at the Cannes Film Festival. Mitchell's previous film had been the angry but exuberant musical *Hedwig and the Angry Inch* (2001) about a transsexual rock star. Eager to encompass explicit sex as a means of treating "themes of connection and love and fear," but weary of the European films in this tradition that end with violence and death,[25] Mitchell's innovation is to deploy the language of sex much the same way that the language of music is used in a musical. Acutely aware of all the traditions he is negotiating—European hard-core art, American hard-core pornography, the new realism of musicals that still want to belt out a song—Mitchell set out to make a uniquely American film of hard-core art that might leave his viewers with a feel-good afterglow.

The film opens to the cool jazz of "Is You Is or Is You Ain't My Baby?" The camera pulls out from the nose of the Statue of Liberty and flies through a stylized, cartoonish model of a post-9/11 Manhattan and adjacent boroughs (figure 115). Peeking into a number of windows, we are introduced to a cast of characters, most of whom are already in medias sex. In the first live action scene we see a man in a bathtub filming his penis as it floats in the water. For a nation that has become positively phobic of any sightings of erect penises outside the ghetto of pornography, this is a very canny beginning. The penis is only a little erect, and the way it bobs in the water is rather endearing and entirely benign (figure 116). We see it in full view, both as attached to the man in the bathtub and also framed in the digital camera's screen. We even see a little yellowness in the water as the

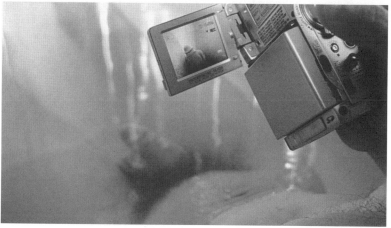

Shortbus (dir. John Cameron Mitchell, 2006)

115: Post-9/11 Manhattan

116: A benign penis filmed in the bath

man pees. Body organs and functions are not horrific or anything to be ashamed of, these first shots of the film seem to say; so let's see what else can be done with them!

Over the first hump of this initial penis sighting, the film proceeds to introduce its cast of characters. A dominatrix sternly whips her young client who tries to make small talk about the war in Iraq and to question her about the quality of her orgasms. The man from the bath, still filming himself, attempts, through a series of yoga exercises, to perform fellatio on his own penis (figure 117). Another man excitedly watches him through binoculars from a window across the way. An Asian Canadian woman and a white man have vigorous sex (cunnilingus, hand job, and coitus) in a variety of athletic positions all over their apartment—on the piano, against a glass wall, even in bed—in a series of athletic positions seemingly designed to give movement to Ludovico Ariosto's famously illustrated positions (figure 118).

Like Winterbottom and Breillat, Mitchell reveals character through the performance of sexual acts. Unlike these European directors, however, this sex is funny and carnivalesque. Mitchell humorously celebrates the crescendo of orgasms by rapidly intercutting the climax of each of these scenes into a stylized tongue-in-cheek nod to the conventions of hard core: The man from the bath comes on his own face, the female half of the heterosexual couple moans in concert with her partner in a way that loudly signals orgasm, the client whipped by the dominatrix ejaculates forcefully and inadvertently onto the multicolored drips of a Jackson Pollock–style action painting hung above his bed. His ejaculate joins all the other little dribbles (figure 119). With this crescendo of comedic climaxes, Mitchell's film breaks the sexual ice while flirting with our certain familiarity with the money shot convention of hard core. We know at once, however, from the clever intercutting, the Pollock gag, and the overathletic comedy of positions, that despite the presence of erections, insertions, and even visible ejaculate that this is too playful, too witty, too rapidly cut, and too little intent on engendering arousal to be porn, even while the pornographic imperative to demonstrate orgasm is observed.

If we did not recognize this fact from the witty comedy of sex, we would certainly recognize it from the mood change that follows. Behind all these strenuous and diverse sexual acts lurks the deep melancholy of characters who aspire to goals of sexual connection that never measure up. We learn, for example, that Sofia (Sook-Yin Lee), the Asian woman who works as a sex therapist, has been faking her orgasms to Rob (Raphael Barker), her husband. And after the self-fellator ejaculates on to his own face he sobs. His acrobatic feat proves symptomatic of a larger inability to allow himself to be penetrated or symbolically touched by anyone other than himself. We later learn that this man, James (Paul Dawson), has been filming himself not out of narcissistic pleasure but as a farewell suicide tape to his lover. Finally, we learn that the dominatrix, Severin (Lindsay Beamish), is an alienated sex worker who goes home alone to a cramped storage container and sadly soaks her tired feet.

Shortbus

117: Autofellatio

118: Vigorous couple

119: Jackson Pollock ejaculate

Shortbus's narrative thus operates in knowing counterpoint to the utopianism of American hard-core pornography. As we saw in chapter 3, Linda Lovelace in *Deep Throat* confessed to her doctor-therapist a failure to orgasm. The pornotopic solution provided by that film was to discover her clitoris in her throat and to prescribe more and better sex: "diff'rent strokes" in the form of deep-throat fellatio leading to earthshaking, world-shattering orgasms. Such is the pattern of hard-core pornography of the classic era: sex is the problem; (more and better) sex is the (simplistic) solution.[26] Mitchell's film expands the range of possible "diff'rent strokes" to include female-female, male-male sex, orgies, and S/M, but he adheres to the fundamental pornotopian notion that the solution to the problem of sex is more or better sex. Thus while *Shortbus* does not imitate the form of pornography, it upholds its orgasmic imperative by also seeking solution in orgasm, though nothing quite so mechanical as that achieved in a single sexual act or position. What is new about this approach is an at least tacit understanding that the proliferation of pornography itself has been part of the problem of everyone's performance anxiety. In an interview, Mitchell notes that because young people today tend to learn about sex from porn, they can become very insecure in their own ability to live up to its hyperboles. His solution to this problem is not to eschew pornography, but to refunction some of its conventions to more polysexual spontaneous ends.[27]

Thus the character of Sofia can be seen to take over where the sexually questing female hero of much classic-era hard-core pornography left off in her quest for the big O. During a therapy session Sofia blurts out to her clients, the gay couple James (the self-fellator from the beginning) and his partner Jamie (P. J. DeBoy) that she is "preorgasmic." "Does that mean that you are about to come?" asks the naive Jamie. "No. That means I've never come," responds Sophia. Though the film is smart enough not to insult its female protagonist by identifying any single technique or philosophy as the solution to her preorgasmic status, and though it has a lot of fun offering Sofia a wide range of contradictory advice and philosophy—from the exercise of Kegel muscles to sensory deprivation, from the idea that orgasm represents immense solitude to the idea that in it one is "finally not alone"—its narrative nevertheless imitates the pornographic quest for pleasure. However, it harnesses that quest to the larger social goal of forming a community of "permeable," unafraid beings. Modeled on the quintessential pornographic narrative, *Shortbus* thus also operates as a corrective to the isolation and fixation on bodies and techniques that solitary porn can engender.

James and Jamie send Sofia to Shortbus, a bohemian sex club and cabaret, modeled on a number of actually existing venues.[28] The club gives as much space to screening avant-garde film on 16 mm as it does to "The Pussy Room," a place for dykes and other women to vent. There is another room for general mixing, another for music, and another for orgies that bring together all kinds of bodies in all kinds of sexual combinations. Queer-friendly but not queer-exclusive, Shortbus welcomes the old, the straight, the transgendered, and the swingers who want more than one partner. Named for that other school bus—the short one that takes the "different," challenged kids to school, *Shortbus* the movie, like Shortbus the cabaret, pays homage to yet another of the groundbreaking films of the porno chic era: *Behind the Green Door* (dir. Artie and Jim Mitchell, 1972) as well as its 1986 sequel (dir. Artie and Jim Mitchell).[29] In both those pornotopias, ordinary people—truck drivers, flight attendants, Vietnam vets—enter a magical cabaret of sexual abundance in which multiple styles of sexual pleasure are celebrated and observed in complexly staged orgies that culminate in glorious communal orgasms.

Like the world "behind the green door," *Shortbus* is a sexually and racially diverse community that is a utopian idea of New York City. Extending beyond the island of Manhattan, it is the place where one can go to be "permeable," as one memorable character who claims to be the ex-mayor of New York puts it. This character tells us that New Yorkers are "permeable and sane" because they are willing to bend over to let in the new and the old. New Yorkers thus are seen to represent America's hope. Claiming for his city and his nation a desirable status of philosophical and sexual permeability, Mitchell then plays out this opposition in the drama of three characters whose impermeability needs fixing.

Sofia shows up at Shortbus, where she encounters all the sexual actors from the beginning: James and partner Jamie are searching to find the right person to make up their threesome; and Severin, the dominatrix, hangs out in the "Pussy Room" avoiding her john. Sofia, the newcomer, is shown around by the MC (Justin Boyd). The film's most quoted line—"It's just like the sixties only with less hope"—uttered by the MC to Sofia, has been cited as a mark of cyncism. But it actually belies how much faith Mitchell actually seems to place in the liberatory utopian ideals of the 1960s. As Richard Corliss, reviewing the film for *Time*, put it, *Shortbus* is "so retro, it seems sparkling new."[30]

But *Shortbus* is no throwback. When Sofia confesses to a failure to orgasm and to a general lack of sexual experience (having only had sex with her husband), she initially sounds like Linda Lovelace who in *Deep*

Throat also asserted that she loved "getting laid," but lamented the fact that there were no "bells ringing, dams bursting" and "bombs going off." Sofia's confession begins in the same way: "Sex feels terrific; I love it a lot, it's a great workout." Unlike Linda, however, and in the security of the "Pussy Room" with only other women listening, she further confesses, "But it's a lot of pressure, and sometimes I feel like somebody's going to kill me, and I just have to smile and pretend to enjoy it." The women who hear this confession have just described their best orgasms to Sofia in exalted terms: "A shooting out of creative energy and it feels like there is no war"; "I was finally not alone"; "It feels like talking to the gods." Though the entire Shortbus establishment is enlisted in the project of showing Sofia the road to orgasm, the film is not so didactic as to believe it can illustrate the way to it. Nor is it so happy-go-lucky as to imagine that Sofia's practice of "smiling and pretending to enjoy" has not had its emotional costs.

The emotional costs of bad sex are indeed everywhere to be seen in *Shortbus*, whose three main characters are all in the line of alienated sex work—for what else should we call Sofia's occupation as a sex therapist and couples counselor? James, the suicidal former male escort, suffers from a problem similar to Sofia's: the inauthenticity of having had to pretend to enjoy. He cannot connect with anyone. Even the invitation to Ceth (Jay Brannan) to join his relation with Jamie proves to have the ulterior motive of providing an alternative partner for Jamie after he is dead. Thus the good-spirited, three-way daisy chain we see these men perform—though comical in its rousing singing of the national anthem into Ceth's anus—is actually more of an acrobatic feat than a sexual event. The men respectfully adjust positions, give proper feedback to one another, and Ceth uses Jamie's penis as a mock microphone, but although they are properly erect and perfectly congenial, no one ever comes, and all three collapse in giggles in the end (figure 120).

Two of *Shortbus*'s main characters thus cannot find pleasure in sex and are unhappily impermeable. When Sofia makes her devastating confession about "smiling and pretending to enjoy" to the other women in the "Pussy Room," the dominatrix from the opening scene, Severin, snaps her picture with a Polaroid and gives it to Sofia with the word "Sorry" inked over it. Soon the two women become friends. Another alienated sex worker, this dominatrix coaches Sofia on her masturbatory technique while they are immersed side by side in a sensory deprivation tank. But Sofia proves to be a klutzy masturbator. Severin, for her part, has no difficulty getting off, but the ability to orgasm in her case refutes the film's metaphoric use of orgasm as a form of connection. She, too, is emotionally impermeable.

120: *Shortbus*, the daisy chain

Connection is everything. Justin Boyd, playing the congenial, gay master of ceremonies uses the metaphor of a "motherboard filled with desire that travels all over the world. That touches you. That touches me. . . . You just have to find the right connection."

In the second evening at Shortbus, Sofia brings along her husband, Rob, having finally informed him of her problem and of the potential solution to be found in the cabaret's "realm of the senses." Sofia has also armed herself with a powerful technological aid that is the film's comedic homage to Oshima's film: a vibrating egg labeled "In the Realm of the Senses" is inserted into her vagina. But husband Rob, given the remote control for the vibrator, proves negligent and loses the device; another man plays it thinking it is a video game. Sofia thus spends the rest of the evening comically vibrating in inappropriate situations, though still not coming. At one point Severin even gets off on the device's vibrations during a moment of intimacy between the two friends, only proving once more Severin's sexual facility and Sofia's incapacity. The legacy of Oshima looms large, but in an era of commodified sex toys, a real realm of the senses seems unattainable.

How, then, is the problem of sexual disconnection and impermeability solved? In further homage to pornography, it is solved as are all problems in porn, with more, and better, sex. James finally attempts the suicide he has been planning all along. But his plan is foiled by a last-minute rescue from the man who has been his faithful voyeur and stalker since the beginning. This benign voyeur pulls him out of the pool where he has tried to drown, nurses him back to health, and asks how someone who is loved so much could ever want to end it all. James replies that he knows Jamie loves him, but that he cannot feel it: "It stops at my skin." Having already bridged the voyeuristic gap that separated him from the object of his desire and thus breached his own impermeability, penetrates James anally in a way that is finally felt. As in hard-core pornography: if sex is the problem then the solution lies in more or better sex. Here the sex offered to James is tender, caring, *and* explicit in a way that very few filmmakers have managed to show outside the world of avant-garde film or hard-core pornography.

Meanwhile, Sofia projects herself into a fantasy in which she finds herself alone by the sea on a park bench in an area flooded with water (figure 121). She masturbates on this bench and seems to come close to orgasm until the power goes out all over New York. This is the film's device for bringing Sofia, Rob, James, Jamie, Ceth, the benign voyeur, Severin, and all the previous denizens of the Shortbus cabaret back together for a happy-ending, candlelit finale that will be capped at the end by Sofia's literally earthshaking orgasm. It is to be noted, however, that this orgasm is not the result of better technique; rather, it is the result of better community and trust for which sex now becomes a metaphor. The MC leads the group in the finale's song ("as your last breath begins / you find your dreams, your best friend / and we all get it in the end"). "Getting it in the end" is the sexual metaphor for permeability that will allow the film to end happily and for New Yorkers to have their share of the revolutionary hope of polymorphous perversity begun in the sixties, now revived at least momentarily in the good feeling of the immediate post-9/11 era under the sign of the circuitry of a motherboard. The orgy commences and everyone becomes permeable, if not literally penetrated, then at least open and available. Sofia finally discovers that she can "get it in the end," not by working hard but by letting herself go with strangers (in this case a particular heterosexual couple she had frequently admired and envied whenever she spied on the activities in the orgy room) (figure 122). Her eventual orgasm will not be a clinical image of female ejaculation or any of the other possible unsimulated involuntary convulsions so central to hard-core pornography. Rather, it will be, as with Jane Fonda, the old standby of the orgasmic woman's face. It is not a face placed next to another sexual organ, like Linda Lovelace's, but the face of a woman who is momentarily beside herself with ecstacy (figure 123). With Caleb, the voyeur's curative interference, we also now find that James and Jamie can get back together

Shortbus

121: Sophia almost comes

122: Sophia swings in the orgy room

123: Sophia's orgasm

124: Everyone joins in

and that James, too, will now "get it in the end." Caleb, the voyeur who has saved James, also finds a partner in Ceth, and even the lonely Severin seems to be happy for once as part of the crowd. A marching band restarts the song and everyone joins in as Sofia's orgasm reconnects the motherboard and the lights turn back on in New York (figure 124).

A retro, sixties-style orgy, though one amply supplied with condoms and lube, is thus not only the place for pleasure but also for understanding, permeability, and even forgiveness. The enemy of this ethic is the fear that closes us off and makes us impermeable. Permeability—a willingness to get it (and take it) in the end, and every other possible way—is the retro sexual revolutionary faith in a world in which sex might be "good again."[31] It is practiced at Shortbus in both sexual and nonsexual ways and constitutes this film's particular philosophy in the bedroom. *Shortbus* might be a better film if it could take the despair of its characters a little more seriously, but if it did, it might not be the quintessentially American sex film it is, and it certainly could not function as the breakthrough film for American hard-core art that it is.

When *Shortbus* premiered in its midnight screening at Cannes, the *Daily Variety* critic called Mitchell's film "unquestionably the most sexually graphic American narrative feature ever made outside the realm of the porn industry."[32] Had the film's distributors taken its NC-17 rating to the multiplexes, it might have found the controversy that would have propelled it to greater publicity and sales. However, I am writing this just at the end of the film's theatrical run in the United States, where it has generated some very good reviews but no big controversy and thus no big audiences. The same reviewer who pronounced the film sexually graphic also condemned it to small recognition when he noted that though the film might be an "immediate must-see for certain audiences, especially gays, in limited theatrical release, it will find its true and lasting home on DVD."[33] One wonders what might have happened had the distributors not believed this prediction.

Distributed by ThinkFilm, the same company that did such a fine job finessing the difficulties of marketing *The Aristocrats* (dir. Paul Provenza, 2005), Mitchell's film has been much more cautiously marketed and only to art houses. Multiplexes have not been eager to book the unrated film for fear that audiences might wander in from another screen. As Mark Urman, ThinkFilm's domestic distribution head, put it, "We've been keeping the film where it belongs"—at festivals and film societies—"We can't be needlessly provocative."[34] No similar concern was registered regarding the similarly unrated *The Aristocrats*, a funny, raunchy film about the long history of a single dirty joke. In the story of the different marketing of these two films by the same company, we face, in a nutshell, differing American attitudes toward the word and the (moving) image. Bold with words, timid with images, especially when those images "speak" explicit sex, ThinkFilm's failure to provoke means that American audiences have mostly not had a chance to see what still remains anomalous on American screens: hard-core art that is not foreign, that is, in fact, aggressively American—from its opening on the Statue of Liberty to its singing of the Star-Spangled Banner.

The films discussed above are only the tip of the iceberg of an international phenomenon of hard-core art cinema.[35] In the United States we have grown so used to the separation of pornography from art that we tend to assume—sometimes rather hypocritically—that any arousal response is antithetical to art and any emotionally complex art automatically antithetical to arousal. Much of the negative critical reaction to what I have been calling hard-core art films has been premised on the assumption that pornography's function is to elicit arousal and art cinema's function is solely aesthetic.

Consider, for example, the *Los Angeles Times* critic Kenneth Turan's fairly typical reaction to Breillat's *Romance*. Turan argues that "those deluded enough to go to *Romance* for its unapologetic scenes of masturbation, oral sex, intercourse and intricate bondage are going to be even angrier and disappointed by the torpid, uninvolving quality they exude. Distant sex, no matter how explicit, and bogus posturing turn out to be a deadly cinematic combination."[36] According to Turan, explicit sex makes any response to it, *other than* sexual arousal, seem like "bogus posturing."[37]

What Turan objects to, in a review typical of the film's American critical reception, is precisely the presence of Marie's female voice-over trying to make philosophical, political, and emotional sense of her various sexual humiliations. It is as if, for Turan, the French tradition of philosophy in the bedroom spoils the pure pleasure of the sex. But it is precisely the firewall between philosophy, politics, and emotion, on the one hand, and pure pornography, on the other, that hard-core art cinema is breaking down, forging new ways of presenting and visually experiencing cinematic sex. To Turan it would seem that anything other than arousing sex is pure pretension and an automatic turnoff. But what kind of moving-image art do we condemn ourselves to if sex must be so compartmentalized? I would argue that the even greater pretension may be the very idea that sex is mindless. If it seems pretentious to Turan to mix ambivalent emotions and philosophical thought with sex, it is also simplistic to assume that sex is monopathic and totally without thought.

We live in a world in which directors like Winterbottom, von Trier, Chéreau, Breillat, and Mitchell make themselves vulnerable to the charge of being pornographers when they depict explicit sex. To defend themselves, these directors have often vehemently protested that they are *not* pornographers. Chéreau's defense, interestingly, has been to distinguish *Intimacy* from what he would term the greater pornographic sensationalism of the French women directors whose explicit works emerged at about the same time as his own. Thus he argues that while Breillat's *Romance* and Virginie Despentes and Coralie Trinh's *Baise-moi* (2000) *are* prurient, *his* film is not. Breillat, for her part, when accused of being a pornographer, argues provocatively that there is no such thing as pornography. What exists instead, she claims in an interview, "is censorship which defines pornography and sets it off from the rest of film. . . . Pornography is the sexual act taken totally out of context, and made into a product for consumption, by using the most debased feelings or emotions of people, when in fact in daily life sexual acts are surrounded by emotions, consideration for the partner, pleasure and so on, which do not come within the pornographic depiction."[38] Mitchell, for his part, claims to enjoy pornography but asserts that his sex is more metaphoric than real.

So where Oshima had argued, as we saw in chapter 5, that "pornographic cinema should be authorized, immediately and completely," as a means to fight censorship and outmoded concepts of obscenity, Breillat claims, to the contrary, that pornography is an artifact of censorship. Most of all, she fights against the hypocrisy of putting a moral value—either as liberation or as condemnation—on the question of whether performers really do it:

> If you look at what most mainstream actors are doing now, more and more the love scenes are very intimate and very frank, so it's hypocrisy to ask "Do they really penetrate or not?" Actors do not simulate: they don't simulate emotions, so at the same time they cannot simulate pleasure—they have to act it. So as they are not going to be able to simulate pleasure, they are going to have to act pleasure. After that it's just really a physical detail.

Simulation, as Breillat uses the term, seems to consist of going through the motions without feeling the feelings (what I earlier called acting). Simulation is an imitation that creates a more or less credible appearance. But Breillat's "acting," or what I prefer to call performing, involves feeling the emotions generated between the actors, who are not just putting on an appearance but, on some level, necessarily feeling.

I do not expect the directors defending themselves against the charges of pornography to agree on their terms, and there may even be a value to claiming to make a new kind of pornography. This, in fact, is what Oshima did when he created *In the Realm of the Senses*. At issue, as it so often happens in film, is the vexed question of the fundamental realism of the medium: the fact that cameras and sound recorders register actions that take place before them even if they are also components in larger fictions and even when some of the acts registered are faked.

Recall that Bazin's reaction to the dilemma of presenting sexual action at the movies was to ask: If one could demand real sex from movies, then should one not also demand real violence? Since he deemed such a demand both immoral and obscene, Bazin's uneasy solution was to pronounce that even though nothing is "*a priori* prohibited on the screen," artists must resort to "the capacity for abstraction in the language of cinema, so that the image never takes on a documentary quality."[39] This caveat fudges Bazin's belief in the fundamental indexicality of the medium, so intensely celebrated elsewhere in his writing. What Bazin's realist imagination does not allow him to consider is the degree to which every sex act that might be placed before a camera is also a document of a performance: It is both real—something that actually happens—and, as we saw most vividly in Warhol's *Blue Movie*, it is fake, staged for the camera and sound equipment. Neither the directors of pornography nor the directors of hard-core art from Warhol forward document real sex in the sense of what people do alone, in private. Warhol's "ghosts" are always present. Perhaps Bazin's "capacity for abstraction" means the introduction of film art in the depiction of sex situations; perhaps it is the way the art of the cinema works to frame, light, edit, and coach performances as we have seen in all of the films discussed here.

The error that Bazin, like George Steiner, makes when he says that "we must stay in the imagination" is to assume that the imagination cannot itself work with more explicit representations of sex acts. It is also to assume that these more explicit representations are not themselves the products of a directorial and performative imagination. The imagination does not suddenly lose its vocation when confronted with a wet, "excessively long" kiss, or with a penis, a vagina, or a blow job, or with the many possible ways of performing—not just acting or simulating—sex. The imagination and the ability to fantasize will always occupy that place at which the film's necessarily limited vision fails. We do it a great disservice when we presume that it cannot deal with more to see than previous convention allows. Chéreau's *Intimacy* suggests that sexual intimacy in its more naturalistic representations has been barely broached in film art. He himself has said: "When people reproach me for showing too much, I claim that sexuality remains as much a mystery as it has always been. Perhaps more. The question is always asked, 'Where can you go from here?' No one should worry, because there will always be something that remains hidden."[40]

Whether the current trend toward more explicit sex will be a lasting feature of contemporary moving images remains to be seen. Certainly the difficulties posed to actors are great. It is hard to imagine any established male American star exposing himself, erect or unerect, for the benefit of film art. Such actors run the risk, among other things, of being compared to the Rocco Siffredis of this world. But perhaps this is exactly the point. Only a realist approach to screening sex can get over the idealized comparisons of body types—male or female—the standards of pornography. And perhaps only familiarity with many different kinds and moods of sexual performance—not just the exotic foreign examples that come to American screens from the outside to seduce or offend us, but the homegrown kind that can speak to our more American identities and experiences—will break down the prolonged adolescence of American film. I can't help but think that in an era in which even the notoriously puritanical American public finds the discussion of explicit sex acts unavoidable—whether in legal cases such as *Lawrence v. Texas*, or in rape hearings that must explicitly detail what penises have precisely done—the continued avoidance of the emotional nature and physical specificity of the sex acts that so importantly punctuate our public and private lives is going to seem increasingly odd in our movies.

Now, a variety of screens—long and wide and square, large and small, composed of grains, composed of pixels, lit by projected light, cathode-ray tube, plasma, LCD—compete for our attention without any convincing arguments about hegemony.
—ANNE FRIEDBERG,
The Virtual Window from Alberti to Microsoft

conclusion

Now Playing on a Small Screen

near You!

We have seen that sex can be blatantly revealed (as in well-lit hard-core pornography) or more subtly concealed (as in the simulated sex acts of mainstream American cinema that arose in the late 1960s). We have also seen that the history of sexual representation in American culture since the invention of moving-image technology has been a process by which acts once considered ob/scene (literally, off scene) have come on/scene. We saw the encroachment of on/scenity in our discussion of *Deep Throat* and *Boys in the Sand* in chapter 3. Yet as the previous chapter indicated, hard-core pornography did not long remain on the big screen and did not, at least in the United States, develop into a thriving form of hard-core art. The peculiar "long adolescence" of American cinema has meant that first, the Hollywood Production Code, then later the byzantine rules of the MPAA, remained in force. Today most Americans, even those quite young, are very familiar with pornography. But since it is now consigned to a space of supposed privacy and is not acknowledged as part of the cultural mainstream, it has become a kind of elephant in the room. We all know it is there, but its familiar poses, gestures, and secretions are often treated as unofficial knowledge. With the exception of the still rarified hard-core art films discussed in chapter 7 we now have two very different experiences of screening sex, one on large public screens, one on smaller private ones. Let us begin by looking at the importance of these screens themselves.

Little Screens: Does Size Matter?

By 1986 (the year of David Lynch's *Blue Velvet*), half of American households had VCRs and thus began to watch movies when they wanted: no longer on television with commercial interruption or at theaters only at designated times.[1] Today Americans screen much more in the "privacy" of the home than in the "public" place of the movie theater.[2]

The shift to home viewing, however, has not meant a wholesale privatization of the experience of screening. Rather, as we shall see below, it has meant a reconfiguration of the relative meanings of public and private. What was once considered private—the space of home—has become more public as the multiple connectivities that characterize the Internet have entered it and as cell phones bring private conversations to the street, airport, train, car, and bus. Conversely, what was once considered public (the movie theater) can now be brought into the home. Computers, telephones, Microsoft's new touch-activated surfaces, and movies have converged. We can now "chat" online, manually manipulate images, and watch and be watched by telepresent webcams.[3] On one level we have entered a world of many small screens.

As we saw in the first chapter, no one paid much attention to Thomas Edison's 1896 film, *The Kiss*, when it was initially projected in the small peephole device of the Kinetoscope. Only when it was magnified through big screen projection did critics perk up, either positively in praise of its anatomy lessons, or negatively in criticism of its obscene "monstrosity." Only when the *magnified* projection of real bodies in movement began to constitute the defining experience of movies did the potential eros or horror of these larger-than-life bodies become both apparent and controversial.

Big screens, and the larger-than-life bodies they reveal, can seem to "engulf" the viewer, but this impression actually relies on the maintenance of a physical gulf between where we sit and the screens themselves as well as a temporal gulf between the time of shooting and the time of screening.[4] We may identify with characters and we may sympathetically respond to the acts they perform with jumps, jolts, strong emotions, arousal, or disgust, but we never fully enter into or touch their world. Rather, we perceive them and "know" them through an always-mediated embodied relation to their bodies and their world as it relates to our knowledge of our world and our own bodies' experiences in it. Our imagination and our bodies relate to these images, but we remain aware, as I have been arguing, of our bodies *here* and those larger-than-life, virtual bodies *there*, and of the unbridgeable gulf between their oversized grandeur and our relative smallness.

A scene in Almodóvar's *Bad Education (La mala educación,* 2004) can serve as a handy allegory of the structure of screening sex I have thus far been examining. Two boys sit before the large movie screen of a provincial Spanish movie theater in 1969 watching the Spanish star Sara Montiel in a scene from the film *Esa mujer* (dir. Mario Camus, 1969). Montiel was a famous pop singer and movie star just beginning her transformation from a general icon of female suffering into a focus of gay pop worship.[5] As Almodóvar frames it, the two boys, seen from behind, are engulfed by the larger-than-life image. They are aroused by Sara, and that arousal plays itself out in the theater as they discover one another's erections. From our discreet viewing position behind them, we see how their seats shake as they masturbate one another (figure 125).

This image of the two boys seen from behind infers a metaphorical getting hold of Sara through their getting hold of one another. This inferred mutual masturbation is an amusing defiance of the usual decorum of the movie theater. Historically, this image is something of an anachronism: while masturbation or even mutual masturbation *could* take place in certain sparsely populated theaters, it was probably rare in Franco's Spain.[6] Nor was masturbation an activity that could be represented *in* mainstream films, Spanish or American, at the date depicted in this film. Nevertheless, we can take this image of Almodóvar's boys in sexual thrall to the glamorous female bodies of the big screen as an emblem of the centrality of sex to the moviegoing experience—a centrality that could not be more directly revealed in movies until the eighties and beyond.

How, then, might we picture screening sex once it has moved into the privacy of the home? Once again it is Almodóvar who provides the appropriately perverse picture. In his 1986 film *Matador* a credit sequence introduces the ecstatic face of the main character intercut with grisly images and sounds from horror films showing the slashing and dismemberment

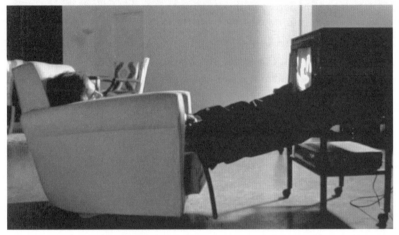

125: *Bad Education* (dir. Pedro Almodóvar, 2004), the boys look at Sara on the big screen and discover their own bodies before it.

126: *Matador* (dir. Pedro Almodóvar, 1986), Diego masturbates astride the television monitor

of female victims. Just how our as-yet-undisclosed hero sees these grisly images is not made clear until we see the final shot of the credit sequence that reveals a side view of his entire body: he is sprawled in a chair with his feet propped up on either side of a television monitor. Diego, the ex-matador turned woman-killer, is not only presumed to be masturbating, he almost seems to be having sex with his TV and it is as if the television monitor has been engulfed by his body (figure 126).

127: *Videodrome* (dir. David Cronenberg, 1983), Max enters the screen of the television monitor as if it were the woman herself

An earlier figuration of this perverse, excited masturbatory relation to small screen appears in David Cronenberg's *Videodrome* (1983).[7] The film is about a cable channel director who, in seeking new soft-core porn and horror material for his station, happens on a possible live snuff show whose video signals appear to produce both violent hallucinations and actual bodily changes in the viewer. Seduced and "infected" by the show's signals, this man himself becomes an appendage of video technology.[8] He discovers a woman with whom he has previously had sex now located in the television monitor. Her lips protrude from the monitor as she beckons him to come to her. The television itself begins to throb and breathe. Cronenberg's antihero embraces, caresses, and "enters" the screen. Even more than Almodóvar's matador, whose own body surrounds the screen, this character bridges the gulf that has traditionally separated the body of the viewer from the bodies imaged on the screen (figure 127).[9] In both these examples, the body of the viewer and the body on the screen seem to merge.

It is hardly surprising that big-screen cinephiles like Almodóvar and Cronenberg depict the human interaction with the small screen in the privacy of the home as both malevolent and horrific. Film-makers love to vilify the small screen experience. In both narratives, solitary, obsessed men become even more antisocial through their absorption into the small television screen. As the media scholar Sean Cubitt put it in 1991, "video seems more likely [than film] to be used for solitary or slightly illicit viewing—by housewives during coffee-breaks, by teenagers late at night."[10]

And, indeed, the small screen has delivered a great many forms of erotic moving images both as soft-core genres aimed primarily at arousal as well as in the many serialized, multi-season shows aimed at depicting new sexual lifestyles. These recent hits include: *Sex and the City* (HBO, 1998–2004), which, like Mike Nichols in the late sixties, preferred to satirically talk about rather than to depict sex; the gay-themed *Queer as Folk* (Showtime, American-Canadian production, 2000–2005), which more boldly displayed the sex of its protagonists (a first episode depicted simulated anal sex accompanied by an illustration and pedagogic explanation of rimming); the lesbian-themed *The L-Word* (Showtime, 2004–), which followed *Queer as Folk* into the realm of serialized drama with steamy simulated sex; or the currently popular *Tell Me that You Love Me* (HBO, 2007–), also a serialized drama, this one about straight, middle-class, white couples. What is new in this show is quasi explicit sex as a key to understanding character. Like the films of hard-core art discussed in chapter 7, new levels of explicitness serve new levels of psychological revelation.[11]

While the hard-core nature of *Tell Me that You Love Me* is new, soft-core sex on cable television extends back to the early nineties. Critic Dave Andrews reminds us that "softcore," as he calls it, was first spawned on cable television as early as 1992 with Zalman King's *Red Shoe Diaries*, which was widely imitated. Andrews locates cable and direct-to-video soft core as a subset of a continuing sexploitation tradition that, like the hard-core feature, punctuates its narrative with frequent sex scenes, albeit ones that avoid all displays of penetration and erect penises.[12] Unlike most hard-core pornography, soft core has historically been marketed to women every bit as much as to men. Linda Ruth Williams calls this soft core the cinematic equivalent of *coitus interruptus*.[13] Both critics have shown how this form of soft-core titillation became linked to the mainstream as well as the low budget erotic thriller.

Cable channels and on-demand soft-core pornography are thus typical television—in the sense of regular series that come into the home—and yet they are "not television" in the sense that they often deal with sex in both adult and titillating ways anathema to the older understanding of the medium as "broadcast." While most of the cable experience may be tamer and more domesticated than the wild world of the Internet (discussed below), and while it may refrain from or go only to the edge of "real sex," it is likely that all these shows contribute both to potential masturbatory uses as well as to frank conversations about sex—whether in the bedroom or at the water cooler.

If the rise of adult viewing material on cable and VCR has facilitated the consumption of sexual moving images for purposes of sometimes immediate sexual gratification, it is worth considering the changed status of masturbation in this new world. The onetime "vice" of "onanism" no longer carries the stigma of self-pollution that Thomas Laqueur tells us it quite suddenly acquired in the early eighteenth century and which it continued to carry throughout the following two centuries. However, even the more recent rehabilitation of solitary sex has been an uneven process.[14] Dave Andrews notes, for example, that in the soft-core erotic films and series shown on cable it became conventional to depict masturbation within the soft-core drama, but only as performed by "clitoral-discovering" women. Masturbating men, though perhaps the primary viewers addressed, were not depicted on the small screen.[15]

Private screening takes us out of public scrutiny and gives us control over what, when, and where we screen. Such screening is often a literal and metaphorical form of what Geoffrey King, in a recent book about New Hollywood cinema, calls "Embracing the Small Screen." Though King speaks metaphorically of the shift to home viewing, it is indeed something like a literal embrace—a kind of "having sex" with the physical screen itself—that is pictured in the phobic and masculine examples of the big-screen cineastes noted above.[16] Where Almodóvar's boys at the movies enjoy a social, public experience, even in their furtive gestures of mutual masturbation, Almodóvar and Cronenberg's men merge onanistically with their screens. Small-screen phobia is facilitated by the fact that the small screen is itself a physical object and that what is pictured in it is often, in the case of television-screen close-ups, roughly life-size. Unlike the large film screen, this small screen can be straddled, kissed, embraced, and manipulated with direct or remote controls. As Catherine Zimmer has argued, the screen on which I view the video, DVD, cablecast, or moving images downloaded from a server *is* a literal object with heft and depth that can be physically touched and embraced.[17] Instead of being engulfed by the immaterial moving images of the film screen, my body can surround the material object that carries the image. There is also the enhanced sense of liveness, whether actual or illusory, associated with the television itself and its ability to broadcast or telecast events while they happen. Cronenberg's antihero enters the video screen through the lure of the outsized "live" woman whose lips protrude.

Almodóvar and Cronenberg found it easy to picture the small screen as the repository of lurid images of sex and gore because it was precisely such images that had pioneered the early practice of home viewing.[18] As Stephen Prince asserts in his history of American cinema in the 1980s, the shift to video enabled the adult industry to expand its output, reach a larger audience, and enjoy enormous profits.[19] The porn industry soon saw the advantage of avoiding theatrical releases altogether, and by 1986 there were only two hundred surviving adult theaters. Hollywood, on the other hand, did not venture to invest in video transfers from 35mm film until the adult film industry had conclusively proven the economic viability of the rented or purchased videocassette. Thus the home video revolution that put VCR and cassettes, laser discs and DVDs into our living rooms and bedrooms—and now into our mobile hands and laps—was initiated more by the drive to see a film like *Deep Throat* and its progeny than by the drive to see *The Godfather* (dir. Francis Ford Coppola, 1972). Clearly one of the important differences of home viewing, along with the ability to stop, start, replay, and otherwise more actively manipulate the image—and despite often very real losses of dimension, quality, and fidelity—is the fact that the VCR, and the small screen in general, "amplifies and individualizes the association of movies with sex."[20]

In the 1980s Cronenberg's video viewer physically broached the divide between his own flesh and that pictured on the video monitor by entering into the image, while Almodóvar's ex-bullfighter planted the monitor between his legs and surrounded it. By the mid-1990s, however, these phobic images of the relation to the small screen were supplanted by something even more sinister: a full-body embrace of a new kind of monitor of a computer equipped with keyboard (figure 128). In this digitally rendered image of the relation of the Internet *user—viewer* no longer seems quite the right word!—to new digital technologies, the very gulf between "viewer" and image that I have emphasized in the theatrical model and that lessens with the television seems to be eliminated altogether. A naked, vulnerable, androgynous but male body embraces the screen of the monitor while perched atop an illuminated keyboard. This image, much discussed by new media scholars, was the infamous centerfold of a 3 July 1995 *Time* article about the dangers of a new thing called cyberporn. Unlike the figures of unseemly proximity discussed above, this image is no longer an analog photograph, but itself the product of computer manipulation. The digital artist Matt Mahurin figures the relation to the computer screen as a full-fledged embrace.[21]

In this image of the human-computer interface, it is even less possible

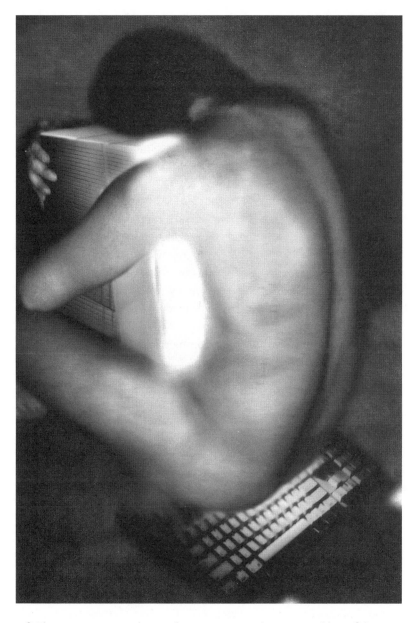

128: The young person embraces the computer monitor as an emblem of the dangers of cyberporn. Matt Mahurin, *Time*, 3 July 1995

to tell where the screen, in the form of the computer monitor, ends and where the body of the viewer or user begins.[22] Zabet Patterson, for example, notes how the relationship between the body and the networked computer is pictured as "unwholesomely dissolute."[23] Dissolute in this context means not only indulging in sensual pleasures or vices, in this case including a possibly incorrect object choice, but simply dissolved—the person who so engages is not whole.

Mahurin's image was one of several that accompanied a panic-inducing *Time* article titled, "On a Screen Near You, Cyberporn: A New Study Shows How Pervasive and Wild It Really Is."[24] The next year Congress passed the Communications Decency Act. Although the act was subsequently struck down by the Supreme Court, it represented the first time any governmental agency attempted to regulate Internet content. As with the 1980s home video revolution, pornographic sexual content once again drove technological innovation. In this case, as Wendy Chun notes, the success of cyberporn sites convinced many American corporations that Internet users were willing to pay with credit cards online.[25] Cyberporn can thus be seen to have "paved the way for the 'Information Superhighway,'" causing both government and commercial companies to debate the status of the Internet as a mass medium.[26]

The panic over Internet porn suggests how ready the public was—perhaps even how primed it had already been by earlier film images of the addictive, perverse embrace of the small screen—to blame pornography as the evil invader of the privacy of the home. This figure of the corruptible adolescent too closely touched by the new technology of cyberporn, along with a cover image of a powerless, susceptible child, became the new face—or perhaps we should now say bodily figuration—of screening sex for the 1990s. What horrifies in this figure is not so much the content—as with the giant lips that fill the television screen Cronenberg's antihero physically enters—but the human interaction with networked technology itself: what new media scholars and users call the inter*face* has actually become something more like an inter*body* relation.[27] In this relation bodies are exposed promiscuously and perversely through the medium of the screen to any number of other bodies, though not necessarily, as Chun perceptively notes, in the spectacular fashion of an earlier cinematic "frenzy of the visible" as portrayed in hard-core pornography.[28] Hard-core sex acts are certainly visible on these small screens, but less spectacularly so. Fiber-optic networks, as Chun puts it, both enable and frustrate the cinematic model of an all-pervasive visuality. Touch, as we see illustrated in this figure, seems more important than sight, which is often simply an effect employed, Chun notes, to make "jacking in," or now simply activating a screen through touch, sexy.[29]

Does screen size matter to screening sex? I think it does, but mostly as it connects with constantly fluctuating issues of privacy and publicity and to what I have described earlier, borrowing from Miriam Hansen and Walter Benjamin's claim that the body is energized as a "porous interface." Home screens have grown larger, movie theaters have grown smaller, and mobile screens and now touch screens of laptops, cell phones, and iPods complicate the whole issue by bringing the once private, small screen out into a public space that is simultaneously more privatized.[30] To hinge the argument about our bodies' relation to media on screen size alone may also not go to the heart of the much-vaunted future "convergence" of all media made possible by the computational nature of digital information. In this future convergence, so the story goes, the specificity of media will end, and our bodies will become interfaces to pure flows of information. The eroticism of being "jacked in" may not be so much about being immersed in a single gigantic visual spectacle but may rather foretell an interaction with promiscuous, proliferating relations to other bodies through the various screens of our lives. How, then, to characterize beyond the hyperbole of utopic or dystopic connections the experience of this embrace of the small screen in comparison to the engulfment by the old-fashioned movie?

Recall Walter Benjamin's claim that the technological reproduction of cinema permits us to "get hold of an object at close range in an image."[31] Benjamin is well aware that there is no literal "getting hold," no actual "grasp," of the object "in an image." Only insofar as it is mediated as image do we experience the illusion of being physically close enough to get hold. But now that new media forms of screening sex make possible both real and illusory interactions that often mime literal grasping and touching, and now that these interactions can take place in the privacy of the home, is it possible to say that screening sex has become a kind of having sex? What does it mean to get hold of an object at close range in an image in a new-media era of screening sex?

Embodiment, New Media, and Cyberporn

Every contemporary theorist of media must now contend with both the fact and the fantasy of a new media age governed by patterns of information instead of analogical representation. Virtual realities always seem about to displace physical realities. For example, Lev Manovich's land-mark *Language of New Media* predicts that one day virtual reality technologies may cease to be cumbersome helmets, goggles, and gloves and be "reduced to a chip implanted in the retina and connected by wireless transmission to the Net." At this moment we will always "be in touch," always "be plugged in," and at this moment, Manovich predicts, the "retina and the screen will merge," the screen itself will disappear.[32]

Yet predictions of the triumph of the virtual belong to what the media critic and skeptical historian Phillip Rosen calls the "rhetoric of the forecast."[33] The forecast is one of the most familiar tropes of all discussions of new media as a journey toward "pure" digitation resulting in the abandonment of the analog. As we get closer to a state of ubiquitous information flow, and as media converge, their specificity will presumably no longer matter. Rosen's main critique of this rhetoric is that we will never quite arrive at this future state. It is another form of Platonic ideal. He characterizes this rhetoric of the forecast as entailing three main promises: (1) the infinite ability to *manipulate* enabled by computational media; (2) the ultimate *convergence* of all media—telephone, film, television, computer—made possible by the free passage of any kind of message among a multiplicity of machines and media; and (3) finally, infinite manipulability and convergence lead to the ultimate achievement of *interactivity* in which the receiver of information can potentially interact with it in the very process of reception. Rosen's skepticism about virtual reality is primarily that infinite manipulation, convergence, and interactivity will never quite arrive. We persist in a permanent interregnum between old and new media.[34]

Vivian Sobchack, whose notion of embodiment in relation to cinema has been important throughout this book, is also no fan of the digital. She argues that the electronic is experienced "not as a discrete, intentional, body-centered mediation and projection in space but rather as a simultaneous, dispersed and insubstantial transmission across a network or web that is constituted spatially more as a materially flimsy latticework of nodal points than as the stable ground of embodied experience." The electronic constructs a metaworld, a system of simulation and of copies that lack an "original ground."[35] Caught up in discrete bits of a perpetually instant present, Sobchack asserts that the only thing that holds identity together in this regime is the ongoing affirmation of our connections to these media themselves. In this flattened, superficial space lacking both temporal thickness and bodily investment, the dominant "techno-logic" of the electronic leaves us diffused and disembodied.[36]

But perhaps Sobchack's objection to a presumed disembodiment caused by new media goes too far. Perhaps it is not a question of leaving the body, humanity, and our relation to screens behind. In two recent books, *New Philosophy for New Media* and *Bodies in Code: Interfaces with Digital Media*,[37] Mark Hansen has insisted on the centrality of the body as the "framer" of information—as the material basis of all perceptual information, whether analogical or coded.[38] In a sense, Hansen tells us what we already know, or at least what we already feel if we are not too caught up in dualistic thinking about mind and body: that we relate to moving images in much the same way that we relate to real bodies. My body sympathetically relates to the bodies I see on screen, but when I am screening sex I do not "have" sex with the bodies I see there. Nor do I slavishly imitate what I see them do. Over time, I have been arguing, we become *habituated* to this screening and to our sympathetic relations to the sex of others as a kind of carnal knowledge felt in our own bodies. The techniques of cinema have led us to an embodied relation to movies that allows us to play with these moving images even while sitting immobile in our theater seats or holding an image on a mobile device in our laps. My irreducible bodily basis of experience has thus been conditioned by the technical dimension of movies. "Mixed reality" is Hansen's term for the fact that there is no escape "into" the virtual, no leaving the body behind, no complete going through the virtual window—only increased awareness of imaging, and of active relations to images, as an originary element of our organism's very being.

Where Hansen explains the embodiment of digital media through analyses of rarefied digital artworks nearly impossible to see because they only exist in museum installations or on ephemeral Web sites, I will briefly explore embodiment in digital media through some quite readily available and popular examples of cyberporn by considering Rosen's categories of infinite manipulability, convergence, and especially interaction. Cyberporn has been called the "great industry of the internet."[39] All pornography, and especially moving-image pornography, offers a dramatic tension between fantasy (for example, the idea that people are always ready to have sex at the drop of a hat) and reality (the supposedly documentary quality of this sex, the fact that in hard core the sex must "really" happen). But in the case of cyberporn, the further tension between analog and digital, real and virtual, complicates this initial tension. Because pornography, as we saw in chapter 3, provokes the bodies that use it to react in the form of arousal, it can be a very real embodied experience *if* we are so aroused. The gay media critic Richard Dyer puts it best: "No other genre can be at once so devastatingly unsatisfactory when it fails to deliver . . . and so entirely true to its highly focused promise when it succeeds."[40]

Since the era of *Deep Throat*, however, there has been a significant escalation in the expectation of what pornography delivers. Where I had once argued of theatrically screened hard core that it was marked with "the primary intent of *arousing viewers*,"[41] Dyer now writes: "The point of porn is to assist the user in *coming to orgasm*."[42] This expectation may be the essential difference between the big screen and the small screen, between public and private screening of sex. Where the big screen configures me as a spectator or viewer, the small screen configures me as a user-participant invited to do more than just watch a moving image across the gulf between me and the screen. As with Dyer—and not only in the realm of gay pornography—there is an assumption that masturbation is the very point of the human-screen interface, and it is not accidental that the video Dyer discusses the most, Ryan Idol's *Ryan Idol: A Very Personal View* (1990),[43] is itself a celebration of masturbation. In this video, Ryan Idol speaks directly to the viewer of the video about a typical day in his life, a day filled with numerous opportunities to masturbate with us watching. As in a great many works of pornography in the electronic era, a user interacts with a porn performer who speaks directly to him or her. And this user may also infinitely manipulate—even though in this predigital video instance manipulation only amounts to the ability to repeat sections and to coincide his or her own arousal and coming with Idol's.

If this escalation from arousal to coming is pervasive in contemporary expectations of the experience of screening hard-core sex, it represents a significant change in what pornography is expected to deliver since the big-screen theatrical viewing days of *Deep Throat*. While the gay video pornography Dyer uses in this instance is not technically cyberporn—it is not delivered online, it is not *infinitely* manipulable, and it is, strictly speaking, not digital, which is to say it is also not yet converged—it formally anticipates many qualities of contemporary cyberporn: it offers direct address to the viewer-user; it cares very little about narrative; and it is real rather than fictional in the sense that the porn star really does masturbate himself to orgasm several times as the main action, sharing his pleasure, articulating its nature to us as he does so. What is real about Idol is certainly not that he is an ordinary person who anticipates the proliferation of many amateur forms of pornography. Rather, he is real in another sense: he acknowledges our own aroused, possibly masturbatory connection to him through the camera. He speaks to us, he grows aroused for us, he comes *for* us. He even seems to expect us to come *with* him. In him we see an anticipation of the cybersex idea of having so-called tele-present sex with a person not physically available to the body of the user.

The media critic Stacy Gillis defines cybersex—as distinct from cyber-porn—as having sex with someone who is not physically present in our space but connected through the computer. Cybersex is a "synchronous sexual exchange" between two people across a distance.[44] For Gillis, this sexual exchange is necessarily only textual—an exchange of written words in real time. In an open chat room, for example, "Laurie" proposes to "Gregory" that they "try anal." Gregory responds that that is his specialty: "Get the head in there with circular motion, and don't put the entire penis in there, or Laurie will lie on her stomach for three days. It's real tight but the relaxation is the key."[45] Part hypothetical action, part sex education, this exchange selectively describes what Laurie and Gregory feel about the act of anal sex, as well as what they feel toward one another while they virtually do it. Of course no physical connection between them—except as they imagine it to be taking place in cyberspace, except as they relate to one another through their screens—is possible.[46] Nevertheless there is a textual exchange that takes place in real time.

Cybersex in this model is a telling of fantasies in "the present active tense of doing and feeling."[47] While Laurie and Gregory, who choose the words they exchange via the computer, are engaged in cybersex, those of us who read the exchange as it unfolds in the chat room, or later as pub-lished in Gillis's article, are experiencing cyberporn—a *representation* of sexual acts.[48] No one, not Laurie, not Gregory, not the "voyeurs" in the chat room not the readers who experience the exchange as cyberporn, exactly knows where the sexual act takes place. The logical answer—that they are in cyberspace, a virtual alternative to the physical world—might satisfy the mind-body dualists who give priority to mind, but it unfortu-nately gives very short shrift to these stubborn bodies still sitting before the computer. Gillis wisely rejects the notion of cyberspace as an alterna-tive to the physical world, and she equally rejects the often accompanying metaphor of the cyborg as the human-machine that we become in an era of converging media, infinite manipulation, and interactivity. However, her conclusion that we experience a "redrawing of the body via the key-board, on the screen" and that this redrawing "empties out" our physical and sensory existence into that other place, cyberspace, where subjectivi-ties are not defined by corporeality, seems dubious.[49]

Gillis's argument relies on notions of the postmodern body as "miss-ing matter" and thus points us away from the phenomenological insight that all media experiences are embodied.[50] Her ultimate conclusion that cybersex is "masturbation, mutual masturbation, erotica, pornography and sex all at the same time (although not in the same place)" is too imprecise. However, it does point us to the important question of both time and space. For not only does the couple use the medium of the screen to get "closer" to one another, but what seems to be most exciting is that they are doing it "together" at the same time.

Cyberporn exists in many different forms, some of it very much like ordinary porn. I have been arguing, however, that the one common denominator of small-screen pornography in a new media era has been the expectation that one might be more likely to use this pornography, not just for arousal but also now "to come." Whether most cyberporn users *do* use it in this way I cannot confirm, but it does seem incontrovertible that much of the pornography out there today has a built-in expectation that users will be "in touch" with themselves and often masturbating before their computer or television monitors or new touch screens.[51] What follows is an impressionistic survey of contemporary pornographies from the perspective of Rosen's never quite achieved qualities of convergence, practically infinite manipulation, and the ever-developing forms of sexual interaction.

In the introduction to this book I cited the example of *Pirates* (dir. Joone, 2005), a work of contemporary pornography available on DVD. Proudly advertised as the most expensive porn film ever, it represents the big-production, professional movie-like end of a continuum whose opposite end is represented by thousands of free, or initially free, adult Web sites offering all manner of amateur sexual poses, performances, and fetishes. Produced by the combined forces of two of contemporary porn's most established studios (Digital Playground and Adam and Eve Productions) and combining the talents of no less than five "contract" girl players, *Pirates* comes packaged in an expensive ($50 to $70) three-disc box set. One disc is the film with a running time of 129 minutes, shot on high-definition video in 5.1 Dolby surround sound in a wide-screen format. Another disc includes special features—a blooper reel, a voice-over commentary from the anonymous director Joone, and a "making-of" documentary. A third disc offers a second, high-definition version of the film that can only be played on proper high-definition machines.[52] The film was heavily promoted, and swept the Adult Video News (AVN) Awards (winning a record eleven, including best video feature, best DVD, best director, best actor, best supporting actor, and best actress). Of course a sequel is in the works.

Pirates is the contemporary example of moving-image pornography that most carries on the narrative tradition begun by *Deep Throat*. Not surprisingly, it offers only minimal evidence of media convergence. It is a digital work aspiring to the big-screen condition of film and harking back to the heyday of porno chic. Though its online marketing campaign won an AVN award, and though it is as full of expensive special effects as the *Pirates of the Caribbean* franchise it affectionately parodies, these computer-generated special effects are primarily devoted to sea battles and the animated bones of pirate skeletons. The sex itself, as I claim in the introduction, is devoted to hard-core pornography's usual maximum visibility of organs and acts. Nor is the experience of screening *Pirates* (whether on a computer or television screen) very interactive, at least not in the way webcam chat rooms (discussed below) or encounters imitating the interactions of cybersex noted above are interactive. The most I can do to interact with *Pirates* is to select sequences from twenty possible chapters, each of which gives me a glimpse of the sexual action as viewed in a small screen-like box. Using the chapter selections, I can easily skip over the badly delivered, though often endearingly comical, dialogue to get down to the sexual business and repeat scenes, gestures, and ubiquitous money shots. On the other hand, if I enjoy this spectacle of a porn movie imitating the Hollywood mainstream, I myself am more likely to ignore the chapter divisions and just watch the whole thing, as if it were a movie. Manipulations are not infinite, interactions are minimal, convergence moves backward to the condition of film, not forward to that of the computer—but they also confirm the impression that the porn industry has always been at the forefront of technological advancement. For example, the porn industry has been a key player in the decision about which format of high definition video will be adopted.[53] And, as we have seen, it has also been at the forefront of the new technology of paying online to screen sex.

Where, however, might one go for more interaction, manipulation, and convergence? Obviously to the Internet, which is rapidly cutting into the once unprecedented profits of the traditional porn industry whose pride and joy is a film like *Pirates*, not the interloping upstart Web sites purporting to offer more "interactive" experiences. For the closest possible experience of interaction with live humans at the other end of the line in real time—an interaction that approaches the condition of cybersex—one goes to the adult Web sites that advertise some variation of cam.whores. Cam.whores are persons paid to sit in front of Webcams attached to computer screens. At these screens they receive messages from paying customers who may ask them to undress or perform various masturbatory gestures. In this experience, I can see the cam.whore, but the cam.whore cannot see me. I select a cam.whore from a thumbnail pose, enter a chat room, and type messages that can be read by both the cam.whore and the others who are online paying court. I can then, for a fee, move to a private one-on-one session.

Zabet Patterson, Wendy Chun, and Victor Burgin have all analyzed the nature of the interactivity of these online Webcam experiences.[54] Cam.-whores are the cyberporn experience that most closely resemble Laurie and Gregory typing away at their keyboards in real time, with the difference, of course, that whatever Laurie and Gregory do, and despite the fact that they cannot see one another, their interactions are reciprocal. In contrast, my interaction with the cam.whore is more one-sided. I request an action or a display that the cam.whore performs. What the experience lacks in terms of exciting spectacle it makes up for in the experience of live simultaneity—the idea, if not always the fact, that this is happening right now and that other people may be watching right along with me.[55] It is the nature of the experience that one is effectively buying time with a real person, though at a distance. This real person's authenticity might in this case be measured by his or her very ordinariness and lack of porn luster compared to the contract player porn starlets of *Pirates* or their well-endowed male costars.

If *Pirates*'s imitation of an old-fashioned movie offers the sexual fantasy of spectacular male and female bodies in action, then these Webcam slices of life place emphasis on the real, whose authenticity is often marked by a lack of glamour and gloss. In online cyberporn, an amateurish low resolution rules, whether in the presentation of ordinary or freakish people (dwarves, fat people, lactating women, hairy men, etc.) In general, however, online porn sacrifices arresting spectacles of nudity, masturbation, and sex for more everyday activities like brushing hair and primping. Zabet Patterson calls this "the abolition of the spectacular in favor of other models of relationality."[56]

Although one can interact with the cam.whore in an experience that represents a kind of convergence of telephone and computer, one cannot highly—let alone infinitely—manipulate this interaction. For more infinite manipulation one might turn to a range of virtual sex experiences called Interactive Sex Simulators (ISS) sold online and as DVDs. "Are you bored with porn? Do you wish it were more interactive?" reads a recent ad, "With *Virtual Eve*, you're the director, camera man and star of your very own virtual production." Interactive Sex Simulators include the popular Digital Playground's *Virtual Sex with* . . . (say, Jenna Jameson), or Digital

Sin's *My Plaything* . . . (say, Jewel DeNyle) series.[57] In both examples, a male avatar whose face is never seen has graphic sex with the female porn body. The "user-player" clicks on icons that choose positions (missionary, doggy, etc.) or camera angles (including a choice between the point of view of the avatar or a second camera angle showing *"what it looks like from the other side!"*).[58]

Like cam.whore experiences, Interactive Sex Simulators claim to be more realistic than ordinary pornography, in this case because of the illusion of greater proximity: they put a virtual you—your avatar—into the scene. Unlike cam.whore experiences, however, the scene you enter through the avatar's body is prerecorded: it is not happening now. Manipulation of various controls determines the kind of activity your avatar and the female porn body perform. This manipulation, while not infinite, is certainly multiplied.[59] Such, it seems, is the trade-off for interacting with a body that is not live, that is not "interacting" with me now. In *Virtual Sex with Jenna Jameson*, for example, I choose, or perhaps it is best to say, I direct, the activity my avatar will enjoy with her (either foreplay that allows "me" to use my fingers, a vibrator, or my mouth; or sex in which "Jenna gets a mouthful of me," or I penetrate her in one of the above positions). I can also choose Jenna's sexual mood, up to a point. For example, if I am already in the "foreplay fingers" mode and then click on "I" instead of "N" in the choice menu, Jenna will say, "Oh, that feels so good," when I direct my avatar's single finger to press into her vagina. But if I then click on the I/N choice again, Jenna changes: "Oh yeah! Jam your fingers in my cunt . . . fuck my little pussy harder!" I/N, it turns out, stands for the choice between innocent (actually just polite) and nasty (actually just a woman who bluntly commands what she wants). Unlike the repeatable but hardly manipulatable sex acts of *Pirates*, there is no necessary linear progression from one activity, position, or affect to another. My avatar will keep sticking his fingers into Jenna in the foreplay-fingers mode until I click on another activity, and Jenna will keep on being "innocent" until I tell her to be "nasty."

The empty, black space of "my" encounter with Jenna is significantly devoid of detail. In this space Jenna seems to float in a state of supreme readiness for whatever prefabricated actions are chosen, calling to mind Sobchack's statement that electronic media have a tendency to liberate the "spectator/user from the pull of what might be termed moral and physical *gravity*—and, at least in the euphoria of the moment, the weight of its real-world consequences."[60] But what is odd about this cyberporn portrayal of release in the encounter between Jenna and my avatar is not that it takes

129: *Virtual Sex with Jenna Jameson*, a digital money shot that shoots longer and farther than any real-life ejaculation ever could

on the conventional phallic form of that most enduring of pornographic conventions—the money shot—which we have perhaps learned to expect in most pornography since the seventies aimed at male viewers. What is odd, rather, is that this particular one is quite obviously computer generated. This money shot shoots longer, farther, and straighter than any real-life one ever could (figure 129). Although my avatar pulls out of Jenna in order to come much the way male porn performers have been doing since *Deep Throat*, this money shot is a special effect, or better, following Ben Hadden, it is a "sexual effect," pairing a conventional sexual event with a technologically new means of representation, in this case animated computer-generated images (CGI).[61]

While we tend to think of special effects as new, they are much older than moving pictures and perhaps only perceived as "special" when they are still relatively unknown.[62] *Deep Throat*'s money shots, along with those in *Boys in the Sand* and *Behind the Green Door*, all discussed in chapter 3, were also, in their own day, "sexual effects." All offered fast-cut montages of sexual climax.[63] In each case, the "old" cinematic sexual effect of the money shot prolongs and exaggerates a climax that—if looked at in real time and without these looping repetitions, fast montages, extreme close-ups, and optical enhancements—might only be a brief squirt, perhaps only a little dribble.[64]

The "new" electronic cyberporn money shot thus does what all money shots do: it aids the impression of the great duration and force of the ejaculation while minimizing aspects that might be much less spectacular, making the ejaculation look on the outside of the body something like what it feels like on the inside (powerful, bursting, explosive, climactic).

Like Jenna's obviously silicon-injected breasts, it is a patent exaggeration of the sexual body that performs at my command. I can end any scene by simply clicking ORG and watching my avatar squirt. In a genre that has historically placed great value on the authenticity of involuntary bodily confessions of pleasure and that, as we saw in chapter 3, relentlessly and unfailingly uses the spectacle of real male orgasm to stand in for the less visible and presumably less spectacular manifestation of pleasure in the female body, this new sexual effect may surprise. Perhaps, in an era of AIDS, the rationale for this digital money shot is that it offers the benefit of not being wet, messy, or in any way biological.[65] This ejaculate could neither impregnate nor infect. It is less biological, and more cybernetic. Wetness, as Hadden notes, is the very sign of humanity.[66]

On the surface this cyber money shot would seem to be the very ex-emplification of Jean Baudrillard's dystopic "ecstasy of communication." Baudrillard defines this new, passionless, sexless ecstasy as "no longer the obscenity of the hidden, the repressed, the obscure, but that of the visible, the all-too-visible, the more-visible-than-visible."[67] It is tempting to agree with Baudrillard and all the other harbingers of the condition of the post-human that such a patently fake sexual effect mixing real body and CGI cannot be good for real human sex.

The media critic Kevin Wynter, for example, claims that the Interactive Sex Simulator, like the flight simulator on which it is modeled, is a "train-ing apparatus where the experience of sexuality is configured as a kind of lucid dreaming in which the body that the "participant" is asked to identify with ostensibly has no identity."[68] To Wynter this experience, which claims to be the most "realistic sexual encounter ever," offers a kind of dementia of disembodiment in which male identity is eschewed in "favor of purely phallic representations."[69] Where I had once commented in relation to an earlier generation of sex simulation games that one receives the un-canny experience of being both here and there, Wynter concludes that the game would seem to succeed in its goal of not only arousing the user but of satisfying a feeling of interacting with another person not actu-ally there. However, this is where Mark Hansen's notion of mixed reality might help put a finer point on the embodied experience of interactive cyberporn.

Masturbation is a self-stimulating act (here) in which we project our-selves into a fantasmatic and imagined relation to another (there), often leaving us with some bodily fluids (back here). It is a motor activity in-creasingly performed, as Richard Dyer and others attest, while watching moving images, in some kind of timed relation to the movements viewed on the screen. In ordinary masturbation, we know in the end that we are alone with ourselves. The ISS form of play seems to integrate an expectation of masturbation as a matter of timing one's own sexual rhythms to the chosen ones of the avatar and the sexual object. This play reformulates masturbation as something less solitary than previously understood—no longer quite sex for one yet not quite sex for two. I do not go "there;" I am not immersed in the world of Jenna. Though my motor activity here in my physical space may converge with Jenna's activity there, my body remains, as Hansen puts it, the "absolute here,"[70] in relation to which all my perceptions of there are organized. While the ISS offers masturbation in the guise of having sex with another person, and thus construes it as a less solitary act, it is not an experience of entering into an illusory space. The realism promised by the ISS is never the reality of immersive thereness, nor could it be so long as my own masturbation and coming here is the goal.

If Sex Simulators turn the involuntary confession of pleasure that is the money shot into a cybernetic performance that I can command and control, does this mean as Wynter argues that phallic pleasures still rule in the land of cyberporn? In many ways they do, every bit as much as in the era of *Deep Throat*. But now, the cheaper, the more amateurish, and the more "real" the porn, the more likely it is that one will encounter variants to the usual phallic expectations. The remarkable variety of sexual effects now available online has led to a situation in which the one effect that I had believed consigned to invisibility in an era of filmed and videotaped professional porn has suddenly, and quite spectacularly, though in a small-screen sort of way, been rendered visible in the bodies of amateurs.

Tucked away modestly among the myriad sex Web sites that one might browse for free so long as one claims to be an adult is www.the-female-orgasm.com. This Web site states: "We film women having real orgasms any which way they can truly cum . . . you'll find all shapes and sizes, hairy and shaven, close up and full body views, toys and fingers, inside and outdoors . . . just about anything you could desire. And most importantly, they are all really cumming, almost all with nice and clearly visible orgasmic contractions!" Though I can become a member and have prolonged access to these female orgasms, I can also browse for free and see enough to confirm that the involuntary confession of pleasure that I once argued, following Freud too closely, was an absence, a "nothing to see," is, if one just looks enough on today's Internet, quite visible as an involuntary spasm, often induced by masturbation. The women who give up these orgasms for all to see are hardly porn stars. For the most part it is only their clitorises, vulvas, and sometimes their anuses that we see in the frame, some-times accompanied by a hand, a finger, or a convulsion-inducing vibrator.[71] The point, compared to the command and control game mentality of the Interactive Sex Simulators, is that these pulsating vulvas may be harder to find, less immediately visible, and not involved in any goal-oriented game. Nevertheless, they are part of the variety of sexual revelation now available on the small screen and one kind of (modest) answer to the ubiquity of masculine money shots in the realm of hard-core.

Experiences of cyberporn today might entail the renting or purchasing of a DVD, downloading a game online, logging onto a cam.whore site, engaging in one-shot-only pay for play, visiting any number of Web sites offering any number of sexual shows or orientations, or integrating virtual sex through the bodies of avatars into the daily life of "massively multi-player online" games such as *Second Life*.[72] While a DVD like *Pirates* repre-sents the mainstream of the porn industry, it seems quite possible that this DVD-oriented professional end is now in for a serious challenge by these diverse and often cheaper amateur sites. In 2006, for the first time, sales and rentals of pornographic videos in the heretofore burgeoning industry fell, while online and often free Web sites have flourished.[73]

Conclusion

"Every day the urge grows stronger to get hold of an object at close range in an image"[74]—if the small-screen examples of cyberporn discussed here do not afford an actual grasp of objects except insofar as they remain physical bodies, they do afford a greater closeness to the objects and a greater sense of "getting hold" because the objects themselves remain rela-tively small and unspectacular compared to those on the big screen. This is one of the most striking qualities of the Interactive Sex Simulators: the gulf between my body and the screen that made possible the impression of my own engulfment by the larger-than-life movie image has given way here to a closeness that puts me right up against Jenna's genitals either through the body of an avatar whose gestures I control or through an ability to move all around the sexual activity. Walter Benjamin surely saw the ways technological reproducibility was, with film and photography, bringing us into "close range." He is the scholar who has most eloquently articulated how closeness and reproducibility work against qualities of uniqueness and aura.

My point is not to disparage the inevitable urge to get closer, or, as the ad for another variation on the experience with Jenna puts it, to "simulate what stimulates."[75] Rather, it is to understand that the embrace of the computer technology depicted so sinisterly in Almodóvar (figure 126), Cronenberg (figure 127), and Mahurin (figure 128) is a pleasure of converged, manipulative, interactive play to those who engage in it. Though I personally would rather occupy the position of Almodóvar's boys in a public place before the big screen, the point is not so much to focus on the size of the screen but the imaginative and newly temporalized connectivities of the various screens which, as Anne Friedberg notes in the epigraph, "compete for our attention." No one kind of screen can now be said to have hegemony. Screening sex today can encompass pointing, clicking, typing, choosing. It can mean an absorption into images that appear to abolish the gulf between me and the old-fashioned movie screen, images which require my own eroticized orchestration of hand-eye coordination. It is also an activity that can put me increasingly in the place of the film director, choosing acts, scenes, interactions. It is an ideal of connectivity and relation, whether with a cam.whore or with "a piece of ass in a software package,"[76] and even if my only "real" tactile connection is through the fingers before the screen doing that pointing, clicking, typing, or screen-touching. But is it "having" sex?

Here we might do well to recall the argument of the First Amendment scholar Frederick Schauer, who argued that a "close-up colour depiction of the sexual organs of a male and female who are engaged in sexual intercourse" is, when viewed, "nothing more than a sex aid." Schauer found the fact that the viewer had no physical contact with the images contained in it, "only fortuitous."[77] He saw no real difference between screening a sex act and having sex instantaneously with the bodies represented in the images. I have so far strenuously resisted this argument in this book with respect to film. The question is whether Schauer's objections have an increased validity now that new media have made possible a kind of "having sex" with ourselves via our machines.

Schauer's claim that the lack of physical contact with the images of hard-core moving-image pornography is "only fortuitous" takes on a special relevance in the above examples of Interactive Sex Simulators. Recall that Schauer seemed to want to say that real sex viewed on the screen would automatically induce real sex in the audience:

> Imagine a motion picture of ten minutes duration whose entire content consists of a close-up colour depiction of the sexual organs of a male and female who are engaged in sexual intercourse. The film contains no variety,

no dialogue, no music, no attempt at artistic depiction, and not even any view of the faces of the participants. The film is shown to paying customers who, observing the film, either reach orgasm instantly or are led to masturbate while the film is being shown.[78]

In this passage Schauer locates obscenity in the fact of the supposedly direct mimicry by the screening body of the screened bodies. I noted in this book's introduction that this description represented one legal scholar's Platonic ideal of obscenity—an ideal of the unacceptable limit of sexual representation that is in fact always complicated by both medium and message. Schauer's example minimizes any difference between screening sex and having sex, between watching and doing. Indeed, he equates the sale of such a film (in a public screening) and the sale of a "plastic or vibrating sex aid," or the sale of a "body through prostitution" (not unlike the virtual experience of a cam.whore), to the sex act itself. In each case, what is obscene to Schauer is the very idea that *public* audience members might orgasm to the image in a public place, in the presence of others. They might as well be having sex, he seems to suggest, right there in the audience.[79] Of course, now Schauer's outrage at the violation of public space would have to be mitigated by the fact that with the "small screen" we are no longer dealing with a public audience, but with a more privatized, though never entirely private, player. What is perhaps most changed in this new situation is that public space gives way to a new kind of public time: users and viewers connected to Jenna, the cam.whore, the Web site with pulsating vulvas are not present to one another in the same space, but they may be connected through these stimulating images to one another in the same time. Indeed, one of the more remarkable features of these screening experiences may be not the connection to the images of the act themselves but the idea of the greater connectivity to a public dispersed in space but sometimes united in time.

But Schauer does not consider time, he considers space, and he would probably say that he wins my running argument with him because of the greater apparent closeness of viewers (now called users, players, and participants) to the acts mediated by the screen. However, I maintain that it is essential to the nature of all relations to screened images that the bodies screened—however close, however I may feel *here* what they or an avatar supposedly feel *there* and however I may feel now what they supposedly also feel now—are still ungraspable. If my own body is graspable, and perhaps no longer just by my own hands in some recent examples of games with hardware attachments that render the figure of being "jacked-in" quite literal,[80] this still does not mean that screening sex and having sex become identical; they just, as Benjamin understood, get a little closer both temporally and spatially. If sex simulators bring us closer, and if they are to some players the perfect masturbatory sex aid precisely because they seem not to be masturbatory—because they offer a simulation of sex with another—they are neither a replacement for the spontaneity and fleshy touch of sex with another nor are they an absence of touch or connection altogether. After more than a century of screening sex the very act of screening has inevitably affected, through habituation to different screening practices, our very sense of what sex can be.

Utopian faith in the possibilities of virtual reality sometimes suggests that a break with the culture of the screen is imminent as once passive, immobile spectators become active and mobile. Manovich, for example, in a passage that insists on the ubiquity of screens, nevertheless ambivalently adds that when true virtual reality is achieved, the user's body will become a "giant mouse, or more precisely, a giant joystick."[81] Yet despite this promise of a future virtual reality in which screens themselves will become passé, Manovich ends his chapter entitled "The Interface" with the acknowledgment that we still live, at least for the time being, "in the society of the screen."[82]

I think we will continue to live in such a society for a very long time. Even if we interface with a cam.whore, a vixen, a virtual Jenna, or a convulsing clitoris, or with the more imaginative personae we may construct and control as they interact with other virtual bodies constructed and controlled by a real other person, or even if we just watch cable television or DVDs with a remote control in hand, such interfacing, or now interbodying, will always take place through media. Getting hold of something by means of its likeness is not the same thing as getting hold of the thing itself, though it does generate embodied feelings that we do well to acknowledge. Whatever mimesis occurs in our bodies is never the kind of slavish imitation Schauer imagines. What we see in that same or other time and distant (but now closer) space may rebound back upon our own bodies in the more solipsistic and masturbatory way Sobchack describes, or it may, as Benjamin held out, offer an imaginative form of play that can lead us back into the world.

As Jane Juffer puts it, computer consumption of pornography is "intensely private." It occurs not only in the privacy of one's "home (or cubicle/office at work) but also in the isolated, ephemeral interaction of user and screen." Yet as Juffer continues, it is also "intensely public, in that information proliferates and spreads to numerous sites, transgressing the physical boundaries that make other kinds of porn outlets, such as bookstores and theaters, much more easily identifiable and regulatable."[83] When the private men's-only consumption of ob/scenities in the stag era gave way to the public consumption of on/scenities in the theatrical film era, pornography became something every adult could screen, not just private clubs of men.[84] As I have already argued, it was this shift from restricted, private, men-only screenings to a general public of sexually interested adults that opened up the contemporary proliferation of online on/scenities in our electronic video-computer age.[85] I continue to think that this shift is at least as significant as that from film pornography to cyberporn. The move "back" to what seems to be a more private viewing venue—the home, though also the office computer or the laptop that goes anywhere—does not engage the same privacy as that of the gentlemen-only stag era. Pornography online or HBO on demand, even if screened in the home, is never really private—both technically, in that our movements (and purchases) are traced, and philosophically, in that the Internet itself is fundamentally, as Wendy Chun argues, an "indeterminate and pornographic" space.[86]

The publication of sex in all the forms I have examined in this book has never been a making public of that which properly belongs to the private—George Steiner's "night words" shouted from the rooftops. As we saw, perhaps most forcefully in the examination of *Brokeback Mountain*'s publicity campaign, a movie about two cowpokes who think their sexual pleasure is "nobody's business" but their own, offered gay anal sex its widest publicity. Publicity is not necessarily the exposure of something that is more properly private. It does not contaminate "an otherwise sealed interiority."[87] It is, as Thomas Keenan has said, what belongs to everyone and to no one in particular.[88] Publicity is promiscuous, it exposes us to, it involves us with, others, even and perhaps especially others who are not physically present to us there with us in the same time and space.

The carnal knowledge that we gain from screening sex is, finally, not a matter of seeing "it." It is not a matter of arriving at an ultimate degree of frankness, explicitness, and least of all maturity. However much I have been rooting, throughout this book, for American moving images to grow up and integrate hard-core art into the fabric of adult narratives beyond the various ghettoes of pornography and to put an end to the awkward "long adolescence of American movies," we cannot cure the dishonesty and bad faith about sex with more explicitness. And however much I would root for the sight of a few more convulsing clitorises to answer the seeming ubiquity of money shots, I do not really believe that more realistic depictions of female pleasure are the answer.

After more than a century of screening sex, perhaps the most important lesson I would like to draw from the last stage of this impressionistic chronicle is that the very act of screening has become an intimate part of our sexuality. The point therefore should not be to discover that screening sex brings us so much closer, spatially or temporally, to "real sex." Rather, it should be to discover that viewers, and now users, have become habituated to these new forms of mimetic play with, and through, screens. The very act of screening is desirable, sensual, and erotic in its own right. Screening sex, from Edison's kiss to the simulated squirts aimed at various parts of Jenna Jameson's anatomy, has, at each new stage, proffered an opportunity to see and to know what has not previously been seen so closely. This carnal knowledge never fully reveals the scratch we imagine "it" to be, but the itch that keeps us screening.

notes

Introduction

1 Williams, *Television: Technology and Cultural Form*, 59.

2 Debord, *Society of the Spectacle*, 7.

3 Williams, *Hard Core: Power, Pleasure and the 'Frenzy of the Visible,'* 281. See also *Porn Studies*, 3.

4 See Escoffier's introduction to his excellent anthology of documents, *Sexual Revolution*, pp. xi-xxxvi.

5 Giddens, *The Transformation of Intimacy: Sexuality, Love and Eroticism in Modern Societies*; D'Emilio and Freedman, *Intimate Matters: A History of Sexuality in America*; Luker, *When Sex Goes to School: Warring Views on Sex—And Sex Education—Since the Sixties*.

6 Luker, 76–77.

7 See Kristin Luker's discussion of the difference between these revolutions, pp. 37–79.

8 In *Hard Core* I understood the emergence of hard-core pornography in the early seventies as part of the phenomenon described by Michel Foucault: an historically new "immense curiosity about sex, bent on questioning it, with an insatiable desire to hear it speak . . . ." Foucault's point is that sex is a discursive construct more than it is a preexisting object. Foucault, *The History of Sexuality: An Introduction, Volume 1*, 178; Williams, *Hard Core*, 2.

9 Eric Schaefer makes this argument in his forthcoming book, *Massacre of*

Pleasure: A History of Sexploitation Film, 1960–1979. I am indebted to Schaefer for communicating an unpublished paper that forms part of this manuscript. Unpublished talk delivered at the Society for Cinema and Media Studies, March 2007.

10 Susan Gal, "A Semiotics of the Public/Private Distinction," 78.

11 Cited in Susan Gal, "A Semiotics of the Public/Private Distinction," 79.

12 "Shadowy right to privacy" is the term of Stefano Scoglio, *Transforming Privacy: The Transpersonal Philosophy of Rights*, 138. In the *Griswold* decision Justice William O. Douglas famously argued that "zones of privacy are present as penumbras not only in the first Amendment but also in the Third, in the Fourth and the Fifth, and in the Ninth." Cited in Schaefer, unpublished talk.

13 I allude here to Supreme Court Justice Potter Stewart's famous non-definition of pornography: "I don't know what it is but I know it when I see it." As with pornography, obscenity proves to be an elusive thing.

14 See the excellent discussion of this particular sexual act in Sasha Torres's "On Graphic Language and the Modesty of Television News," in Lauren Berlant and Lisa Duggan, eds., *Our Monica, Ourselves: The Clinton Affair and the National Interest*, 111.

15 Some of the relevant works by and about Foucault include Michel Foucault's *The History of Sexuality: An Introduction, Volume 1*; *The History of Sexuality Vol. 2: The Use of Pleasure*; *The History of Sexuality Vol. 3: The Care of the Self*; *The Lives of Michel Foucault*; and Eve Kosofsky Sedgwick's *Epistemology of the Closet*.

16 Foucault writes of "lifting of prohibitions, an irruption of speech, a reinstating of pleasure within reality." *The History of Sexuality: Volume 1, An Introduction*, 5.

17 Ibid., 7.

18 Ibid., 11.

19 Ibid., 44.

20 Ibid., 47.

21 Bersani, *The Freudian Body: Psychoanalysis and Art*, 34.

22 Ibid., 34.

23 Bataille, *Erotism: Death and Sensuality*, 29–55. Counterintuitively, Bataille links life with discontinuity and death with continuity. Death is not the end of connection with life but the end of discontinuity. When we die, we resume connection with the continuity of the inanimate. We are discontinuous beings, individuals who perish in isolation in the midst of an incomprehensible adventure, but we yearn for our lost continuity and sexual eroticism is one place we get it. Through descriptions of physical, emotional, and religious eroticism, Bataille argues that all substitute for the individual's isolated discontinuity a feeling of profound continuity.

24 Bataille, *Erotism*, 36.

25 Benjamin, "The Work of Art in the Age of Its Technological Reproducibility: Second Version," 105.

26 Taussig, *Mimesis and Alterity*, 21.

27 Schauer, *Free Speech: A Philosophical Enquiry*, 181.

28 Ibid., 181.

29 Benjamin, "The Mimetic Faculty," 333–336.

30 Benjamin, "The Work of Art in the Age of Its Technological Reproducibility: Second Version," 104.

31 Hansen, "Benjamin and Cinema: Not a One Way Street," 313.

32 Ibid., 317.

33 Ibid.

34 Benjamin, "The Work of Art in the Age of Its Technological Reproducibility: Second Version," 127.

35 The following few paragraphs are an adaptation of a previous discussion of Sobchack's notions of embodied viewing published in the epilogue to Williams, *Hard Core: Power, Pleasure and the "Frenzy of the Visible,"* 289–291.

36 Sobchack, *Carnal Thoughts: Embodiment and Moving Image Culture*, 57.

37 Ibid., 59. See also Sobchack's *The Address of the Eye*.

38 Sobchack, *Carnal Thoughts: Embodiment and Moving Image Culture*, 76–77.

39 Ibid., 66.

40 See Mulvey 1975, 1981; Doane 1982 and Williams 1989.

41 As, for example, numerous seventies film theorists have done. See Baudry, "The Apparatus: Metapsychological Approaches to the Impression of Realism in the Cinema," 299–318. For a brilliant critique of this perspective and for the introduction of another way of considering embodied viewing see Crary, *Techniques of the Observer: On Vision and Modernity in the Nineteenth Century.*

42 Another important proponent of the embodied nature of film viewing is Anne Rutherford. Rutherford speaks of film viewing as a movement of the body toward "a corporeal appropriation of or immersion in a space, an experience, a moment" (Rutherford, "Cinema and Embodied Affect," 138). Once again, the body that screens is viewed as "groping towards a connection" that is not literal touch but a movement "of our beings towards potency. It is an erotics of the image, a dilation of the senses, a nervous excitation—an eye-opening sure—but more than that an opening of the pores, a quickening of the pulse" (Rutherford, 138). Another theorist-critic of embodied viewing is Laura Marks, who approaches it through avant-garde films that emphasize the surface qualities of their images, inviting the viewer to "dissolve his or her subjectivity in the close and bodily contact with the image" (*Touch*, 13). For Marks certain kinds of images—those haptic ones that emphasize surface qualities and their own materiality, or those we may not be able to see clearly—invite us to dissolve our subjectivity in a close and bodily contact with the image. Like Sobchack, Marks does not mean that we literally touch the immaterial image. Rather, she argues that some images invite us to interact up close to the extent that figure and ground commingle and we lose our sense of separateness. Marks adds that the oscillation between a viewer who is "distant, distinct, and disembodied" and one who haptically engages creates an erotic re-

lation, a "shifting between distance and closeness" that overcomes the kind of distance that operates in the purely ocular relation.

Chapter 1: Of Kisses and Ellipses

1 Richard Alapack writes that a kiss is a transcendence of self through the connection to an other whom one both "faces" and "tastes" for the first time. Alapack, "Adolescent First Kiss," 63.

2 I recognize that there are difficulties with the terms *Code era* (e.g., era of the Hollywood Production Code's enforcement) and *pre-Code* (the whole of American mainstream cinema history until that enforcement became somewhat effective), but it will prove necessary in this discussion of kisses. The Hollywood Production Code was created in 1930 as a way for the film industry to regulate itself so as to avoid controversial subjects that might alienate the general audience. It was authored by the Motion Picture Producers and Distributors of America and contained a list of "General Principles" (e.g., "No picture shall . . . lower the moral standards of those who see it") and particular applications, including nine points about the sorts of sex scenes or acts that were forbidden. Although written in 1930, it was by many accounts not enforced until 1934, when the Catholic Legion of Decency threatened to boycott films if the Code was not enforced and Joseph Breen was brought in to do the enforcing. However, it is not strictly true that pre-Code films went entirely unregulated, as Lea Jacobs, Tino Balio, and Richard Maltby have shown. Nor am I interested in this chapter in establishing a strict dividing line between the two eras, or in arguing that the pre-Code era was a wild period of freedom and the Code era one of strict regulation. However, as far as kisses are concerned, films from the time before about 1933 and from the time of the Code's greater enforcement do differ. The kisses that interest me most in the pre-Code era will not be those of the transition period, but those that precede the transition in the silent era. See Maltby, "More Sinned Against than Sinning"; Balio, *Grand Design*; and Jacobs, *Wages of Sin*.

3 For reasons consonant with my topic, I will continue to call it *The Kiss*. Charles Musser, for reasons consonant with his topic, may prefer to call it *The May Irwin Kiss*. See Musser, "The May Irwin Kiss," 97.

4 Musser, *Thomas A. Edison*, 199.

5 Charles Musser has unearthed a number of important facts about this kiss in relation to the beginnings of projected cinema as we know it. Most striking among these is the relation between other stage kisses and this film and the possibility that the fifteen-second *The Kiss* may have included more action. Musser, "The May Irwin Kiss." Musser's forthcoming book on the kiss will discuss further mysteries about this fascinating film, including possible missing footage.

6 Musser also notes that while the Irwin-Rice stage kiss itself was not controversial, Olga Nethersole's extended multiple kisses in *Carmen* had been extremely

so the previous year. The film kiss may thus have been referring in general to the controversy about the propriety of prolonged stage kisses, as Nethersole's apparently were. See Musser, "The May Irwin Kiss," 99–104.

7 Jane Gaines calls it "an awkward two-shot, two faces pressed quickly together, both facing out-toward the camera." Gaines, *Fire and Desire*, 88. Writing about the conflicts between sexual show and sexual event in the genre of moving-image pornography, I have argued that the compulsion to display the maximum visibility of sexual acts often results in a tension between the exhibitionistic display of sex and the often less visible event. This first screen kiss perfectly manifests this tension. Linda Williams, *Hard Core*, 60–72.

8 Qtd. in Musser, "The May Irwin Kiss," 103.

9 Musser tells us that short films of this era were looped. He also notes, citing Henri Bergson, that repetition itself can be considered funny. On a deeper level a potentially comic repetition might humorously clash with the quasi-scientific analytical observation that made reference to, but did not itself imitate, the presumably more torrid scandal of other stage kisses. Ibid., 104.

10 For these remarks themselves, see Lenne, *Sex on the Screen*, 151; and Lewis, *Hollywood v. Hard Core*, 86. The remarks have often been attributed to the editor of the *Chap Book*, Herbert Stone, but they were actually written by the then young painter John Sloan. According to the memory of his second wife, Sloan wrote the unsigned review in the 15 July 1896 issue of *Chap Book*. It is all the more interesting that an artist whose own paintings would later capture the social mix and vitality of audiences at the nickelodeon would object so strenuously here to the monstrosity of exactly the sorts of risqué movie scenes he would later depict himself. See Zurier, "City, Stage, and Screen," 179.

11 Kracauer, *Theory of Film*, 48.

12 Phillips, *On Kissing*, 97.

13 See Gunning, "Cinema of Attractions"; and, "Aesthetic of Astonishment."

14 See Mayne, "Uncovering the Female Body," 66; Gaines, *Fire and Desire*, 87–90; Courtney, *Hollywood's Fantasy of Miscegenation*, 24; Best, *Fugitive's Properties*, 228–37; Stewart, *Migrating to the Movies*, 81–84.

15 Susan Courtney shows that a great many films of early cinema "openly flirted with miscegenation" and that almost all of them offered variations on a similar gag in which a white man is punished for lusting after a white woman with the unintended kiss or touch of a black woman. A variation on this gag includes that of the substituting of black babies for white. Courtney, *Hollywood's Fantasy of Miscegenation*, 24.

16 Gaines, *Fire and Desire*, 90.

17 Jacqueline Stewart, following Miriam Hansen, suggests that the joke may even have been played *by* the black woman on the white man, in collusion with the mistress. Stewart, *Migrating to the Movies*, 82.

18 *Birth* is especially remarkable, despite the elision of interracial kisses, in its suggestive gyrations of the hips of its "mulatto" villain, Silas Lynch, when sexually

threatening the white virgin, Elsie Stoneman. It is precisely this kind of lustful genital allusion that would soon disappear from American screens even in pre-Code Hollywood. See my *Playing the Race Card*, 96–135.

19 Leff and Simmons, *Dame in the Kimono*, 287.

20 Bataille, *Erotism*, 36. For work on Production Code Administration (PCA) censorship, see especially Jacobs, *Wages of Sin*; and Leff and Simmons, *Dame in the Kimono*.

21 In the now-forgotten introductory verse it is Einstein, "new invention," and "fourth dimension" that represent this change; in the context of *Casablanca*'s narrative, it is World War II. The songwriter is Herman Hupfeld.

22 Dyer, *White*, 122.

23 Sam is important to the narrative not only for the music he provides but also as proof of Rick's democratic spirit. That spirit is not consistent, however. At one moment Sam drinks with the couple, while at another moment he is servile and attends to their needs, and sometimes he simply disappears.

24 Richard Dyer writes that it is not "just a matter of a different disposition of light on women and men, but the way the light constructs the relationship between them. The sense of the man being illuminated by the woman is a widespread convention, established in classic Hollywood cinema . . . but still current today." Dyer, *White*, 134.

25 Part of the guilt derives from the fact that we do not know, at this point in the movie, whom Ilsa "really loves." Indeed, as Umberto Eco stresses in his fascinating study of the film, Ilsa is a kind of token and intermediary in the platonic love of the two men: "She herself does not bear any positive value (except, obviously, Beauty)," and she basically does what she is told to do. Eco, "Casablanca," 208.

26 This ellipsis is discussed at length by Maltby in *Hollywood Cinema*, 344–51.

27 Some kisses do conclude, but they tend not to be the big, dramatic ones.

28 Maltby, *Hollywood Cinema*, 349.

29 Qtd. in ibid., 350.

30 This kiss offers a blatantly perverse tension between fear and desire because of its suggestion of necrophilia—Stewart believes Novak to be dead. There is also the remarkable, slightly slow-motion kiss with Grace Kelly in *Rear Window* (dir. Alfred Hitchcock, 1954) that awakens Stewart like a sleeping beauty.

31 This film's unerotic credentials would seem to be confirmed by the fact that it has long screened on television each Christmas season, making it, rather like *The Wizard of Oz*, a perennial family favorite.

32 William Cane describes the *orbicularis oris* muscle as responsible for four distinct movements of the lips, usually described in relation to speech, but equally important in kissing: pressing together, tightening and thinning, rolling inward between the teeth, and, for more "lascivious kisses" thrusting forward. Cane, "Orbicularis Oris of the Face and Mouth."

33 Eve Babitz writes: "In more ways than one, taste is everything in kissing." Babitz, "Sex, Love, and Kissing," 160.

34 Freud, *Three Essays on the Theory of Sexuality*, 48.

35 Ibid., 45–46.

36 Ibid., 50.

37 Nursing, the giving and taking of nurture, is the prototype of many of the sex acts we will examine in this book, especially kissing and fellatio, since both recall the pleasure of the child's oral groping, tasting, and sucking as a crucial originary moment of satisfaction.

38 For an excellent discussion of the two-way street of this satisfaction and excitation, see St. John, "Mammy Fantasy."

39 Freud, *Three Essays on the Theory of Sexuality*, 16.

40 Freud acknowledges, for example, that the kiss is well recognized as an example of certain "intermediate relations to the sexual object . . . which lie on the road towards copulation and are recognized as being preliminary sexual aims." He recognizes that such a relation is in itself pleasurable and that it works to intensify the excitation, "which should persist until the final sexual aim is attained." Pointing out that "contact between the mucous membranes" is held in high esteem by some of "the most highly civilized" nations of the world, he nevertheless emphasizes that these membranes do not actually form a part of the sexual apparatus, but "constitute the entrance to the digestive tract." Ibid., 16.

41 "If a perversion, instead of appearing merely *alongside* the normal sexual aim and object . . . ousts them completely and takes their place in *all* circumstances—if, in short, a perversion has the characteristics of exclusiveness and fixation—then we shall usually be justified in regarding it as a pathological symptom." Ibid., 27.

42 Bersani, *Freudian Body*, 34.

43 Ibid.

44 Ibid., 36.

45 Phillips, *On Kissing*, 96.

46 Of course, for the child, sensual sucking is hardly a one-way street: the mother is a partner in the intimate relation. D. W. Winnicott stresses the mother's sensitive adaptation to the infant's needs and her ability to provide the "illusion that her breast is part of the infant." Winnicott, "Transitional Objects and Transitional Phenomena," 11.

47 Winnicott, *Playing and Reality*, 11.

48 Laplanche, *Jean Laplanche*, 190.

49 As Adam Phillips writes, "Kissing on the mouth can have a mutuality that blurs the distinctions between giving and taking." Phillips, *On Kissing*, 97. See also Coward, *Female Desires*, 97; and Gaines, *Fire and Desire*, 87.

50 Rosalind Coward writes: "Kissing is a voracious activity, an act of mutual penetration. Kissing offers women the chance actively to penetrate. . . . Kissing is probably for women the most sensational activity, representing the height of erotic involvement. Precisely because of its transgressive nature, crossing boundaries between people, engaging sensations usually kept at bay, kissing clearly produces 'excitement.'" Coward, *Female Desires*, 97. And just as clearly, it is an excitement that women, more than men, enjoy. I doubt that I would ever have stayed up late on a summer night to watch movies with romantic kisses with my father!

51 It would also certainly be a mistake to presume, just because a cigarette is a potentially phallic object, that the cigarette in this instance serves as a phallic marker of sexual difference. For even if one wanted to note its phallic shape, it is clear that as soon as this object has done its work of opening up two similar mouths to one another, it has no further value and is thrown away. The pleasures of kisses, and the pleasures of screening kisses, thus do not seem to be those of diametrically opposed penetrator and penetrated.

52 Phillips, *On Kissing*, 97.

53 Buster Keaton's two-reeler, *The Paleface* (1922), offers an ingenious gag based on just this limitation in the representation of sex acts. In a brilliant parody of a final clinch, Buster takes the pretty "Indian Squaw" in his arms and kisses her in the classic position of the man leaning over an extremely leaned-back woman. An intertitle reads "Two years later," but we see the same couple in the exact same position. As the gag well understands, there is nothing else that can be officially depicted!

54 Heartfelt thanks to Yuri Tsivian for pointing out this film, and its kiss, to me.

55 Phillips, *On Kissing*, 97.

56 And, of course, all film vampires, from *Nosferatu* (dir. F. W. Murnau, 1922) on, cross this line between sustaining and actually consuming what they kiss.

57 I am excluding a long list of films, many of them post-Code, in which eating blatantly stands in for sex acts: *Tom Jones* (dir. Tony Richardson, 1963), *La Grande Bouffe* (dir. Marco Ferreri, 1973), *Tampopo* (dir. Juzo Itami, 1985), and so on.

58 This is a gesture we saw Bergman use on Bogart in *Casablanca* as well.

59 The same is true of a later kiss performed by Grant's Devlin on Bergman's Alicia. The kiss is offered as a decoy to make Alicia's ex-Nazi husband, Alex (Claude Raines), believe that Devlin is in love with Alicia rather than hot on the trail of the nefarious uranium hidden in the wine bottles. However, the kiss is also real in the sense that it expresses the passion of both kissers.

60 *A Place in the Sun* (dir. George Stevens, 1951) is another Code-era film that powerfully connects sexual hunger, class hunger, and the oral drive. Elizabeth Taylor, a sexually alluring young socialite, and Montgomery Clift, a sexually and materially hungry factory worker, dance at a formal party in a crowded room in a set piece culminating in one of the most memorable of fifties' screen kisses, an era in which an overt Freudianism had permeated American cinema. On the dance floor, Clift blurts a sudden confession of love. Taylor, suddenly terrified of being seen, pulls him to a more private terrace, where she too confesses love. Little beads of sweat become visible on Clift's brow as he explains how much he loves her, and how much he wishes that he could "tell all." These beads of sweat are eloquent signs that the sex both of them hunger for is primal and dangerous. Indeed, the "all" that he cannot tell is his responsibility toward another woman of his own class whom he has made pregnant. Taylor does not understand what this "all" means, but she responds to the intensity of his desire in a striking line that invites his kiss: "Tell mama, tell mama all." By inviting confession in this eroticized yet maternal way, Taylor turns Clift into an abject infant longing for the maternal breast. It is for this kiss, and all the oral satisfaction it promises in these mammary-obsessed fifties, that Clift's George will soon plot to kill his unwanted girlfriend and for which he will ultimately die. Most of the time Clift's shoulder blocks the view of their mouths, rendering moot the issue of whether they are open or closed. However, the shot is framed so tightly that when Taylor pulls away from the kiss we see that it is open in the beginning fade-out. We are left with the distinct impression that sexual hunger has sealed a forbidden and fateful union.

61 Maurice Merleau-Ponty describes seeing as "to have at a distance." Merleau-Ponty, "Eye and Mind," 166.

62 Kracauer, *Theory of Film*, 48.

63 Proust, *The Guermantes Way*, 77.

64 See Sobchack's *Address of the Eye* and *Carnal Thoughts*.

65 The usual projection speed for sound film is twenty-four frames per second. Thus Warhol shoots at a normal speed and slows the image down slightly in the projection.

66 Though it is not as epic as the six-hour *Sleep* (1963) or the eight-hour *Empire* (1964), *Kiss* is eminently more watchable.

67 Tony Rayns admits that this may only be a legend, but he adds, "There is no doubt that Warhol's earliest films were materially governed by the technical limitations of the equipment in use, much as Edison's pioneering experiments in cinematography had been. Warhol started out with a hand-wound 16mm Bolex camera, which takes 100-foot rolls of film (approximately 2 3/4 minutes when projected at 24 frames-per-second). . . . He then added a motor, which enabled him to run 100 feet of film continuously." Rayns, "Death at Work," 164.

68 Koch, *Stargazer*, 43.

69 It is possible to know who many of these kissers are through information given in various filmographies. I will not dwell on this information, even when known, since for my purposes the kissers' fame or lack of it does not seem crucial to our reception of the film. It is worth knowing, however, that Naomi Levine is the woman in the first two kisses, as well as in kisses 7 and 13. All of the kisses of Naomi Levine were screened together at the Gramercy Arts Theatre in September 1963 under the title *Andy Warhol Serial*. The man in this first kiss is not known. Apra, *Andy Warhol*, 37–38.

70 Wayne Koestenbaum argues, in his fine short book on Warhol, that we do not know the gender of these kissers until the camera pulls out. While it is true that we might not recognize that both are male given the pattern of heterosexual kisses thus far, I did suspect it on initial viewing and imagine that others do as well. Koestenbaum, *Andy Warhol*, 81.

71 Unlike Proust's narrator, women seem to more willingly relinquish the compulsion to see and touch at the same time.

72 Warhol, *Philosophy of Andy Warhol*, 44.

73 Though they do rather resemble the beginning of Larry Clark's *Kids* (1995).

74 Kael explains that these words, which she saw on an Italian movie poster, "are perhaps the briefest statement imaginable of the basic appeal of movies. This appeal is what attracts us, and ultimately what makes us despair when we begin to understand how seldom movies are more than this." Kael, *Kiss Kiss, Bang Bang*.

75 The stage direction reads: "The Queen lays her head on the block, supporting herself with her hands. The Executioners on each side bend down and remove the hands. The axe is raised amid general weeping, and the curtain falls. THE END." Blake, *Mary Queen of Scots*. Thanks to Scott Combs for this reference.

76 Recall that *The Kiss* was shown in both the small-image, peephole Kinetoscope and by the projecting Vitascope. Only the latter projection aroused interest and scandal.

77 It is frequently claimed that Brown said, "Violence is as American as apple pie," although this is a misquote. On 27 July 1963, in the wake of urban rioting, President Lyndon B. Johnson appointed the Kerner Commission, charged with assessing the causes of the violence. That same day, Brown, the former head of the Student Nonviolent Coordinating Committee, held a news conference in Washington, DC, in which he urged local blacks to arm themselves, saying, "Violence is necessary. It is as American as cherry pie."

78 Bazin, "Marginal Notes," 173.

79 Ibid., 173.

80 Ibid., 174. We must note Bazin's automatic assumption that woman is the sexual object, and man both the caresser and the spectator—all conventions we see upheld in Edison's *The Kiss* and countless sex scenes to come.

81 Ibid., 174.

82 Ibid., 175.

Chapter 2: Going All the Way

1 For example, Jeanne Moreau's exquisite facial performance of orgasm in Louis Malle's *Les Amants* (1958) as her lover's head descends below the frame for an unseen genital kiss.

2 Freud's useful term *screen memory* describes a particularly vivid childhood memory whose analysis covers a compromise formation made up of the mix of indelible real experiences and childhood fantasies. Struck by the way screen memories both evoke and screen out possibly repressed memories, Freud argues that such memories constitute important records not so much of the real past but of retroactively projected fantasies whose shape and form offer significant keys to the past. I invoke Freud's term here mostly for the value of considering how the memory of one image can block out a more powerful one. Freud, "Seven Memories," *Standard Edition of the Complete Psychological Works*, 307.

3 In his study of the "Wolf Man," for example, Freud first suggests that the child understands the act of coitus as the father's aggression on the mother; then he suggests that the scene may be cause for the child's excitation and, since the child is always male to Freud, incite fears of castration. Finally, presuming the (male) child's sexual ignorance, he suggests that the child presumes the coitus to be anal. See Freud, "From the History of an Infantile Neurosis." See also Laplanche and Pontalis, *Language of Psychoanalysis*, 335.

4 Laplanche and Pontalis, "Fantasy and the Origins of Sexuality," 16.

5 Laplanche, *Life and Death in Psychoanalysis*, 42.

6 Wilhelm Reich's book *The Sexual Struggle of Youth* introduced the term during an era of social reform in Germany in the twenties. The English title, when published in 1945 in the United States, was *The Sexual Revolution: Toward a Self-Governing Character Structure*. See Allyn, *Make Love Not War*, 4–5.

7 I borrow this term from the subtitle of Niklas Luhmann's *Love as Passion: The Codification of Intimacy*. Luhmann's book examines how the semantics of literary expressions of love evolved from the courtly love of the Middle Ages through the Romantic era to contemporary notions of intimacy that require neither an idealization of the object nor ascetic postponements of the sex act. In this evolution, the old semantic content of "romantic" and Romanticism have been clandestinely replaced by ideas of sexual performance or the notion of simply "being there for one another" (159). The intimacy whose codification Luhmann traces thus evolves from a highly idealized *amour passion* to a contemporary situation in which sexual relations have become the key to intimacy itself. Through a slow process of the "revaluation of sexuality" Luhmann shows how European culture moved from sublimation of sexual emotions that did not necessarily revolve around intimate knowledge of the love object to increasing valuations of intimacy as good in themselves. Intimacy is thus fundamentally a process of "interpersonal interpenetration" that includes the sexual (158). The Victorian age, having lost the battle to negate sexuality, is replaced by a "barely conscious, but all the more manifest semantics of sport": sex becomes a matter of performing and of improving performance. The capacity for improvement in turn requires effort and attentiveness and, as several of the films discussed in this chapter will demonstrate, "training." Luhmann adds, "As in sport, resorting to a form of physical behavior that is socially defined as meaningful makes it possible to evade the uncertainties of meaning in all other domains of life" (161). He argues that passion thus comes to an end and idealization of the love object no longer battles with the paradoxical existence of animal sexuality. Intimacy becomes less a fusion into a unity than a finding of meaning in

the world and the inner experience of another. In the transition from the Hollywood Production Code to the movies of the post-Code era we can locate much of the "revaluation of sexuality" of which Luhmann speaks: the triumph of animal sexuality without necessary idealizations, literal and figural interpenetrations, anxieties and triumphs of performance, and, in the very narrative of the era's most well-known porn film (discussed in the next chapter), the very embodiment of the concept of training.

8 See Leff and Simmons, *Dame in the Kimono*; and Lewis, *Hollywood v. Hard Core*.

9 Schaefer, *Bold! Daring! Shocking! True!*, 4.

10 I will be arguing in what follows that it is rarely possible to separate neatly titillation or arousal from other ways of being moved at the movies even though the courts, and most film historians, would act as if this were the case. See, for example, Wyatt, "Stigma of X," 238.

11 This phrase originated in the 1968 song, "Everyday People," popularized by Sly and the Family Stone. It was then picked up as a line indicating sexual permissiveness in *Deep Throat* (1972). In 1978 it was redeployed as the title of a sitcom.

12 Vivian Sobchack's two books on embodiment and cinema have been extremely helpful in my attempt to fathom the carnal knowledges offered up by films. See her *Address of the Eye* and *Carnal Thoughts*.

13 I discuss this question in relation to the "intimate sounds" of postdubbed sex in *Hard Core*, 122–26. See also Chion, *Audio-Vision*.

14 Taylor and Segal disappear for a while and are seen in silhouette at a bedroom window. Their spouses suspect that "humping" is what they are doing, but later it is not clear if the act really took place.

15 Qtd. in Leff and Simmons, *Dame in the Kimono*, 264.

16 Dick uncovers some of the notoriously secretive deliberations of the ratings board.

17 By 1967 60 percent of the films with Production Code seals of approval would bear the "mature audiences" caveat. Leff and Simmons, *Dame in the Kimono*, 270.

18 To this day Nichols remains the master of a certain kind of provocative talk about but avoidance of showing sex, as evidenced in his recent film, *Closer* (2005).

19 This case opened the way for most R-rated films to go unchallenged by the courts in the future. See Lewis, *Hollywood v. Hard Core*, 264–65.

20 Feiffer, *San Francisco Chronicle*.

21 See Leff and Simmons, *Dame in the Kimono*, 270; and Lewis, *Hollywood v. Hard Core*, 218.

22 Part of the joke on Mrs. Robinson seems to be the fact, embodied in Dustin Hoffman's very being, that Benjamin is not, by any movie-star criteria of the time, automatically desirable. The other, crueler, joke is that although Bancroft played and has gone down in history as the lasciviously villainous "older woman," she was, in fact, only one year older than Hoffman at the time.

23 Nichols has been quoted as saying that Hoffman's distinctive and quite literal whimper was modeled on his own helpless whimpering in long meetings with Jack Warner, arguing over the language in his previous film, *Who's Afraid of Virginia Woolf.* When Warner began to tell jokes, Nichols reported, he involuntarily whimpered. See Leff and Simmons, *Dame in the Kimono,* 249.

24 The rest of the sequence shows Benjamin in the hotel bed alone. He gets up and closes the door to the hotel bathroom—where, in what should be the bathroom, his parents sit at the dinner table, confounding the two spaces. "The Sounds of Silence" ends, and another song, "April Come She Will," begins. Now it is Mrs. Robinson who moves, passing quickly before Benjamin, dressing and leaving while Benjamin smokes in full postcoital mode.

25 Metz, *Film Language,* 179. Stam, *Film Theory,* 116.

26 An example would be the "Can't Buy Me Love" montage of the 1964 Beatles film *A Hard Day's Night* (dir. Richard Lester). See Jeff Smith, *Sounds of Commerce.* See also Lack, *Twenty Four Frames Under.*

27 Jeff Smith's example is the playful montage to "Raindrops Keep Fallin' on My Head" in *Butch Cassidy and the Sundance Kid* (dir. George Roy Hill, 1969). See his *Sounds of Commerce.*

28 Chion, *Audio-Vision,* 59.

29 Ibid., 61.

30 Another anomaly of X was that while all the other ratings—G, PG, R—were assigned by the MPAA and were, indeed, copyrighted by them, X was not copyrighted and could therefore be self-assigned. Lewis, *Hollywood v. Hard Core,* 193.

31 See Wyatt, "Stigma of X," 243; see also Lewis, *Hollywood v. Hard Core.*

32 Interestingly, this out-of-focus "melting" enacts my false condensed memory of *The Virgin Spring* and *Two Women.*

33 Diegetic music is that whose source is not within the fictional space of the film. Michel Chion uses the terms *onscreen* and *offscreen* to signal this difference, and the term *acousmatic* to describe sound not visualized or given a cause in the image. Chion, *Audio-Vision,* 72.

34 Vitto Russo reads the film as an exercise in gay-hating in his *Celluloid Closet,* 80–86. Interpreted today, however, in the light of much more overtly queer portrayals of such attachments by directors like Pedro Almodóvar, I am inclined to see the unspoken relationship between Joe and Ratso as a melancholic melodrama of the loss of unattainable homosexual erotic attachments. Given the fact that Joe is now hustling to help his friend Ratso get to a better climate in Florida, which will happen melodramatically too late, the undertone of plaintiveness heard in this sex scene almost seems a gentle parody of Joe's performance of heterosexual virility and a hint of the unspoken love between Joe and Ratso. See Linda Williams, "Melancholy Melodrama."

35 Popular examples extend from *Top Gun* (dir. Tony Scott, 1986) to *Cold Mountain* (dir. Anthony Minghella, 2003). Both exemplify the big-budget, tasteful version, constructed as a kind of sampling of vignettes of the sex act. In *Top Gun* Tom Cruise's hotshot flyer couples with his female flight instructor (Kelly McGillis). In a very few brief shots we first see the couple clothed and kissing, then tastefully displayed naked in bed with Cruise on top in the kind of hazy interior soon to become common in sex scenes under the influence of an MTV style that would make everything an interlude.

36 See Linda Williams, *Hard Core*.

37 See the chapter on stag films in ibid., 58–92.

38 Eric Schaefer's definitive book on exploitation cites the impresario David F. Friedman: "All those subjects were fair game for this exploiter—as long as it was in bad taste!" Qtd. in Schaefer, *Bold! Daring! Shocking! True!*, 3. Schaefer briefly discusses sexploitation on 337–39, and his forthcoming book also treats this topic.

39 The European films that focused exclusively on sexual situations, such as Roger Vadim's *And God Created Woman* (1957) with Brigitte Bardot, moved easily, Schaefer notes, from art house to grind house with no necessary changes. Schaefer, *Bold! Daring! Shocking! True*, 336–37. See also Jack Stevenson's forthcoming *Totally Uncensored*.

40 Schaefer, "Does She or Doesn't She?" 5.

41 In the sex scene with the fish, she performs a perversely displaced erotic dance in which she rubs this phallic object all over her clothed body to the accompaniment of loud jazz.

42 In contrast to the women in *Sin in the Suburbs*, Vixen comes to no bad end and is even cured of her racism, though she never overcomes her aversion to having sex with the black war protestor.

43 Courtney, *Hollywood Fantasies of Miscegenation*, 141.

44 As we saw in the previous chapter, before the institution of the Code, white male–black female relations such as the kiss in *What Happened in the Tunnel* could be considered comic if achieved inadvertently. Comedy constituted the only mode for white male–black female sex. There was nothing funny, however, about a black man threatening to kiss, marry, or have sex with a white woman. In the landmark *The Birth of a Nation* (1915) D. W. Griffith flirted with the constant threat of would-be black rapists. See Linda Williams, *Playing the Race Card*, 122–29.

45 See Susan Courtney's discussion of white–Native American, white-Asian, and white-Latin "epidermic drama" in relation to the Code in *Hollywood's Fantasies of Miscegenation*, 103–41. Courtney's brilliant examination of Production Code files emphatically shows that the "social relations" and "erotic looks" most policed were those in which black men (or inconsistently, "native," Asian, or other nonwhite men) "related to" or "looked at" white women (117).

46 Browne, "Race," 8.

47 *Variety* estimated that while blacks constituted 10 to 15 percent of the population, they made up more than 30 percent of the audience in first-run, major city theaters. Hollywood had long been aware of the economic clout of the back audience concentrated in the inner city, but only in the late sixties when the studios faltered and the Code disintegrated did that audience begin to show its power and attract specific genres of film. See Guerrero, *Framing Blackness*, 83.

48 Qtd. in ibid., 74. See also Cripps, "*Sweet Sweetback's Baadasssss.*"

49 Or, as Ed Guerrero notes, even in 1964 when Poitier played a Moorish prince surrounded by "an extensive harem of beautiful women of all races," he remained celibate. He never got to do what James Bond would have done in such a situation. Guerrero, *Framing Blackness*, 72.

50 See Williams, *Playing the Race Card*.

51 *One Hundred Rifles* (dir. Tom Gries, 1969), starring Jim Brown and Raquel Welch, appears to be the first film to have screened a miscegenous kiss, though the fact that Welch played an indigenous Mexican and was herself part Latino muddied the waters a bit.

52 Best-known titles include *Shaft* (1971), *Black Jesus* (1971), *Superfly* (1972), and *Black Caesar* (1973).

53 Thomas Cripps writes, for example, that in the sixties blacks had "proportionally more income to spend on the immediate gratifications of entertainments such as movies." Cripps, "*Sweet Sweetback's Baadasssss*," 242. See also Guerrero, *Framing Blackness*, 82–85.

54 Blaxploitation action heroes, male and female, have sexual desirability and prowess built into their very names, but the male names tend to refer more directly to phallic body parts: Sweetback's back (and frequently visible backside), Shaft's shaft, Superfly's fly. Pam Grier's "foxiness" in the *Foxy Brown* films, for example, is both sexy and smart. But while the male blaxploitation heroes make a point of having sex with both the sisters of the black community and appreciative white women, the female heroes are never portrayed having interracial sex except under duress.

55 It was made for $500,000 (from his own savings and contributed to by Bill Cosby). See Guerrero, *Framing Blackness*, 86.

56 Chaffin-Quiray, "Identity Crisis," 3. Van Peebles also sent a letter to Jack Valenti of the MPAA at the time of the film's release saying that he refused to submit the film for a rating. Nor would he self-apply an X to the film: "I charge that your film rating body has no right to tell the Black community what it may or may not see. . . . White standards shall no longer be imposed on the Black community." Van Peebles, *Sweet Sweetback's Baadasssss Song*, 209.

57 Lewis, *Hollywood v. Hard Core*, 305.

58 Louis Althusser argues that individuals are "interpellated"—hailed by and answer to—particular ideologies through a process that brings them into being by figuratively or literally calling out their name. In Althusser's example, it is a policeman who hails a citizen by calling out "hey you there!" When the citizen turns, he or she is interpellated. Althusser, "Ideology and Ideological State Apparatuses," 170–86.

59 Cecil Brown, who is making a documentary film about Van Peebles and asked him this question, confirms that this meaning preexisted the film.

60 Van Peebles's screenplay suggests a contrast between the boy's initial immobility and the movement that follows after the whore calls for it—"and then the boy's back begins to move. . . . At first she whispers instructions but the boy is a natural." Van Peebles, *Sweet Sweetback's Baadasssss Song*, 136. The actual film, however, shows none of the boy's own movement.

61 See my discussion of the film *Mandingo* in "Skin Flicks on the Racial Border," in Linda Williams, *Porn Studies*, 271–308.

62 See, for example, Richard Fleischer's *Mandingo* (1975).

63 He will do so again, for example, after escaping from the cops, in a brief sexual scene with another black woman—presumably a whore for whom he once pimped. She demands sex as payment for removing his handcuffs. Sweetback dutifully lies down between her legs, but the sex is not depicted.

64 Huey Newton, for example, objects to the minstrelsy of the hat and bow tie but does not mention the penis. Indeed, he goes to great lengths to desexualize and allegorize most of the sex scenes. Newton, "He Won't Bleed Me," c. See further discussion below.

65 Thomas Cripps notes that the emerging Blaxploitation genre often required critics to review the audience right along with the movie, and that the movie, in turn, was reviewed alongside the backstory of the legend of its maker, which Van Peebles carefully cultivated. Cripps writes that for the trades such as *Variety* the practice of reading the audience became de rigueur since the films followed so few of the conventions of dramaturgy: "Close observation of the audience's response [was] an index of the prospects of each new movie. In effect, the reader-response criticism that a new generation of critics had begun to introduce into academic circles became an essential tool of tradepaper critics." One critic noted two camps: white "stony silence" and black "delighted exclamations." Cripps, "*Sweet Sweetback's Baadasssss*," 256.

66 Many white reviewers simply panned the film. Judith Crist, for example, wrote that the film was "a ham-handed sexed-up, chase story for the unthinking, regardless of color or creed," adding that it was amateurishly made (*New York*, 3 May 1971). More typical, however, was the ambivalence of Penelope Gilliatt, who began her review, "Alas!—I mean, hurrah!—there exists a furiously tasteless picture called *Sweet Sweetback's Baadasssss Song*. It was made by a black man for blacks and it is turning into a phenomenon of the industry" (*New Yorker*, 18 June 1971).

67 He adds, "Every time after that when Sweetback engages in sex with a sister, it is always an act of survival, and a step towards his liberation." Newton, "He Won't Bleed Me," c.

68 Bennett, "Emancipation Orgasm," 116.

69 Ibid.

70 He writes: "Who is Sweetback? Is he a white stereotype, the Black Everyman

Stud of the white man's dreams? Or is he a black fantasy figure, the internalized other of the white man's projection?" Ibid.

71 Ibid.

72 Rosello, *Declining the Stereotype*, 38–40.

73 Cripps, "*Sweet Sweetback's Baadasssss*," 252.

74 For a longer discussion of this issue from the point of view of white supremacist, mainstream American culture, see my *Playing the Race Card*.

75 See my discussion of this film and the black buck of American racial melodrama in ibid., 96–134.

76 Van Peebles, *Sweet Sweetback's Baadasssss Song*, 29.

77 Ibid., 60, 62.

78 Ibid.

79 See my essay, "Skin Flicks on the Racial Border: Pornography, Exploitation, and Interracial Lust," in Linda Williams, *Porn Studies*, 271–308.

80 See also Gordon Parks's *Shaft* (1971), in which Richard Roundtree has prolonged romantic sex with a black woman, and abrupt sex with a white woman.

81 McMillan, "Thoughts on *She's Gotta Have It*," 19.

82 Gates, "Jungle Fever," 163.

83 The extent to which they did this has been beautifully argued by Ara Osterweil in chapter 2 of a Ph.D. dissertation entitled "Flesh Cinema." I am indebted to Osterweil for many of the following insights about the fleshy attractions of American avant-garde cinema. I refer anyone interested in a full analysis of the carnal interest of avant-garde cinema of the sixties to Osterweil's second chapter, "Experimental Intercourse: Documenting the Sex Act."

84 See ibid., 5–7; MacDonald, "Confessions of a Feminist Porn Watcher," 5.

85 The film shows a black-and-white close-up of the changing face of a handsome young man during what may, or may not, be the eponymous action. See Roy Grundeman's fascinating book-long discussion of its many possible interpretations in *Andy Warhol's "Blow Job."* See also Osterweil, "Andy Warhol's *Blow Job*," in Linda Williams, *Porn Studies*, 431–60.

86 Waugh, "Cockteaser"; Osterweil, "Flesh Cinema."

87 I remember, as an undergraduate at the University of California at Berkeley, that the film, then still entitled *Fuck*, showed somewhere on or near campus. I remember because it was the occasion of one of the very first dirty puns I ever made. (When a friend asked me if I was going to see *Fuck*, I prided myself on what I thought to be a witty answer: "Conceivably," I said, but then found, unfortunately, that I had to work that night.)

88 Blue movies were not themselves tinted blue, but one theory as to the origin of the term is that the small-format projectors on which they were often shown had a bluish cast. However, since the early nineteenth century, the color blue connoted indecent or obscene.

89 Koestenbaum, *Andy Warhol*, 141.

90 Ibid.

91 Wayne Koestenbaum writes that the film "redeems heterosexuality, which had never been top on his list of cinematic treats. . . . Here for the first time in Warhol's work, heterosexuality is not a joke" (ibid., 154). Koestenbaum goes further, asserting that after the shooting, the bullet-wounded, black and blue body of Warhol finds itself definitively excluded from the "replete" spectacle of heterosexual coupling staged in this film. No political radical proponent of queerness, Warhol's own sexual radicalism, Koestenbaum argues, derives from his own sense of failed masculinity. He knew and acted better, but he viewed homosexuality as a problem—an interesting, productive, fascinating problem. In his universe "straight men were real men" (155). Koestenbaum concludes, "I believe that *Blue Movie*—his summa, his key to all mythologies—may have proved decisively to him that he was not a real man; peering more closely at the secrets of other people's bodies than ever before, he removed himself from his own irreversibly ruptured body. *Blue Movie*, which records two bodies intertwining, seals Andy's rupture from his body—his premature exile from organs, those irrelevant irritants." Ibid., 155–56.

92 Miller writes that consensual sex means the mutual transgression of disgust-defended boundaries: "We simply will do things or let things be done to ourselves in love and sex that violate all the norms the violation of which would trigger disgust if unprivileged, if coerced, or even if witnessed. And to do such and to have such done to us is much of what sexual intimacy is." William Ian Miller, *Anatomy of Disgust*, 132, 139.

93 James, *Allegories of Cinema*, 69.

94 Warhol, *Philosophy of Andy Warhol*, 26–27.

95 Viva, for example, would later write: "Because Andy was so shy and complexed about his looks, he had no private life. In filming, as in 'hanging out,' he merely wanted to find out how 'normal people' acted with each other. And I think my own idea about *Blue Movie* (or *Fuck* as it had originally been called) wasn't, as I believed at the time, to teach the world about 'real love' or 'real sex,' but to teach Andy." Wrenn, *Andy Warhol*, 64.

96 Ara Osterweil notes that the film is unusual in its portrayal of domesticity. Where other films had tended to remove their chosen activities from their usual contexts, here sex takes place in a home among bourgeois, heterosexual domestic rituals. Osterweil, "Flesh Cinema," 44–46.

97 This realism often includes aspects of the negotiation that takes place around the sex act as in that between Candi Barr and the man who picks her up in *Smart Alec*. See my discussion of the frequent absence of climactic endings in stag film in *Hard Core*, 72.

98 Koestenbaum quotes a diary entry from November 1978: "I said that I wasn't creative since I was shot, because after that I stopped seeing creepy people." Koestenbaum, *Andy Warhol*, 159.

99 It has since shown occasionally, but it was not included in the 1994 Warhol retrospective. Only those able to travel to the Warhol Museum in Pittsburgh can view it, and then only on videotape. The image included here is from the degraded bootleg dubbed into German.

Chapter 3: Going Further

1 Kael, "Tango," 130.

2 The *Rite of Spring* was originally performed as a modern ballet divided into two halves. The first part, "The Adoration of the Earth," is a pagan celebration of spring that reaches one climax when a Wise Elder plants a kiss on the newly flowering earth and the pagan tribes are seized with a mystic terror that culminates in the "Dance of the Earth." The second part is entitled "The Sacrifice" and culminates with the sacrifice of a young maiden to the god of spring.

3 "The ballet's scenic evocation of pagan Russian rituals elicited from Stravinsky a score of unprecedented primitive force, in which music seemed to be distilled to its rhythmic essence, hammered out by the orchestra with unrestrained percussive intensity. Shaken by the radical nature of both score and ballet, the opening-night audience was in an uproar from the beginning, with those both for and against shouting at one another in heated debate. . . . the sensational aspect of the event placed Stravinsky at the forefront of the musical revolutions of the time." Robert Morgan, qtd. in Taruskin, "Myth of the Twentieth Century," 13.

4 Some of Nijinsky's movements in the ballet, choreographed by his lover Diaghilev, have been described as masturbatory.

5 Kael, Tango," 130; emphasis added.

6 Recall here the two rape scenes that had so affected me in *The Virgin Spring* (1959) and *Two Women* (1960).

7 When the film was shown in Cleveland in defiance of a local police order, the manager-projectionist Nico Jacobellis was arrested on charges of exhibiting obscenity. Jacobellis famously fought back, and his contestation of this local obscenity ruling would become the basis of an important later Supreme Court ruling that not only overturned his conviction but proved instrumental in establishing the concept that films no longer needed to be acceptable to all age groups, thus dealing an important blow to the Production Code's dedication to this idea. Lewis, *Hollywood v. Hard Core*, 133.

8 The full quote reads: "Brando cashes the check Stanley Kowalski wrote for us twenty-five years 'ago—he fucks the heroine standing up. It solves the old snicker of how do you do it in a telephone booth?—he rips her panties open." Mailer, "Transit to Narcissus," 203.

9 Bertolucci, *Last Tango in Paris*, 37.

10 Bataille, *Erotism*, 103–4.

11 "I moved the story to Paris, and gave it the title *La Petite morte* (sic), which is the eighteenth-century Libertine expression for orgasm. I was reading a lot of

Georges Bataille, including *Le Bleu du ciel*, which really impressed me." Qtd in David Thompson, *Last Tango in Paris*, 11.

12 Ibid., 103.

13 Ibid., 42.

14 Though as I showed in the last chapter, what we think of today as an ordinary X—the one that would attach automatically to hard-core pornography—was only at this moment becoming common.

15 Kael, "Tango," 130; emphasis added.

16 Ibid.; emphasis added.

17 The review was published a few months before Kael's. *Screw* magazine, considered by some to have been the apotheosis of bad taste, was begun by Goldstein in 1968. It combined dirty photos with political commentary and sexually tinged satire. Described by Goldstein as a "MAD comics for sex," it ceased publication in 2003.

18 This was Goldstein's term for his own personalized rating system gauged, presumably, by his own degree of erection.

19 Qtd. in Richard Smith, *Getting into Deep Throat*, 31–32.

20 Al Goldstein, qtd. in Richard Smith, *Getting into Deep Throat*, 32.

21 Kael, "Tango," 130.

22 The Hollywood films with markedly adult content released that year include *The Godfather* (dir. Francis Ford Coppola), *Deliverance* (dir. John Boorman), and *Cabaret* (dir. Bob Fosse). This was also an important year for Blaxploitation following the X-rated success of the 1971 *Sweet Sweetback's Baadasssss Song* with *Superfly* (dir. Gordon Parks Jr.).

23 Kael, "Tango," 130.

24 Ibid., 134.

25 Schauer, *Law of Obscenity*, 96.

26 Qtd. in ibid., 97.

27 Ibid., 101–2.

28 The so-called Peter Meter was not an actual device; rather it was a metaphor, employed by reviewers of hard-core films to indicate the degree of arousal elicited by a given film. The Peter Meter assumes the turn-on to be an exclusively male province. The following chapter will address the question of the female turn-on.

29 Kael, "Tango," 134.

30 For example, in a 1985 case that attempted to clarify the definition of *prurient* as that which "incites lasciviousness or lust," the Supreme Court decided that "lust" referred to "normal" while "lascivious" referred to "abnormal" sexual responses and redrew the line between acceptable and censorable as that between normal lust and abnormal lasciviousness. See Downs, *New Politics of Pornography*, 29; and Linda Williams, "Second Thoughts on Hard Core," 47.

31 Schauer, *Free Speech: A Philosophical Enquiry*, 181.

32 Taussig, *Mimesis and Alterity*, 21.

33 Of course I had seen naked men and women in real life, and I had seen a few "dirty pictures" in magazines. But except for a few isolated penises drawn on the walls of public toilets, I had not really *seen* sex from the point of view of a spectator.

34 We may have gone so far as to say whether we found it arousing, but polling some of these friends recently, I discovered that at least one of the men was quite worried that he was aroused, fearing a feminist wrath that may not have really been much in evidence until later. Phillip Roth's 1997 novel, *American Pastoral*, depicts a dinner conversation among upper-middle-class couples in New Jersey. "At dinner the conversation was about Watergate and about *Deep Throat*. Except for the Swede's parents and the Orcutts, everybody at the table had been to see the X-rated movie." When one of the parents asks why they let it into their lives, another answers: "It leaks in . . . whether we like it or not. Whatever is out there leaks in. . . . It's not the same out there anymore, in case you haven't heard." Roth, *American Pastoral*, 345–46.

35 William Miller, *Anatomy of Disgust*, 105.

36 *Report of the Commission on Obscenity and Pornography*, 11.

37 Schaefer also notes that the new, franker 16mm movies "marked the convergence of the revolution in film aesthetics and the sexual revolution." Schaefer, "Gauging a Revolution," 386.

38 Ibid., 387.

39 Interestingly, what *Mona* did *not* pioneer was the convention of the money shot to signal climax.

40 Schaefer, "Gauging a Revolution," 393.

41 Ralph Blumenthal, "Porno Chic," *New York Times Magazine*, 21 January 1973, 28–34.

42 It is striking, for example, how much the early articles on the so-called porno chic phenomenon, both that written initially for the *New York Times Magazine* by Ralph Blumenthal in January of 1973 and one written by Bruce Williamson later that summer for *Playboy* with the same title, stress the names of the many celebrities—from Johnny Carson's lowbrow sidekick Ed McMahon who stood out front of the theater with a case of beer, to more sophisticated fans like Mike Nichols and Truman Capote and movie stars like Jack Nicholson and Sandy Dennis—all of whom viewed the film with interest.

43 This information derives from an as yet unpublished paper by film historian Jon Lewis titled "Real Sex." I thank him for making it available to me.

44 *Blue Movie* is about a bored and blasé Hollywood director who joins forces with a successful producer and an adventurous female star to produce the most expensive porn movie of all time. In 1974, two years after *Last Tango*, Warner Bros. actually optioned Southern's book and signed Mike Nichols to direct. Of course the film was never made, and even if it had been it is not clear it would have been made in a hard-core version. Hollywood's last taboo, as John Waters has noted, remains today as it was then visible penetration. See Lewis, "Real Sex": "There is only one taboo left . . . penetration. Let the golden age of censor-free independent film begin."

45 He writes, "The film has been in reach of the greatness Kael has been talking about, but the achievement has only been partial. . . . We are being given a fuck film without the fuck. It is like a Western without the horses." Mailer, "Transit to Narcissus," 213.

46 *Report of the Commission on Obscenity and Pornography*; the first reference to a "New Genre" is on 11.

47 Bruce Williamson, for example, wrote in *Playboy* in the summer of 1973 that many earnest and ambitious pornographers were aiming at "deeper characterization, stronger stories with a social or psychological slant, and the superior production values that are a concomitant of higher budgets." Williamson, "Porno Chic," 16. And William Rotsler similarly wrote, "Erotic films are here to stay. Eventually they will simply merge into the mainstream of motion pictures and disappear as a latent sub-division. Nothing can stop this." Rotsler, *Contemporary Erotic Cinema*, 11.

48 There are, of course, exceptions to every rule, and a few auteurs have emerged in the contemporary adult video world feted at Adult Video Awards ceremonies. Chief among these in the heterosexual narrative category is, whose videos are aesthetically ambitious and well directed, often with complex narratives and spectacular MTV-style musical numbers. However, the highly edited sexual performances lack warmth, and the acting never comes close to that in mainstream or independent films. In the more gonzo style of nonnarrative heterosexual pornography, John Stagliano's fetish-oriented pseudodocumentaries have captured a more seemingly authentic off-the-street look that often manages to depict sexual heat and connection. And in the realm of gay video, Christian Bjorn has engineered some of the most mind-boggling and slick orgies imaginable. See Cante and Restivo, "'World' of All-Male Pornography," 110–26. Nowhere, however, is the dream of a dramatic cinema that is not pornography but that does include actual sex realized.

49 This was an era when feature-length, narrative, sound and color film pornography with scripts like regular movies, with award-winning direction and performances discussed by critics and discerning viewers, seemed possible. This golden age included all the films of Radley Metzger, some of the later films of Gerard Damiano, Henry Pachard, Joe Sarno, Chuck Vincent, and Anthony Spinelli, as well as performers like Georgina Spelven, Annette Haven, Veronica Hart, Jamie Gillis, and John Leslie. Although many of these original films are now available on video or DVD, almost none are available on film, nor have they been preserved and restored the way other American films of the era have been. For discussions of pornography's auteurs, see O'Toole, *Pornocopia*, 75–96. See also Linda Williams, *Hard Core*, 134–52.

50 Damiano quoted in Bruce Williamson, "Porno Chic," *Playboy*. Reprinted in *Flesh and Blood*, 14.

51 This codification would function at least for the seventies; see Ziplow, *Film Maker's Guide to Pornography*. This how-to-do-it manual would insist on ten money shots and a wide variety of sexual numbers: masturbation, straight sex, a lesbian scene, oral sex, a ménage à trois, and anal sex.

52 Hollywood calls the shot for which it pays the most money, and which delivers the greatest degree of spectacle, the "money shot": the chariot race in *Ben Hur*, the burning of Atlanta in *Gone with the Wind*. The porn industry follows suit in its fashion, adding money shot to the repertoire of slang terms that constitute its biggest spectacle. I prefer this term because of its resonance with money and the fetishistic overvaluation of one partial element of the whole sex act. See Linda Williams, *Hard Core*, 103–19.

53 This was much less the case in gay pornography, which was equally committed to fellatio as a privileged sexual act but committed as well, at least in its earlier incarnations, to the alternation of fellatio (e.g., *Boys in the Sand*).

54 Qtd. in Richard Smith, *Getting into Deep Throat*, 14.

55 See, for example, my discussions of the films of Radley Metzger (aka Henri Paris) in *Hard Core*, 134–51.

56 See Linda Williams, *Hard Core*; O'Toole, *Pornocopia*; and McClintock, "Gonad the Barbarian." See also the 2005 documentary film *Inside Deep Throat* (dir. Randy Barbados and Fenton Bailey).

57 She has freckles, irregular teeth, high cheekbones, and smallish breasts. She does not, in other words, have what would solidify in the eighties as a porn-star body: big breasts, small waist, big hips.

58 See Flint, *Babylon Blue*, 31.

59 It is worth recalling that the feminist arguments about the objectification of women came in the latter part of the decade.

60 When asked in the documentary *Inside Deep Throat* whether he thought it was a very good film, Damiano sighed, "No."

61 Bersani, *Freudian Body*, 38.

62 Niklas Luhmann has noted the prevalence of the semantics of sport in late twentieth-century treatises on sexual pleasure, from Masters and Johnson to any number of sexual advice manuals. "It is a matter of performing and improving performance, not because one has to, but because one wants to do so voluntarily. The capacity improvement in turn requires effort and attentiveness and—as in the case of all physical achievement—training." Luhmann, *Love as Passion*, 160–61.

63 See my extended discussion of the comparative invisibility of female pleasure vis-à-vis male pleasure in *Hard Core*, 93–119.

64 Judith Crist, for example, called it "awful," "idiot" moviemaking; Vincent Canby called it "junk" and cleverly listed the pitfalls of every critical approach from the "haughty (it's boring)" to the "golly-gee-whiz (They've gone as far as they can go!)"; and Andrew Sarris found it "joyless." The problem for many, as Richard Smith notes, "was to express distaste for the film without giving ammunition to the forces of censorship." Indeed, "much of the verbiage that resulted displayed the tortured introspection of a law-and-order liberal who has just been mugged." All citations in Richard Smith, *Getting Into Deep Throat*, 12–13.

65 Qtd. in ibid., 13–14.

66 Of course this *is* what the husband wants his wife to do, and he ends up marrying another woman who does. Updike, *Couples*, 248.

67 See, for example, the talking heads interviewed in *Inside Deep Throat*—the men tend to suggest they knew about it but also knew it was dirty; the women tend to suggest they had never heard of it before they saw the film. Of course these talking heads do not offer a representative cross section of Americans; most are sexually aware types: Hugh Heffner, John Waters, Norman Mailer are representative of the men, and Erica Jong, Helen Gurley Brown, and Camille Paglia are representative of the women. Nevertheless all suggest that the film offered a new legitimation of an act once vaguely classified as abnormal.

68 Kinsey, Pomeroy, and Martin, *Sexual Behavior in the Human Male*, 578.

69 See the excellent discussion of orality in the Clinton scandal in Berlant and Duggan, *Our Monica, Ourselves*, 254–56.

70 Roth, *Dying Animal*, 9. Roth's sixty-year-old narrator, a lover of many younger women, speculates that the rise of fellatio is linked to the resurrection of the condom in the early seventies. After the end of the sixties, when the pill had been the predominant form of birth control, condoms became once again popular, as they now are even more so in an era of AIDS. Writes Roth: "What man can say he enjoys sex with a condom the way he does without? . . . That's why the organs of digestion have, in our time, come to vie for supremacy as a sexual orifice. The crying need for the mucous membrane." Roth, *Dying Animal*, 68.

71 Foucault, *History of Sexuality*, 1:12.

72 Qtd. in Daphne Merkin's obituary for Lovelace, *New York Times Magazine*, 29 December 2002, 30.

73 "'Missionary' position? . . . That is a very interesting term you use." Toward the end of the trial he gratuitously instructs an expert witness that "normal intercourse" means "the missionary position." Substantial excerpts from the questioning of each of five expert witnesses are offered in Richard Smith, *Getting into Deep Throat*, 120, 213.

74 Ibid., 210.

75 Ibid., 212.

76 Ibid., 284.

77 Ultimately, most of the judgments made against the film, including the conviction by a Memphis court of the actor Harry Reems, were overturned and the film went on to earn a reported $600 million nationwide, none of which went to the director or performers.

78 Anne McClintock begins her tale by comparing the paucity of slang terms for the clitoris compared to those for the penis and then recounts the story of one Renaldus Columbus who claimed to have "discovered" the female penis some sixty years after Columbus "discovered" America. McClintock, "Gonad the Barbarian," 115–16.

79 Freud, *Three Essays on the Theory of Sexuality*, 50.

80 Irigaray, *This Sex Which Is Not One*, 23–33.

81 See the discussion of orality between Jane Gallop and Lauren Berlant in *Our Monica, Ourselves*, 254–60, in which both discussants stress the importance of the pleasure of sucking and of being sucked.

82 The psychoanalytic theorist Maria St. John has argued that Freud has a tendency to view the breast of infantile sucking as "being *for* the baby rather than *of* the woman." St. John notes further that psychoanalysis in general has not concentrated sufficiently on the breast as an organ—certainly nothing like the way it has concentrated on the penis as the ultimate subject of sexual pleasure. Had it done so, it might have been equipped to theorize sexual pleasures themselves as a mutual give-and-take. St. John, *Mammy Fantasy*, 70–91.

83 He writes, "I once put forward the view that there was no need to be too much horrified at finding in a woman the idea of sucking at a male organ. This repellent impulse, I argued, had a most innocent origin, since it was derived from sucking at the mother's breast." Freud, "Analysis of a Phobia," 7. In another essay he writes: "So we see that this excessively repulsive and perverted phantasy of sucking at a penis has the most innocent origin." Freud, "Fragment," 52.

84 St. John, *Mammy Fantasy*, 9.

85 *Deep Throat*'s absurd conceit of the clitoris located in the throat is thus one way the film attempts to restore the idea of pleasure to the fellator as well as to the fellatee.

86 Most sources claim that *Deep Throat* cost $25,000 to make (a big budget and something of a gamble for a pornographic film just transitioning from the stag era) and eventually grossed, if one believes FBI figures, as much as $600 million. What is sure is that in its initial thirty-nine-week run in New York at only one theater, it grossed $1,300,000. See the documentary *Inside Deep Throat*; and Flint, *Babylon Blue*, 33.

87 David Thompson, *Last Tango in Paris*, 20.

88 Marcus, *Other Victorians*, 269.

89 D'Emilio and Freedman, *Intimate Matters*, 323.

90 Foucault, *History of Sexuality*, 1:100–101.

91 It opened at the Fifty-fifth Street Playhouse in New York on 29 December 1971 and ran for nineteen weeks. It later ran for nine weeks at the Paris Theater in Los Angeles. It was the first gay film to point the way "to a mostly untapped profitable market: gay men starved for positive, out-of-the-closet movie representations of their selves and their (explicit) sexuality." Burger, *One-Handed Histories*, 16. According to Kenneth Turan and Stephen Zito, it "almost single-handedly legitimized the gay hard-core film." Turan and Zito, *Sinema*, 197.

92 According to Turan and Zito, the film cost $8,000 to make and grossed $400,000 (*Sinema*, 212). According to John Burger's more recent study, it cost

$20,000 to both make and market and, after nineteen weeks at its initial New York venue, had grossed $140,000. This compares to *Deep Throat*'s initial cost of $25,000 and gross of what some claim to be as high as $600 million. Like *Deep Throat, Boys in the Sand* was advertised in mainstream newspapers, reviewed in *Variety*, and included in the magazine's top-fifty gross list.

93 Chauncey notes that in the first six months of 1921, sixty-seven men were arrested for homosexual solicitation in movie theaters in Manhattan, including forty-five men at a single theater on Sixth Avenue, near Twenty-second Street. Chauncey, *Gay New York*, 194–95.

94 Thomas Waugh, personal conversation, May 2005, Berkeley, Calif. For more histories of gay film viewing, see Samuel R. Delany's account of cruising Times Square film theaters, gay and straight, during the early seventies in *Times Square Red, Times Square Blue*. And for an excellent discussion of the homosocial experience of stag films, see Waugh, "Homosociality in the Classical American Stag Film."

95 Dyer, *Now You See It*, 172.

96 *Maximum visibility* is the term I have used to describe the imperative of all pornography to prove that real sex takes place. It includes the privileging of close-ups of body parts over other shots, the overlighting of otherwise easily obscured genitals and, of course, with the rise of feature-length porno in the early seventies, the money shot. See Linda Williams, *Hard Core*. Richard Dyer's more recent, and more vivid, term, *plumbing shots*, describes a similar phenomenon, but Dyer uses it particularly to describe the kind of "spatial lability" that might place the camera on the floor, the better to "look up the legs of one man fucking another," or "looking up into the dangling balls at the penis moving back and forth into the arsehole." Most vividly, John Waters has noted that such shots are what make porn look to him like "open-heart surgery." Both in Dyer, "Idol Thoughts," 104. *Boys in the Sand*, I am arguing, does not participate in this clinical aesthetic.

97 Foucault, *History of Sexuality*, 1:100–101.

98 Rich Cante and Angelo Restivo prefer the term *male-male* to *gay* pornography because the "gay" desire of such films is never assured in an era of "gay for pay." Cante and Restivo, "'World' of All-Male Pornography," 111.

99 McClintock notes that the convention originated in gay porn: "Emerging first in gay porn the shot became *de rigueur* in straight porn during the seventies." Though *Boys in the Sand*'s 1971 date, one year before *Deep Throat*, makes this assertion plausible, one would need to look closely at the first conventionalizations of the shot in all-male as well as heterosexual pornography of the early seventies to back up this assertion. McClintock, "Gonad the Barbarian," 123.

100 Cante and Restivo, "Cultural-Aesthetic Specificities," 142.

101 Poole, *Dirty Poole*, 157.

102 Ibid., 156.

103 Ibid.

104 Fanon, *Black Skin/White Masks*, 11.

105 Much the way the black man played by Johnny Keyes in *Behind the Green Door* (dir. Artie Mitchell and Jim Mitchell, 1972) is fetishized for his racial-sexual characteristics.

106 He writes, "The whole film features high-profile homosexuality with no guilt—and includes an interracial cast." Poole, *Dirty Poole*, 157.

107 Bataille, *Erotism*, 27.

108 In "Skin Flicks on the Racial Border: Pornography, Exploitation, and Interracial Lust," I argue that interracial sex acts inscribe the tension of the forbidden into their fantasies and depend on some kind of continued awareness of the taboo they transgress. Linda Williams, 274–75.

Chapter 4: Make Love, Not War

1 Indeed, I married him, at a time when marriage seemed a very bourgeois institution, to be able to visit him in prison. He was one of the lucky ones never prosecuted, partly because there were so many other draft resisters at the Oakland Induction Center. Other friends were not so lucky and, like the soldiers who went to war, came back very different people.

2 Allyn cites Larry Bercowitz, the star of another off-Broadway countercultural production, *Che*, which opened several months after *Hair*. Where the *Hair* cast had appeared naked without being arrested, that of *Che* was. From behind bars Bercowitz wrote: "Killing and violence are OBSCENE, not Art or Love, or simulated Love. . . . WAR IS OBSCENE!!! Frustration and repression leads to violence. Lack of love mental and physical leads to violence, then to war. . . . MAKE LOVE NOT WAR!!!" Allyn, *Make Love, Not War*, 127.

3 Marcuse, *Eros and Civilization*, 174, 184.

4 Ibid., 184.

5 Segal, *Straight Sex*, 31.

6 Gathorne-Hardy, *Sex, the Measure of All Things*, 121.

7 Kinsey pointed out "that the clitoris at this point is stimulated, thus providing the erotic stimulation necessary for the completion of the act on the part of the female." Qtd. in ibid., 126.

8 Kinsey discovered, as Gathorne-Hardy notes, that the "mere fact of *saying* sexual intercourse, coitus, masturbation, clitoris, orgasm, etc., in a society where even the word sex was barely mentionable, and in which 'venereal disease' had just been banned on radio, was enough to shock his audiences into electrified attention." Ibid., 126.

9 Ibid., 171.

10 Segal, *Straight Sex*, 90. See also Kinsey et al., *Sexual Behavior in the Human Female*.

11 Gathorne-Hardy, *Sex, the Measure of All Things*, 308; Kinsey et al., *Sexual Behavior in the Human Female*, 634.

12 Gathorne-Hardy, *Sex, the Measure of All Things*, 307.

13 Wardell Pomeroy, qtd. in ibid., 315.

14 According to Gathorne-Hardy, Kinsey had a sexual liaison with Spears and they remained friends for many years after. Ibid., 315.

15 Ibid., 333.

16 Judith Reisman, the leader of a group called Restoring Social Virtue and Purity to America, has particularly targeted Kinsey as the cause of a pro-sex agenda that has been, as one of her books puts it, *Crafting 'Gay' Children*. These claims give Kinsey an awful lot of credit—as if one man could cause a sexual revolution, let alone an epidemic of sexually transmitted diseases. Reisman's argument that Kinsey based a portion of his research on a sexually voracious pedophile blames the researcher for acts committed and entered in a diary long before Kinsey began his work.

17 Jones, *Alfred C. Kinsey*, 4, 75, 83.

18 Waugh, *Hard to Imagine*, 398.

19 Ibid., 400.

20 Albert Goldbarth's poem, "The Origin of Porno," says, "Studying the horse, we understand / how hard-core followed the invention of photography." I cite this poem at the beginning of my study of hard-core pornography to emphasize Foucault's understanding of the transfer points of knowledge, power, and pleasure in modern discourses of sexuality. It does not seem surprising to me that Kinsey's quest for the knowledge of sex should also, as Foucault puts it, have been a place for the osmosis of a pleasure feeding power and a power feeding pleasure. See Foucault, *History of Sexuality*, 1:44–45; Linda Williams, *Hard Core*, 35.

21 Kinsey et al., *Sexual Behavior in the Human Female*, 606.

22 Ibid., 580.

23 He writes, "There is no evidence that the vagina responds in orgasm as a separate organ and apart from the total body." Ibid., 582–83.

24 They write, "the female is capable of rapid return to orgasm immediately following an orgasmic experience" and "the female is capable of maintaining an orgasmic experience for a relatively long period of time." Masters and Johnson, *Human Sexual Response*, 131. Lynne Segal comments: "They in fact recorded so many physiological differences between men and women that their decision to emphasize similarities was clearly ideological." Segal, *Straight Sex*, 93.

25 Masters and Johnson, *Human Sexual Response*, 67.

26 Ibid., 132.

27 Sherfey, "Theory of Female Sexuality," 91.

28 Ibid., 93.

29 Koedt, "Myth of the Vaginal Orgasm," 199. See also Masters and Johnson, *Human Sexual Response*; Sherfey, "Theory of Female Sexuality;" Seaman, "Is Woman Insatiable?"

30 Koedt, "Myth of the Vaginal Orgasm," 101.

31 Seaman, "Is Woman Insatiable?" 133.

32 Qtd. in Williamson, "Porno Chic," 14.

33 Especially in his work with John Ford—in *Young Mr. Lincoln* (1939), in *The Grapes of Wrath* (1940), and in several westerns.

34 She is credited with publicly exposing Nixon's potential strategy of bombing the dikes, which would have endangered hundreds of thousands of civilians. Fonda toured the country and made numerous radio speeches to American pilots, informing them of the devastation they were wreaking on the country. She was called a liar and, after being photographed sitting on anti-aircraft turrets, was accused of treason. But her efforts did expose and avert the plan to bomb the dikes. Fonda, *My Life So Far*, 291–333.

35 Ibid., 128.

36 This film stars Fonda as a woman whose quasi-incestuous affair with her husband's son proves her undoing.

37 Compare, for example, Hollywood's 1960 "celebration" of Elizabeth Taylor's sexual charms in Daniel Mann's *Butterfield 8*, which could only end with the demise of Taylor's high-class call girl.

38 We will need to remember this curling of hair. In an era as obsessed with hair as the sixties, curled hair on women and long hair on men would prove a reliable indicator of predilection for pleasure.

39 Seaman, "Is Woman Insatiable?" 133.

40 Sherfey, "Theory of Female Sexuality," 91.

41 Marcus, *Other Victorians*, xiii–xiv.

42 According to Marcus, nineteenth-century pornography was marked by the wish-fulfilling expenditure of the scarce resource of male semen, "spent" as a utopian reversal of a social and economic economy of scarcity. Now the multiply orgasmic woman pleasured by an electrical device is no longer a wish-fulfilling reversal of economic reality, but the somewhat scarier embodiment of that reality itself: postindustrial consumption. I have argued elsewhere that Marcus invokes a curious double standard in his utopian model of nineteenth-century (male economic) pornotopia and his comparatively dystopian (female economic) pornography that implicitly represents pleasurable female self-sufficiency as a depressing reality. See Linda Williams, *Hard Core*, 108–10 and Marcus, *The Other Victorians*, xiii–xiv.

43 See Linda Ruth Williams's discussion of the film in *Erotic Thriller in Contemporary Cinema*, 118.

44 Both Kael and Haskell praise the psychological nuances of Fonda's performance. Kael, "Mythologizing"; Haskell, "Review of *Klute*."

45 For example, in hard-core pornography, European art film, and the American avant-garde—not to mention Nicholas Roeg's remarkably adult "pensive" coupling in *Don't Look Now* (1973).

46 Koedt, "Myth of the Vaginal Orgasm," 101.

47 And like Jeanne in *Last Tango* (and also like Barbarella), her sexual awakening is measured by hair that goes suddenly curly.

48 Contrast *The Graduate*: Benjamin slams the door, the screen grows dark, and the film then shows everything but what happens in the bed between the couple.

49 Fonda, *My Life So Far*, 371.

50 Ibid.

51 Ibid., 375.

52 Annie Potts, "The Day the Earth Stood Still," in *The Science Fiction of Sex*, 79–100.

53 Bersani, *Freudian Body*, 34.

54 Vincent Canby, "Coming Home," *New York Times*, 16 February 1978.

55 Kael, "Mythologizing," 120.

56 James, "Rock and Roll," 90.

57 Jeff Smith, *Sounds of Commerce*.

58 In fact, there is just the faintest possible sound of music, presented as if from an offscreen diegetic source, playing ever so softly under this scene. I have not been able to recognize it.

Chapter 5: Hard-Core Eroticism

1 I paraphrase Richard Corliss: "Sex is too important to be left to the sex-film industry. The erotic impulse and its consequences are crucial. Lovemaking is a powerful experience, the most convulsive emotional and physical drama in most people's lives. And it warrants as much artful attention from film auteurs as space operas or teen revenge fantasies." Corliss, "In Defense of Dirty Movies," 74.

2 Susan Sontag's groundbreaking essay, "The Pornographic Imagination," which discusses only pornographic literature, not film, is helpful on this point. Sontag argues that literary pornography's aim of inducing sexual excitement is not at odds with supposedly more "detached involvement" evoked by genuine art. She points out that many certified masterpieces from Geoffrey Chaucer to D. H. Lawrence have excited readers sexually and that many other works of literary pornography—*Story of O*, *Story of the Eye*, *The Image*—mix art and arousal. Sontag, *Georges Bataille*, 37.

3 Bazin writes that pornographic films are an "expiation, or at least in payment of a debt that we owe for sixty years of cinematographic lies about love." Reading Henry Miller, he "suffered at the idea that cinema lagged so far behind his books as well as behind reality. Unhappily, I still cannot cite an erotic film that is the equivalent of Henry Miller's writing (the best films, from Bergman to Bertolucci, have been pessimistic)." Bazin, "What Do Critics Dream About?" 7.

4 For example, *The Night Porter* (dir. Liliana Cavani, 1974), *The Devils* (dir. Ken Russell, 1971), *Swept Away* (dir. Lina Wertmüller, 1975), and the early films of Catherine Breillat.

5 Note that *Caligula* (dir. Tinto Brass, 1980), the much-hyped end-of-decade

American entry in this competition, proved a big disappointment. It so radically bracketed its nonactor, *Penthouse*-style orgy participants from its high-class British cast that it seemed like two different movies.

6 Joan Mellen's original review and subsequent British Film Institute book on the work are particularly insistent on the point that Oshima's film is foreign to both Western sexuality and pornography. See her "Is 'Senses' in the Realm of Pornography?" (*New York Times*, 31 July 1977) and *In the Realm of the Senses*, 36. In the latter work, perhaps to counter the judgment that the film is mere pornography, she is particularly insistent that the film "permits little vicarious arousal by a spectator" (36). Of course, each of us must be our own judge of that. Peter Lehman's chapter on the film in *Running Scared* also stresses the film's difference from pornography—visually its lack of meat and money shots, and aurally its divergence from the patently dubbed-over sound of so much hard-core pornography (178).

7 Maureen Turim's fine book, *The Films of Oshima Nagisa*, offers the best defense of the film as a new kind of pornography, while cautioning that "there is never any clear line between generic pornography and the sophisticated erotic text" (267). Turim goes on to say that many of Oshima's films refuse to exist either inside or outside pornography's territory but that "in treating explicit sexuality directly they lay a claim on pornography construed in a positive sense as the uncensored viewing of sex acts" that are structured in opposition to the "expected coding of pornography" (267).

8 Oshima, *Cinema, Censorship, and the State*, 261.

9 In addition to the Mellen, Turim, and Lehman books mentioned above, see also Grindon, "In the Realm of the Censors"; and Russell, *Narrative Mortality*, 105–36.

10 As the film critic Judy Stone put it in a review, Oshima's film "is to hard-core dirty movies what an Utamaro print is to dirty pictures" (*San Francisco Chronicle*, 15 April 1977).

11 In the late 1980s I finally tackled it by including it in a discussion, I now think inappropriately, of sadomasochistic pornography in my book *Hard Core*. It was thus through the lens of hard-core pornography that I first debated it, not as art cinema.

12 This was *The True Story of Abe Sada* (dir. Tanaka Norburu, 1975)—a more conventionally told, though still sensational, story with no graphic sex.

13 Tony Rayns says six years, Oshima himself says four. However, according to William Johnston's informative biography, she served five. See Rayns, "Interview with Nagisa Oshima," 34–35. See also Johnston, *Geisha, Harlot, Strangler, Star*, 147.

14 Qtd. in Turim, *Films of Oshima Nagisa*, 18.

15 The Meiji period (1868–1912) achieved the rapid modernization of Japanese economic, political, and social institutions at the cost of instituting a large number of reforms that imitated Western models, including the model of sexual prudery that ran counter to Japan's thriving premodern sex culture.

16 Oshima, *Cinema, Censorship, and the State*, 247.

17 For example, Oshima quotes a piece of graffiti, written on a wall at the Sorbonne during France's May 1968 revolution: "The greater your labor of love, the more overwhelming your desire for revolution. The more you revolt, the more overwhelming your desire to engage in a labor of love" (ibid., 247). Sex behind the barricades, like the group sex that purportedly once existed in farm villages prior to the Meiji period, are, to Oshima, examples of revolutionary attacks on the "myth of sexual exclusiveness and possessiveness" (ibid.)

18 Ibid.

19 Grindon, "In the Realm of the Censors," 294; Oshima, *Cinema, Censorship, and the State*, 256–57.

20 Oshima, *Cinema, Censorship, and the State*, 260.

21 Ibid.

22 I am making a distinction here between feature-length hard-core narrative art film and hard-core experimental films such as Andy Warhol's *Couch* (1964) or *Blue Movie* (1968), both of which had hard-core action but neither of which could be categorized as a narrative art film.

23 For example, he declares, in this same essay, that on 26 April 1975, "France launched a complete legalization of pornography. Cannes, naturally, was overflowing with it." See "On Trial for Obscenity," in Oshima, *Cinema, Censorship, and the State*, 257. Cannes was not really overflowing with hard-core pornography, though that year did include a documentary interview film, entitled *Exhibition* (dir. Jean Francois Davy), in which Claudine Becarrie described and then acted out some sexual scenes from her life. The year also included the soft-core *The Story of O* (dir. Just Jaeckin), the bestiality of Thierry Zéno's *Vase de noces* (*The Wedding Trough*), and the sex-obsessed yet entirely simulated Hollywood comedy *Shampoo* (dir. Hal Ashby)—all of which may have seemed, from the distance of Japan, to have been "overflowing." The important point, of course, was that the following year Oshima's film would outdo all the above.

24 During this period the merchant culture that had supported *shunga* died and the reprinting of Edo erotica was prohibited. As all nudity was proscribed, Japanese authorities became fig-leaf aficionados. In 1918 laws were amended to permit the display of pubic areas, but without anatomical details. Jay Rubin believes that this reticence about anatomical detail is the basis for current prohibitions about penises and pubic hair (*Injurious to Public Morals*, 44). It would seem that Japanese culture embraced Meiji censorship because it saw Victorian morality as a means of escaping the colonized fate of the rest of Asia and Africa. Thanks also to Deborah Shamoon, Miryam Sas, and Allan Tansman for explaining many of these intricacies to me.

25 Noël Burch, Peter Lehman, and Maureen Turim have all asserted the importance of the once suppressed tradition of *ukiyo-e* erotic prints. See Burch, *To the Distant Observer*, 343; Turim, *Films of Oshima Nagisa*, 128; Lehman, *Running Scared*, 181–84.

26 On 4 May 1977, *Variety* estimated that a third of the film's content was "obliterated" in the version shown in Japan (49, 63).

27 These photos did not actually show sex organs. Rather, the prosecutor charged that they were "scenes that allow one easily to perceive the fact that men and women are engaged in sexual intercourse . . . or sex play. Moreover, the fact that the still photos were photographed during the process of filming the movie . . . strongly produces a very real feeling and consequently, excessively stimulates sexual desire." Qtd. in Cathers, "Great Censorship Trials," 172.

28 Oshima, *Cinema, Censorship, and the State*, 261.

29 In 2001, on its twenty-fifth anniversary, for the first time a complete uncut version of the film was released in Japan on video. While the original expurgated footage was restored, clouds obscuring genitals were imposed. See Cathers, "Great Censorship Trials," 134–35. Contemporary Japanese censorship is marked by a rather amazing toleration of violence and violent sex and an absolutely puritanical effacement of anything having to do with genitals or pubic hair. As Nicolas Bornoff has noted, some of the most violent and extreme sexual fantasies can be viewed in Japanese comics, or *manga*, and cartoons, or anime, as long as realistic genitals and pubic hair, especially the latter, remains invisible. Snakes and steam locomotives can take the place of penises, and tunnels and mollusks can take the place of female genitals. Today, thousands of hard-core videos are shot in Japan and freely rented or sold so long as the genitals are digitally obscured. Bornoff, *Pink Samurai*, 594.

30 On 4 May 1977 *Variety* reported: "It is now considered to be a bit of one-upmanship for Japanese to see the uncut version when they travel abroad and it has been estimated that about 20,000 locals have seen the film in Paris alone. There was also, believe it or not, a charter flight from Tokyo to Cannes during the 1976 festival, and another package tour to Paris. It is considered a major tourist attraction by Japanese" (63).

31 The print shown to the press had arrived from Los Angeles, where customs officials did not screen it. Customs officials in New York, however, questioned the propriety of this seemingly backdoor, West-to-East entry and so demanded to be present at the New York press screening. The organizers then canceled the film, though they gave a rain check to the audience gathered for the first festival screening once the film was "freed" from customs. Bouras, "In the Realm of the Censors," 32.

32 Oshima, *Cinema, Censorship, and the State*, 260.

33 As Turim puts it, Sada is "singing her pleasure." Turim, *Films of Oshima Nagisa*, 132.

34 *Floating world* is a term that originally referred to the Buddhist doctrine of impermanence and detachment but that eventually came to refer to the sinful world of the pleasure quarters, and from that to signify the pleasures of urban life in general.

35 See Turim, *Films of Oshima Nagisa*, 148; Mellen, *In the Realm of the Senses*,

65–66; Heath, *Questions of Cinema*, 158; McCormick, "*In the Realm of the Senses*," 34.

36 In a fine review of the film, Ruth McCormick writes that the slightly world-weary Kichi is portrayed as a product of the old floating world of the pleasure districts, "which by 1936 had become an anachronism." Before the incursions of Western morality, these districts had been devoted to the "pleasure-givers"—geishas, artists, musicians, actors, and prostitutes. McCormick, "*In the Realm of the Senses*," 33. Mellen, in her monograph on the film, points out that this spectacle of two Japans—"one lonely and abandoned" walking without direction, another a "modernized and militarized" threat that "proceeds with grim defiance, having supplanted a tradition of freedom, sexual refinement and pleasure"—would seem all the more poignant to those aware of Japanese history: 1936, the year of the film's events, also marked the year of a failed coup by military officers opposed to the mounting military expansionism of the emperor. The coup failed, the officers were executed, and Japan marched off to war. Mellen, *In the Realm of the Senses*, 33–34.

37 Peter Lehman correctly argues that both Turim and Burch exaggerate the equivalencies of the two and fail to note the crucial fact of the vastly exaggerated penis size in *shunga*. I agree with Lehman that penis size is importantly not exaggerated in *Realm of the Senses*, but I do not agree with him that "penetration shots are entirely lacking" in the film (*Running Scared*, 180, 183). They may only seem lacking and deemphasized compared to *shunga* or to Western cinema's hard-core pornography.

38 Foucault writes somewhat romantically of the *ars erotica* tradition that pleasure in it is "evaluated in terms of its intensity, its specific quality, its duration, its reverberations in the body and the soul." But he makes this generalization without differentiating the traditional *ars erotica* of China, Japan, India, Rome, and Arab Muslim societies. This version of the knowledge of pleasure is to Foucault always just a little secret; it is divulged by a master who guides a disciple's progress. Foucault, *History of Sexuality*, 1:57.

39 Foucault does not resolve this issue, but he leaves us with the impression that *ars erotica* does persist in the West and that, by implication, a *scientia sexualis* may equally be located in modern examples of the *ars erotica*. Ibid., 1:71–72.

40 In *shunga* adulterous sex might take place rather casually in the same room with a sleeping husband or under the eyes of servants. Peter Lehman discusses this similarity in *Running Scared*, 181–83.

41 Japanese artistic traditions, not to mention the country's own mores, underwent a profound shift even before the country opened up to the West in 1864.

42 In *Injurious to Public Morals*, Jay Rubin describes one of the first attempts to bring European nude art to Japan in 1901. In a gesture not unlike that of the U.S. attorney general John Ashcroft, who in 2002 covered the naked breast of a twelve-foot-high Art Deco statue of Justice, the police covered the lower parts of the nudes with maroon curtains. In another exhibition in 1903 they pasted fig leaves onto the canvasses and sawed the penis off a statue (44). In other words, by this time the Edo tradition had already been lost. Rubin notes that in 1918 the law was amended to state that the pubic area could be shown, but that anatomical details were not allowed (44). Another scholar, Deborah Shamoon, argues that the Japanese embrace of Puritanism arose from the desire to accept Victorian morality as a means of escaping colonization. The Japanese realized that unless they could prove to the West that they were a civilized nation, they would end up like China and the rest of Asia and Africa (personal communication, 2006).

43 Marco Fagioli writes that many of the lovers depicted in *shunga* were known figures—famous actors and courtesans: "Astounding though it may seem, many of these famous couples were represented in explicit sexual encounters in many *Shunga* books." Fagioli, *Shunga*, 12. Of course it is only "astounding" in a culture such as our own in which sexual activity is considered shameful. Bornoff writes of a "macabre print of the decadent period" showing "the aftermath of a double suicide" that sounds every bit as bloody as what we shall see in *Realm of the Senses*. Bornoff, *Pink Samurai*, 285. Oshima, however, eschews the double suicide tradition and instead opts for a heroine who wants to live.

44 McCormick, "*In the Realm of the Senses*," 34.

45 Nineteen paragraphs of the police investigation into Abe Sada's crime were devoted to her previous sexual behavior and strong sexual appetite, and there was internal disagreement as to whether this appetite constituted normal or abnormal behavior. Perhaps ironically, her "diagnosis" tipped toward "normality" because in the end, as the report said, "her activities in foreplay, in sexual intercourse, and even in acts of cruelty were ultimately aimed at achieving sexual pleasure in a normal sense; it is impossible to say that she is sexually perverted." Qtd. in Johnston, *Geisha, Harlot, Strangler, Star*, 129.

46 At one point Kichi calls Sada "insatiable," not as a reproach but as a compliment; "I hope you are incurable," he adds. The English subtitles also use the word *sensitive* (in some prints, *hypersensitive*). In all cases there is no implication of sexual aberration. In Western terms Sada's condition could be described as an extreme case of what the previous chapter cited from American feminist psychoanalyst Mary Jane Sherfey: "Theoretically, a woman could go on having orgasms indefinitely if physical exhaustion did not intervene." Sherfey, "Theory on Female Sexuality," 91.

47 Bataille, *Erotism*, 103.

48 Of course, the still images of *shunga* depicted many similar activities, but only rarely happening simultaneously with sex; due to the limits of the still-image medium that could not portray sex over time, the everyday acts of the couples were more often portrayed as interrupted by, rather than ongoing with, sex.

49 We might compare the continuousness of these "acts of love" to the elaborately casual boredom of Linda Lovelace's roommate who smokes while her partner diligently "eats" her. Even at their most casual, these are intensely physical acts of love, not acts of rote sexual performance.

50 Indeed, it is as if Sada makes the organ her own, learning to make it move herself. Strangulation, as was well known in the era of public executions by hanging, could produce erections caused by the decrease in the flow of blood to the brain. This is the same form of cerebral hypotension induced by the use of amyl and butyl nitrates in more contemporary sexual practices. Peter Lehman notes that having deemphasized penis size throughout the bulk of his film, Oshima suddenly emphasizes it at the end, depicting Kichi's engorged, severed penis shortly after showing his limp penis on the dead body. Though I do not believe the discrepancy is enormous, I agree with Lehman that Oshima is negotiating important contradictions between the critique and the celebration of a phallocentric culture. Lehman, *Running Scared*, 188–190.

51 Sada is the real name of the woman who was found wandering the streets with her lover's member. No Japanese-speaking critic seems to think that the name has any significance.

52 Ruth McCormick points out that "not once is pain per se ever inflicted by either of the lovers on the other," and draws the lesson that it would therefore be a mistake to call the film sadomasochistic. McCormick, "*In the Realm of the Senses*," 33. I would say, to the contrary, that pain is inflicted—Kichi hits Sada and Sada's strangulation of Kichi does inflict pain—but that this pain is mixed with pleasure. Sadomasochistic sex is never about the experience of pure pain, nor about the infliction of it on another. *Sadomasochism* is a term that keeps in play the oscillations between active and passive and male and female subject positions, rather than fixing one pole or the other as the essence of the pleasure offered up by the pornographic fantasy. The presence of violence in a sexual relation does not mean that it is either essentially sadistic or masochistic.

53 Bataille, *Erotism*, 11.

54 Bersani, *Freudian Body*, 34.

55 Ibid., 87.

56 Ibid.

57 Some prints say, less acutely, "Let's be happy forever."

58 Bataille, *Erotism*, 105.

59 A less eloquent subtitle on another print reads, "It's like I was inside you again; I see everything."

60 Joan Mellen translates the girl as saying "Where are you now?" and the man answering, "I'm not there yet." Mellen, *In the Realm of the Senses*, 68.

61 Grindon, "In the Realm of the Censors," 308.

62 For example, the film reviewer Stanley Eichelbaum wrote in the *San Francisco Examiner* of 15 April 1977: "We've had nothing since 'Last Tango in Paris' to send critics scrambling for words with more desperate ambivalence than Nagisa Oshima's *In the Realm of the Senses*" ("A Landmark in Hard-core Eroticism," 24).

63 McCormick, "In the Realm of the Senses," 34.

64 Mellen, *In the Realm of the Senses*, 37.

65 Ibid.

66 For example, Bersani writes: "If sexuality is by definition something excessive, a psychic shattering due to the gap between the level of stimulation to which the ego is exposed and its structuring capacities, then the ego's hatred of external objects, its invasion by stimuli from these objects, *and* its need to incorporate loved objects, can also be identified with *masochism*. We have perhaps become willing to think of sadism as a projection of masochism; must we now conceive of sado-masochism as a form of narcissism?" Bersani, *Freudian Body*, 88–89. See also Bataille, *Erotism*, 94.

67 Oshima writes that of the small number of people who had seen his film at the time of writing (in June 1976), "nearly all the male viewers, who constitute the majority, comment that the moment they see O-Sada cut off Yoshizo's penis, they feel pain in their own sexual organ." He adds that a woman critic, Kawakita Kazuko, faced with these male expressions of pain countered that when women have light bulbs or a pole stuck up inside them: "I bet you guys never felt pain then." Oshima, *Cinema, Censorship, and the State*, 261.

68 Sontag, *Georges Bataille*, 103.

69 Oshima, *Cinema, Censorship, and the State*, 261.

70 Sontag, *Georges Bataille*, 103.

71 Ibid.

72 Jameson, *Signatures of the Visible*, 1.

73 Oshima, *Cinema, Censorship, and the State*, 260.

74 See epigraph to Chapter 7, Michael Winterbottom, interview by James Brown, *Independent*, 13 May 2004, www.independent.co.uk/.

75 André Breton, *L'Amour Fou*.

Chapter 6: Primal Scenes on American Screens

1 Kinder, "Reinventing the Motherland," 257.

2 Almodóvar himself uses the words *front* or *blindfold*. He writes, "I invented 'Shrinking Lover' as a kind of blindfold" to what is "really happening in Alicia's room." From the pressbook for *Talk to Her*, www.sonyclassics.com/talktoher/talktoher.pdf (accessed 2 Nov. 2007).

3 We have seen that screening sex moves in both directions at once, as overt display and as a mask or concealment of display. In the introduction and first chapter I cited Freud's essay on "screen memories"—false memories that have come to replace actual events of the past, screening out uncomfortable memories with seemingly indifferent ones. These indifferent early memories thus conceal, but also paradoxically reveal, the memory of later events. In this case, the silent movie offers a way of rendering a more "benign" version of the rape of Alicia, but one that is also true to Benigno's deluded experience.

4 These films—the last of its kind was Sam Peckinpah's *Straw Dogs* (1971)—view rape as something a woman will come to enjoy. By "old style" Clover means the sort of film in which the woman either "asks for it" or humiliates the man and thus seems to deserve her fate. In *Straw Dogs* the woman, played by Susan George, is portrayed as "asking for it." Clover, *Men, Women, and Chain Saws*, 152.

5 In Almodóvar's *Tie Me Up! Tie Me Down!* (1990) another male character, again played by Banderas, forces himself on a woman he has been stalking, ties her up, and then waits for her to fall in love with him. Though he pointedly does not rape her, and in fact undergoes many trials that leave his body covered with bruises, the situation of coercion turns into one in which the woman learns to love his bruised body. In a telling scene, she asks him to tie her up so that she will not escape, and she does eventually fall in love with and have prolonged (simulated) enthusiastic sex with him. Spaniards had no problem with this film, but the basic situation of bondage seems to have precipitated the MPAA's decision to give an X rating to the film. The *Hollywood Reporter* made much of the comparison between the restrictions on films in the United States and comparative Spanish license to the ruling. See Paul Julian Smith, *Desire Unlimited*, 117. Miramax, the film's American distributor, challenged the X but lost its appeal for the commercially more viable R (this was before the compromise NC-17 had been invented). Americans, it would seem, were used to having their violence ("as American as cherry pie") straight and their sex, however represented, disentangled from violence. This is why the "butter scene" from *Last Tango*—a somewhat rough, though ultimately not coercive act of anal intercourse during which Marlon Brando's Paul speaks rudely to Maria Schneider's Jeanne—had been so scandalous to American audiences. Unlike Europeans, Americans needed to learn to screen sexual pleasures tinged with the emotional tenor of threat and violence. European films were ready to teach them, but I am arguing here that the best lessons for Americans actually came from American films.

6 Foucault, *History of Sexuality*, 1:63.

7 Ibid., 1:65.

8 I thank Rachel Swan for these insights in "Perversions in the Limelight."

9 King Vidor's 1946 film that ends in a sadomasochistic love-death (but without explicit sex) is seen playing on a movie screen that Maria and Diego briefly view.

10 Giddens, *Transformation of Intimacy*, 3, 10.

11 J. Hoberman, "Return to Normalcy," *Village Voice*, 22 September 1986.

12 One student reported watching *Blue Velvet* with her father and younger sisters (aged nine and six). When their mother came home in the middle of the screening, she was horrified. The father excused himself by saying that he had not remembered what the film was like. This student herself only recalled that the movie was "weird and creepy."

13 See Kael; Hoberman, "Return to Normalcy"; Gifford, *Devil Thumbs a Ride*.

14 Pauline Kael, for example, who had written so much about *Last Tango*, now wrote about *Blue Velvet*: "This is American darkness—darkness in color, darkness

with a happy ending. Lynch might turn out to be the first popular surrealist—a Frank Capra of dream logic." Kael, "Blue Velvet," 99. See also Hoberman, "Return to Normalcy." For a feminist reading of the film's misogyny, see Shattuc, "Postmodern Misogyny in *Blue Velvet*." For a stylistic reading of the film's "illegibility" as contemporary art film, see Tim Corrigan, *A Cinema without Walls*, 71–79.

15 Laplanche and Pontalis, "Fantasy and the Origins of Sexuality," 10.

16 Ibid., 9.

17 Atkinson, *Blue Velvet*, 33. Laura Mulvey and Sam Ishii-Gonzales have also pointed out the Freudian qualities of the primal scene in this prolonged and shocking scene. Mulvey, "Netherworlds and the Unconscious"; Ishii-Gonzales, "Mysteries of Love."

18 Laplanche and Pontalis, "Fantasy and the Origins of Sexuality," 19.

19 Ibid.

20 Freud, "From the History of an Infantile Neurosis," 17–21.

21 Ibid., 57.

22 As Ned Lukacher puts it, the primal scene for the "Wolf Man" was this seduction, not the earlier witnessing of parental sex. The dream of wolves merged with a story about a wolf whose tail was pulled off and could be construed as a way for the four-year-old dreaming boy to "think" about seduction and castration in conjunction with whatever primal scene he may have witnessed or fantasized. Freud thus understands that there are two associations with wolves, one in which the wolf is erect as a menacing castrator, another in which the wolf is tailless (the mother's position beneath the father, as castrated). The dream thus portrays the dreadful consequences of the primal scene "thought" both from the position of the mother and that of the father. Lukacher, *Primal Scenes*, 137–67.

23 Ishii-Gonzales, "Mysteries of Love," 49.

24 Michel Chion has observed the parental surrogate role Frank and Dorothy occupy for Jeffrey in *David Lynch*, 92.

25 Lynch's fondness for allusions to *The Wizard of Oz* is not confined to his later *Wild at Heart*. Indeed, the novelist J. G. Ballard has noted that *Blue Velvet* is "like *The Wizard of Oz* re-shot with a script by Franz Kafka and décor by Francis Bacon." Qtd. in Rodley, *Lynch on Lynch*, 56.

26 Ishii-Gonzales, "Mysteries of Love," 52.

27 This is the case a moment later when Dorothy has him stand and walk across the room to a more convenient couch. We only see him from behind. However, at a later moment, when Frank suddenly knocks and Jeffrey must scramble to hide once again in the closet, we very briefly glimpse his flaccid penis as he scampers across the room.

28 In the film's climax, Jeffrey will again hide in this closet, but this time armed with a gun. When Frank opens the door, Jeffrey shoots and kills at close range, thus killing the "Daddy" who, again tanked up with gas, was about to "come home."

29 Michael Atkinson makes the excellent point that what we witness in this scene is not only Jeffrey's primal scene but Frank's as well. He notes that Frank's suffering is so strong that "for the moments he's on the screen, *Blue Velvet* is his feverdream, not Jeffrey's." Atkinson, *Blue Velvet*, 49.

30 Freud, "Uncanny," 220.

31 Ibid., 222, 236, 242.

32 Ibid., 245.

33 Ibid.

34 As Ishii-Gonzales puts it, Dorothy's madness has the last word; it constitutes the lyrics of the song that we finally hear: "I still can see blue velvet through my tears." Ishii-Gonzales, "Mysteries of Love," 57.

35 That Dorothy *is* a mommy is emphasized in the following scene that shows Jeffrey, now clothed and about to leave, playing with little Donnie's beanie.

36 It is thus not surprising that it will be Jeffrey, not the detectives, who will finally kill Frank with a bullet between the eyes when he finds himself hiding, yet again, in Dorothy's closet.

37 Laplanche and Pontalis, "Fantasy and the Origins of Sexuality," 26.

38 Attorney General's Commission on Pornography, *Final Report*.

39 Laplanche and Pontalis, "Fantasy and the Origins of Sexuality," 26.

40 Jameson, *Postmodernism*, 294.

41 Ibid., 295–96.

42 Foucault, *History of Sexuality*, 1:47.

43 In this respect anal sex between men differs from that performed by a man on a woman. Heterosexual anal sex has a more ambivalent status: sometimes it is seen as degrading, but rarely as the utmost in pain and humiliation. Recall the "butter scene" in *Last Tango*. Jeanne is not exactly raped, but the sex is portrayed as degrading. This, indeed, is its point, and the point of the reversal in which Jeanne is required to put her fingers up Paul's anus. In more recent and more mainstream films, however, as in *Basic Instinct* (dir. Paul Verhoeven, 1992), anal sex is marked as over the top, but not necessarily painful. It is what the Michael Douglas character does to his girlfriend played by Jeanne Templeton after he has been driven wild by the unharnessed libido of Sharon Stone's character.

44 Once again, Pedro Almodóvar is in the advance garde with his 1987 *The Law of Desire*, a highly autobiographical film about a gay art film director who engages in an affair with a homophobic previously straight man played by Antonio Banderas. Simulated anal sex—with Banderas as the receiver—occupies a prominent position in this film. In American film, John Boorman's *Deliverance* (1972) is still the benchmark for the "horrors" of anal rape. The plump, out-of-shape city slicker played by Ned Beatty is anally gang-raped by a group of cretinous hillbillies. The tradition continues in prison settings in the nineties. In *American Me* (dir. Edward James Olmos, 1992) and *American History X* (dir. Tony Kaye, 1998) anal rape is what imprisoned men do to humiliate or shame other, more powerless prisoners. The apotheosis of this attitude—though perhaps also a flirtation with the forbidden that represents its limit case—occurs in Quentin Tarantino's *Pulp Fiction*

(1994). In this film, spectacular (simulated) anal rape is the one act of violence that can lead one macho man to take pity on another, who is its victim. Anal rape unites former enemies in a common cause against those who would violate their (anal) virginity. In the very few times that sex between men has been depicted as pleasurable rather than punishing, it has either been staged so as to emphasize its sexy luridness—as in William Friedkin's *Cruising* (1980)—or it has been tastefully vague about what it is the men may actually do, as in Arthur Hiller's *Making Love* (1982).

45 D. A. Miller, "On the Universality of *Brokeback Mountain*."

46 Ibid., 60.

47 For example, Robin Wood points out that the 1982 *Making Love* by Arthur Hiller was a well-meaning Hollywood film about a man who discovers his gayness through his first relationship with another man. He marks it as the first time gay men were shown to kiss on-screen. That kiss elicited groans in the theater. Wood marks the success of *Brokeback* in the absence of groans. Wood, "On and Around *Brokeback Mountain*," 28.

48 Rich also writes, "There has never been a film by a brand-name director, packed with A-list Hollywood stars at the peak of their careers, that has taken an established conventional genre by the horns and wrestled it into a tale of homosexual love emotionally positioned to ensnare a general audience." B. Ruby Rich, "Hello Cowboy."

49 For example, Rich writes that the film "queers the Wyoming landscape as a space of homosexual desire and fulfillment, a playground of sexuality freed from judgment, an Eden poised to restore prelapsarian innocence to a sexuality long sullied by social shame." Ibid., 3.

50 *Lawrence v. Texas*, 539 U.S. (2002), 3.

51 Ibid., 6.

52 This is, of course, only a story, though a fascinating one because it asserts not only that police "caught" the two men *in flagrante delicto* but also that they continued having sex after the light in the bedroom was turned on and after being ordered to stop. Indeed, according to the affidavit of one of the officers, Quinn Tyrone Garner, a black man, was positioned on the bed and Lawrence, a white man, was "standing behind him at the side of the bed" (Carpenter, 7). When ordered to stop, Lawrence reportedly looked the officer in the eye and continued. Because the case itself did not come to trial—the men were only fined and the appeal did not dispute the facts of the case, only the constitutionality of sodomy law—it has not been established in a court of law what actually happened. Like the primal scene itself, this event is intensely subject to revision and even to the possibility, as argued by the Michigan law professor Dale Carpenter, of never having taken place. See Carpenter, "Colloquium," 102.

53 *Lawrence v. Texas*, 539 U.S. (2002), 2.

54 Gore Vidal in *Inside Deep Throat* (dir. Fenton Baily and Randy Barbato, 2005)

55 Ibid., 1.

56 Ibid., 5.

57 Ibid., 18.

58 Ibid., 8; emphasis added.

59 Ibid., 13.

60 See Berlant and Warner, "Sex in Public"; Gayle Rubin, "Thinking Sex"; and Cante and Restivo, "'World' of All-Male Pornography"; and Cante and Restivo, "Cultural-Aesthetic Specificities."

61 Hard-core pornography's X status has made it less public, especially since it became available online. Small-screen cable has also been a source of enormous publicity for simulated gay sex. Witness the American Showtime success of the serial TV show *Queer as Folk* (American series premier December 2000) whose initial episode featured a prolonged simulated scene of first anal sex for a young high school–aged protagonist.

62 Freud, "From the History of an Infantile Neurosis," 36.

63 Edelman, "Seeing Things," 101.

64 Ibid., 103.

65 Laplanche and Pontalis, "Fantasy and the Origins of Sexuality," 10.

66 Wood, "In and Around *Brokeback Mountain*," 28.

67 Ibid., 3.

68 Proulx, *Brokeback Mountain*, 14.

69 Daniel Mendelsohn argues especially against Roger Ebert's claim for the universality of the story. Ebert claimed that the tragedy of the film was not unlike those of characters from different religious or ethnic groups. Mendelsohn, "Affair to Remember," 12–18.

70 Ibid., 3. It is worth noting in the wake of Heath Ledger's death, initially reported as a possible suicide, that this death itself has become a kind of memorialization of familiar themes of queer death and self-loathing.

71 Later in the film Ennis tells a barmaid who likes him that he spent the day "castrating cows."

72 Proulx, *Brokeback Mountain*, 49.

73 Ibid., 50.

74 Ibid., 49.

75 Ennis's father dies while he is young, but not before taking him to witness the mutilated cowboy. Jack's father fails to pass on his rodeo secrets and is, as we see, a cold and forbidding man.

76 Daniel Mendelsohn challenges the value of this "macho" moment in the film, which he compares to an earlier scene that shows Ennis's standing up to bikers at a Fourth of July picnic. For Mendelsohn this later scene is an occasion to link Ennis to all-American iconography. However, I do not think these moments should be equated. Jack's macho stance, I am arguing, is not as an emulation of the father's violence, but a firm standing up to the paternal law through the strength of his own difference—a difference that eventually causes him to show himself as queer, with fatal consequences. Ennis, however, can only repeat the male hysteria that phobically guards against difference. Picking a fight with bikers who speak roughly around women and children is his way of aligning himself with the paternal law that protects women and children, but, like all his paranoid and hysterical outbursts of violence, it does not assert his difference from them. It only repeats over and over his attempted repudiation of the woman he fears he might be.

77 Proulx, *Brokeback Mountain*, 52.

78 Ibid.

79 See Luciano, "Love's Measures," 108.

80 Ibid., 109. The man who bought the shirts said he would never sell them and thus never separate them.

81 Freud, *Three Essays on the Theory of Sexuality*, 20.

82 James Shamus writes: "It is not that . . . we made a great gay movie and then spent the next year insistently trying to stuff it back into the closet. . . . It is that . . . in . . . removing gayness from the closet and 'mainstreaming' it, we disturb the given sites—some closeted, some not—from which gay identities struggle for recognition. *Brokeback* appears in the midst of new, and confusing, displacements of the sites of gay and, more broadly, GLBT identities—in the vast and disorienting space between the closet and the wedding altar." Shamus, Conarroe, and Mendelsohn, "*Brokeback Mountain*," 68–69. See also Sedgwick, *Epistemology of the Closet*.

83 Witness the recent rash of foreign films whose trailers, by not reproducing any language or subtitles, present themselves as if they were English-language films.

84 www.filmmakermagazine.com/blog/2006_03_01_archive.php (accessed 22 April 2008).

85 Bataille, *Erotism*, 37.

Chapter 7: Philosophy in the Bedroom

1 For example, Jane Campion's theatrical release of *In the Cut* (2003) received an R rating, while the DVD showed a brief glimpse of fellatio witnessed by Meg Ryan's character in an early scene.

2 In addition to Kirby Dick's excellent film, see also West and West, "MPAA Ratings, Black Holes, and My Film."

3 Steiner, "Night Words," 77.

4 Ibid.

5 Metz, *Imaginary Signifier*, 77.

6 The *Guardian* makes this claim, listing the sex scenes as unsimulated "fellatio, ejaculation and cunnilingus, many in close-up" (Charlotte Higgens, "Cannes Screening for Most Sexually Explicit British Film," 17 May 2004).

7 Heterosexual pornography has relied on testing its performers. Most gay

pornography in the nineties, by contrast, has used condoms and in some cases eroticized the incorporation of condom use.

8 A new eroticization can also develop around the use, and even the nonuse, of condoms. Sex without condoms—as in the dangerous and defiant gesture with which Romane Bohringer tosses away the condom she was about to use when about to have (simulated) sex with the HIV-positive Cyril Collard in *Les nuits fauves* (*Savage Nights*, dir. Cyril Collard, 1992)—thus becomes a pointed choice, a dramatic decision that suggests new forms of *amour fou*.

9 Michael Winterbottom, qtd. in Brown, "Lights, Camera, Explicit Action," 6–7.

10 "Although you might find the sex scenes graphic, it is certainly not pornography" (*Independent*, 13 May 2004, 6–7).

11 The following discussion of Lars von Trier, Catherine Breillat, and Patrice Chéreau is adapted from my essay, "Cinema and the Sex Act."

12 Thus, for example, props were supposed to grow organically out of the film's location; music could never be added to a film after the fact; superficial action and genres were forbidden, as were special lights.

13 See the official Dogme 95 Web site, www.dogme95.dk (accessed 30 September 2007).

14 Part of the insistence on real sex in *The Idiots* came from the compromises von Trier felt he had had to make in his previous film, *Breaking the Waves* (1996), originally intended as a sex film. He had originally described the project as a hardcore art film that would explore the ambiguities of power through sex along the lines of the Marquis de Sade's *Justine*. The film is about a young female religious fanatic powerfully awakened sexually by the man she marries. When he suffers an accident that renders him impotent, he asks her to have affairs and report back on her pleasures. According to Jack Stevenson, earlier drafts of the script showed the character who came to be called Bess (Emily Watson) enjoying this sex, painting her as a creature of powerful lusts. Later drafts, and the finished film, however, moved away from this "erotic melodrama" into "religious melodrama with erotic overtones." Bess martyrs herself for her husband's needs in repeated scenes of sexual humiliation in which she seems to take no pleasure herself. It is as if to gain sympathy for Bess and to make the film palatable for audiences, von Trier needed to paint her as a sexual victim devoid of sexual pleasure. See Stevenson, *Lars von Trier*, 91–93.

15 The only available version of this film in the United States is a video with ludicrous large black rectangles obscuring all male, and most female, genitalia, thus making it a little hard to tell what actually happens underneath the floating shapes. I am basing this analysis on a Danish DVD without the rectangles.

16 Chéreau has famously staged Richard Wagner's *Der Ring des Nibelungen* (*The Ring of the Nibelung*) at Bayreuth. He has more occasionally made films, including the period drama *Queen Margot* (1994) and the contemporary *Those Who*

Love Me Will Take the Train (1998). His comment is quoted from the press kit for *Intimacy*, 13.

17 Denby, "Current Cinema."

18 Kael, "Tango," 130.

19 Much more typical is Elizabeth Taylor's seeming innocence in *A Place in the Sun* (dir. George Stevens, 1951), an innocence of gesture belied by the sexual allure of her body.

20 Béla Balázs, for example, writes: "We cannot use glycerin tears in a close-up. What makes a deep impression is not a fat, oily tear rolling down a face—what moves us is to see the glance growing misty, and moisture gathering in the corner of the eye—moisture that as yet is scarcely a tear. This is moving, because this cannot be faked." Balázs, *Theory of the Film*, 77.

21 Breillat is inserting her heroine into the tradition begun in the late eighteenth century by the Marquis de Sade's *Philosophy in the Bedroom*, a collection of seven fictional dialogues that take place among a group of two male and one female libertine as they initiate a young girl into the pleasures of sex. Metaphysical speculations on morality, history, and religion are interspersed with scenes of sex in which the young girl proves an apt pupil. See Sade, *Justine*. Marie is the modern heroine inserted into this tradition of sex talk and sex acts.

22 Constable, "Unbecoming Sexual Desires," 672–95.

23 See, for example, Todd Solondz's *Storytelling* (1998) and *Happiness* (2002), or Gaspar Noé's *Seul contre tous* (*I Stand Alone*; 1998) and *Irréversible* (2002).

24 As such, I would argue that Breillat's films are infinitely more feminist than Virginie Despentes and Coralie Trinh's feminist rape-revenge odyssey, *Baise-moi* (2000), though I know that some would disagree.

25 This is an indirect quote from Cox, "Sex on the Brain."

26 This is an axiom of golden-age pornography of the 1970s and early 1980s. See Linda Williams, *Hard Core*, 134–52.

27 Mitchell notes that "young people learn sex nowadays from porn rather than multiple sources—from life or friends or whatever. They become very insecure about how they look and they just don't enjoy it. They figure they have to do this and then follow it with being rimmed and then follow it with coming on someone's back. Sex is supposed to be surprising and spontaneous, and instead it's become another fucking marketing niche." Qtd. in Kennedy, "Return of Free Love," 46.

28 It is called Dumba—a queer performing arts collective and occasional site for orgies in Brooklyn—where some of the scenes were actually filmed. See Lee, "Shortbus," 71. However, other models from the nineties are a rock and roll drag party called Squeezebox, where Mitchell's original stage play for *Hedwig and the Angry Inch* began, as well as another venue in the East Village with which the Shortbus MC Justin Bond was associated. Kennedy, "Return of Free Love," 46.

29 It is called *Behind the Green Door: The Sequel* (1986).

30 Corliss, *Time*, 6 October 2006.

31 Foucault, *The History of Sexuality*, 1:7. In making this statement, Foucault dismissed a long tradition of supposedly salubrious anti-Victorianism, in which the fight against repression would liberate a good, healthy sexuality. Along with Foucault, and whether they read him or not, this generation is more likely to believe that prohibition and censorship are not the only ways in which power is exercised in the realm of sex. Similarly, these filmmakers seem to have absorbed Georges Bataille's once novel lesson of the complicity of law with its violation and no longer believe that the breaking of a taboo means freedom from it. See Bataille, *Erotism*, 36.

32 McCarthy, *Variety*, 21 May 2006, 33, 34.

33 Ibid.

34 Qtd. in Mohr, "*Shortbus* on Low-Key Ride."

35 Other titles include, for example, Marco Bellocchio's very early depiction of fellatio *Devil in the Flesh* (1986); Gaspar Noé's *Seul contre tous* (*I Stand Alone*; 1998); Leos Carax's *Pola X* (1999); Virginie Despentes and Coralie Trinh's groundbreaking *Baise-moi* (2000); Bertrand Bonello's *Le pornographe* (2001); Catherine Breillat's *Anatomy of Hell* (2004); Julio Medem's *Lucía y el sexo* (*Sex and Lucia*; 2001); Carlos Reygadas's *Japón* (2002) and *Batalla en el cielo* (*Battle in Heaven*; 2005); Ulrich Seidl's *Dog Days* (2001); Götz Spielmann's *Antares* (2004); Mathias Glasner's *Der Freie Wille* (2006); Bruce La Bruce's *The Raspberry Reich* (2004); and most recently Ang Lee's *Lust, Caution* (2007), which walks a very fine line between hard-core and non-hard-core art in two of its later scenes. The above list is not meant to be complete, but an indication of the range of art films that now include, often quite unsensationally, hard-core sex acts.

36 Kenneth Turan, "A Crowning Effort," *Los Angeles Times*, 1 Oct. 1999, F1, F8.

37 Ibid.

38 Qtd. in Linda Ruth Williams, "Edge of the Razor."

39 Bazin, "Marginal Notes on Eroticism in Cinema," 174.

40 Qtd. in Porton, "Elusive Intimacy," 18.

Conclusion

1 In that same year revenues from videocassette sales equaled theatrical box-office grosses. Subscription cable services also rose from 13.4 million in 1982 to 41.5 million in 1998. King, *New Hollywood Cinema*, 229, 230.

2 However, the portability of the smaller screens also means that they can fluidly move from place to place, including back out into public spaces.

3 See, for example, Mark Poster's discussion of the changing meanings of public and private in a chapter entitled "CyberDemocracy." Poster, *What's the Matter with the Internet*, 178–83.

4 Dudley Andrew, a cinephile if ever there was one, writes in "Film and Society" that if, as Walter Ong claims, TV has returned us to an oral culture, then movies need to be considered as "reigning briefly at the end of an essentially nineteenth-century fascination with engulfing illusions. Hollywood called for and rewarded concentrated viewing. . . . Spectators paid to lose themselves in such engulfing images" (161–62).

5 See Marvin D'Lugo's discussion of Montiel's place in Spanish popular culture and in this film in "Post-nostalgia."

6 See my discussion of *Boys in the Sand* in chapter 3.

7 Cronenberg's justly famous cult film has been much commented on. Here I am only using it to touch on the new figuration of the closeness of the television screen to our bodies and our lives, on the bridging of the gulf.

8 In the words of the guru of the new world produced by the new technology, "The television is the retina of the mind's eye, therefore the television screen is part of the physical structure of the brain" (*Videodrome* [dir. David Cronenberg, 1983]).

9 See W. J. T. Mitchell's discussion of this scene in his insightful *What Do Pictures Want*, xv.

10 To Cubitt, video, at least when it was still new, appeared as "an alibi—not a surrogate for company but an alternative to it—for more or less intensively introverted pleasure." Cubitt, *Timeshift*, 42. Why Cubitt chooses to only vilify housewives and teenagers is not quite clear. He could have easily included media scholars on his list!

11 While all sex is simulated in the earlier shows, *Tell Me that You Love Me* has so far been especially focused on penises and scrotums.

12 Andrews, *Soft in the Middle*, 159–83.

13 Williams writes, "if hardcore really does it, softcore merely fakes it. If hardcore hangs on the authenticity of the real view (that adolescent shock of seeing people *actually getting off*) softcore holds back, cannot show, kisses but finally does not tell." Williams, *The Erotic Thriller*, 269–70.

14 Laqueur, *Solitary Sex*, 303.

15 Andrews, *Soft in the Middle*, 189–192.

16 This is a subsection of a chapter about various screen sizes in Geoff King's fine introductory book entitled *New Hollywood Cinema* (225).

17 Zimmer, "Long Live the New Flesh," 7. Zimmer also notes that the videotape functions as object more than the film does: "Put it in, take it out. Rent it." With film we buy admission to an event, with video we rent or buy a commodity.

18 So successful was the marketing of X-rated movies on videocassette that the porn industry soon saw the advantage of avoiding theatrical releases altogether. By 1983, when approximately seven hundred adult theaters still operated across the country, videocassettes began their inexorable rise, producing four hundred adult titles. By 1986 there were only two hundred surviving adult theaters, and the revenue share from video and cable constituted 80 percent of the industry's earnings (Prince, *New Pot of Gold*, 359). In that year, adult video sales revenues reached an extraordinary $425 million and fifteen hundred videos were released. Prince, *New Pot of Gold*, 122–23. See also O'Toole, *Pornocopia*, 104. O'Toole notes that in driving this technological change, the porn business was "performing its regular duty as a key driver for the economic emergence of a new technology."

19 Prince, *New Pot of Gold*, 359.

20 Linda Ruth Williams, *Erotic Thriller in Contemporary Cinema*, 254.

21 Mahurin is the same artist who digitally darkened O. J. Simpson's face in another *Time* image.

22 Wendy Chun discusses this image at length in her book, *Control and Freedom*, and notes that what is figured in this influential image is the hunger of a "user" whose desire seems to be less for the images and more for the vague information of "the computer itself" (6, 92).

23 Patterson, "Going Online," 104.

24 *Newsweek* followed suit with an equally alarmist article, also based on the same rather flimsy evidence from a badly researched Carnegie Mellon undergraduate thesis asserting, erroneously, that 83.5 percent of all Usenet images were pornographic. In fact, less than 0.5 percent of Usenet messages contained pornographic images. For the conceptual flaws of the study all-too-credulously taken up by the hysterical media, see Chun, *Control and Freedom*, 78.

25 A *Wall Street Journal* article of 20 August 1997 by Thomas Weber wrote, for example, "find a web site that is in the black, and, chances are, its business and content are distinctly blue." Qtd. in ibid., 78.

26 Ibid., 79.

27 Lev Manovich, "The Interface," *The Language of New Media*, 62–115.

28 Linda Williams, *Hard Core*.

29 "Although Internet pornography is visual, its invisible workings are more significant and its visual impact less than that of cinematic pornography." Chun, *Control and Freedom*, 124.

30 Cell-phone pornography, already big business overseas, is reportedly poised to take off in the United States as well. Web-enabled phones can download porn from the Internet. See Strauss, "Cellphone Technology."

31 Benjamin, "The Work of Art in the Age of Its Technological Reproducibility: Second Version," 105.

32 Manovich, *The Language of New Media*, 114.

33 Rosen, *Change Mummified*, 314.

34 Ibid., 318–37.

35 Sobchack, *Carnal Thoughts*, 154.

36 Ibid., 158.

37 Mark Hansen, *New Philosophy for New Media*; Mark Hansen, *Bodies in Code*.

38 Both of Hansen's books are developed from the philosophy of Henri Bergson, recent work in neuroscience by Antonio Damasio, and the phenomenology of Maurice Merleau-Ponty. Instead of viewing new media as a forecast of the loss of the body to technologies of the virtual, Hansen adapts media artists Monika Fleischman and Wolfgang Strauss to understand how interactive media support the multisensory mechanisms of the body to extend the body's space for play and action. As analog media lose their material specificity—as photography, film, video, television, and telephone converge under the regime of the digital in the production of simulated worlds and bodies with which users interact—bodies do not lose embodiment and vision does not become abstracted from reality. Rather, vision becomes all the more haptic, all the more a product of sense making in the body.

39 Gillis, "Cybersex," 92.

40 Dyer, "Idol Thoughts," 49.

41 Linda Williams, *Hard Core*, 30; italics added.

42 Dyer, "Idol Thoughts," 49; italics added.

43 Dyer calls it *Ryan Idol: A Very Special View*, but I think this title is in error.

44 Gillis, "Cybersex," 92.

45 Ibid., 95.

46 Ibid., 94.

47 Ibid., 95.

48 Ibid., 94.

49 Ibid., 97.

50 Ibid., 98.

51 In the 1999 conclusion to *Hard Core* I had argued that the kind of "busy," gamelike activities of the early CD-ROM games that involved "scoring" on virtual women by making them come before one's avatar did were entirely too busy for pleasure. Apparently I was not the only one to dislike those games. See my *Hard Core*, 307–14.

52 One further sign of the DVD's hubris is that it even released an R-rated version of itself the following year, as if it was such a well-made film that it could commercially flourish without the hard-core sex of its raison d'être. Where most DVDs of films often restore sexual materials censored to receive their R ratings, this porn film deleted sex in hopes that its special effects alone (sans sexual effects) might please. It was not enough.

53 See Lucas Mearian, "Porn Industry May Be Decider in Blu-ray, HD-DVD battle," www.macworld.com/article/50627/2006/05/pornhd.html (accessed 22 April 2008). It appears that Sony's Blu-ray has won the battle. See Dawn Chmielewski and Bruce Wallace, "Blu-ray winner KO in high-definition war," *Los Angeles Times*, www.latimes.com/business/la-fi-bluray20feb20,0,5286548.story (accessed 22 April 2008). Observations about how pornography has historically driven the invention of new media have become a truism in need of much more serious examination. Is it just that each new representational technology suddenly moves into pornography, or is it that pornographic content actually drives the invention? Joseph Slade, for example, writes that "the appeal of pornography—the need to represent and to enjoy those representations—quite literally drives the development of new media." However, his follow-up explanation simply indicates that pornography follows invention: "In previous ages, cave painting led to pictures of vaginas and penises, clay tablets to sexy cuneiform, printing to steamy typographies." These last examples seem tenuous. However, his more recent examples appear more convincing: "During the past two decades, erotic applications fueled the evolution of VCR's and computers." Slade, "Pornography in the Late Nineties," 9.

54 Chun notes that the cam.whores can sometimes choose what and when we see and they can sometimes even fake the illusion of performing in real time. See Chun, *Control and Freedom*, 283–90; Patterson, "Going Online," 112–16; Burgin, "Jenny's Room," 85.

55 Chun, *Control and Freedom*, 284.

56 Patterson, "Going Online," 112.

57 These Interactive Sex Simulators are in many ways similar to the CD-ROM games that I described in the epilogue to *Hard Core* and which I myself played very badly. The main difference is that the CD-ROMs were actual games that depended on the player bringing a woman to orgasm. My judgment of this game was that it was too busy—pitting game play against arousal. In my experience, frenzied game play did not lead to pleasure. See *Hard Core*, 280–316.

58 *User-player* is the term used by Kevin Wynter, whose enlightening essay, "Towards a Theory of Virtual Pornography," is an excellent discussion of phenomenology of this form.

59 Simulation in this case does not refer to non–hard-core sexual acts, as in R-rated films whose simulation avoids hard-core explicitness, but to hard-core simulation of the connection to the female porn body through the body of the avatar. In other words, what is simulated is not the sex, but the viewer-user's relation to it. The sex itself is quite explicit.

60 Sobchack, *Carnal Thoughts*, 154.

61 I am indebted to Ben Hadden for this handy term developed in his unpublished paper, "Sexual Effects."

62 Bukatman, "Artificial Infinite."

63 Recall that *Deep Throat* literalized the figures of speech of "bells ringing" and "rockets firing," and recall that the first episode of *Boys in the Sand* also packed a brief history of the sex scene up to the point of climax. Both films did so in a series of fast cuts, interspersed with the image of the ejaculating penis. In the case of *Behind the Green Door*, the "effect" is slow-motion, distorted, electronic sound and multicolored optical printing that creates a mirror image of the ejaculating penis.

64 Here we might recall that Alfred Kinsey embarked on his long career filming and screening sex to test his theory of how men ejaculated—in dribbles or with projecting force. As noted in chapter 4, Kinsey hired photographers to film three hundred men in New York City masturbating to ejaculation. After eventually collecting films of a thousand men masturbating, Kinsey concluded that in 73 percent of men ejaculate does not spurt but dribbles. Gathorne-Hardy, *Sex, the Measure of All Things*, 308; Kinsey et al., *Sexual Behavior in the Human Female*, 634.

65 This lack of wetness was much complained about by one online reviewer who complained that "it aint porn unless at the end someones gooey" (www .cduniverse.com/productinfo.ask?pid=1595258&style—ice&cart552730665; accessed October 6 2007). In general, computer-generated money shots were not appreciated by three out of five reviewers.

66 Hadden, "Sexual Effects."

67 Baudrillard, *Ecstasy of Communication*, 24.

68 Wynter, "Towards a Theory of Virtual Pornography," 21.

69 Ibid.

70 Mark Hansen, *Bodies in Code*, 5.

71 I am indebted to Lucy van de Wiel, whose unpublished paper, "*In Flagrante Delicto*: Pleasure in Visible Pleasure; The Coming Onscene of the Female Orgasm," not only pointed out the new "coming on/scene" of visible female orgasm but also offered a splendid analysis of its tactile dimensions.

72 *Second Life* is an Internet-based virtual world with over 6 million players. Players custom-build an avatar who then navigates this alternative universe, including buying property and having sex with other avatars.

73 The *New York Times* reports: "After years of essentially steady increases, sales and rentals of pornographic videos were $3.62 billion in 2006, down from $4.28 billion in 2005, according to estimates by AVN, an industry trade publication." This article reports that these recent developments offer an unusual twist on the usual Internet-transforms-industry story. Where the Internet immediately represented a challenge to the music and newspaper businesses, it initially was a boon to pornography, providing easy and anonymous access online. However, as high-speed Internet access has permitted individuals to download free movies and clips more quickly and has allowed amateurs to upload their own creations more easily, free Web sites have represented a serious challenge to the more commercial end of the industry. So while the porn industry proper makes approximately one thousand X-rated DVDs a month and has rarely lost money, for the first time this burgeoning growth is beginning to look like a glut with free sites proliferating. (Matt Richtel, "For Producers of Pornography Internet's Virtues Turn to Vices," A1, C9.) See also Jon Swartz, "Purveyors of porn scramble to keep up with Internet." According to Swartz, the trend described above continues. Sales of porn DVDs are rapidly declining.

74 Benjamin, "The Work of Art in the Age of Its Technological Reproducibility: Second Version," 105.

75 In *VirtuallyJenna* both the body of Jenna and that of my avatar—who can now be designed even as a woman—are animated beings, computer-generated "sexual effects." With whole-body sexual effects whose very features I can design and whose actions and settings I can choose, *VirtuallyJenna* gives me very precise control over all aspects of the sexual scene. In this game, I do not so much fuck Jenna through an avatar as move into and all around the fantasy scene of sex like a kind of exalted film director. I can, for example, choose to move a disembodied hand to stroke her body when she is alone or with the avatar.

76 This is what one of the Virtual Vixens of the earlier CD-ROM game says of herself: "I know I'm not a real woman. I'm just a pleasure matrix, a piece of ass in a software package." Qtd. in Linda Williams, *Hard Core*, 309.

77 Schauer, *Law of Obscenity*, 81.

78 Schauer, *Free Speech*, 181.

79 Ibid.

80 For example, one short-lived CD-ROM product, *The Virtual Sex Machine*, advertised in 2003, offered the experience of watching girls perform on the screen with the added attraction of a "Penis Stimulator Chamber" whose vibration and suction would presumably mimic the movements of the performer you choose on the screen. The salon.com reporter who described its effects noted, "Like a Godzilla movie where the Japanese mouths aren't quite in sync with the English words, the VSM wasn't quite in sync with [the woman's action] on the screen. She zigged, it zagged" (Mike Phillips, "My Date with the Virtual Sex Machine," archive .salon.com-sex/feature/2003/02/05/vsm/index_np.html, accessed 11 May 2007).

81 Manovich, *Language of New Media*, 110.

82 Manovich, *Language of New Media*, 115.

83 Juffer, *At Home with Pornography*, 51.

84 Linda Williams, *Hard Core*, 313.

85 Ibid.

86 Chun, *Control and Freedom*, 126–27.

87 Keenan, "Windows of Vulnerability," 133–34.

88 Ibid, 133.

bibliography

Affron, Charles. *Cinema and Sentiment*. Chicago: University of Chicago Press, 1982.

Alapack, Richard. "The Adolescent First Kiss." *Humanistic Psychologist*, no. 19 (1991): 48–67.

Allyn, David. *Make Love, Not War: The Sexual Revolution, an Unfettered History*. Boston: Little, Brown, 2000.

Althusser, Louis. "Ideology and Ideological State Apparatuses." In *Lenin and Philosophy*, trans. Ben Brewster, 170–86. New York: Monthly Review Press, 1971.

Andrew, Dudley. "Film and Society: Public Rituals and Private Space." In *Exhibition, the Film Reader*, ed. Ina Rae Hark, 161–72. New York: Routledge, 2001.

Andrews, Dave. *Soft in the Middle: The Contemporary Softcore Feature in Its Contexts*. Columbus: Ohio State University Press, 2006.

Apra, Adriano. *Andy Warhol: Four Silent Movies*. Rome: Minerva Pictures Group, 2004.

Ariès, Philippe, and André Béjin. *Western Sexuality: Practice and Precept in Past and Present Times*. Trans. Anthony Forster. Oxford: Blackwell, 1985.

Atkins, Thomas, ed. *Sexuality in the Movies*. New York: Da Capo, 1976.

Atkinson, Michael. *Blue Velvet*. London: British Film Institute, 1997.

Babitz, Eve. "Sex, Love, and Kisses." *Vogue*, February 1996, 160–61.

Balázs, Béla. *Theory of the Film*. Trans. Edith Bone. New York: Dover, 1970.

Balio, Tino, ed. *Grand Design: Hollywood as a Modern Business Enterprise 1930–1939*. New York: Charles Scribner's Sons, 1993.

Bancroft, John. *Human Sexuality and Its Problems*. Edinburgh: Churchill Livingston, 1989.

Barcan, Ruth. "In the Raw: 'Home-Made' Porn and Reality Genres." *Journal of Mundane Behavior* 3.1 (2002): 1–20.

Bataille, Georges. *Erotism: Death and Sensuality*. Trans. Mary Dalwood. San Francisco: City Lights, 1962.

Baudrillard, Jean. *The Ecstasy of Communication*. Ed. Sylvère Lotringer, trans. Bernard and Carolina Schutze. Brooklyn: Autonomedia, 1988.

Baudry, Jean-Louis. "The Apparatus: Metaphysical Approaches to the Impression of Reality Cinema." In *Narrative, Apparatus, Ideology*, ed. Philip Rosen, 299–318. New York: Columbia University Press, 1986.

Baudry, Patrick. *La pornographie et ses images*. Paris: Armand Colin, 1997.

Bazin, André. "Death Every Afternoon." In *Rites of Realism: Essays on Corporeal Cinema*, ed. Ivone Margulies, 27–31. Durham: Duke University Press, 2003.

———. "Marginal Notes on Eroticism in Cinema." In *What Is Cinema?* 2:169–75. Berkeley: University of California Press, 1971.

———. "What Do Critics Dream About?" In *The Films in My Life*, ed. François Truffaut, trans. Leonard Mayhew, 169–75. New York: Simon and Schuster, 1978.

Benjamin, Walter. "On the Mimetic Faculty." In *Reflections: Essays, Aphorisms, Autobiographical Writings*, 333–336. New York: Schocken, 1978.

———. "The Work of Art in the Age of Its Technological Reproducibility: Second Version." In *Selected Writings*, vol. 3, *1935–1938*, ed. Howard Eiland and Michael W. Jennings, trans. Edmond Jephcott and Harry Zohn, 101–33. Cambridge: Belknap, 1999.

Bennett, Lerone. "The Emancipation Orgasm: Sweetback in Wonderland." *Ebony*, September 1971, 107–18.

Berlant, Lauren, and Lisa Duggan. Introduction to *Our Monica, Ourselves: The Clinton Affair and the National Interest*, 1–6. New York: New York University Press, 2001.

Berlant, Lauren, and Michael Warner. "Sex in Public." In "Intimacy," ed. Berlant, special issue, *Critical Inquiry* 24.2 (1998): 547–66.

Bernstein, Matthew. *Controlling Hollywood: Censorship and Regulation in the Studio Era*. New Brunswick: Rutgers University Press, 1999.

Bersani, Leo. *The Freudian Body: Psychoanalysis and Art*. New York: Columbia University Press, 1986.

Bertolucci, Bernardo. *Bernardo Bertolucci's Last Tango in Paris*. New York: Dell, 1973.

Best, Stephen. *The Fugitive's Properties: Law and the Poetics of Possession*. Chicago: University of Chicago Press, 2004.

Bhabha, Homi K. *The Location of Culture*. New York: Routledge, 1994.

———. "The Other Question: The Stereotype and Colonial Discourse." In *The*

Sexual Subject: A Screen Reader in Sexuality, ed. Mandy Merck, 312–31. London: Routledge, 1992.

Black, Joel. *The Reality Effect: Film Culture and the Graphic Imperative*. New York: Routledge, 2002.

Blake, Robert. *Mary Queen of Scots: A Tragedy in Three Acts*. London: Simpkin, Marshall, 1894.

Blumenthall, Ralph. "Porno Chic." *New York Times Magazine*, 21 January 1973, 28–34.

Bornoff, Nicolas. *Pink Samurai: An Erotic Exploration of Japanese Society*. New York: Harper Collins, 1991.

Boulware, Jack. *Sex, American Style: An Illustrated Romp through the Golden Age of Heterosexuality*. Venice, Calif.: Feral House, 1997.

Bouras, James. "In the Realm of the Censors." *Film Comment*, no. 13 (1977): 32–33.

Brathwaite, Brenda. *Sex in Video Games*. Boston: Charles River Media, 2006.

Breton, André. *L'Amour Fou*. Paris: Gallimard, 1937.

Brown, James. "Lights, Camera, and Explicit Action." *Independent*, 13 May 2004, 6–7.

Browne, Nick. "Race: The Political Unconscious of American Film." *East-West Film Journal* 6.1 (1992): 5–16.

Bukatman, Scott. "The Artificial Infinite: On Special Effects and the Sublime." In *Alien Zone II: The Spaces of Science-Fiction Cinema*, ed. Annette Kuhn, 249–75. London: Verso, 1999.

Burch, Noël. *To the Distant Observer: Form and Meaning in the Japanese Cinema*. Rev. and ed. Annette Michelson. Berkeley: University of California Press, 1979.

Burger, John R. *One-Handed Histories: The Eroto-Politics of Gay Male Video Pornography*. New York: Harrington Park, 1995.

Burgin, Victor. "Jenny's Room: Exhibitionism and Solitude." *Critical Inquiry* 27:1 (2000): 77–99.

Butler, Heather. "What Do You Call a Lesbian with Long Fingers? The Development of Lesbian and Dyke Pornography." In *Porn Studies*, ed. Linda Williams, 167–97. Durham: Duke University Press, 2004.

Canby, Vincent. "Coming Home." *New York Times*, 16 February 1978, C20.

Cane, William. "Orbicularis Oris of the Face and Mouth." face-and-emotion.com/dataface/expression/orbicularis_oris.html (accessed 10 August 2003).

Cante, Rich, and Angelo Restivo. "The Cultural-Aesthetic Specificities of All-Male Moving-Image Pornography." In *Porn Studies*, ed. Linda Williams, 142–66. Durham: Duke University Press, 2004.

———. "The 'World' of All-Male Pornography: On the Public Place of Moving-Image Sex in the Era of Pornographic Transnationalism." In *More Dirty Looks: Gender, Pornography, and Power*, ed. Pamela Church Gibson, 110–26. London: British Film Institute, 2004.

Carpenter, Dale. "Colloquium: The Boundaries of Liberty After *Lawrence v. Texas*:

The Unknown Past of *Lawrence v. Texas*." *Michigan Law Review*, no. 102 (2004): 1464.

Cathers, Kirsten. "The Great Censorship Trials of Literature and Film in Postwar Japan, 1950–1983." Ph.D. diss., University of California, Berkeley, 2004.

Chaffin-Quiray, Garrett. "Identity Crisis and Sweetback's Bellyful of a Three-Day Watermelon Man." *Senses of Cinema* (March 2003). www.sensesofcinema.com/ contents/directors/03/van_peebles.html.

Chauncey, George. *Gay New York: Gender, Urban Culture and the Making of the Gay Male World, 1890–1940*. New York: Basic, 1994.

Chion, Michel. *Audio-Vision: Sound on Screen*. New York: Columbia University Press, 1994.

———. *David Lynch*. London: British Film Institute, 1995.

Chun, Wendy Hui Kyong. *Control and Freedom: Power and Paranoia in the Age of Fiber Optics*. Cambridge: MIT Press, 2006.

Clover, Carol J. *Men, Women, and Chain Saws: Gender in the Modern Horror Film*. Princeton: Princeton University Press, 1992.

Coleman, Horace. "Melvin Van Peebles." *Journal of Popular Culture*, no. 5 (1971): 368–84.

Comfort, Alex. *The Joy of Sex*. New York: Crown, 2002.

Constable, Liz. "Unbecoming Sexual Desires for Women Becoming Sexual Subjects." *MLN* 119, no. 4 (2004): 672–95.

Corliss, Richard. "In Defense of Dirty Movies." *Time*, 5 July 1999.

Corrigan, Timothy. *A Cinema without Walls*. New Brunswick: Rutgers University Press, 1991.

Courtney, Susan. *Hollywood's Fantasy of Miscegenation: Spectacular Narratives of Gender and Race, 1903–1967*. Princeton: Princeton University Press, 2005.

Coward, Rosalind. *Female Desires: How They Are Sought, Bought, and Packaged*. New York: Grove, 1985.

Cox, Jeremy. "Sex on the Brain." *Pajiba*, 21 October 2006, www.pajiba.com/ shortbus.htm.

Crary, Jonathan. *Techniques of the Observer: On Vision and Modernity in the Nineteenth Century*. Cambridge: MIT Press, 1990.

Cripps, Thomas. "*Sweet Sweetback's Baadasssss Song* and the Changing Politics of Genre Film." In *Close Viewings: An Anthology of New Film Criticism*, ed. Peter Lehman, 238–261. Tallahassee: Florida State University Press, 1990.

Cubitt, Sean. *Timeshift: On Video Culture*. London: Taylor and Francis, 1991.

Debord, Guy. *Society of the Spectacle*. Detroit: Black and Red, 1983.

Delaney, Samuel R. *Times Square Red, Times Square Blue*. New York: New York University Press, 1999.

D'Emilio, John, and Estelle Freedman. *Intimate Matters: A History of Sexuality in America*. New York: Harper and Row, 1988.

Denby, David. "The Current Cinema: Unsheltered Lives." *New Yorker*, 29 October 2001, 92–93.

Diamond, Jared. *Why Is Sex Fun? The Evolution of Human Sexuality*. London: Orion House, 1997.

D'Lugo, Marvin. "Post-nostalgia in Almodóvar's *La mala educación*: Written on the Body of Sara Montiel." In *All about Almodóvar*, ed. Brad Epps and Despina Kakoudaki. Minneapolis: University of Minnesota Press, forthcoming.

Doane, Mary Ann. "Film and the Masquerade: Theorizing the Female Spectator." *Screen* 23.3–4 (1982): 74–88.

Downs, Donald Alexander. *The New Politics of Pornography*. Chicago: University of Chicago Press, 1989.

Dudley, Andrew. "Film and Society: Public Rituals and Private Space." *East-West Film Journal* 1.1 (1986): 7–22.

Dyer, Richard. "Don't Look Now: The Male Pin-Up." In *The Sexual Subject: A Screen Reader in Sexuality*, ed. Mandy Merck, 261–64. London: Routledge, 1992.

———. "Idol Thoughts: Orgasm and Self-Reflexivity in Gay Pornography." In *More Dirty Looks: Gender, Pornography, and Power*, ed. Pamela Church Gibson, 102–9. London: British Film Institute, 2004.

———. *Now You See It: Studies on Lesbian and Gay Film*. New York: Routledge, 1990.

———. *White*. New York: Routledge, 1997.

Eco, Umberto. "Casablanca: Cult Movies and Intertextual Collage." In *Travels in Hyperreality: Essays*, 197–211. Trans. William Weaver. San Diego: Harcourt Brace Jovanovich, 1986.

Edelman, Lee. "Seeing Things: Representation, the Scene of Surveillance, and the Spectacle of Gay Male Sex." In *Inside/Out: Lesbian Theories, Gay Theories*, ed. Diana Fuss, 93–116. New York: Routledge, 1991.

Ellis, John. "On Pornography." In *The Sexual Subject: A Screen Reader in Sexuality*, ed. Mandy Merck, 146–70. London: Routledge, 1992.

Ericksen, Julia A., with Sally A. Steffen. *Kiss and Tell: Surveying Sex in the Twentieth Century*. Cambridge: Harvard University Press, 1999.

Escoffier, Jeffrey, ed. *Sexual Revolution*. New York: Thunder's Mouth, 2003.

Fagioli, Marco. *Shunga: The Erotic Art of Japan*. New York: St. Martin's, 1998.

Fanon, Franz. *Black Skin, White Masks*. Trans. Charles Lam Markmann. New York: Grove, 1967.

Feiffer, Jules. *San Francisco Chronicle*, 22 August 1971, Datebook.

Flint, David. *Babylon Blue: An Illustrated History of Adult Cinema*. London: Creation, 1998.

Fonda, Jane. *My Life So Far*. New York: Random House, 2005.

Foucault, Michel. *The History of Sexuality*. Vol. 3, *The Care of the Self*. Trans. Robert Hurley. New York: Pantheon, 1986.

———. *The History of Sexuality*. Vol. 2, *The Use of Pleasure*. Trans. Robert Hurley. New York: Pantheon, 1985.

———. *The History of Sexuality*. Vol. 1, *An Introduction*. Trans. Robert Hurley. New York: Pantheon, 1978.

Freedberg, David. *The Power of Images: Studies in the History and Theory of Response*. Chicago: University of Chicago Press, 1989.

Freud, Sigmund. "Analysis of a Phobia in a Five-Year-Old Boy." In *Standard Edition of the Complete Psychological Works*, 10:5–149. Ed. and trans. James Strachey. London: Hogarth, 1955.

———. "Fragment of an Analysis of a Case of Hysteria." In *Standard Edition of the Complete Psychological Works*, 7:7–112. Ed. and trans. James Strachey. London: Hogarth, 1955.

———. "From the History of an Infantile Neurosis." In *Standard Edition of the Complete Psychological Works*, 17:7–122. Ed. and trans. James Strachey. London: Hogarth, 1955.

———. "Screen Memories." In *Standard Edition of the Complete Psychological Works*, 3:315–16. Ed. and trans. James Strachey. London: Hogarth, 1955.

———. *Three Essays on the Theory of Sexuality*. Ed. and trans. James Strachey. New York: Basic, 2000.

———. "The Uncanny." In *Standard Edition of the Complete Psychological Works*, 17:217–56. Ed. and trans. James Strachey. London: Hogarth, 1955.

Friedberg, Anne. *The Virtual Window from Alberti to Microsoft*. Cambridge: MIT Press, 2006.

———. *Window Shopping: Cinema and the Postmodern*. Berkeley: University of California Press, 1993.

Gagnon, John H., and William Simon. *Sexual Conduct: The Social Sources of Human Sexuality*. Chicago: Aldine, 1973.

Gaines, Jane. "Competing Glances: Who Is Reading Robert Mapplethorpe's *Black Book*?" *New Formations*, no. 16 (1992): 24–39.

———. *Fire and Desire: Mixed-Race Movies in the Silent Era*. Chicago: University of Chicago Press, 2001.

Gallop, Jane, with Lauren Berlant. "Loose Lips." In *Our Monica, Ourselves: The Clinton Affair and the National Interest*, ed. Berlant and Lisa Duggan, 246–67. New York: New York University Press, 2001.

Gates, Henry Louis, Jr. "Jungle Fever; or, Guess Who's Not Coming to Dinner." In *Five for Five: The Films of Spike Lee*, ed. Spike Lee, 163–67. New York: First Glance, 1991.

Gathorne-Hardy, Jonathan. *Sex, the Measure of All Things: A Life of Alfred C. Kinsey*. Bloomington: Indiana University Press, 1998.

Giddens, Anthony. *The Transformation of Intimacy: Sexuality, Love, and Eroticism in Modern Societies*. Stanford: Stanford University Press, 1992.

Gifford, Barry. *The Devil Thumbs a Ride and Other Unforgettable Films*. New York: Grove, 1988.

Gillis, Stacy. "Cybersex." In *More Dirty Looks: Gender, Pornography, and Power*, ed. Pamela Church Gibson, 92–100. London: British Film Institute, 2004.

Gitlin, Todd. *Media Unlimited: How the Torrent of Images and Sounds Overwhelms Our Lives*. New York: Metropolitan, 2003.

Grindon, Leger. "In the Realm of the Censors: Cultural Boundaries and the Poetics of the Forbidden." In *Word and Image in Japanese Cinema*, ed. Dennis Washburn and Carole Cavanaugh, 293–317. Cambridge: Cambridge University Press, 2001.

Grundeman, Roy. *Andy Warhol's "Blow Job."* Philadelphia: Temple University Press, 2003.

Guerrero, Ed. *Framing Blackness: The African American Image in Film*. Philadelphia: Temple University Press, 1993.

Gunning, Tom. "An Aesthetic of Astonishment: Early Film and the (In)Credulous Spectator." In *Viewing Positions: Ways of Seeing Film*, ed. Linda Williams, 114–33. New Brunswick: Rutgers University Press, 1995.

———. "The Cinema of Attractions: Early Film, Its Spectator, and the Avant-Garde." In *Early Cinema: Space, Frame, Narrative*, ed. Thomas Elsaesser, with Adam Barker, 56–62. London: British Film Institute, 1990.

Hadden, Benjamin. "Sexual Effects: A Brief History of Special Effects Onscreen." Unpublished paper.

Hales, N. Katherine. *How We Became Posthuman: Virtual Bodies in Cybernetics, Literature, and Informatics*. Chicago: University of Chicago Press, 1999.

Hansen, Mark B. N. *Bodies in Code: Interfaces with Digital Media*. New York: Routledge, 2006.

———. *New Philosophy for New Media*. Cambridge: MIT Press, 2004.

Hansen, Miriam. "Benjamin and Cinema: Not a One-Way Street." *Critical Inquiry* 25.2 (1987): 306–43.

Haskell, Molly. Review of *Klute*. *Village Voice*, 15 July 1971, 55.

Heath, Stephen. *Questions of Cinema*. Bloomington: Indiana University Press, 1981.

Heim, Michael. *The Metaphysics of Virtual Reality*. New York: Oxford University Press, 1993.

Hickman, Tom. *The Sexual Century: How Private Passion Became a Public Obsession*. London: Carlton, 1999.

Hoberman, Jim. "Return to Normalcy." *Village Voice*, 22 Sept. 1986, 62.

Irigaray, Luce. *This Sex Which Is Not One*. Trans. Catherine Porter. Ithaca: Cornell University Press, 1985.

Ishii-Gonzales, Sam. "Mysteries of Love: Lynch's *Blue Velvet*/Freud's Wolf-Man." In *The Cinema of David Lynch*, ed. Erica Sheen and Annette Davison, 48–60. London: Wallflower, 2004.

Jacobs, Lea. *The Wages of Sin: Censorship and the Fallen Woman Film, 1928–1942*. Madison: University of Wisconsin Press, 1991.

James, David. *Allegories of Cinema: American Film in the Sixties*. Princeton: Princeton University Press, 1989.

————. "Rock and Roll in the Representation of the Invasion of Vietnam." *Representations*, no. 29 (1990): 78–98.

Jameson, Fredric. *Postmodernism; or, the Cultural Logic of Late Capitalism*. Durham: Duke University Press, 1991.

————. *Signatures of the Visible*. New York: Routledge, 1990.

JanMohamed, Abdul. "Sexuality on/of the Racial Border: Foucault, Wright, and the Articulation of Racialized Sexuality." In *Discourses of Sexuality*, ed. Donma Stanton, 94–116. Ann Arbor: University of Michigan Press, 1992.

Johnston, William. *Geisha, Harlot, Strangler, Star: A Woman, Sex, and Morality in Modern Japan*. New York: Columbia University Press, 2005.

Jones, James H. *Alfred C. Kinsey: A Public/Private Life*. New York: W. W. Norton, 1997.

Juffer, Jane. *At Home with Pornography: Women, Sex, and Everyday Life*. New York: New York University Press, 1998.

Kael, Pauline. "Blue Velvet." *New Yorker*, 22 Sept. 1986, 99.

————. *I Lost It at the Movies*. New York: Bantam, 1965.

————. *Kiss Kiss, Bang Bang*. New York: Bantam, 1969.

————. "Mythologizing the 60s: *Coming Home*." *New Yorker*, 20 Feb. 1978, 119.

————. "Pipe Dream." *New Yorker*, 3 July 1971, 40.

————. "Tango." *New Yorker*, 28 October 1972, 130–38.

Keenan, Thomas. "Windows of Vulnerability." In *The Phantom Public Sphere*, ed. Bruce Robbins, 121–41. Minneapolis: University of Minnesota Press, 1993.

Kendrick, Walter. *The Secret Museum: Pornography in Modern Culture*. New York: Viking, 1987.

Kennedy, Sean. "The Return of Free Love." *Advocate*, 24 October 2006.

Kincaid, James R. "It's Not about Sex." In *Our Monica, Ourselves: The Clinton Affair and the National Interest*, ed. Lauren Berlant and Lisa Duggan, 73–85. New York: New York University Press, 2001.

Kinder, Marsha. "Reinventing the Motherland: Almodóvar's Brain Dead Trilogy." *Journal of Spanish Cultural Studies*, no. 5 (2004): 245–60.

King, Geoff. *New Hollywood Cinema: An Introduction*. New York: Columbia University Press, 2002.

Kinsey, Alfred C., et al. *Sexual Behavior in the Human Female*. Philadelphia: W. B. Saunders, 1953.

Kinsey, Alfred C., Wardell B. Pomeroy, and Clyde E. Martin. *Sexual Behavior in the Human Male*. Philadelphia: W. B. Saunders, 1948.

Koch, Stephen. *Stargazer: The Life, World, and Films of Andy Warhol*. New York: Marion Boyars, 1991.

Koedt, Anne. "The Myth of the Vaginal Orgasm." In *Sexual Revolution*, ed. Jeffrey Escoffier, 100–110. New York: Thunder's Mouth, 2003.

Koestenbaum, Wayne. *Andy Warhol*. New York: Penguin, 2001.

Kracauer, Siegfried. *Theory of Film: The Redemption of Physical Reality*. Princeton: Princeton University Press, 1997.

Kristeva, Julia. "Ellipsis on Dread and the Specular Seduction." Trans. Dolores Burdick. In *Narrative, Apparatus, Ideology: A Film Theory Reader*, ed. Philip Rosen, 236–43. New York: Columbia University Press, 1986.

Lack, Russell. *Twenty Four Frames Under: A Buried History of Film Music*. London: Quartet, 1997.

Laplanche, Jean. *Jean Laplanche: Seduction, Translation, and the Drives*. Trans. Martim Stanton. London: Institute of Contemporary Arts, 1992.

———. *Life and Death in Psychoanalysis*. Trans. Jeffrey Mehlman. Baltimore: Johns Hopkins University Press, 1976.

Laplanche, Jean, and J. B. Pontalis. "Fantasy and the Origins of Sexuality." In *Formations of Fantasy*, ed. Victor Burgin, James Donald, and Cora Kaplan, 5–34. New York: Methuen, 1986.

———. *The Language of Psychoanalysis*. Trans. Donald Nicholson-Smith. New York: W. W. Norton, 1973.

Laqueur, Thomas. *Solitary Sex: A Cultural History of Masturbation*. New York: Zone, 2003.

Laumann, Edward O., et al. *The Social Organization of Sexuality: Sexual Practices in the United States*. Chicago: University of Chicago Press, 1994.

Lee, Nathan. "Shortbus." *Film Comment* (2006): 71.

Leff, Leonard J., and Jerold L. Simmons. *The Dame in the Kimono: Hollywood, Censorship, and the Production Code from the 1920s to the 1960s*. New York: Anchor, 1990.

Lehman, Peter. *Masculinity: Bodies, Movies, Culture*. New York: Routledge, 2001.

———. *Running Scared: Masculinity and the Representation of the Male Body*. Philadelphia: Temple University Press, 1993.

———, ed. *Close Viewings: An Anthology of New Film Criticism*. Tallahassee: Florida State University Press, 1990.

Lenne, Gerard. *Sex on the Screen: Eroticism in Film*. New York: St. Martin's, 1978.

Lev, Peter. *American Films of the 70s: Conflicting Visions*. Austin: University of Texas Press, 2000.

Lewis, Jon. *Hollywood v. Hard Core: How the Struggle over Censorship Saved the Modern Film Industry*. New York: New York University Press, 2000.

———. "Real Sex." Unpublished manuscript.

Loftus, David. *Watching Sex: How Men Really Respond to Pornography*. New York: Thunder's Mouth, 2003.

Luciano, Dana. "Love's Measures." GLQ 13.1 (2007): 107–8.

Luhmann, Niklas. *Love as Passion: The Codification of Intimacy*. Trans. Jeremy Gaines and Doris L. Jones. Stanford: Stanford University Press, 1998.

Lukacher, Ned. *Primal Scenes: Literature, Philosophy, and Psychoanalysis*. Ithaca: Cornell University Press, 1980.

Luker, Kristin. *When Sex Goes to School: Warring Views on Sex—and Sex Education—Since the Sixties*. New York: W. W. Norton, 2006.

MacDonald, Scott. "Confessions of a Feminist Porn Watcher." *Film Quarterly* 36.3 (1983): 10–17.

Macey, David. *The Lives of Michel Foucault*. New York: Vintage, 1993.

MacKendrick, Karmen. *Counterpleasures*. Albany: State University of New York Press, 1999.

Mailer, Norman. "A Transit to Narcissus." In *Last Tango in Paris*, by Bernardo Bertolucci and Franco Arcalli, 203. New York: Delacorte, 1972.

Maltby, Richard. *Hollywood Cinema*. Oxford: Oxford University Press, 1995.

———. "More Sinned Against than Sinning: The Fabrications of 'Pre-Code Cinema.'" *Senses of Cinema* 29 (2003). www.sensesofcinema.com/contents/03/29/pre_code_cinema.html.

Manovich, Lev. *The Language of New Media*. Cambridge: MIT Press, 2002.

Marcus, Steven. *The Other Victorians: A Study of Sexuality and Pornography in Mid-Nineteenth Century England*. New York: New American Library, 1974.

Marcuse, Herbert. *Eros and Civilization: A Philosophical Inquiry into Freud*. New York: Vintage, 1955.

Marks, Laura. *Touch: Sensuous Theory and Multisensory Media*. Minneapolis: University of Minnesota Press, 2002.

Masters, William, and Virginia Johnson. *Human Sexual Response*. New York: Bantam, 1966.

Mayne, Judith. "Uncovering the Female Body." In *Before Hollywood: Turn-of-the-Century Film from American Archives*, ed. Jay Leyda and Charles Musser, 63–68. New York: American Federation of the Arts, 1986.

McCarthy, Todd. "Shortbus." *Variety* 403, no. 2 (2006): 33–34.

McClintock, Ann. "Gonad the Barbarian and the Venus Flytrap: Portraying the Female and Male Orgasm." In *Sex Exposed: Sexuality and the Pornography Debate*, ed. Lynne Segal and Mary McIntosh, 111–31. London: Virago, 1992.

McCormick, Ruth. "An Interview with Nagisa Oshima," *Cineaste* 4, no. 2 (1976–77): 34–35.

———. "*In the Realm of the Senses*." *Cineaste* 4, no. 2 (1976–77): 32–34.

McMillan, Terry. "Thoughts on *She's Gotta Have It*." In *Five for Five: The Films of Spike Lee*, ed. Spike Lee, 19–29. New York: First Glance, 1991.

McNair, Brian. *Striptease Culture: Sex, Media, and the Democratization of Desire*. London: Routledge, 2002.

Mellen, Joan. *In the Realm of the Senses*. London: British Film Institute, 2004.

———. "Is *Senses* in the Realm of Pornography?" *New York Times*, 31 July 1977, B1.

Mendelsohn, Daniel. "An Affair to Remember." *New York Review of Books*, 23 Feb 2006, 12–13.

Mercer, Kobena. "Imaging the Black Man's Sex." In *Photography/Politics: Two*, ed. Pat Holland, Jo Spence, and Simon Watney, trans. Carleton Dallevy, 61–69. London: Comedia/Methuen, 1987.

———. "Skin Head Sex Thing: Racial Difference and the Homoerotic Imaginary."

In *How Do I Look? Queer Film and Video*, ed. Bad Object-Choices, 169–222. Seattle: Bay, 1991.

———. *Welcome to the Jungle: New Positions in Black Cultural Studies*. New York: Routledge, 1994.

Merck, Mandy. *In Your Face: Nine Sexual Studies*. New York: New York University Press, 2000.

———, ed. *The Sexual Subject: A Screen Reader in Sexuality*. London: Routledge, 1992.

Merleau-Ponty, Maurice. "Eye and Mind." In *The Primacy of Perception*, ed. James M. Edie, 159–90. Evanston: Northwestern University Press, 1964.

———. *The Phenomenology of Perception*. Trans. C. Smith. London: Routledge, 1982.

Metz, Christian. *Film Language: A Semiotics of Cinema*. Trans. Michael Taylor. New York: Oxford University Press, 1974.

———. *The Imaginary Signifier: Psychoanalysis and Cinema*. Trans. Celia Britton et al. London: Macmillan, 1982.

Miller, D. A. "On the Universality of *Brokeback Mountain*." *Film Quarterly* 60.3 (2007): 50–81.

Miller, Toby. "The First Penis Impeached." In *Our Monica, Ourselves: The Clinton Affair and the National Interest*, ed. Lauren Berlant and Lisa Duggan, 116–33. New York: New York University Press, 2001.

Miller, William Ian. *The Anatomy of Disgust*. Cambridge: Harvard University Press, 1997.

Mitchell, W. J. T. *What Do Pictures Want?* Chicago: University of Chicago Press, 2005.

Mohr, Ian. "*Shortbus* on Low-Key Ride." *Variety*, 5 October 2006.

Mohr, Richard D. *Gays/Justice: A Study of Ethics, Society, and Law*. New York: Columbia University Press, 1988.

Monaco, Paul. *The Sixties: 1960–1969*. Berkeley: University of California Press, 2001.

Mulvey, Laura. "Netherworlds and the Unconscious: Oedipus and *Blue Velvet*." In *Fetishism and Curiosity*, 137–154. Bloomington: Indiana University Press, 1996.

———. "Visual Pleasure and Narrative Cinema." *Screen* 16.3 (1975): 6–18.

Murray, Jacqueline, ed. *Constructing Sexualities*. Windsor, Ont.: Humanities Research Group, University of Windsor, 1993.

Musser, Charles. *The Emergence of Cinema: The American Screen to 1907*. New York: Scribner's, 1990.

———. "The May Irwin Kiss: Performance and the Beginnings of Cinema." In *Visual Delights Two: Exhibition and Reception*, ed. Vanessa Toulmin and Simon Popple, 98–115. London: John Libbey, 2005.

———. *Thomas A. Edison and His Kinetographic Motion Pictures*. New York: Scribner's, 1995.

Neale, Steve. "Masculinity as Spectacle." In *The Sexual Subject: A Screen Reader in Sexuality*, ed. Mandy Merck, 277–87. London: Routledge, 1992.

———. "The Same Old Story: Stereotypes and Difference." *Screen Education*, no. 33 (1979): 80.

Newton, Huey P. "He Won't Bleed Me: A Revolutionary Analysis of *Sweet Sweetback's Baadasssss Song*." *Black Panther Party Intercommunal News Service*, 19 June 1971.

Oshima, Nagisa. *Cinema, Censorship, and the State: The Writings of Nagisa Oshima*. Cambridge: MIT Press, 1992.

Osterweil, Ara. "Andy Warhol's *Blow Job*: Toward the Recognition of a Pornographic Avant-Garde." In *Porn Studies*, ed. Linda Williams, 431–60. Durham: Duke University Press, 2004.

———. "Flesh Cinema: The Corporeal Avant-Garde, 1959–1979." Ph.D. diss., University of California, Berkeley, 2005.

O'Toole, Laurence. *Pornocopia: Porn, Sex, Technology, and Desire*. London: Serpent's Tail, 1998.

Patterson, Zabet. "Going Online: Consuming Pornography in the Digital Era." In *Porn Studies*, ed. Linda Williams, 104–23. Durham: Duke University Press, 2004.

Paul, Pamela. *Pornified: How Pornography Is Transforming Our Lives, Our Relationships, and Our Families*. New York: Times, 2005.

Peavy, Charles. "An Afro-American in Paris: The Films of Melvin Van Peebles." *Cineaste* 3, no. 1 (1969): 2–3.

Petersen, James R., ed. *The Century of Sex: Playboy's History of the Sexual Revolution; 1900–1999*. New York: Grove, 1999.

Petro, Patrice. *Fugitive Images: From Photography to Video*. Bloomington: Indiana University Press, 1995.

Phillips, Adam. *On Kissing, Tickling, and Being Bored*. Cambridge: Harvard University Press, 1993.

Pomeroy, Wardell B. *Dr. Kinsey and the Institute for Sex Research*. New York: Harper and Row, 1972.

———. *Taking a History*. New York: Free Press, 1961.

Poole, Wakefield. *Dirty Poole: The Autobiography of a Gay Porn Pioneer*. Los Angeles: Alyson, 2000.

Porton, Richard. "Elusive Intimacy: An Interview with Patrice Chéreau." *Cineaste* 27.1 (2001): 18–25.

Poster, Mark. *What's the Matter with the Internet?* Minneapolis: University of Minnesota Press, 2001.

Potts, Annie. *The Science/Fiction of Sex: Feminist Deconstruction and the Vocabularies of Heterosex*. New York: Routledge, 2002.

Prince, Stephen. *A New Pot of Gold: Hollywood under the Electronic Rainbow, 1980–1989*. Berkeley: University of California Press, 2000.

———. "True Lies: Perceptual Realism, Digital Images, and Film Theory." *Film Quarterly* 49.3 (1996): 27–37.

Proulx, Annie. *Brokeback Mountain*. New York: Scribner's, 2000.

Proust, Marcel. *The Guermantes Way*. Trans. C. K. Scott Moncrieff. New York: Modern Library, 1933.

Rayns, Tony. "Death at Work: Evolution and Entropy in Factory Films." In *Andy Warhol: Film Factory*, ed. Michael O'Pray, 160–69. London: British Film Institute, 1989.

———. "An Interview with Nagisa Oshima." *Film Comment* (1976): 34–38.

Reich, Wilhelm. *The Sexual Revolution: Toward a Self-Governing Character Structure*. New York: Farrar, Straus and Giroux, 1935/1951.

Reisman, Judith. *Crafting 'Gay' Children*. www.rsvpamerica.org/

Rembar, Charles. *The End of Obscenity: The Trials of "Lady Chatterley," "Tropic of Cancer," and "Fanny Hill."* New York: Random House, 1969.

The Report of the Commission on Obscenity and Pornography. New York: Bantam, 1970.

Rich, B. Ruby. "Hello Cowboy." *Guardian*, 23 September 2005.

Rich, Frank. "Naked Capitalists." *New York Times Magazine*, 20 May 2001, 51–56, 80–82, 92.

Robinson, Paul. "The Case for Dr. Kinsey." *Atlantic Monthly*, May 1972, 99–102.

———. *The Modernization of Sex: Havelock Ellis, Alfred Kinsey, William Masters, and Virginia Johnson*. Ithaca: Cornell University Press, 1989.

Rodley, Chris, ed. *Lynch on Lynch*. London: Faber and Faber, 1997.

Rosello, Mireille. *Declining the Stereotype: Ethnicity and Representation in French Cultures*. Hanover: University Press of New England, 1998.

Rosen, Philip. *Change Mummified: Cinema, Historicity, Theory*. Minneapolis: University of Minnesota Press, 2001.

Roszak, Theodore. *Flicker*. Chicago: Chicago Review, 1991.

Roth, Philip. *American Pastoral*. New York: Vintage, 1997.

———. *The Dying Animal*. New York: Vintage, 2001.

Rotsler, William. *Contemporary Erotic Cinema*. New York: Ballantine, 1973.

Rubin, Gayle. "Thinking Sex: Notes for a Radical Theory of the Politics of Sexuality." In *Pleasure and Danger: Exploring Female Sexuality*, ed. Carole S. Vance, 267–319. London: Routledge and Kegan Paul, 1984.

Rubin, Jay. *Injurious to Public Morals: Writers and the Meiji State*. Seattle: University of Washington Press, 1984.

Russell, Catherine. *Narrative Mortality: Death, Closure, and New Wave Cinema*. Minneapolis: University of Minnesota Press, 1994.

Russo, Vito. *The Celluloid Closet: Homosexuality in the Movies*. New York: Harper and Row, 1981.

Rutherford, Anne. "Cinema and Embodied Affect." *Senses of Cinema*, no. 25 (2003).

Sade, Marquis de. *Justine, Philosophy in the Bedroom, and Other Writings*. Trans. Richard Seaver and Austryn Wainhouse. New York: Grove, 1965.

St. John, Maria. "How to Do Things with the *Starr Report*: Pornography, Performance, and the President's Penis." In *Porn Studies*, ed. Linda Williams, 27–49. Durham: Duke University Press, 2004.

———. "The Mammy Fantasy: Psychoanalysis, Race, and the Ideology of Absolute Maternity." Ph.D. diss., University of California, Berkeley, 2004.

Schaefer, Eric. *Bold! Daring! Shocking! True! A History of Exploitation Films, 1919–1959*. Durham: Duke University Press, 1999.

———. "Does She or Doesn't She?" Unpublished paper, delivered at the Society for Cinema and Media Studies Conference. Denver, Colorado, 24 May 2002.

———. "Gauging a Revolution: 16mm Film and the Rise of the Pornographic Feature." In *Porn Studies*, ed. Linda Williams, 370–400. Durham: Duke University Press, 2004.

Schauer, Frederick F. *Free Speech: A Philosophical Enquiry*. Cambridge: Cambridge University Press, 1982.

———. *The Law of Obscenity*. Washington: Bureau of National Affairs, 1976.

Schlosser, Eric. *Reefer Madness: Sex, Drugs, and Cheap Labor in the American Black Market*. New York: Houghton Mifflin, 2003.

Schneider, Steven Jay. "The Essential Evil in/of *Eraserhead* (or, Lynch to the Contrary)." In *The Cinema of David Lynch: American Dream, Nightmare Visions*, ed. Erica Sheen and Annette Davison, 5–18. London: Wallflower, 2004.

Seaman, Barbara. "Is Woman Insatiable?" In *Free and Female: The Sex Life of the Contemporary Woman*. New York: Fawcett, 1972.

Sedgwick, Eve Kosofsky. *Epistemology of the Closet*. Berkeley: University of California Press, 1990.

Segal, Lynne. *Straight Sex: Rethinking the Politics of Pleasure*. Berkeley: University of California Press, 1994.

Segal, Lynne, and Mary McIntosh, eds. *Sex Exposed: Sexuality and the Pornography Debate*. London: Virago, 1992.

Shamus, James, Joel Conarroe, and Daniel Mendelsohn. "*Brokeback Mountain*: An Exchange." *New York Review of Books*, 6 April 2006, 1–4.

Shattuc, Jane. "Postmodern Misogyny in *Blue Velvet*." *Genders*, no. 13 (1992): 73–89.

Sherfey, Mary Jane. "A Theory on Female Sexuality." In *Sexual Revolution*, ed. Jeffrey Escoffier, 91–99. New York: Thunder's Mouth, 2003.

Shipman, David. *Caught in the Act: Sex and Eroticism in the Movies*. London: Elm Tree, 1985.

Slade, Joseph W. *Pornography and Sexual Representation: A Reference Guide*. 3 vols. Westport: Greenwood, 2001.

———. "Pornography in the Late Nineties." *Wide Angle* 19.3 (1997): 1–12.

Smith, Jeff. *The Sounds of Commerce: Marketing Popular Film Music.* New York: Columbia University Press, 1998.

Smith, Paul Julian. *Desire Unlimited: The Cinema of Pedro Almodóvar.* New York: Verso, 2000.

Smith, Richard. *Getting into "Deep Throat."* Chicago: Playboy, 1973.

Sobchack, Vivian. *The Address of the Eye: A Phenomenology of Film Experience.* Princeton: Princeton University Press, 1992.

———. *Carnal Thoughts: Embodiment and Moving Image Culture.* Berkeley: University of California Press, 2004.

Sontag, Susan. *Georges Bataille: Story of the Eye.* New York: Penguin, 1986.

Southern, Terry. *Blue Movie.* New York: Grove, 1970.

Stam, Robert. *Film Theory: An Introduction.* Malden, Mass.: Blackwell, 2000.

Steiner, George. "Night Words." In *Language and Silence: Essays on Language, Literature, and the Inhuman,* 68–77. New York: Atheneum, 1967.

Stern, Lesley. "The Body as Evidence." In *The Sexual Subject: A Screen Reader in Sexuality,* ed. Mandy Merck, 197–222. London: Routledge, 1992.

Stevenson, Jack. *Dogme Uncut: Lars von Trier, Thomas Vinterberg, and the Gang That Took Hollywood.* Santa Monica: Santa Monica Press, 2003.

———. *Lars von Trier.* London: British Film Institute, 2002.

———. *Totally Uncensored! The Wild World of Scandinavian Sex Cinema: The Myth, the Movies, the Happenings.* Forthcoming.

Stewart, Jacqueline. *Migrating to the Movies: Cinema and Black Urban Modernity.* Berkeley: University of California Press, 2005.

Straus, Gary. "Cellphone Technology Rings in Pornography in USA." *USA Today.* www.usatoday.com/tech/products/services/2005-12-12-pornography-cellphones_x.htm (accessed 22 April 2008).

Swan, Rachel. "Perversions in the Limelight: Weird Sex and Spanishness in the Films of Pedro Almodóvar." Honors Thesis, University of California, Berkeley, 2003.

Swartz, Jon. "Purveyors of porn scramble to keep up with Internet." www.usatoday.com/tech/techinvestor/industry/2007-06-05-internet-porn_N.htm (accessed 21 May 2008).

Taruskin, Richard. "A Myth of the Twentieth Century: The Rite of Spring, the Tradition of the New, and 'The Music Itself.'" *Modernism/Modernity* 2.1 (1995): 1–26.

Taussig, Michael. *Mimesis and Alterity: A Particular History of the Senses.* New York: Routledge, 1993.

Thompson, Bill. *Soft Core: Moral Crusades against Pornography in Britain and America.* London: Cassell, 1994.

Thompson, David. *Last Tango in Paris.* London: British Film Institute, 1998.

Torres, Sasha. "Sex of a Kind: On Graphic Language and the Modesty of Television News." In *Our Monica, Ourselves: The Clinton Affair and the National Interest,* ed. Lauren Berlant and Lisa Duggan, 102–15. New York: New York University Press, 2001.

Truffaut, François, ed. *The Films in My Life*. Trans. Leonard Mayhew. New York: Simon and Schuster, 1978.

Turan, Kenneth, and Stephen Zito. *Sinema: American Pornographic Films and the People Who Make Them*. New York: Praeger, 1974.

Turim, Maureen. *The Films of Oshima Nagisa: Images of a Japanese Iconoclast*. Berkeley: University of California Press, 1998.

Updike, John. *Couples*. New York: Ballantine, 1968.

Van de Wiel, Lucy. "*In Flagrante Delicto*: Pleasure in Visible Pleasure: The Coming Onscene of Female Orgasm." Unpublished paper (May 2007).

Van Peebles, Melvin. *Sweet Sweetback's Baadasssss Song: A Guerilla Filmmaking Manifesto*. New York: Thunder's Mouth, 2004.

Voltaire. *The Philosophical Dictionary*. Trans. H. I. Woolf. New York: Alfred A. Knopf, 1924.

Warhol, Andy. *The Philosophy of Andy Warhol: From A to B and Back Again*. New York: Harcourt Brace Jovanovich, 1975.

Warner, Michael. *The Trouble with Normal: Sex, Politics, and the Ethics of Queer Life*. Cambridge: Harvard University Press, 1999.

Waugh, Thomas. "Cockteaser." In *Pop Out: Queer Warhol*, ed. Jennifer Doyle, Jonathan Flatley, and José Esteban Muñoz, 51–77. Durham: Duke University Press, 1996.

———. *Hard to Imagine: Gay Male Eroticism in Photography and Film from Their Beginnings to Stonewall*. New York: Columbia University Press, 1996.

———. "Homosociality in the Classical American Stag Film: Off-Screen, On-Screen." In *Porn Studies*, ed. Linda Williams, 127–41. Durham: Duke University Press, 2004.

Weitzer, Ronald, ed. *Sex for Sale: Prostitution, Pornography, and the Sex Industry*. New York: Routledge, 2000.

West, Joan, and Dennis West. "MPAA Ratings, Black Holes, and My Film: An Interview with Kirby Dick." *Cineaste* 23.1 (2006): 14–37.

Willeman, Paul. "Letter to John." In *The Sexual Subject: A Screen Reader in Sexuality*, ed. Mandy Merck, 171–83. London: Routledge, 1992.

Williams, Linda. "Cinema and the Sex Act." *Cineaste* 27.1 (2001): 20–25.

———. "Corporealized Observers: Visual Pornography and the 'Carnal Density of Vision.'" In *Fugitive Images: From Photography to Video*, ed. Patrice Petro, 3–41. Bloomington: Indiana University Press, 1995.

———. "Film Bodies: Gender, Genre, and Excess." *Film Quarterly* 44, no. 4 (1991): 2–13.

———. *Hard Core: Power, Pleasure, and the "Frenzy of the Visible."* Exp. ed. Berkeley: University of California Press, 1999.

———. "Melancholy Melodrama." In *All about Almodóvar*, ed. Brad Epp and Despina Kakoudaki. Minneapolis: University of Minnesota Press, forthcoming.

———. *Playing the Race Card: Melodramas of Black and White from Uncle Tom to O. J. Simpson*. Princeton: Princeton University Press, 2001.

———. "Pornographies On/scene; or, 'Diff'rent Strokes for Diff'rent Folks.'" In *Sex Exposed: Sexuality and the Pornography Debate*, ed. Lynne Segal and Mary McIntosh, 233–65. London: Virago, 1992.

———. "Second Thoughts on Hard Core: American Obscenity Law and the Scapegoating of Deviance." In *Dirty Looks: Women, Pornography, Power*, ed. Pamela Church Gibson and Roma Gibson, 46–61. London: British Film Institute, 1993.

———, "Skin Flicks on the Racial Border: Pornography, Exploitation, and Interracial Lust." In *Porn Studies*, ed. Linda Williams. Durham: Duke University Press, 2004.

———. ed. *Porn Studies*. Durham: Duke University Press, 2004.

Williams, Linda Ruth. "The Edge of the Razor." *Sight and Sound* 9.10 (1999): 12–14.

———. *The Erotic Thriller in Contemporary Cinema*. Bloomington: Indiana University Press, 2005.

Williams, Raymond. *Television: Technology and Cultural Form*. New York: Schocken, 1975.

Williamson, Bruce. "Porno Chic." In *Flesh and Blood: The National Society of Film Critics on Sex, Violence, and Censorship*, ed. Peter Keough, 10–27. San Francisco: Mercury House, 1995.

Winnicott, D. W. *Playing and Reality*. New York: Routledge, 1971.

———. "Transitional Objects and Transitional Phenomena." *International Journal of Psycho-Analysis* 34: 89–97.

Wirenius, John F. *First Amendment, First Principles: Verbal Acts and Freedom of Speech*. New York: Holmes and Meier, 2000.

Wood, Robin. "On and around *Brokeback Mountain*." *Film Quarterly* 60.3 (2007): 28–31.

Wrenn, Mike. *Andy Warhol: In His Own Words (In Their Own Words)*. London: Omnibus, 1991.

Wyatt, Justin. "The Stigma of X: Adult Cinema and the Institution of the MPAA Ratings System." In *Controlling Hollywood: Censorship and Regulation in the Studio Era*, ed. Matthew Bernstein, 238–64. New Brunswick: Rutgers University Press, 1999.

Wynter, Kevin. "Towards a Theory of Virtual Pornography." *CineAction* 72 (2007): 16–22.

Zimmer, Catherine. "Long Live the New Flesh: Embodied Perception and the Video Image." Ph.D. diss., University of California, Berkeley, 2003.

Ziplow, Stephen. *The Film Maker's Guide to Pornography*. New York: Drake, 1977.

Zurier, Rebecca. "City, Stage, and Screen: Joan Sloan's Urban Theater." In *On the Edge of Your Seat: Popular Theater and Film in Early Twentieth-Century American Art*, ed. Patricia McDonnell, 175–88. New Haven: Yale University Press, 2002.

Index

mutual sexual pleasure, 130, 138, 140; prurient interest in, 122–24; avoidance of female genitalia, 137, 141, 155; in contrast to *In the Realm of the Senses*, 187, 206, 210; cultural legitimacy of, 145, 236; always-bedtime atmosphere in, 150; humor in, 131; cost and gross, 351n86

Deliverance (dir. John Boorman), 237

deep throat fellatio: as a means to orgasm, 125, 133, 136, 288; *Deep Throat* visuals, 126, 134, 194; as a cure, 131, 155; as an obscene sexual practice, 138

Demme, Jonathan, 235–36

Denby, David, 270

Dern, Laua, 234–35

desire, 40, 42, 56, 118, 122, 132, 150, 154, 157, 177, 206, 211–12, 219, 227, 235, 255–56, 272, 274, 276, 278, 280, 282, 291–92

Despentes, Virginie and Coralie Trinh, 296

Devil and Miss Jones, The (dir. Gerard Damiano), 199

Dietrich, Marlene, 50

discharge, 46, 48, 122, 132–34, 139, 142, 177, 205–6, 212

disgust, 30, 108, 132, 136–38, 140, 276–77, 301

Dogme 95, 266–67, 270

Don't Look Now (dir. Nicholas Roeg), 87–88, 182

Donovan, Casey (in *Boys in the Sand*), 145–54

Douglas, Melvin, 51–53

drinking, 53, 56, 59, 61, 191, 201

Ducey, Caroline, 276–78, 283, 295

Dyer, Richard, 36, 145, 311–12, 319

eating, 53–54, 131–32, 191, 201, 265

ecstasy, 115, 117, 319

Ecstasy (dir. Gustave Machaty), 114

Edelman, Lee, 241–42

Edison, Thomas: screened kisses produced by, 19, 33, 62–63, 126, 300, 326; development of shorts for exhibition, 26–27; introduction of new screened sex acts, 28, 65

Eisen, Keisai, 196–97

ellipses, 26, 38–40, 42, 50, 59, 73, 79, 81–82, 109, 123, 148, 172, 178, 260, 282

emasculation, 242, 247–48

emotion, 120, 122–23, 130, 244, 273, 275, 282, 290, 295–96, 298, 301

emotional intimacy, 243, 252–53

Ephron, Nora, 125

erotic art, 130, 142, 181, 186, 190, 197–98, 201

erotic fantasy, 150, 153, 275

eroticism, 15, 33–34, 66, 115, 118–19, 121, 130, 132, 150, 161, 173, 182, 184, 190, 196, 200, 205, 212, 256, 271, 273, 304, 309, 314, 326

Esa mujer (dir. Mario Camus), 301–2

Escoffier, Jeffrey, 8, 327n4

European influence, 178, 180, 184, 284

European screen sexuality, 165, 221

European sophistication, 114, 121

Execution of Mary, Queen of Scots, The (dir. Thomas Edison), 63–65, 336n75

Experimental Cinema Group, 104

explicit sex acts, 281–84, 295, 298

explicit sexual content, 105, 260, 296

"Exsexive Machine": as sex tool, 170; crescendo of pleasure, 167–69, 174, 200

Eyes Wide Shut (dir. Stanley Kubrick), 283

face of orgasm, 169, 175, 292, 336n80

Fanon, Franz, 153

fantasy, 72, 151, 201, 206, 213, 225–26, 229, 233, 235–36, 246–47, 292, 309, 311, 313, 319

Fassbinder, Rainer Werner, 238

Fat Girl (dir. Catherine Breillat): sex as humiliation, 278; sexual explicitness, 275; virginity in, 279–83

fear, 42, 120, 122–23, 131–32, 153, 172, 179, 211, 227, 234, 238, 255–56, 280, 284

feature-length pornography, 120, 127–28, 136, 145

Feiffer, Jules, 77

fellatio: in *Boys in the Sand*, 146–48, 151–52; in *Deep Throat*, 120–21, 132; demand for visibility of, 129, 284; initial shock of screening, 136–37; innocence of, 140–41; in *In the Realm of the Senses*, 193–94; maintaining virginity through recourse to, 127; as sex, 137; in *Blue Velvet*, 229; in gay pornography, 349n53; link to resurrection of condom, 350n70; *See also* deep-throat fellatio; *See also* autofellatio

female carnal knowledge, 163

female genitalia, 137–38, 232–33

female orgasm: depiction of, 155–56, 163, 165, 169–73, 199–200, 320; on the Internet, 320–21; rapid return, 354n24

female pleasure, 155–56, 168, 170, 173, 178, 201

feminism, 10, 125, 162–63, 167–68, 180, 199, 283

feminist critique, 171, 176, 218

fetishism, 153, 224, 227, 230–33, 251–52, 314

Fisk, Peter, 145

flesh, 89, 204, 206, 276, 283

Flesh and the Devil (dir. Clarence Brown): orality in, 44–46, 50; perverse pleasures in, 47–48; Garbo's kisses in, 49

Fonda, Jane: as critic of phallocentric sex, 163, 166, 176, 180; mediated public life of, 164, 174–75, 355n34; real orgasms of, 165, 167–70, 174–75; faked orgasms of, 171, 173; sexual performance of, 172, 179, 182; sexual transformation of, 177

Foucault, Michel: *ars erotica*, 195, 198, 360nn38–39; historical constructions of sexuality, 12–13, 241; implantation of perversions, 137–38, 236; role of confessional in constructing the truth of sex, 219, 319–20; focus on sexual acts, 15; discipline into arousal, 18; discourse and power, 144

foreign film, 68, 73, 89, 98, 114, 121, 128, 298

foreplay, 26, 48, 148

Fox, Kerry, 270–74

Foxy Brown (dir. Jack Hill), 93

Freedman, Estelle. *See* D'Emilio, John and Estelle Freedman

French influence, 183, 188, 212, 238, 278, 295

French New Wave, 79, 186

Freud, Sigmund: infantile orality, 46–48, 139–41, 333n40, 351n83; telos of sex and violence, 65, 122, 133, 142, 205–6; civilization's inherent repression of sex, 12, 157–58; primal scenes and fantasies, 72, 225, 241; use of the term 'perversion', 14, 74; on screen memories, 70, 336n2; on clitoral vs. vaginal orgasm, 139, 162; case study of the "Wolf Man", 226, 337n3; digestive orality, 61; motivating force of sexuality, 113; the uncanny, 232–34

Friedberg, Anne, 299, 322

From Here to Eternity (dir. Fred Zinneman), 34, 41

Fuji, Tatsuya, 210, 214; *See also* Ishida, Kichizo

Fugitive Kind, The (dir. Stanley Kramer), 92–93

full frontal nudity, 85, 98

Gaines, Jane, 31

Gal, Susan, 10

Gallo, Vincent, 284

Game Is Over, The (dir. Roger Vadim), 165

Holmes, John, 195

Home of the Brave (dir. Stanley Kramer), 101

home video: revolution, 143, 222, 306, 308; viewing, 300, 309; technology, 164; successful marketing of X-rated material, 373n18

home, 231–33, 248, 257–58, 298, 300

homme facile, L', (writ. Catherine Breillat), 275

homoeroticism, 85, 238, 288

homophobia, 238, 241, 247

homosexual desire, 238, 242–43, 246–47, 249, 254

Hopper, Dennis, 216, 226, 230–31, 233–36, 242, 251

Human Sexual Response (writ. Masters and Johnson), 162

humiliation, 117, 275–76, 278, 281

hunger, 55, 276, 334n60; *See also* eating

hysteria, 91, 120

Idiots, The (dir. Lars von Trier), 266–70

Idol, Ryan, 312

illumination, 44, 79–80

imaginative play, 18–19

Immoral Mr. Teas, The (dir. Russ Meyer), 89

implantation of perversion, 137–38, 141, 143, 222

impotence, 202, 252

In the Realm of the Senses (dir. Oshima Nagisa): in contrast to hard-core pornography, 183, 193–95, 213–14, 297, 357n6; as a breakthrough film, 184, 215, 236, 258, 260; in opposition to traditional Japan, 186–87, 191–92; censorship history of, 188–89, 359n31; graphic sex acts in, 190, 237, 360n37; synthesis of *ars erotica* and *scientia sexualis*, 198–99, 212; prolonged sexual pleasure in, 201, 205–6; juxtaposition of violence and impotence, 202–3, 207; the castrated body in, 209–11; predication upon

itch model of sexual excitement, 15, 48; influence of *shunga*, 196–97; sadomasochisms of, 204, 208; presentation of female orgasm, 200

incest, 89–90, 226; *See also* parental sex

infantile sexuality, 26, 46–49, 53, 56, 72, 140, 206, 224, 235–36, 279

innervation, 17, 19–20

innocence, 223, 239, 242, 279, 317

Inside Deep Throat (dir. Fenton Bailey and Randy Barbato), 127, 145

Interactive Sex Simulators (ISSS), 316–21, 376n57

Internet pornography: dangers of, 306–7, 317; invasion of the home, 308, 321; as the great industry of the medium, 311, 320; direct address of the user in, 312–13, 315–16; as a means to come, 314; money shots in, 318 *See also* cam.whores

interracial sex. *See* miscegenation

intimacy, 115, 269, 283, 291

Intimacy (dir. Patrice Chéreau), 270–74, 296, 298

Intolerance (dir. D.W. Griffith), 30

Irigaray, Luce, 140

Ishida, Kichizo, 184–85, 190–94, 196–11, 214–15, 360n36

Ishii-Gonzales, Sam, 226–27

It's a Wonderful Life (dir. Frank Capra), 42–43, 263

itch, 15, 46, 48, 55, 132–33, 142, 177, 205–6, 326

James, David, 109, 177

Jameson, Fredric, 213, 235–36

Jameson, Jenna: in *Virtual Sex with Jenna Jameson* (ISS), 317–18, 319–21, 324, 326; stimulation through simulation, 322–23; in *VirtuallyJenna* (ISS), 377n75

Jane Fonda Collection: The Complete Workout (1989), 164

Japanese cinema, 183–85, 198, 359n29

Japanese history, 183, 210, 357n15, 360n42
Jones, James, 160
Jones, Justine, 199
Joone, 314
Jørgensen, Bodil, 269–70
Joy of Sex, The (writ. Alex Comfort), 124
Juffer, Jane, 324
Jungle Fever (dir. Spike Lee), 103

Kaas, Nicolaj Lie, 268–69
Kael, Pauline: review of *Last Tango in Paris*, 112–15, 121–22, 128, 130, 200, 214, 271; connection of sex to emotions, 119–20, 123, 173; on sex and violence, 63, 65; review of *Coming Home*, 177–79; review of *Klute*, 171; review of *Blue Velvet*, 365n14
Kane, Carol, 77
Keenan, Thomas, 325
Kinder, Marsha, 216
King, Geoffrey, 305
King, Zalman, 304
Kinsey, Alfred: contribution to sexual revolution, 8, 158; methodological approach to studying orgasm, 159, 376n64; discussion of oral sex in marriage, 137; "attic films" of, 160; as a pornographer, 161; on shock of words, 353n8
Kiss (dir. Andy Warhol), 58–63, 105–6
Kiss, The (dir. Thomas Edison): anatomization of sex act in, 27–28, 58, 135; contemporaneous reaction to, 29–30, 330n6; close-up composition of, 31, 38; as cinematic first, 26; projection on small and large screens, 300
kissing, 25–68, 73, 75, 92–93, 108, 110, 113, 123, 126, 140, 146, 170, 174, 178, 263, 265, 269, 272, 278–79, 297, 305, 326, 333n50
Klute (dir. Alan Pakula), 163, 171–72, 174, 179
knowledge: of the sexual, 26, 68–70,

72, 74–85, 87, 104, 109–10, 120, 142, 156, 165, 170, 179, 224, 226, 238, 269, 311, 313, 325–26; through visuals, 27, 73; of pleasure, 198; of sexual difference, 232
Koch, Stephen, 59
Koedt, Anne, 163, 173
Koestenbaum, Wayne, 105, 110
Koryusai, Isoda, 210–11
Kovic, Ron, 176
Kracauer, Siegfried, 30, 56–57, 65
Kramer, Stanley, 92, 101
Kubrick, Stanley, 68, 128, 188, 283
Kureishi, Hanif, 270
Kurosawa, Akira, 185

L-Word, The (Michele Abbot, Ilene Chaiken, and Kathy Greenberg, Showtime),̆ 304
Lacan, Jacques, 184, 211
Landes, Joan, 10
Laplanche, Jean, 49
Laplanche, Jean and J.B. Pontalis: on origin of human sexuality, 224, 239, 243, 257; on primal fantasy, 225, 235, 242, 247; shift of trauma into knowledge, 72
Laqueur, Thomas, 305
Last Tango in Paris (dir. Bernardo Bertolucci): as modern erotic art, 113–14, 1̆21, 136, 183, 188, 200, 271, 273; display of sex acts in, 115–16, 128–30, 182, 272, 277; sex as death in, 119–20, 142, 210, 213; exploration of anal eroticism, 117–18, 132; prurient interest in, 122–25, 223; parallels to *The Rite of Spring*, 112; sexual pleasure in, 133
Law, John Philip, 166
Lawrence v. Texas (2003), 239–42, 246, 298, 367n52
Ledger, Heath, 216, 237–39, 241–57
Lee, Ang, 222, 237, 242, 245, 257
Lee, Sook-Yin, 286–93
Lee, Spike, 103

LINDA WILLIAMS is a professor of rhetoric and film studies
at the University of California, Berkeley. Her previous books
include *Hard Core: Power, Pleasure, and the "Frenzy of the Visible"*
(1989) and *Playing the Race Card: Melodramas of Black and White
from Uncle Tom to O. J. Simpson* (2001).

Library of Congress Cataloging-in-Publication Data
Williams, Linda, 1946–
Screening sex / Linda Williams.
p. cm. — (A John Hope Franklin Center book)
Includes bibliographical references and index.
ISBN 978-0-8223-4263-2 (cloth : alk. paper)
ISBN 978-0-8223-4285-4 (pbk. : alk. paper)
1. Sex in motion pictures. 2. Erotic films—
United States—History and criticism. I. Title.
PN1995.9.S45W523 2008
791.43'6538—dc22   2008013530